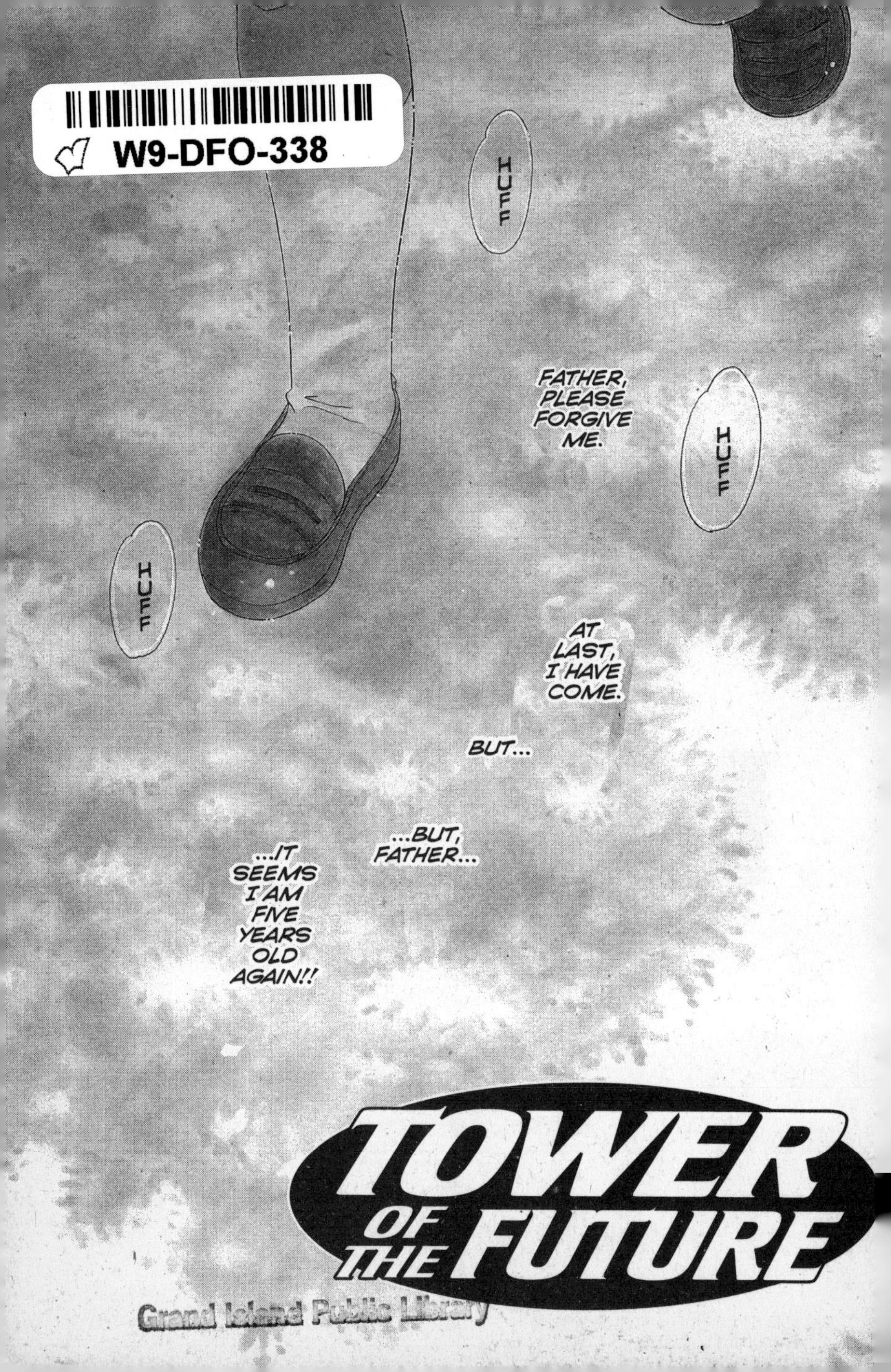
HUFF
HUFF
FATHER, PLEASE FORGIVE ME.
HUFF
AT LAST, I HAVE COME.
BUT...
...BUT, FATHER...
...IT SEEMS I AM FIVE YEARS OLD AGAIN!!
TOWER OF THE FUTURE

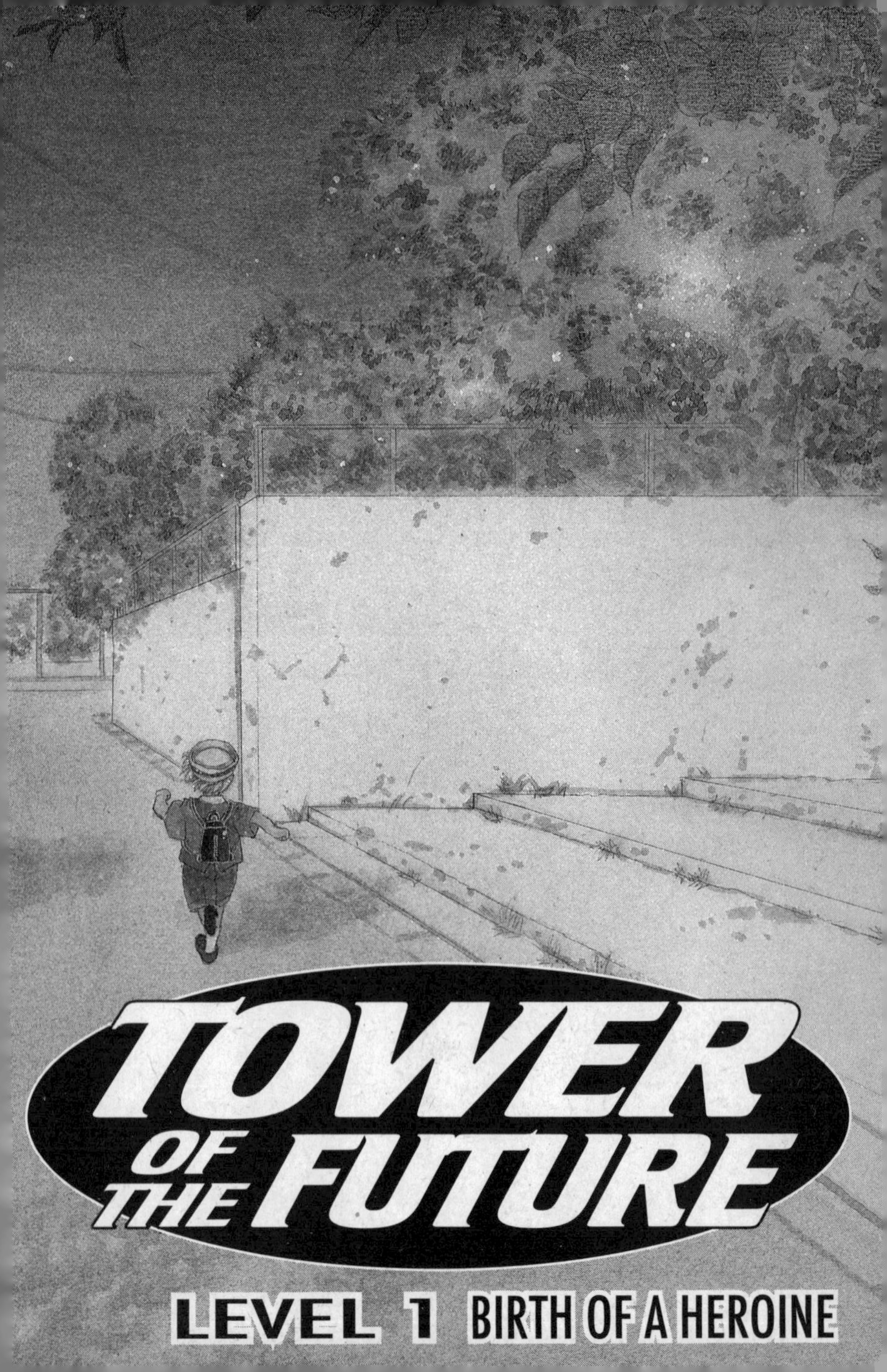
TOWER OF THE FUTURE
LEVEL 1 BIRTH OF A HEROINE

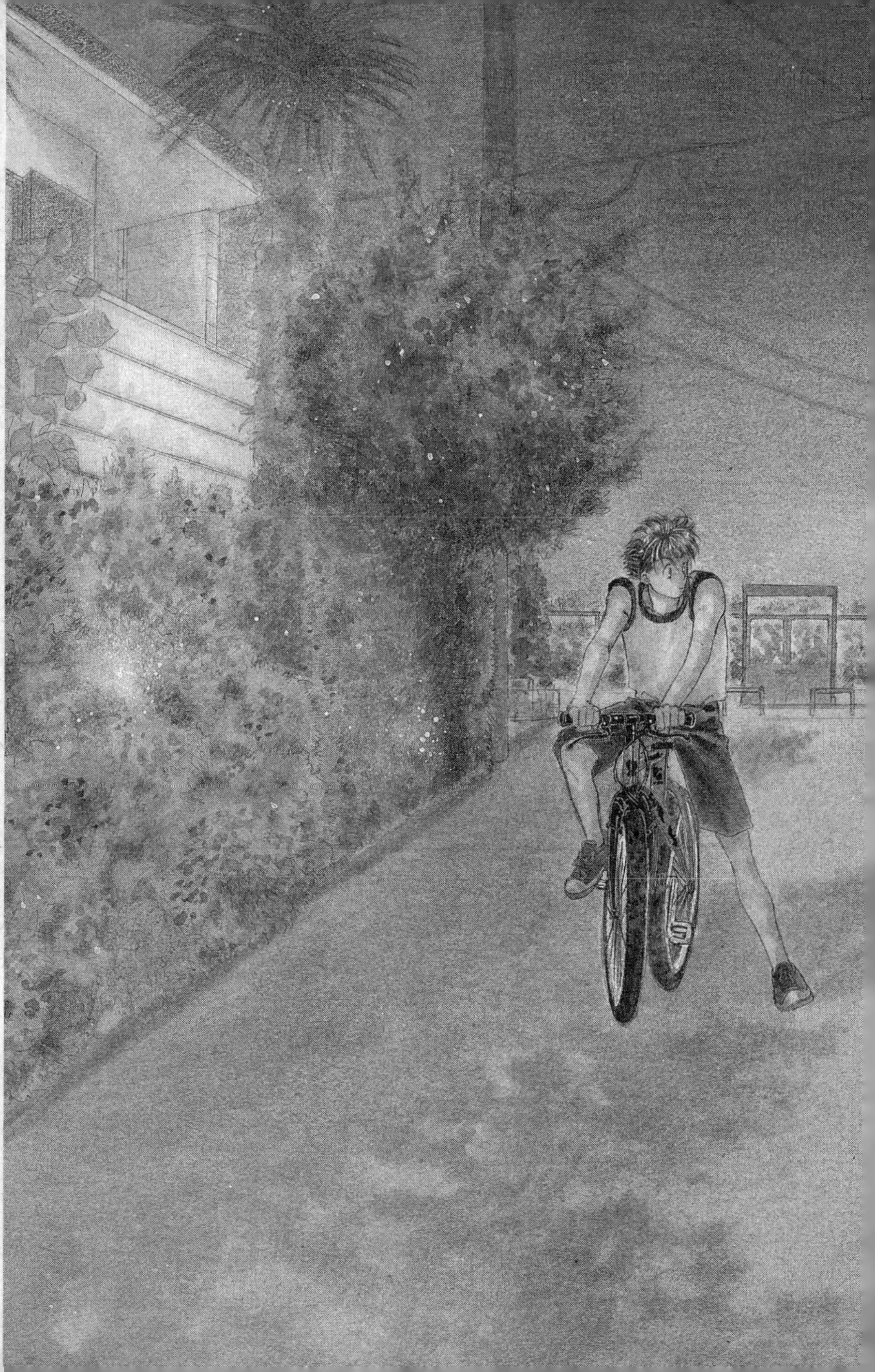

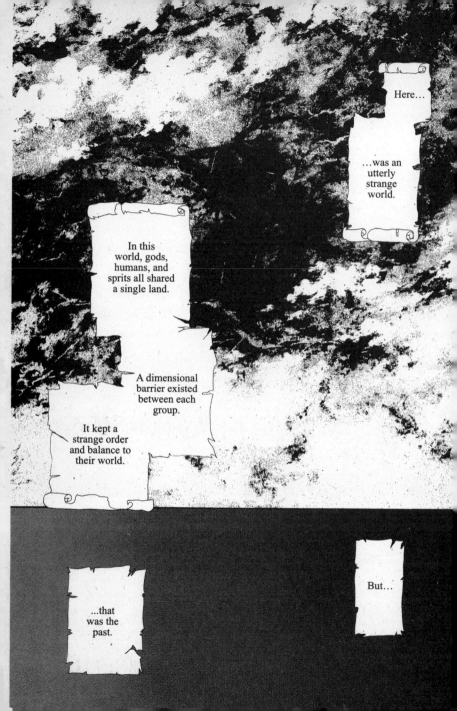

Here…

…was an utterly strange world.

In this world, gods, humans, and sprits all shared a single land.

A dimensional barrier existed between each group.

It kept a strange order and balance to their world.

…that was the past.

But…

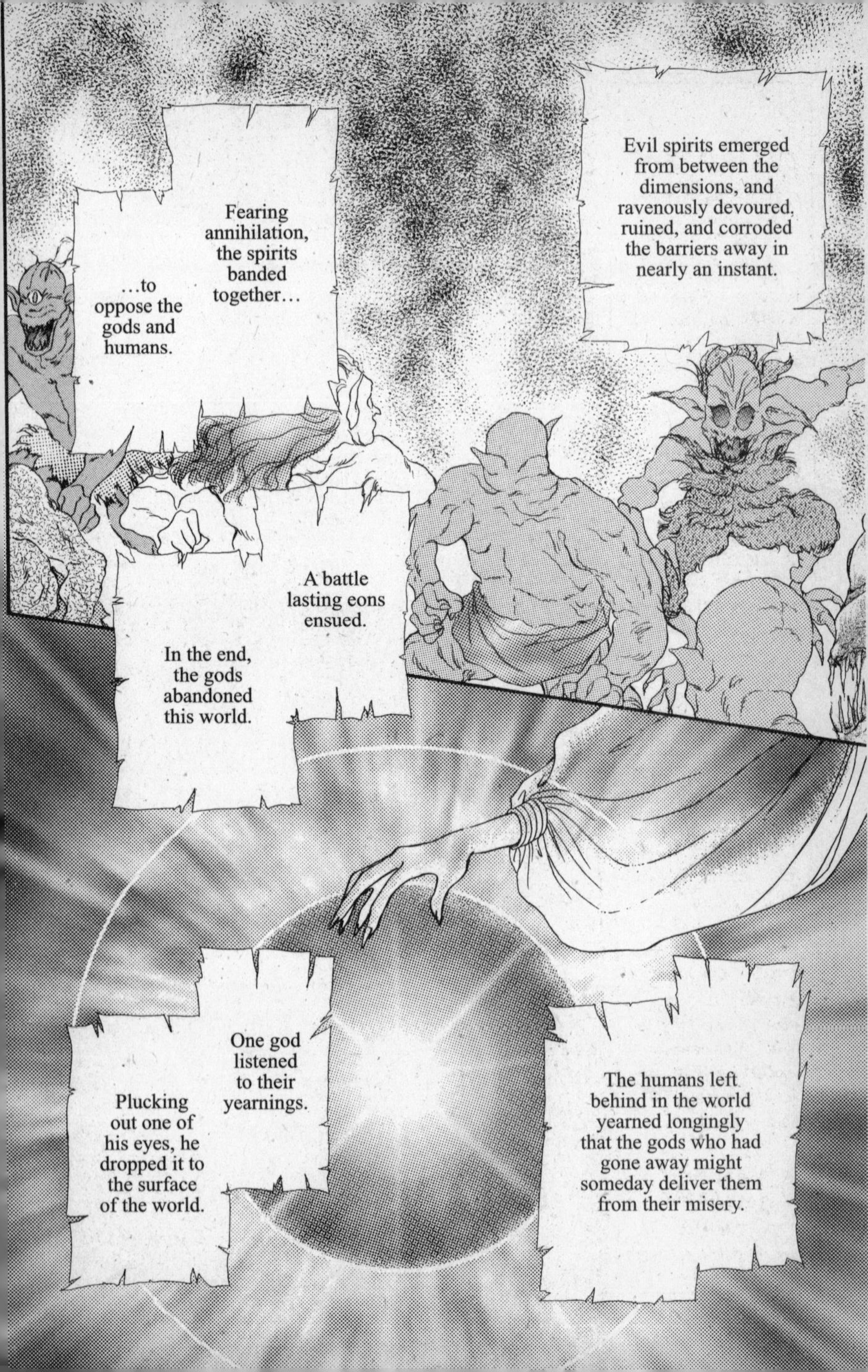
Evil spirits emerged from between the dimensions, and ravenously devoured, ruined, and corroded the barriers away in nearly an instant.
Fearing annihilation, the spirits banded together…
…to oppose the gods and humans.
A battle lasting eons ensued.
In the end, the gods abandoned this world.
The humans left behind in the world yearned longingly that the gods who had gone away might someday deliver them from their misery.
One god listened to their yearnings.
Plucking out one of his eyes, he dropped it to the surface of the world.

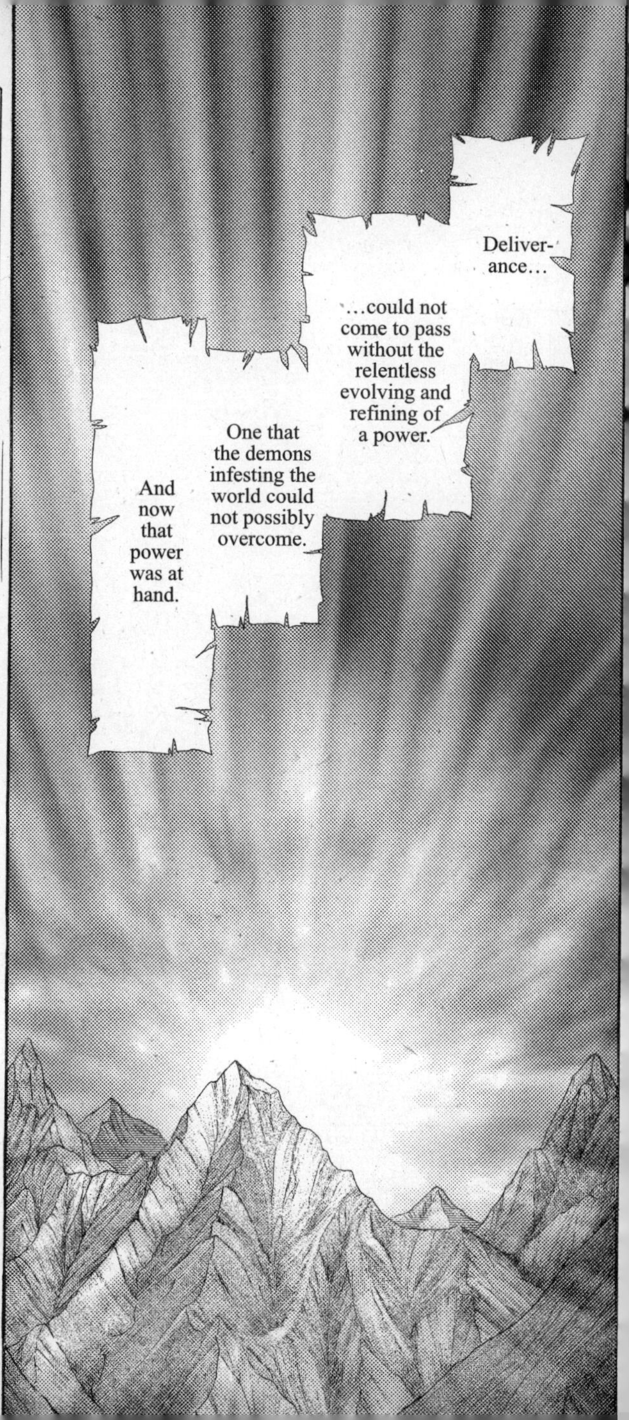
Deliver-ance…
…could not come to pass without the relentless evolving and refining of a power.
One that the demons infesting the world could not possibly overcome.
And now that power was at hand.

1/4 Sidebar No. 1

1

Hi! I'm Saki Hiwatari. Thanks for buying volume 1 of "Tower of the Future." Drum roll... Ta daaa!

Welcome to my very first TOWER OF THE FUTURE SIDEBAR.

If you talked to me about this time last year I'd have told you that I was furiously drawing the climax to Saving My World.
And here's what I thought while I was in the middle of doing that manga: "Save the World" is kind of a typical SF story--and it's really gloomy and a high maintenance project to boot--yet that's what I somehow ended up drawing for seven-and-a-half years.

I WANNA DRAW HAPPY STORIES!!

It's the truth

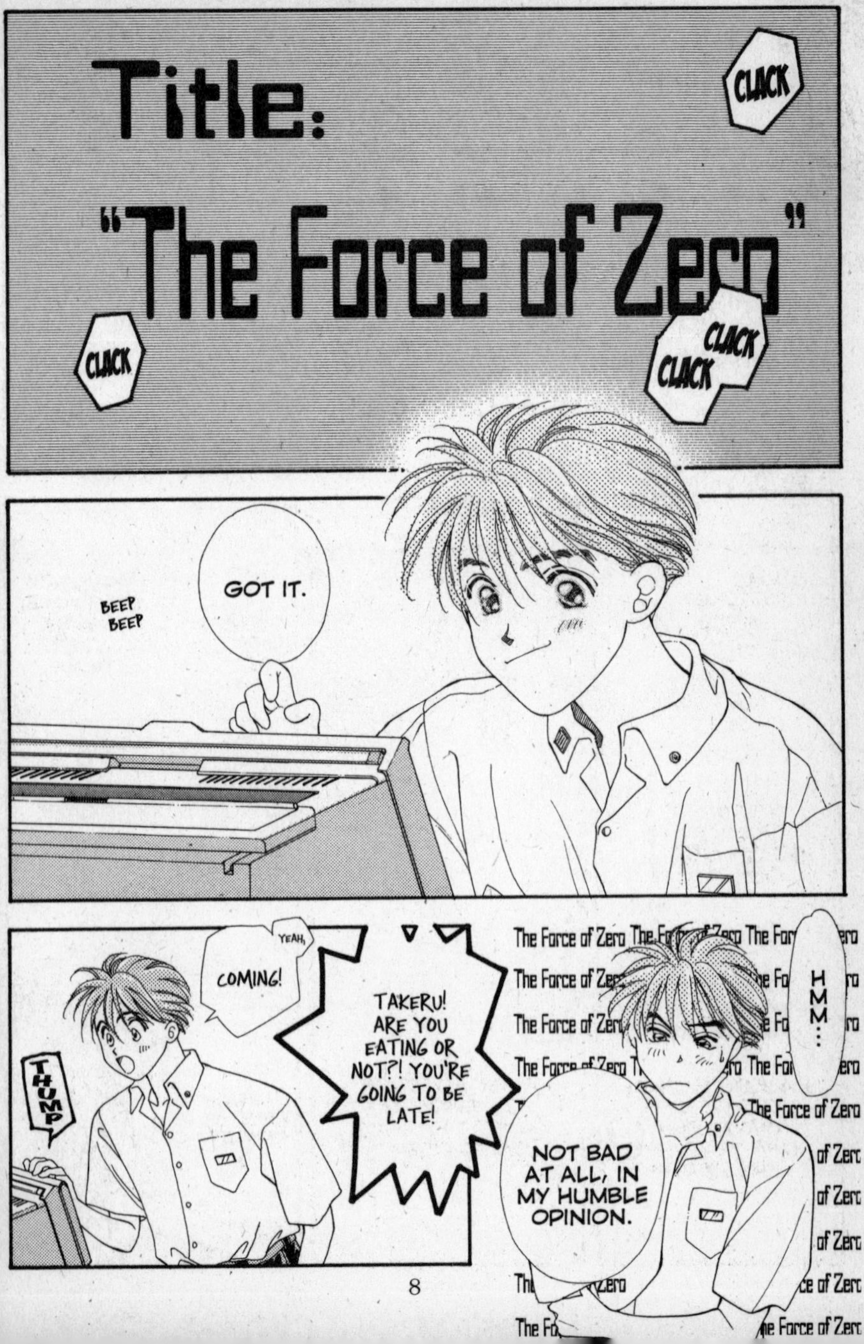
CLACK
Title: "The Force of Zero"
CLACK
CLACK
CLACK
GOT IT.
BEEP BEEP
HMM...
The Force of Zero
NOT BAD AT ALL, IN MY HUMBLE OPINION.
TAKERU! ARE YOU EATING OR NOT?! YOU'RE GOING TO BE LATE!
YEAH,
COMING!
THUMP

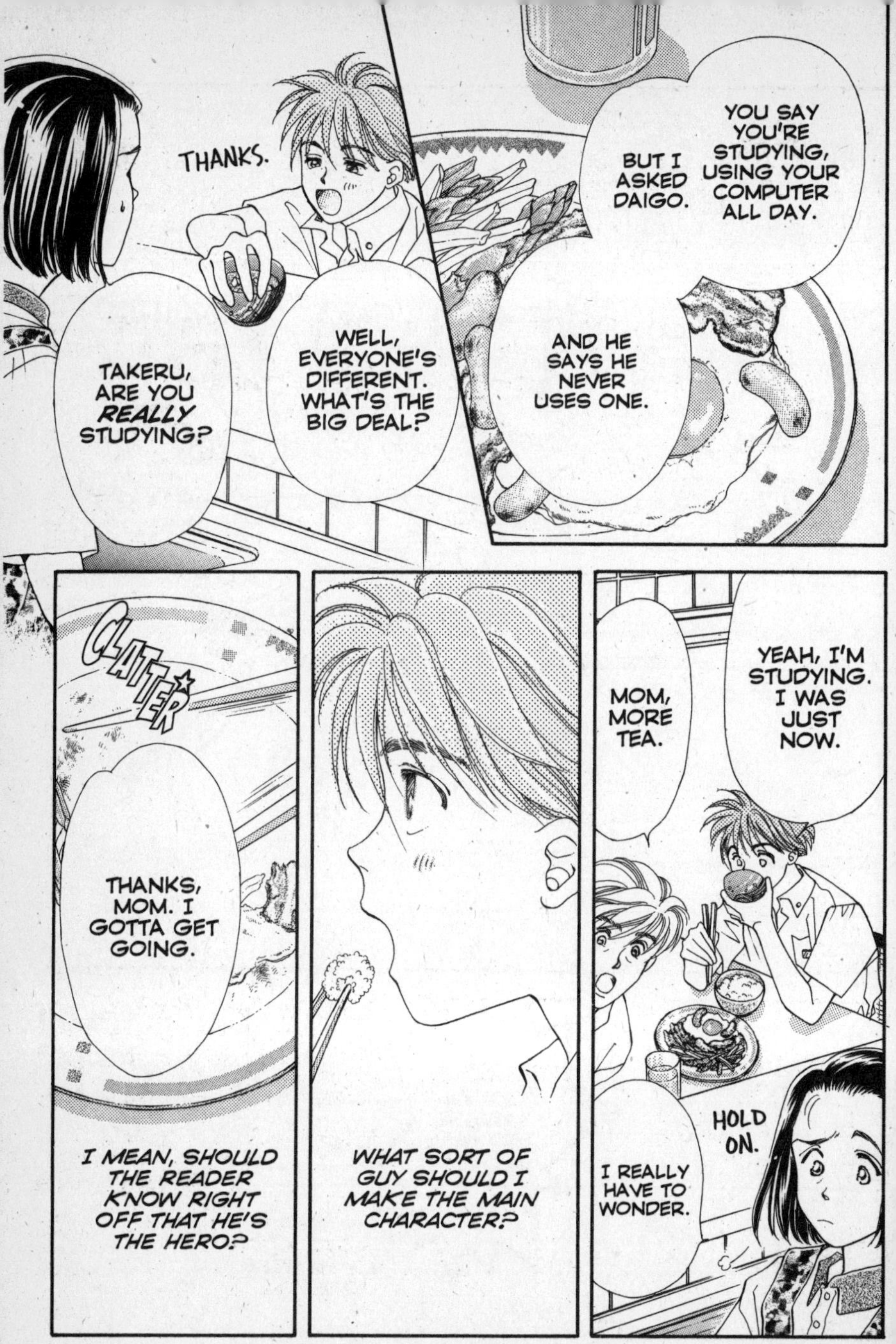
YOU SAY YOU'RE STUDYING, USING YOUR COMPUTER ALL DAY.
BUT I ASKED DAIGO.
AND HE SAYS HE NEVER USES ONE.
THANKS.
WELL, EVERYONE'S DIFFERENT. WHAT'S THE BIG DEAL?
TAKERU, ARE YOU *REALLY* STUDYING?
YEAH, I'M STUDYING. I WAS JUST NOW.
MOM, MORE TEA.
HOLD ON.
I REALLY HAVE TO WONDER.
WHAT SORT OF GUY SHOULD I MAKE THE MAIN CHARACTER?
CLATTER
THANKS, MOM. I GOTTA GET GOING.
I MEAN, SHOULD THE READER KNOW RIGHT OFF THAT HE'S THE HERO?

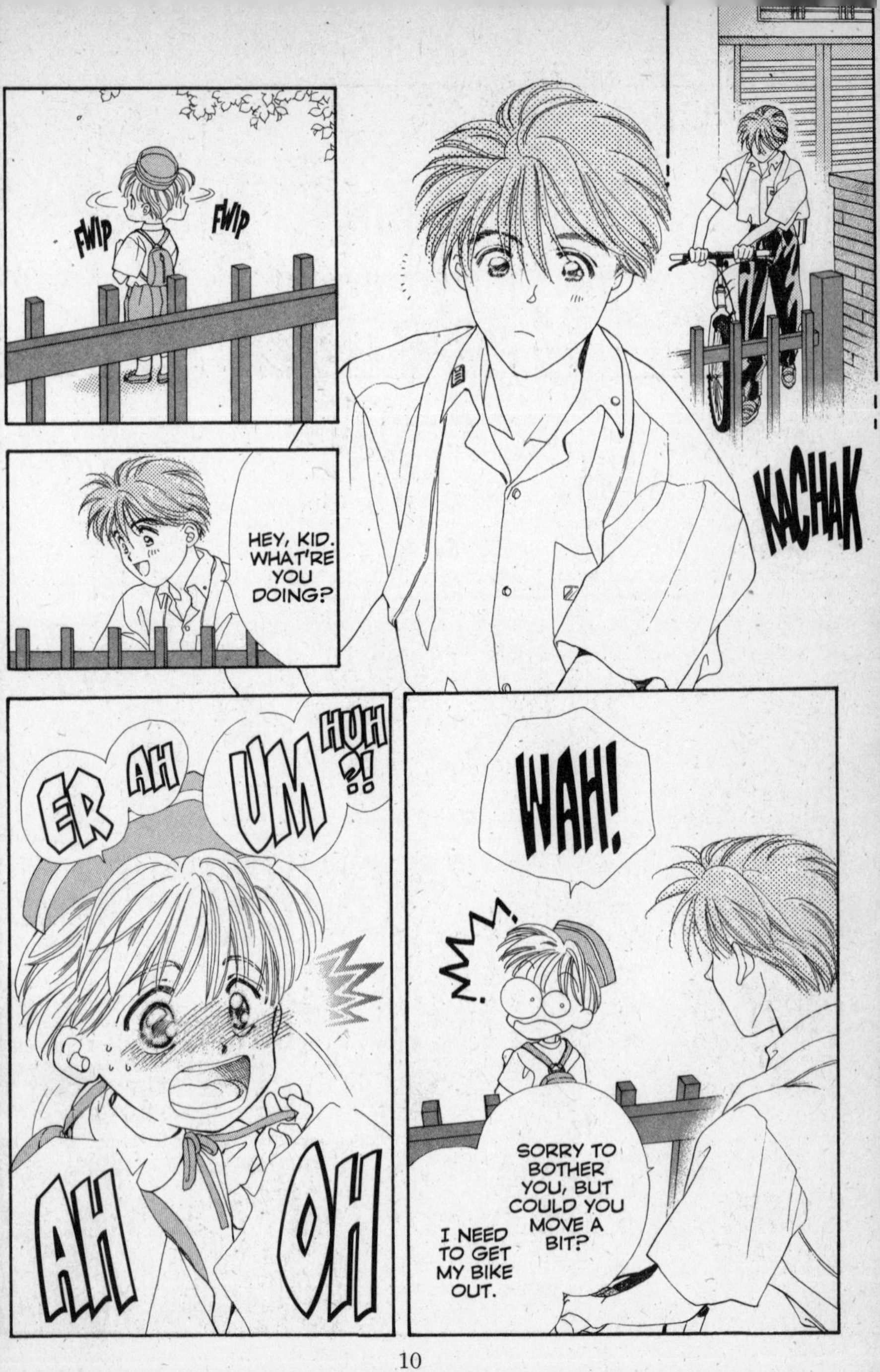
KACHAK
FWIP
FWIP
HEY, KID. WHAT'RE YOU DOING?
WAH!
SORRY TO BOTHER YOU, BUT COULD YOU MOVE A BIT?
I NEED TO GET MY BIKE OUT.
HUH?!
UM
AH
ER
OH
AH

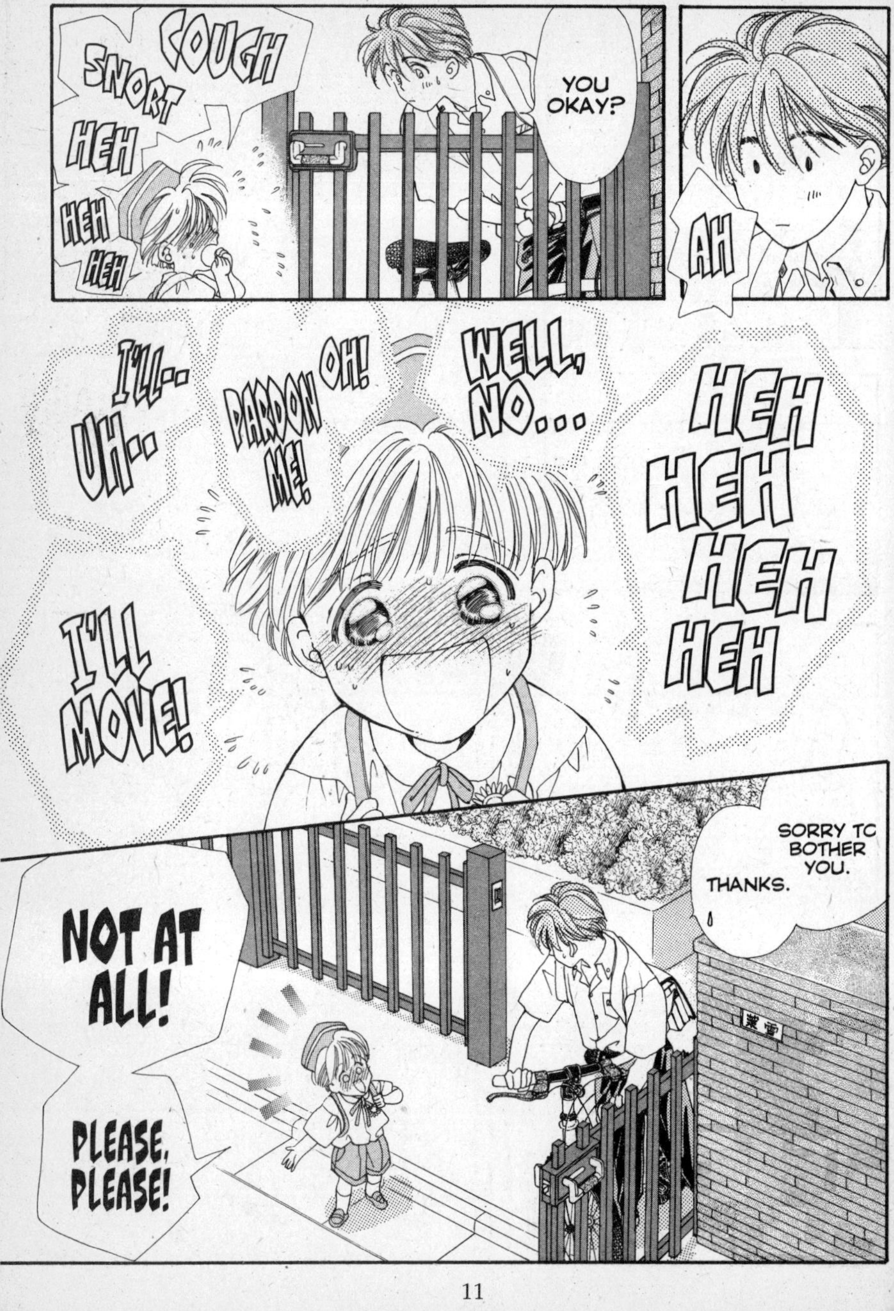
AH
YOU OKAY?
COUGH
SNORT
HEH
HEH
HEH
HEH HEH HEH HEH
WELL, NO...
OH!
PARDON ME!
I'LL.. UH..
I'LL MOVE!
SORRY TO BOTHER YOU.
THANKS.
NOT AT ALL!
PLEASE, PLEASE!

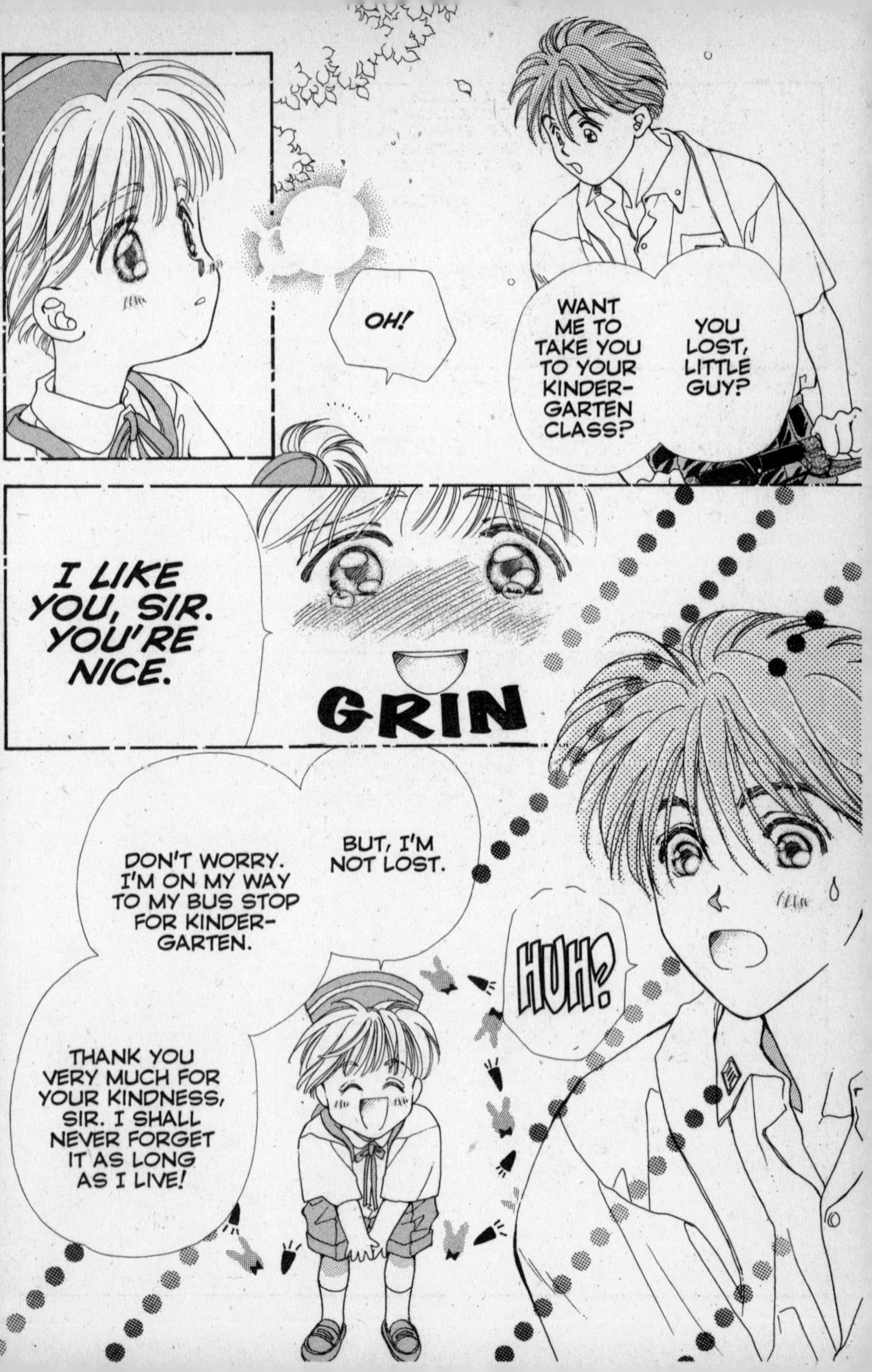

YOU LOST, LITTLE GUY?
WANT ME TO TAKE YOU TO YOUR KINDERGARTEN CLASS?
OH!
I LIKE YOU, SIR. YOU'RE NICE.
GRIN
BUT, I'M NOT LOST.
DON'T WORRY. I'M ON MY WAY TO MY BUS STOP FOR KINDERGARTEN.
HUH?
THANK YOU VERY MUCH FOR YOUR KINDNESS, SIR. I SHALL NEVER FORGET IT AS LONG AS I LIVE!

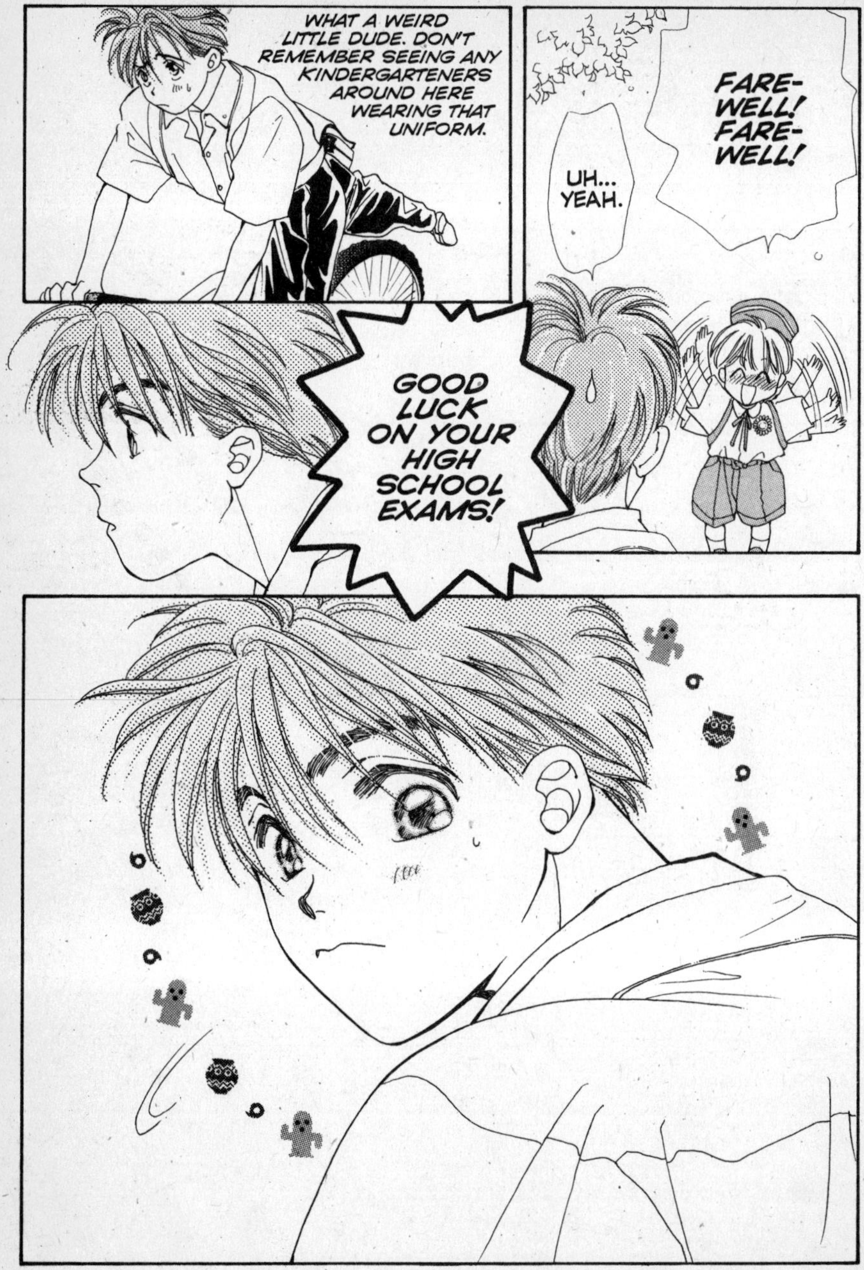

FARE-WELL! FARE-WELL!
UH... YEAH.
WHAT A WEIRD LITTLE DUDE. DON'T REMEMBER SEEING ANY KINDERGARTENERS AROUND HERE WEARING THAT UNIFORM.
GOOD LUCK ON YOUR HIGH SCHOOL EXAMS!

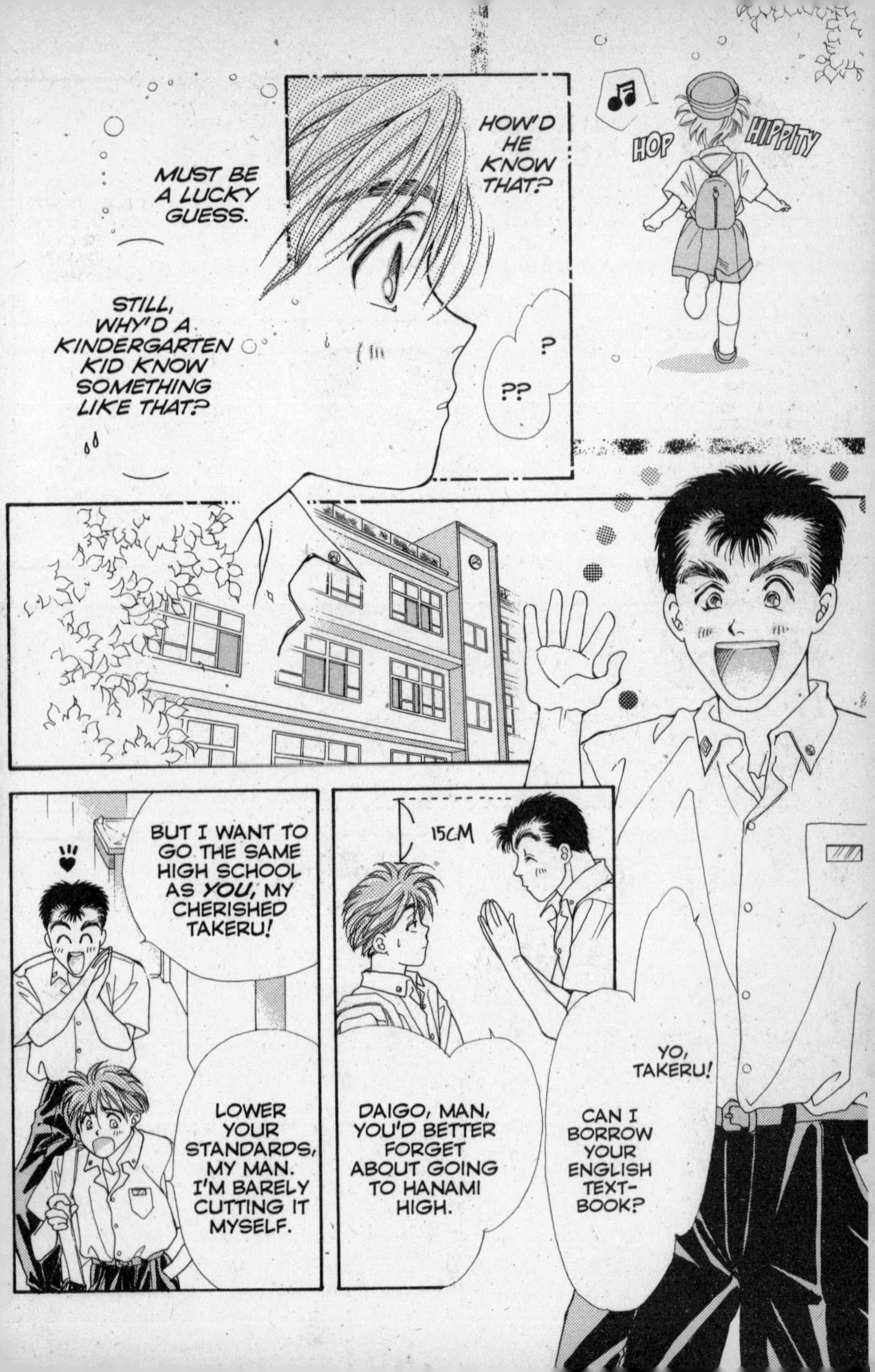
HIPPITY
HOP
HOW'D HE KNOW THAT?
?
??
MUST BE A LUCKY GUESS.
STILL, WHY'D A KINDERGARTEN KID KNOW SOMETHING LIKE THAT?
YO, TAKERU!
CAN I BORROW YOUR ENGLISH TEXT-BOOK?
15CM
DAIGO, MAN, YOU'D BETTER FORGET ABOUT GOING TO HANAMI HIGH.
BUT I WANT TO GO THE SAME HIGH SCHOOL AS *YOU*, MY CHERISHED TAKERU!
LOWER YOUR STANDARDS, MY MAN. I'M BARELY CUTTING IT MYSELF.

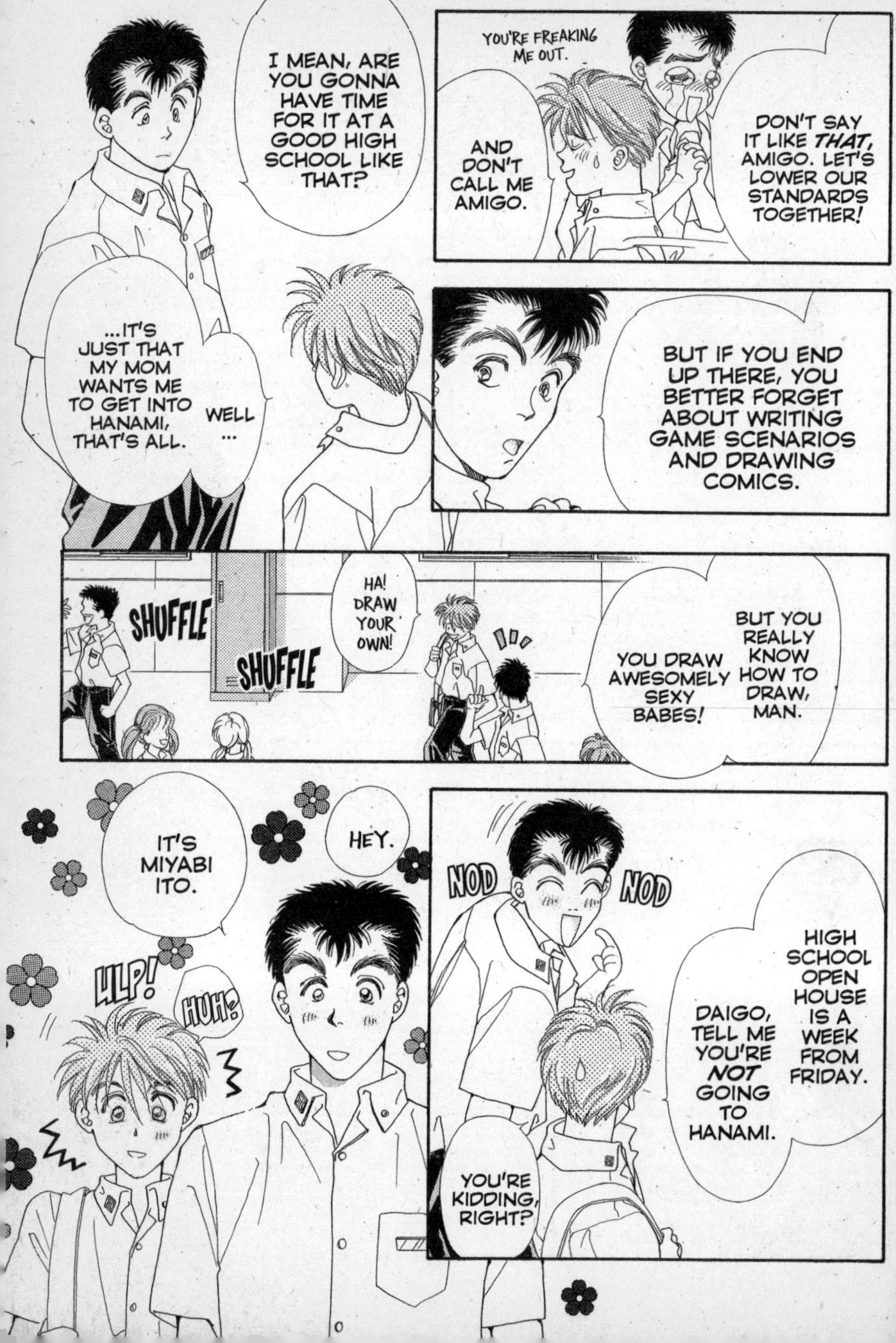
DON'T SAY IT LIKE *THAT*, AMIGO. LET'S LOWER OUR STANDARDS TOGETHER!
AND DON'T CALL ME AMIGO.
YOU'RE FREAKING ME OUT.
BUT IF YOU END UP THERE, YOU BETTER FORGET ABOUT WRITING GAME SCENARIOS AND DRAWING COMICS.
I MEAN, ARE YOU GONNA HAVE TIME FOR IT AT A GOOD HIGH SCHOOL LIKE THAT?
WELL ...
...IT'S JUST THAT MY MOM WANTS ME TO GET INTO HANAMI, THAT'S ALL.
BUT YOU REALLY KNOW HOW TO DRAW, MAN.
YOU DRAW AWESOMELY SEXY BABES!
HA! DRAW YOUR OWN!
SHUFFLE
SHUFFLE
NOD
NOD
HIGH SCHOOL OPEN HOUSE IS A WEEK FROM FRIDAY.
DAIGO, TELL ME YOU'RE *NOT* GOING TO HANAMI.
YOU'RE KIDDING, RIGHT?
HEY.
IT'S MIYABI ITO.
HUH?
ULP!

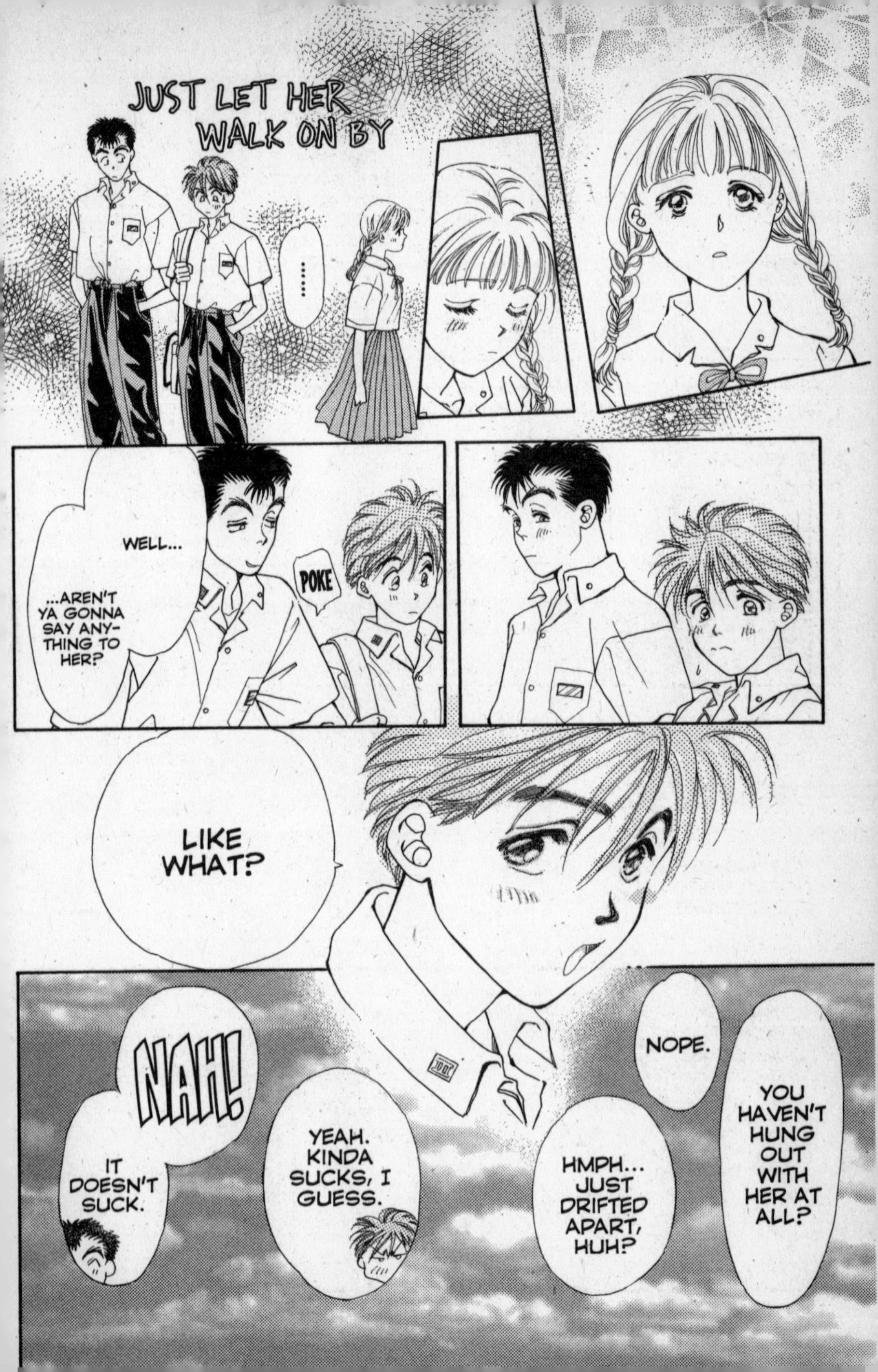
JUST LET HER WALK ON BY
......
WELL...
...AREN'T YA GONNA SAY ANYTHING TO HER?
POKE
LIKE WHAT?
YOU HAVEN'T HUNG OUT WITH HER AT ALL?
NOPE.
HMPH... JUST DRIFTED APART, HUH?
YEAH. KINDA SUCKS, I GUESS.
NAH!
IT DOESN'T SUCK.

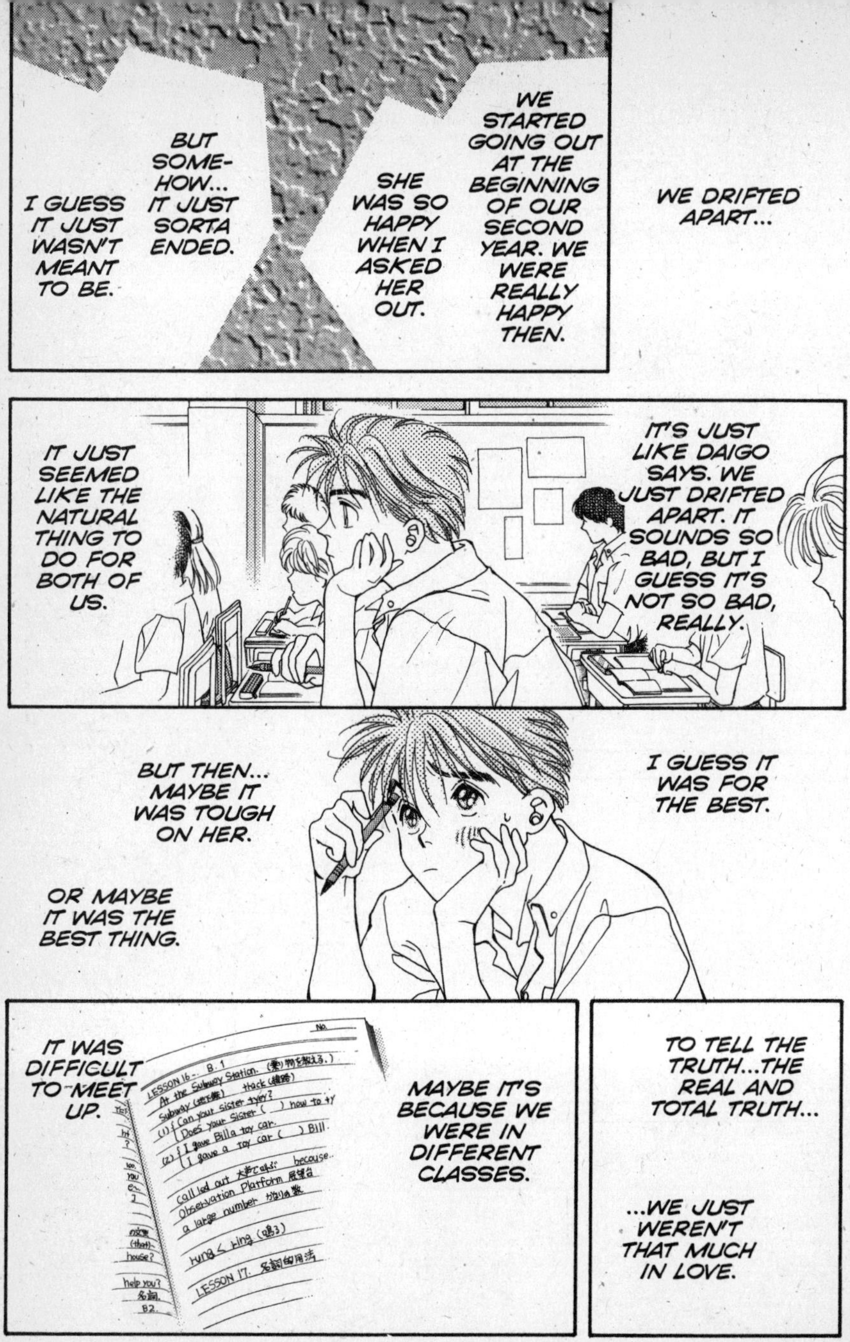
WE DRIFTED APART...
WE STARTED GOING OUT AT THE BEGINNING OF OUR SECOND YEAR. WE WERE REALLY HAPPY THEN.
SHE WAS SO HAPPY WHEN I ASKED HER OUT.
BUT SOMEHOW... IT JUST SORTA ENDED.
I GUESS IT JUST WASN'T MEANT TO BE.
IT'S JUST LIKE DAIGO SAYS. WE JUST DRIFTED APART. IT SOUNDS SO BAD, BUT I GUESS IT'S NOT SO BAD, REALLY.
IT JUST SEEMED LIKE THE NATURAL THING TO DO FOR BOTH OF US.
I GUESS IT WAS FOR THE BEST.
BUT THEN... MAYBE IT WAS TOUGH ON HER.
OR MAYBE IT WAS THE BEST THING.
TO TELL THE TRUTH...THE REAL AND TOTAL TRUTH...
...WE JUST WEREN'T THAT MUCH IN LOVE.
MAYBE IT'S BECAUSE WE WERE IN DIFFERENT CLASSES.
IT WAS DIFFICULT TO MEET UP.

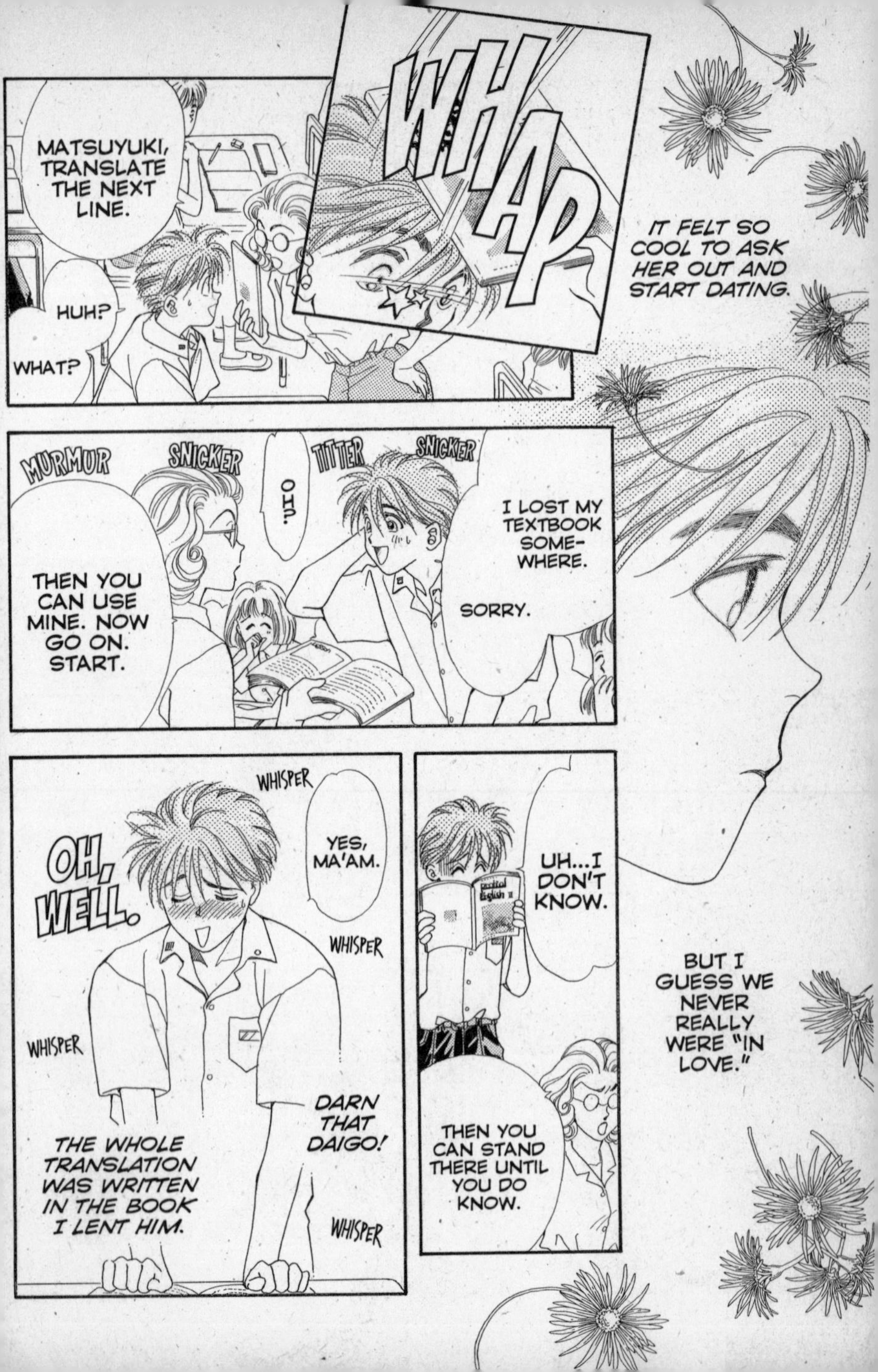
IT FELT SO COOL TO ASK HER OUT AND START DATING.
WHAP
MATSUYUKI, TRANSLATE THE NEXT LINE.
HUH?
WHAT?
SNICKER
TITTER
I LOST MY TEXTBOOK SOME-WHERE.
SORRY.
OH?
SNICKER
MURMUR
THEN YOU CAN USE MINE. NOW GO ON. START.
BUT I GUESS WE NEVER REALLY WERE "IN LOVE."
UH...I DON'T KNOW.
THEN YOU CAN STAND THERE UNTIL YOU DO KNOW.
WHISPER
YES, MA'AM.
OH, WELL.
WHISPER
WHISPER
DARN THAT DAIGO!
THE WHOLE TRANSLATION WAS WRITTEN IN THE BOOK I LENT HIM.
WHISPER

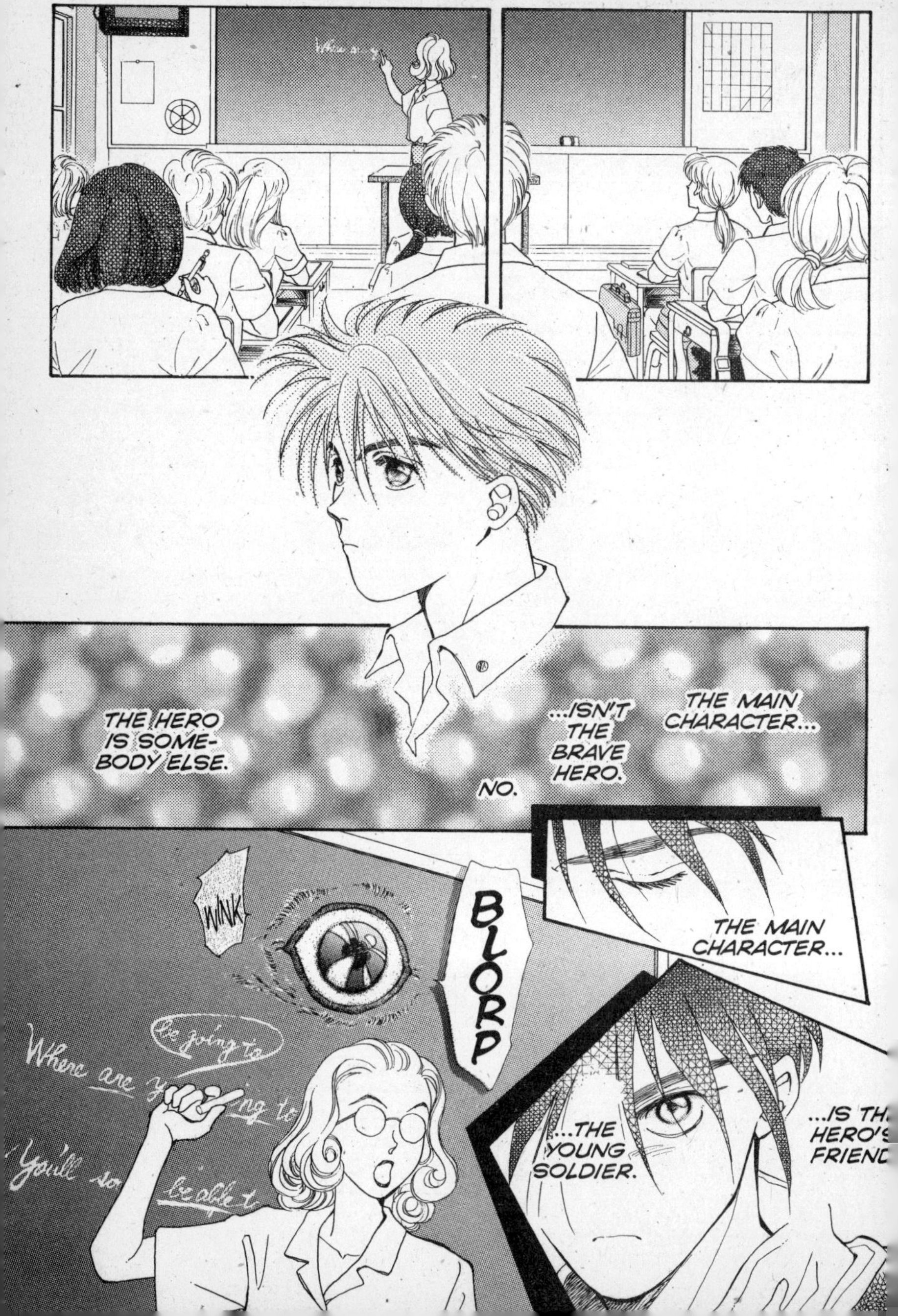
THE MAIN CHARACTER...
...ISN'T THE BRAVE HERO.
NO.
THE HERO IS SOMEBODY ELSE.
THE MAIN CHARACTER...
...IS TH HERO'S FRIEND
...THE YOUNG SOLDIER.
BLORP
WINK

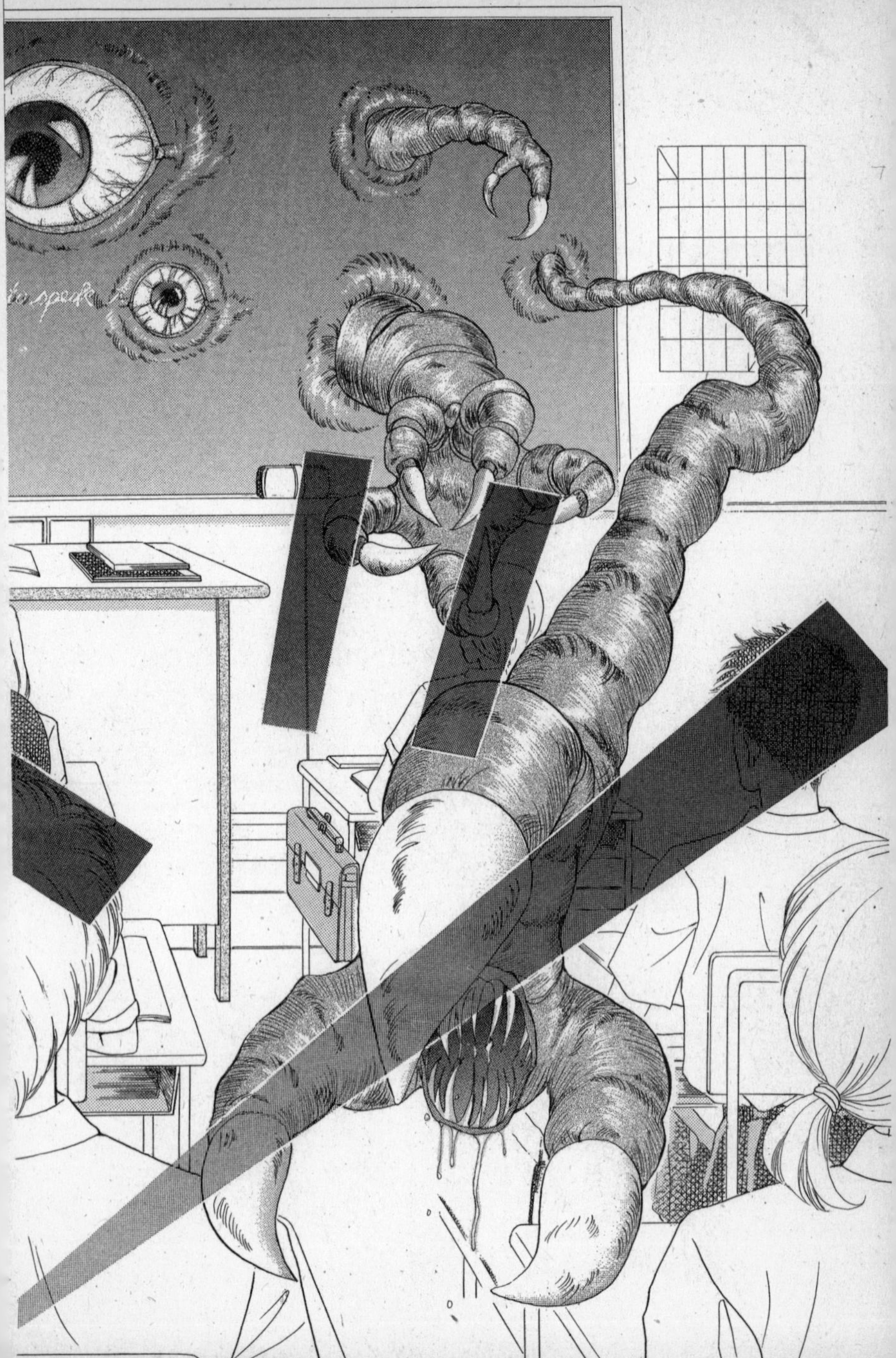
to speak

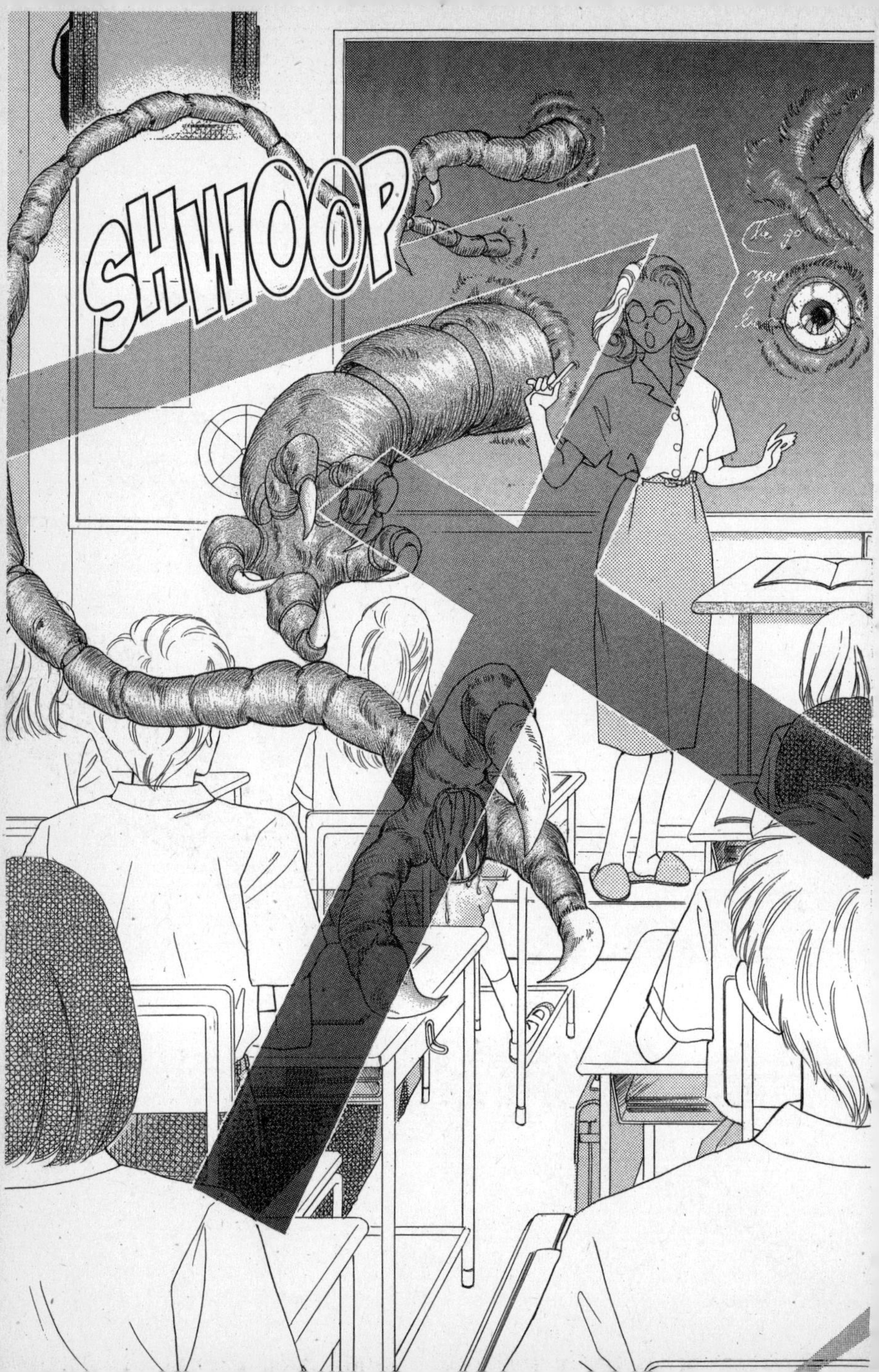
SHWOOP

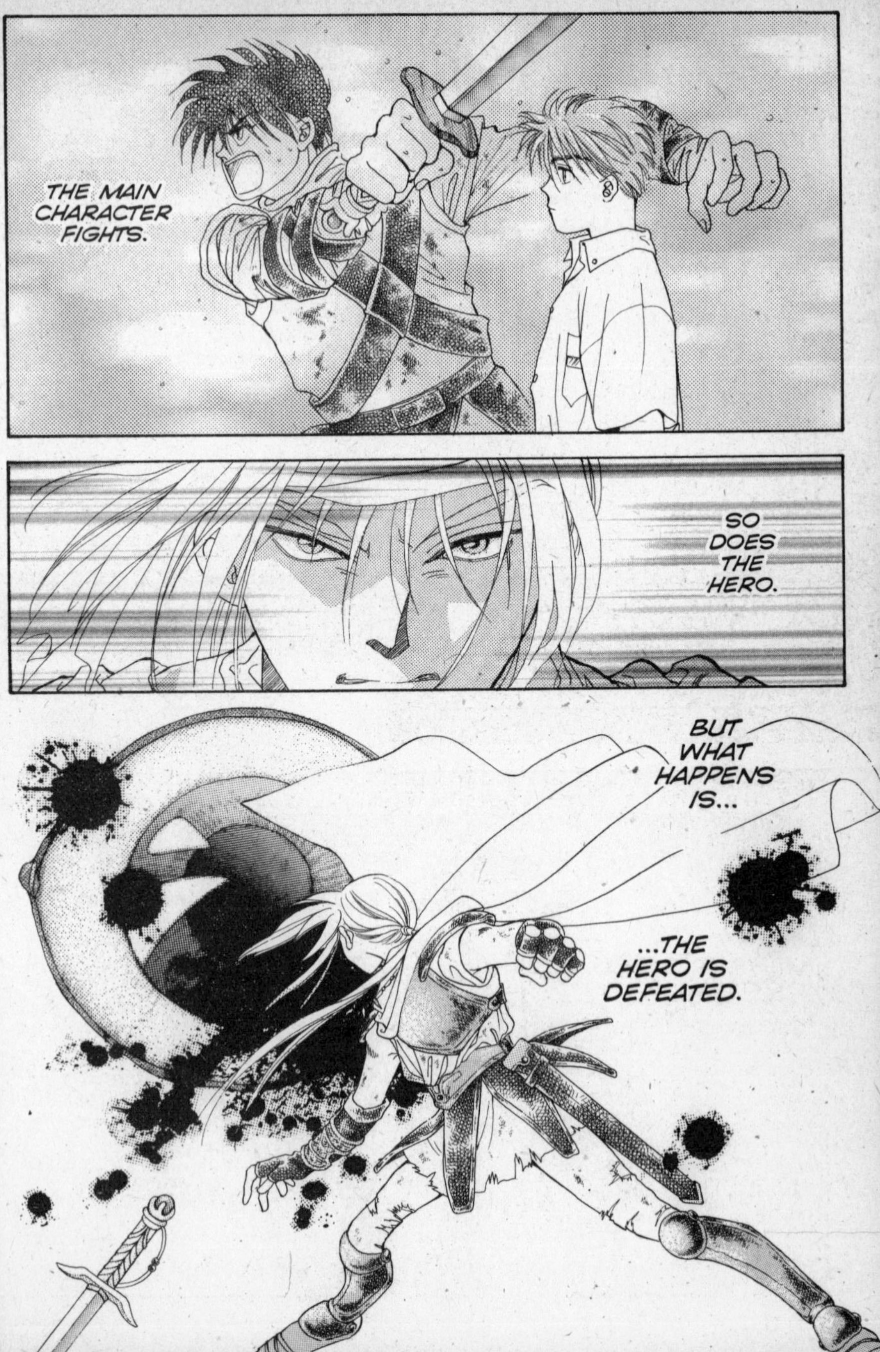
THE MAIN CHARACTER FIGHTS.
SO DOES THE HERO.
BUT WHAT HAPPENS IS...
...THE HERO IS DEFEATED.

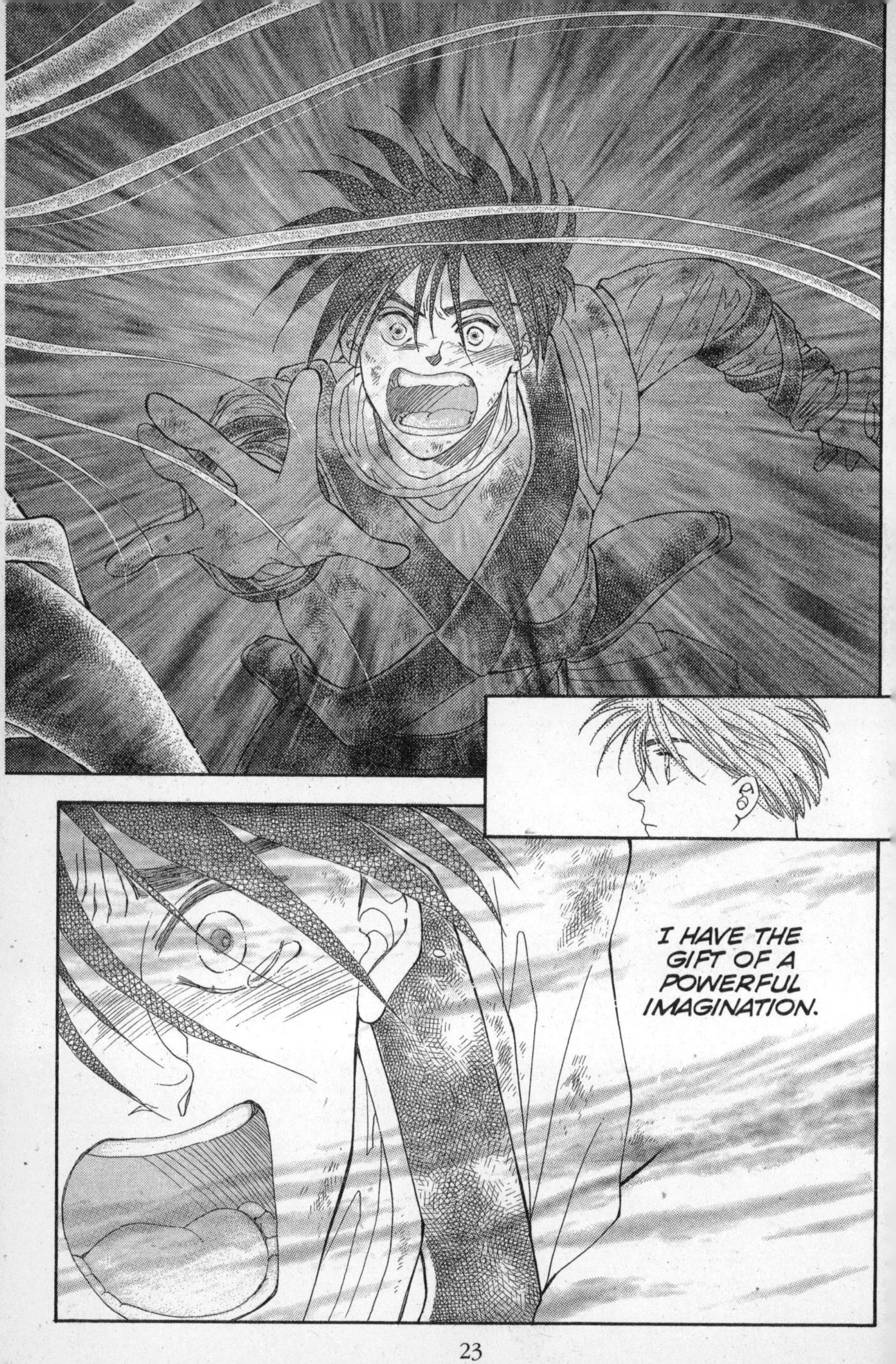
I HAVE THE GIFT OF A POWERFUL IMAGINATION.

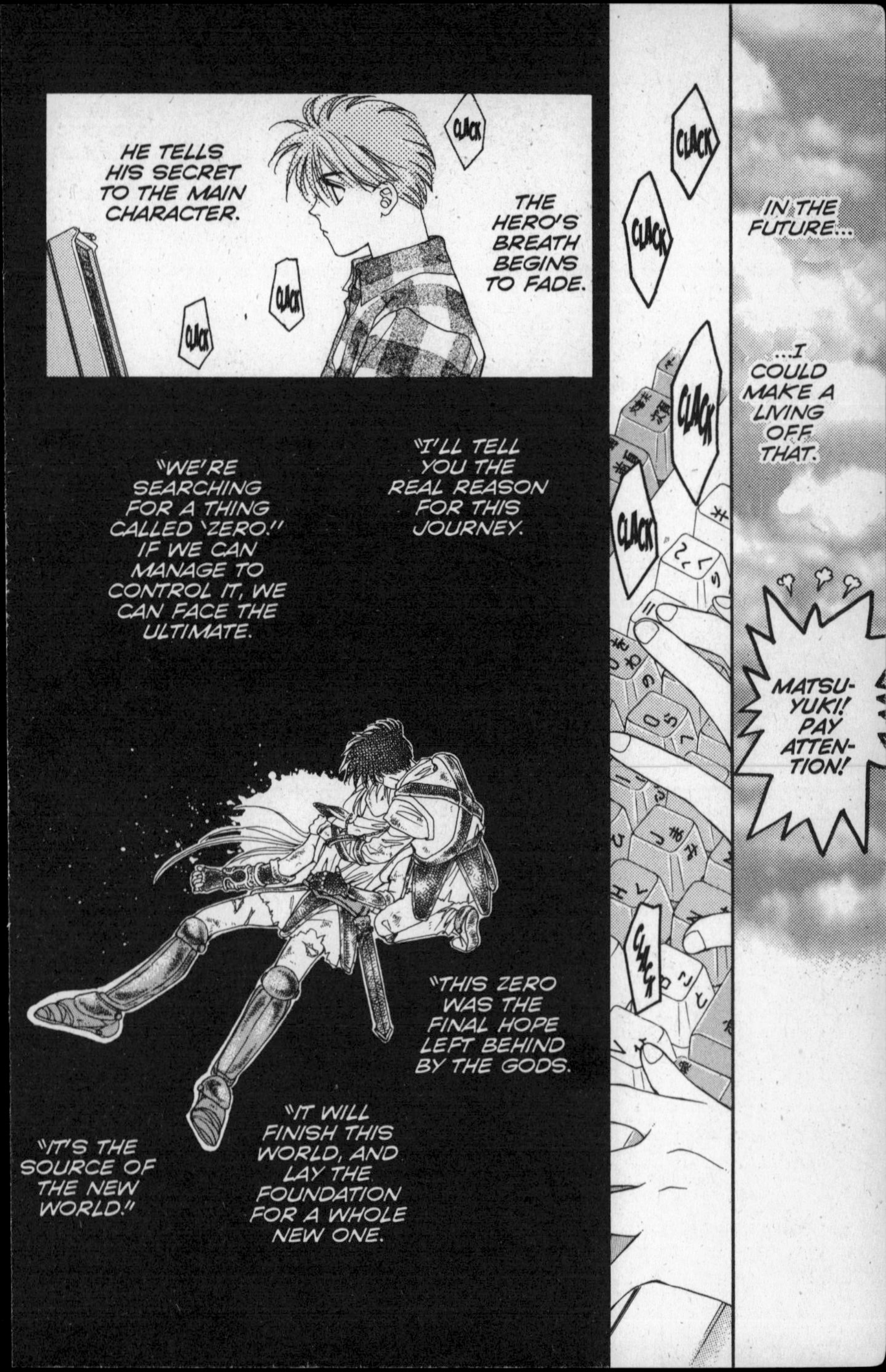
IN THE FUTURE...
...I COULD MAKE A LIVING OFF THAT.
MATSU-YUKI! PAY ATTEN-TION!
CLACK
CLACK
CLACK
CLACK
CLACK
CLACK
CLACK
THE HERO'S BREATH BEGINS TO FADE.
HE TELLS HIS SECRET TO THE MAIN CHARACTER.
CLACK
CLACK
CLACK
"I'LL TELL YOU THE REAL REASON FOR THIS JOURNEY.
"WE'RE SEARCHING FOR A THING CALLED 'ZERO.' IF WE CAN MANAGE TO CONTROL IT, WE CAN FACE THE ULTIMATE.
"THIS ZERO WAS THE FINAL HOPE LEFT BEHIND BY THE GODS.
"IT WILL FINISH THIS WORLD, AND LAY THE FOUNDATION FOR A WHOLE NEW ONE.
"IT'S THE SOURCE OF THE NEW WORLD."

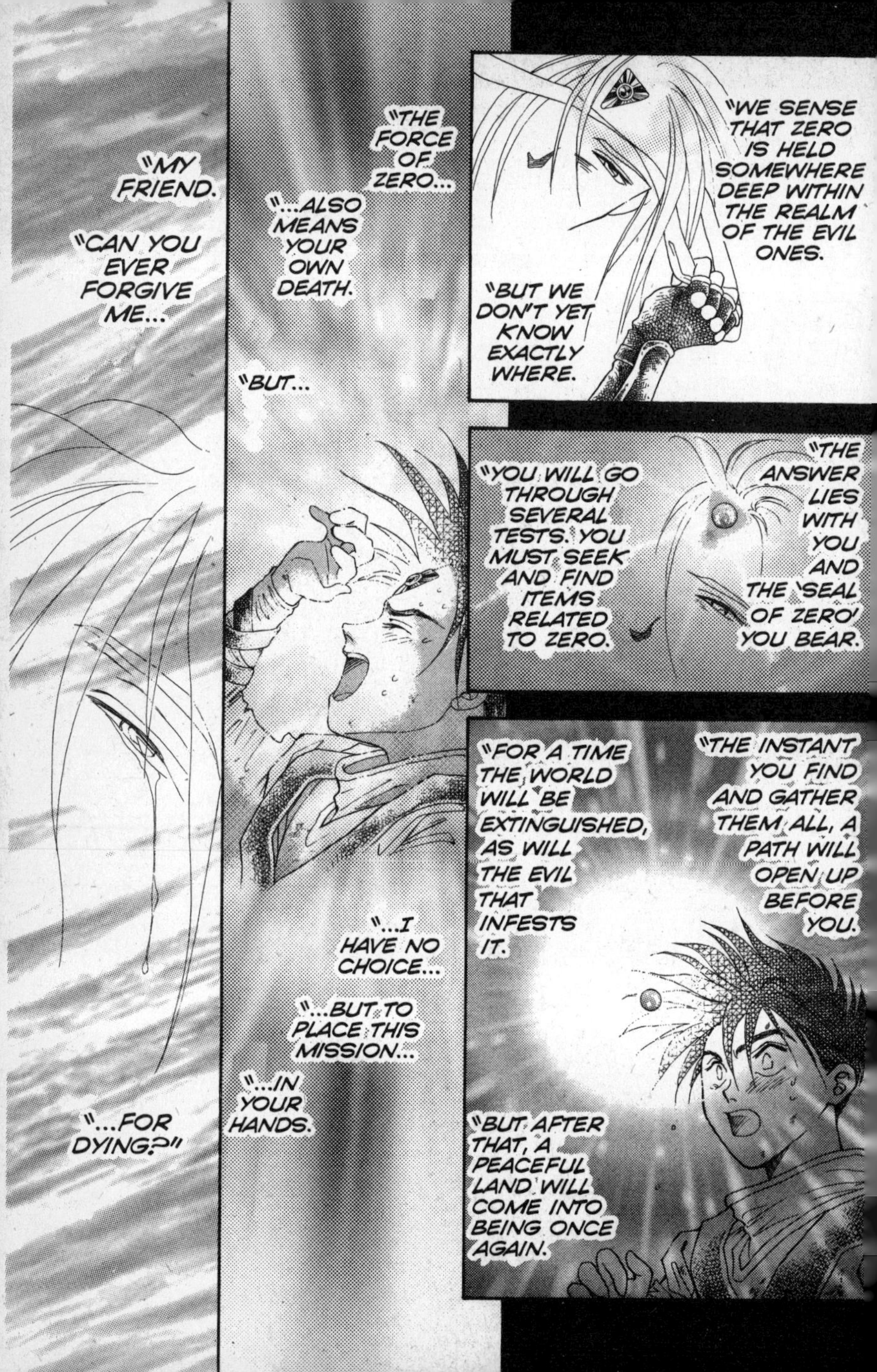
"WE SENSE THAT ZERO IS HELD SOMEWHERE DEEP WITHIN THE REALM OF THE EVIL ONES.
"BUT WE DON'T YET KNOW EXACTLY WHERE.
"THE ANSWER LIES WITH YOU AND THE 'SEAL OF ZERO' YOU BEAR.
"YOU WILL GO THROUGH SEVERAL TESTS. YOU MUST SEEK AND FIND ITEMS RELATED TO ZERO.
"THE INSTANT YOU FIND AND GATHER THEM ALL, A PATH WILL OPEN UP BEFORE YOU.
"FOR A TIME THE WORLD WILL BE EXTINGUISHED, AS WILL THE EVIL THAT INFESTS IT.
"BUT AFTER THAT, A PEACEFUL LAND WILL COME INTO BEING ONCE AGAIN.
"THE FORCE OF ZERO...
"...ALSO MEANS YOUR OWN DEATH.
"BUT...
"...I HAVE NO CHOICE...
"...BUT TO PLACE THIS MISSION...
"...IN YOUR HANDS.
"MY FRIEND.
"CAN YOU EVER FORGIVE ME...
"...FOR DYING?"

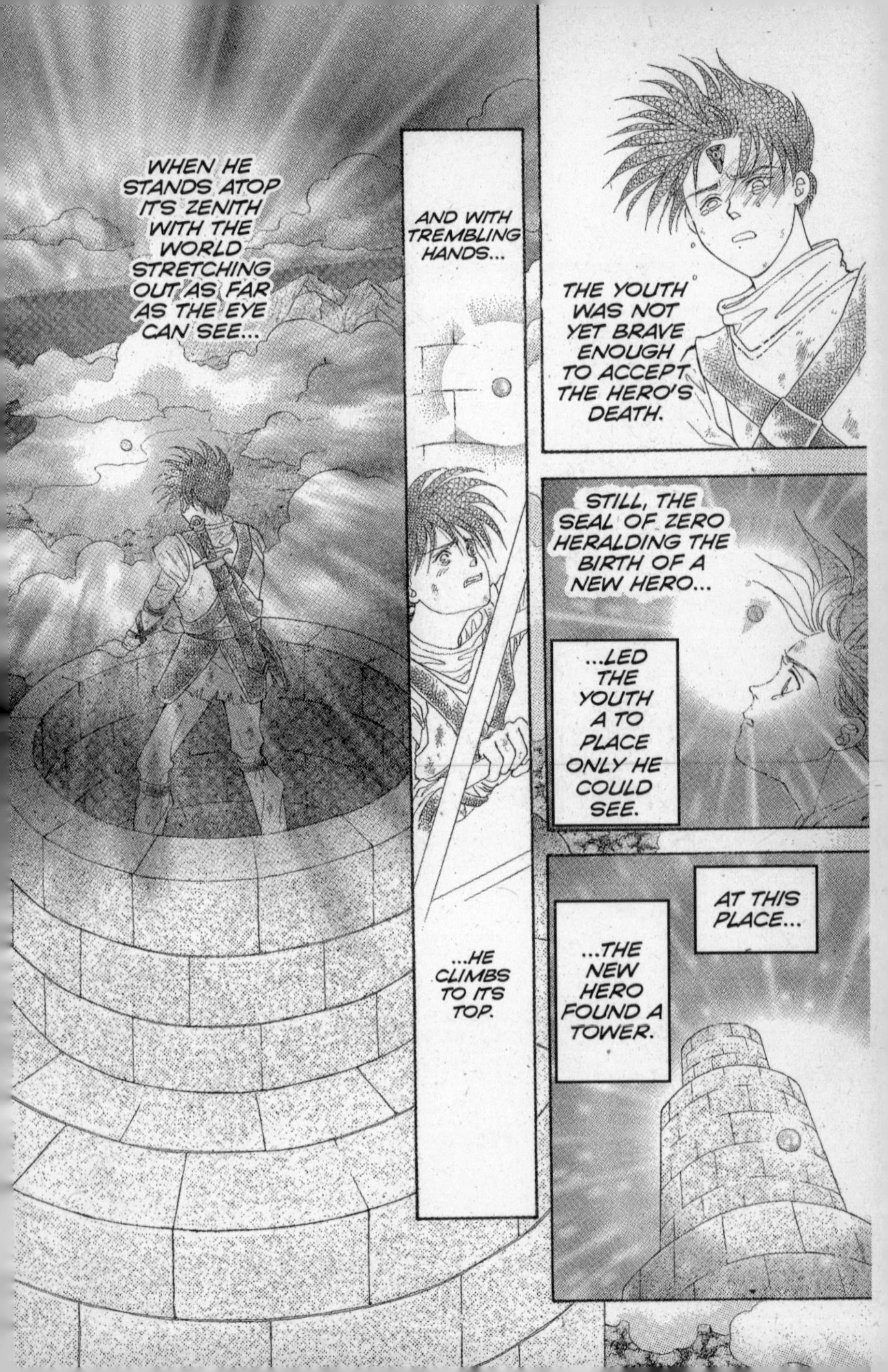
THE YOUTH WAS NOT YET BRAVE ENOUGH TO ACCEPT THE HERO'S DEATH.
STILL, THE SEAL OF ZERO HERALDING THE BIRTH OF A NEW HERO...
...LED THE YOUTH A TO PLACE ONLY HE COULD SEE.
AT THIS PLACE...
...THE NEW HERO FOUND A TOWER.
AND WITH TREMBLING HANDS...
...HE CLIMBS TO ITS TOP.
WHEN HE STANDS ATOP ITS ZENITH WITH THE WORLD STRETCHING OUT AS FAR AS THE EYE CAN SEE...

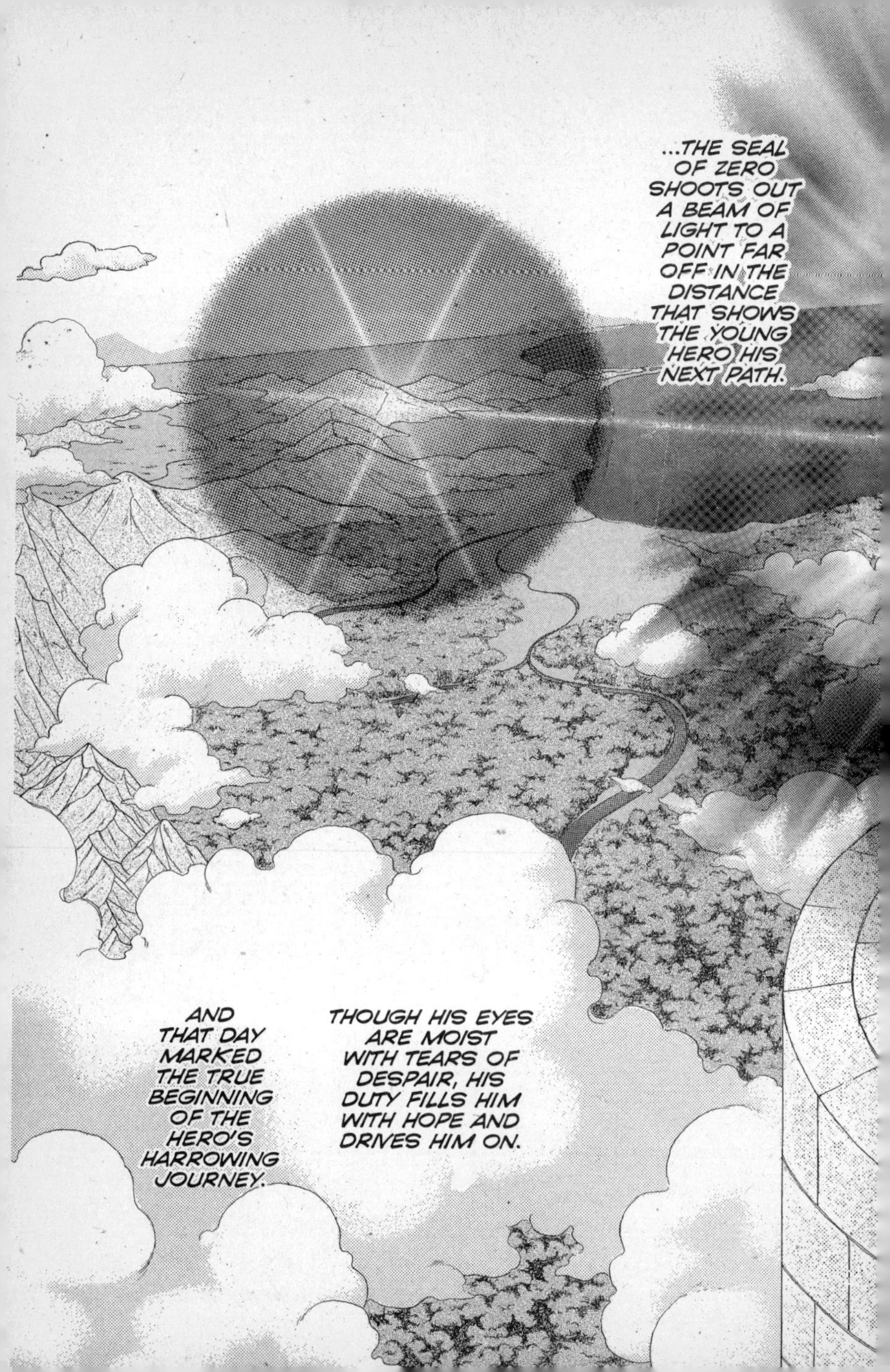
...THE SEAL OF ZERO SHOOTS OUT A BEAM OF LIGHT TO A POINT FAR OFF IN THE DISTANCE THAT SHOWS THE YOUNG HERO HIS NEXT PATH.
THOUGH HIS EYES ARE MOIST WITH TEARS OF DESPAIR, HIS DUTY FILLS HIM WITH HOPE AND DRIVES HIM ON.
AND THAT DAY MARKED THE TRUE BEGINNING OF THE HERO'S HARROWING JOURNEY.

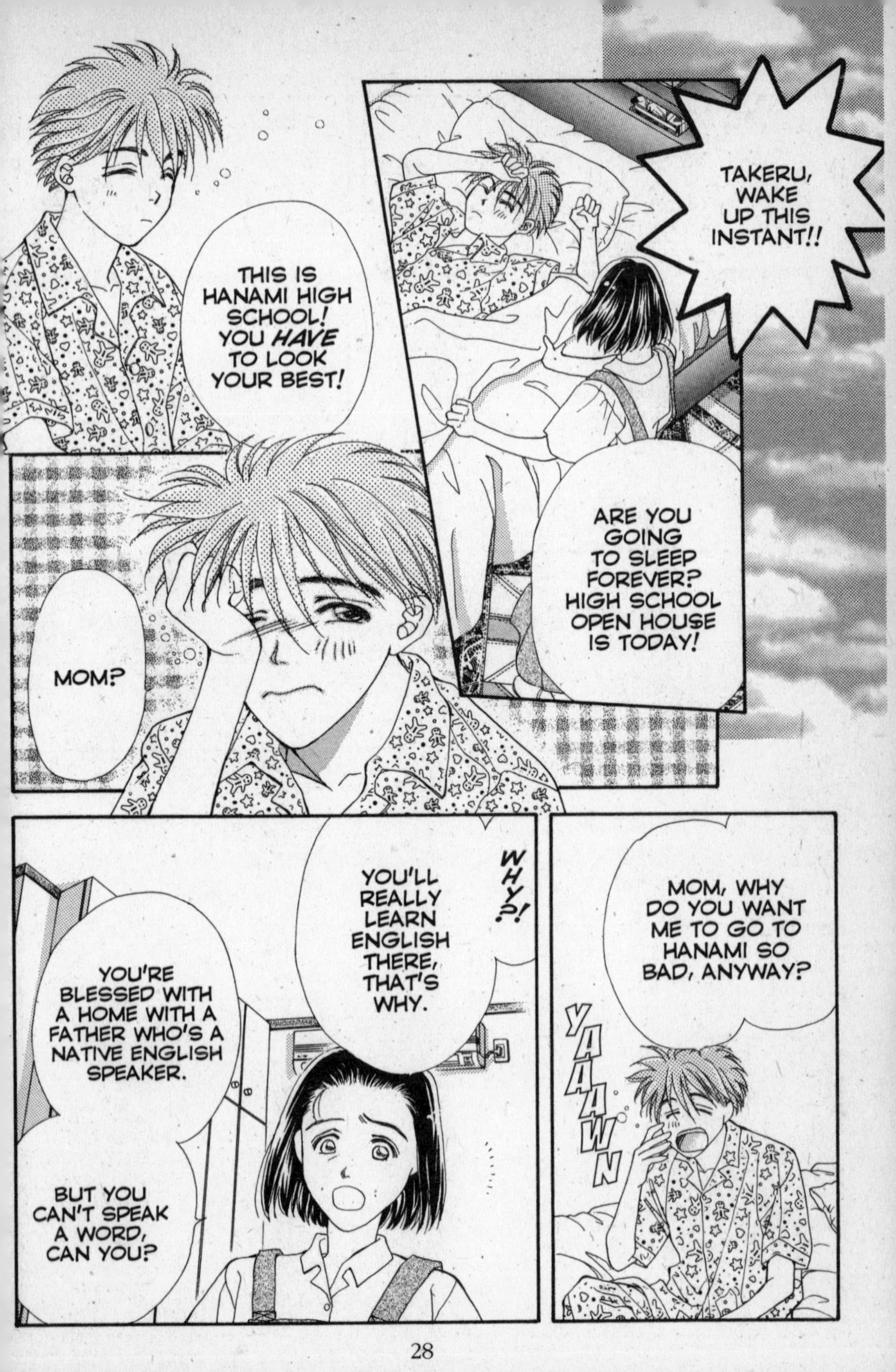
TAKERU, WAKE UP THIS INSTANT!!
ARE YOU GOING TO SLEEP FOREVER? HIGH SCHOOL OPEN HOUSE IS TODAY!
THIS IS HANAMI HIGH SCHOOL! YOU *HAVE* TO LOOK YOUR BEST!
MOM?
MOM, WHY DO YOU WANT ME TO GO TO HANAMI SO BAD, ANYWAY?
YAAAWN
WHY?!
YOU'LL REALLY LEARN ENGLISH THERE, THAT'S WHY.
YOU'RE BLESSED WITH A HOME WITH A FATHER WHO'S A NATIVE ENGLISH SPEAKER.
BUT YOU CAN'T SPEAK A WORD, CAN YOU?

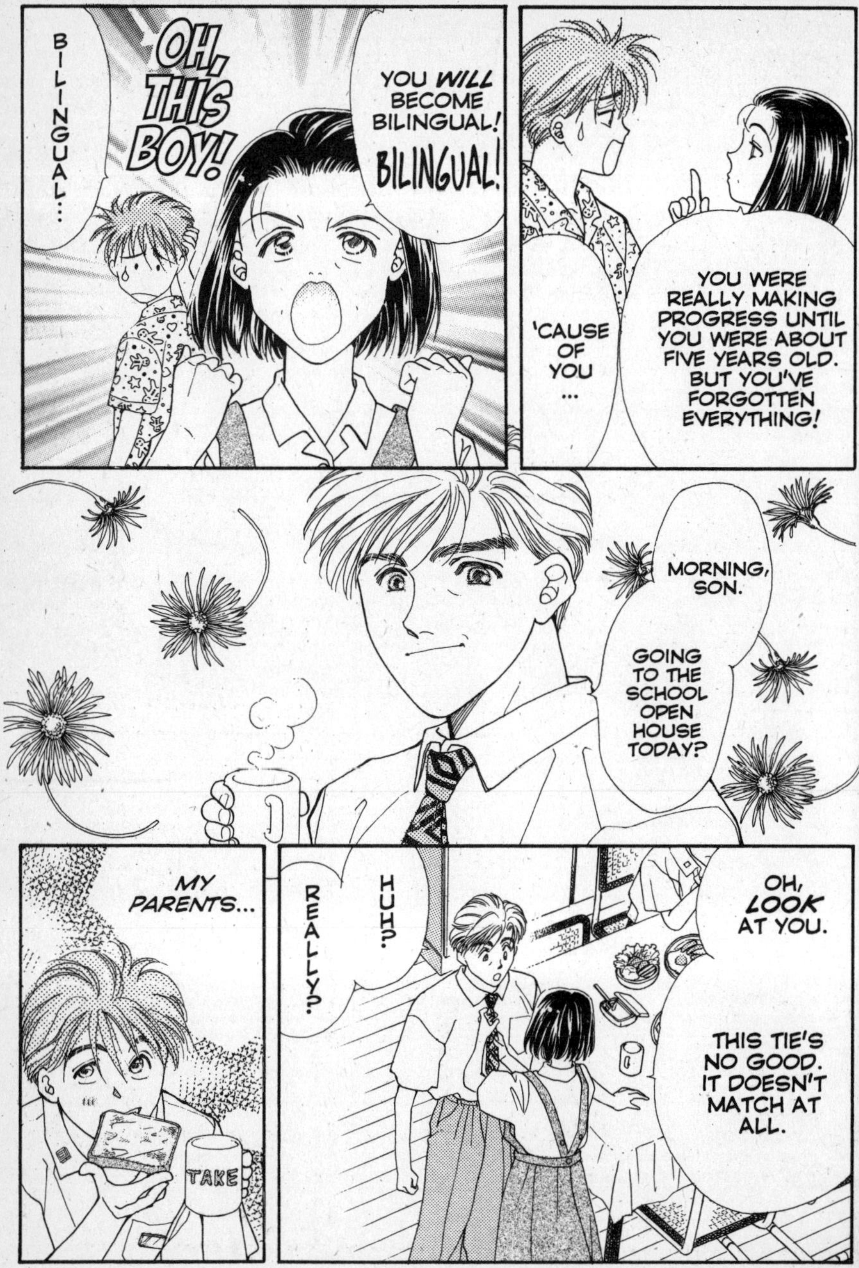
YOU WERE REALLY MAKING PROGRESS UNTIL YOU WERE ABOUT FIVE YEARS OLD. BUT YOU'VE FORGOTTEN EVERYTHING!
'CAUSE OF YOU ...
YOU *WILL* BECOME BILINGUAL! BILINGUAL!
OH, THIS BOY!
BILINGUAL...
MORNING, SON.
GOING TO THE SCHOOL OPEN HOUSE TODAY?
OH, *LOOK* AT YOU.
THIS TIE'S NO GOOD. IT DOESN'T MATCH AT ALL.
HUH?
REALLY?
MY PARENTS...
TAKE

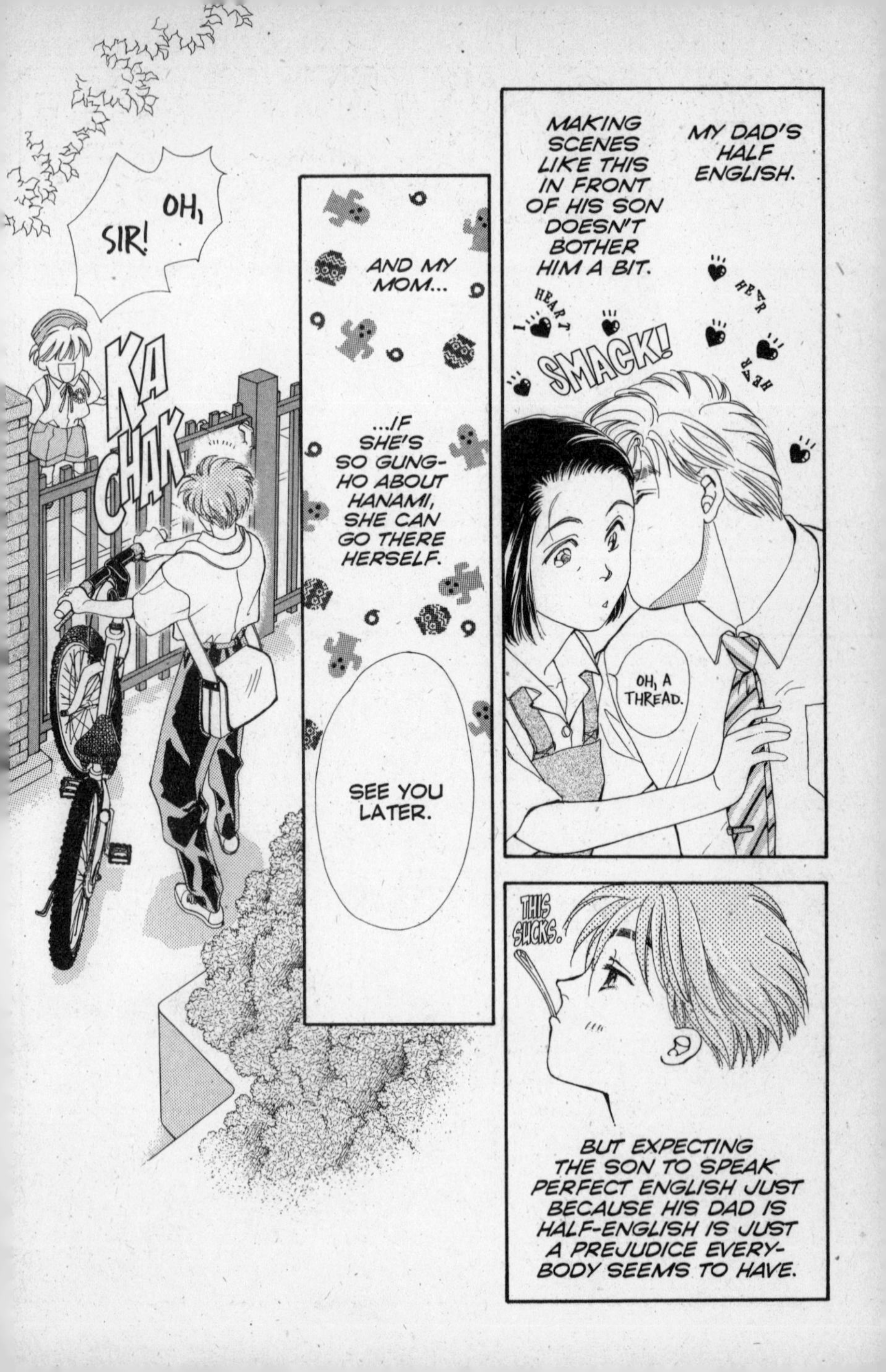
MY DAD'S HALF ENGLISH.
MAKING SCENES LIKE THIS IN FRONT OF HIS SON DOESN'T BOTHER HIM A BIT.
I HEART
SMACK!
OH, A THREAD.
THIS SUCKS.
BUT EXPECTING THE SON TO SPEAK PERFECT ENGLISH JUST BECAUSE HIS DAD IS HALF-ENGLISH IS JUST A PREJUDICE EVERY-BODY SEEMS TO HAVE.
AND MY MOM...
...IF SHE'S SO GUNG-HO ABOUT HANAMI, SHE CAN GO THERE HERSELF.
SEE YOU LATER.
OH, SIR!
KA CHAK

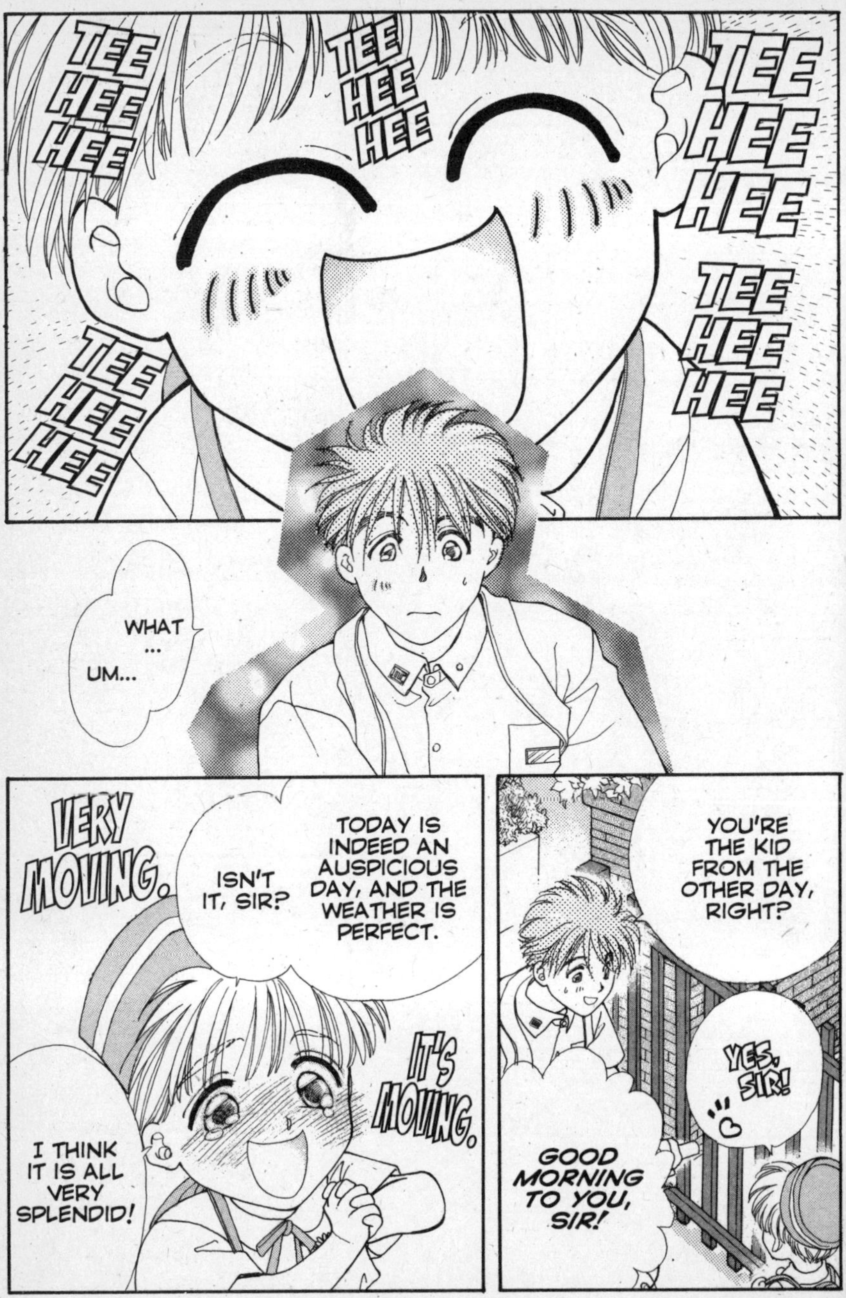
TEE HEE HEE
TEE HEE HEE
TEE HEE HEE
TEE HEE HEE
TEE HEE HEE
WHAT ... UM...
YOU'RE THE KID FROM THE OTHER DAY, RIGHT?
YES, SIR!
GOOD MORNING TO YOU, SIR!
TODAY IS INDEED AN AUSPICIOUS DAY, AND THE WEATHER IS PERFECT.
ISN'T IT, SIR?
VERY MOVING.
IT'S MOVING.
I THINK IT IS ALL VERY SPLENDID!

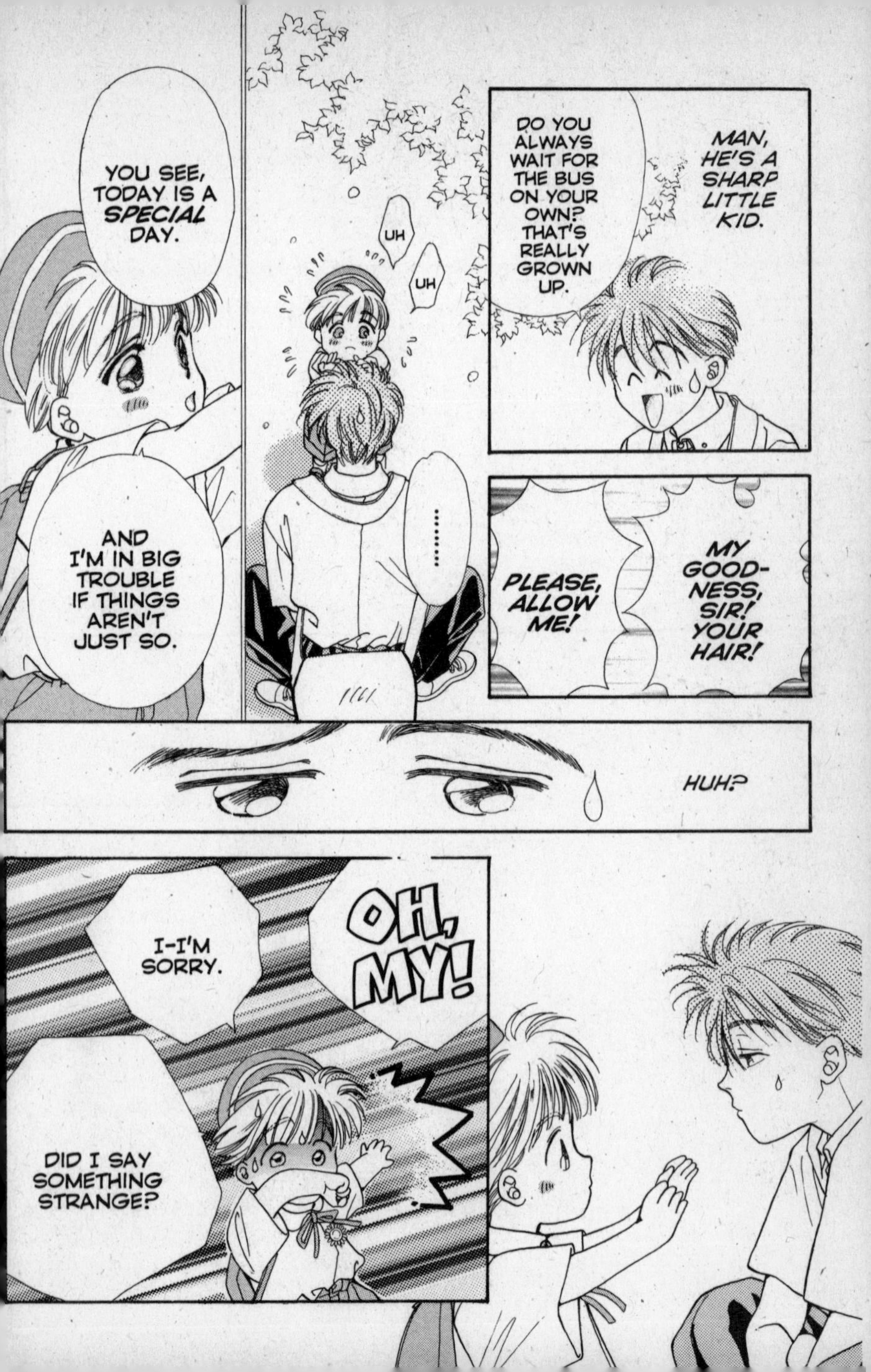
MAN, HE'S A SHARP LITTLE KID.
DO YOU ALWAYS WAIT FOR THE BUS ON YOUR OWN? THAT'S REALLY GROWN UP.
MY GOODNESS, SIR! YOUR HAIR!
PLEASE, ALLOW ME!
UH
UH
......
YOU SEE, TODAY IS A SPECIAL DAY.
AND I'M IN BIG TROUBLE IF THINGS AREN'T JUST SO.
HUH?
OH, MY!
I-I'M SORRY.
DID I SAY SOMETHING STRANGE?

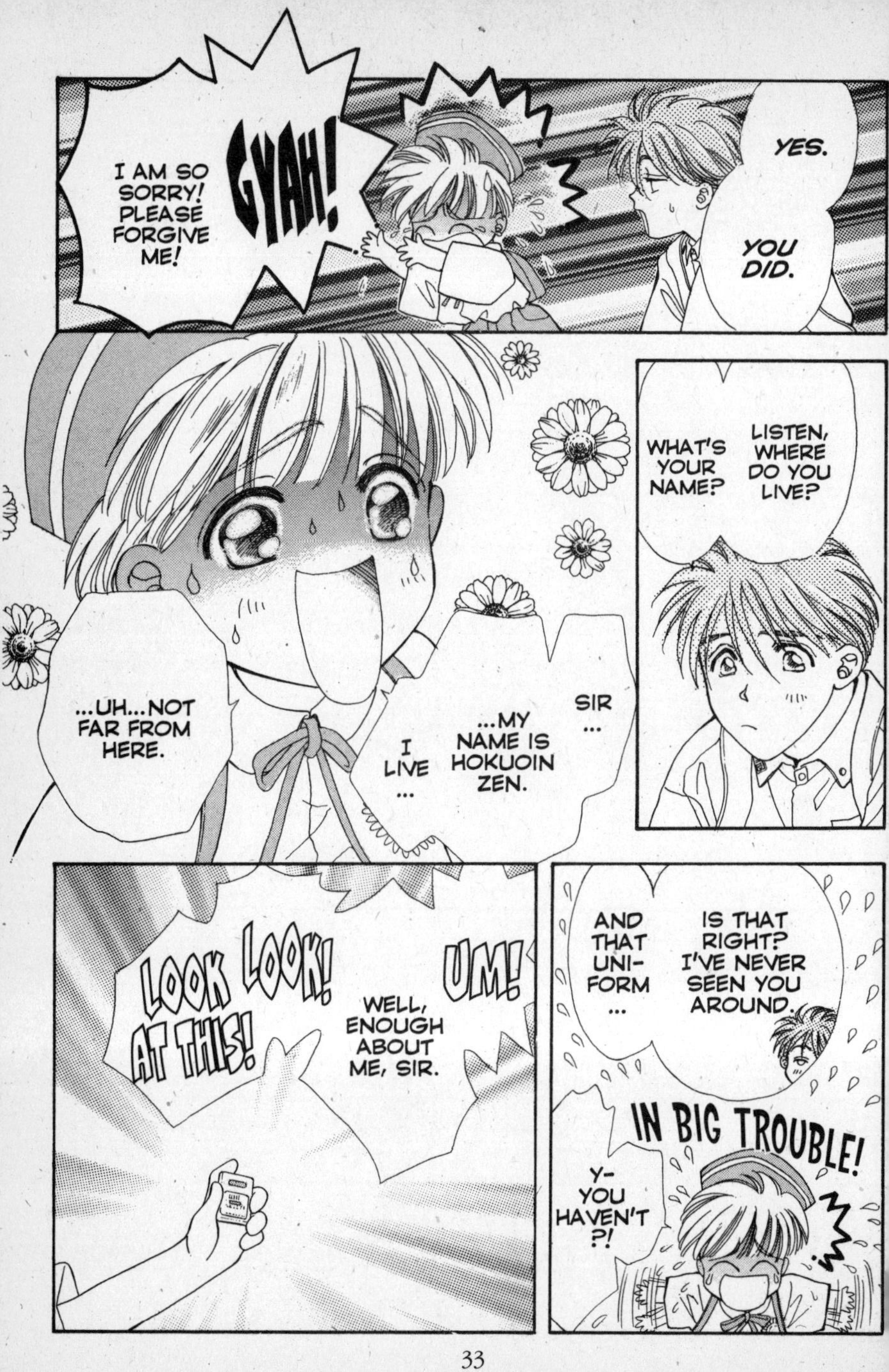
YES. YOU DID.
GYAH!
I AM SO SORRY! PLEASE FORGIVE ME!
LISTEN, WHERE DO YOU LIVE?
WHAT'S YOUR NAME?
SIR ...
...MY NAME IS HOKUOIN ZEN.
I LIVE ...
...UH...NOT FAR FROM HERE.
IS THAT RIGHT? I'VE NEVER SEEN YOU AROUND.
AND THAT UNI-FORM ...
IN BIG TROUBLE!
Y-YOU HAVEN'T?!
UM!
WELL, ENOUGH ABOUT ME, SIR.
LOOK LOOK! AT THIS!

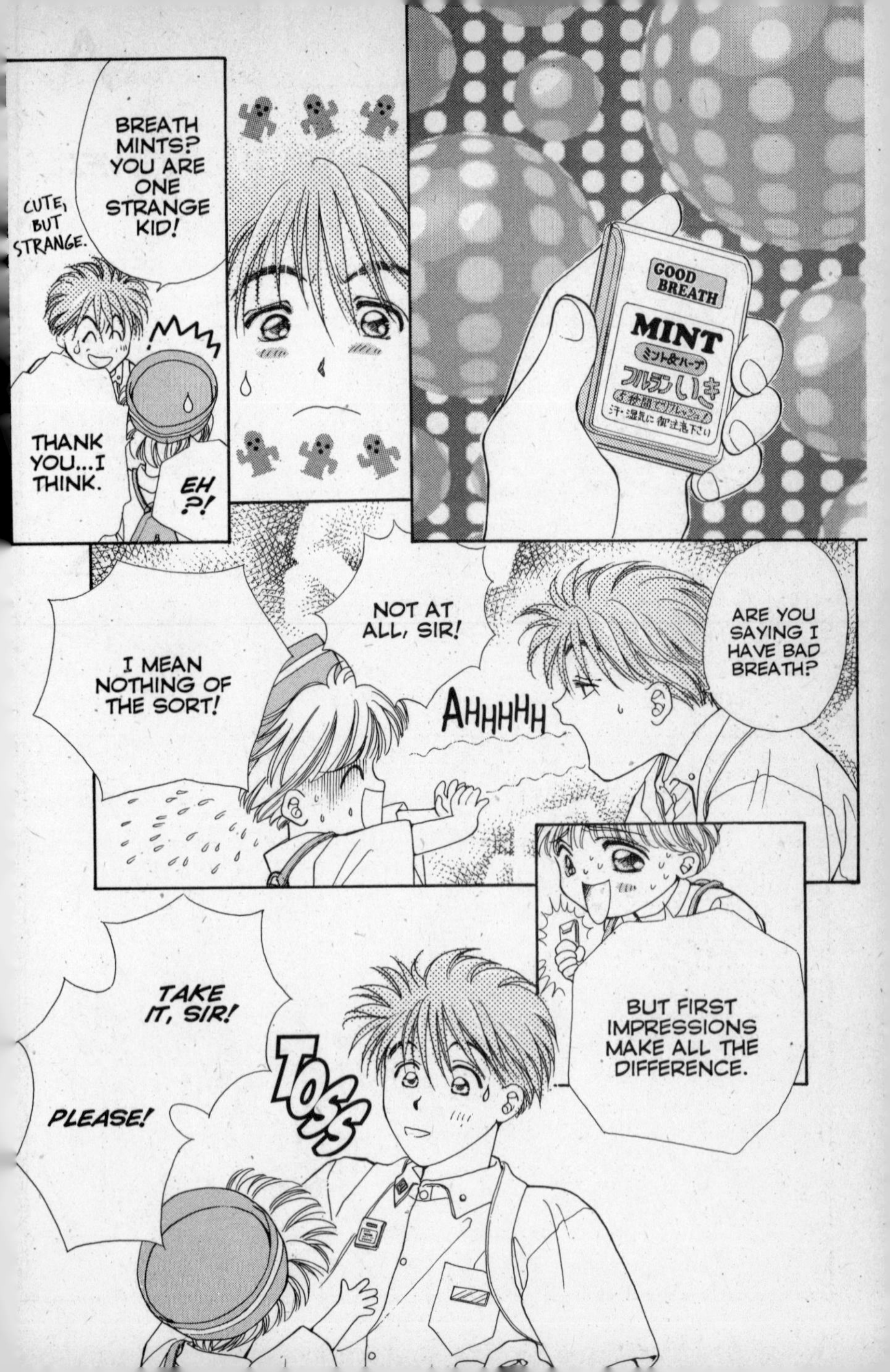
GOOD BREATH
MINT
ミント&ハーブ
BREATH MINTS? YOU ARE ONE STRANGE KID!
CUTE, BUT STRANGE.
EH ?!
THANK YOU...I THINK.
ARE YOU SAYING I HAVE BAD BREATH?
AHHHHH
NOT AT ALL, SIR!
I MEAN NOTHING OF THE SORT!
BUT FIRST IMPRESSIONS MAKE ALL THE DIFFERENCE.
TOSS
TAKE IT, SIR!
PLEASE!

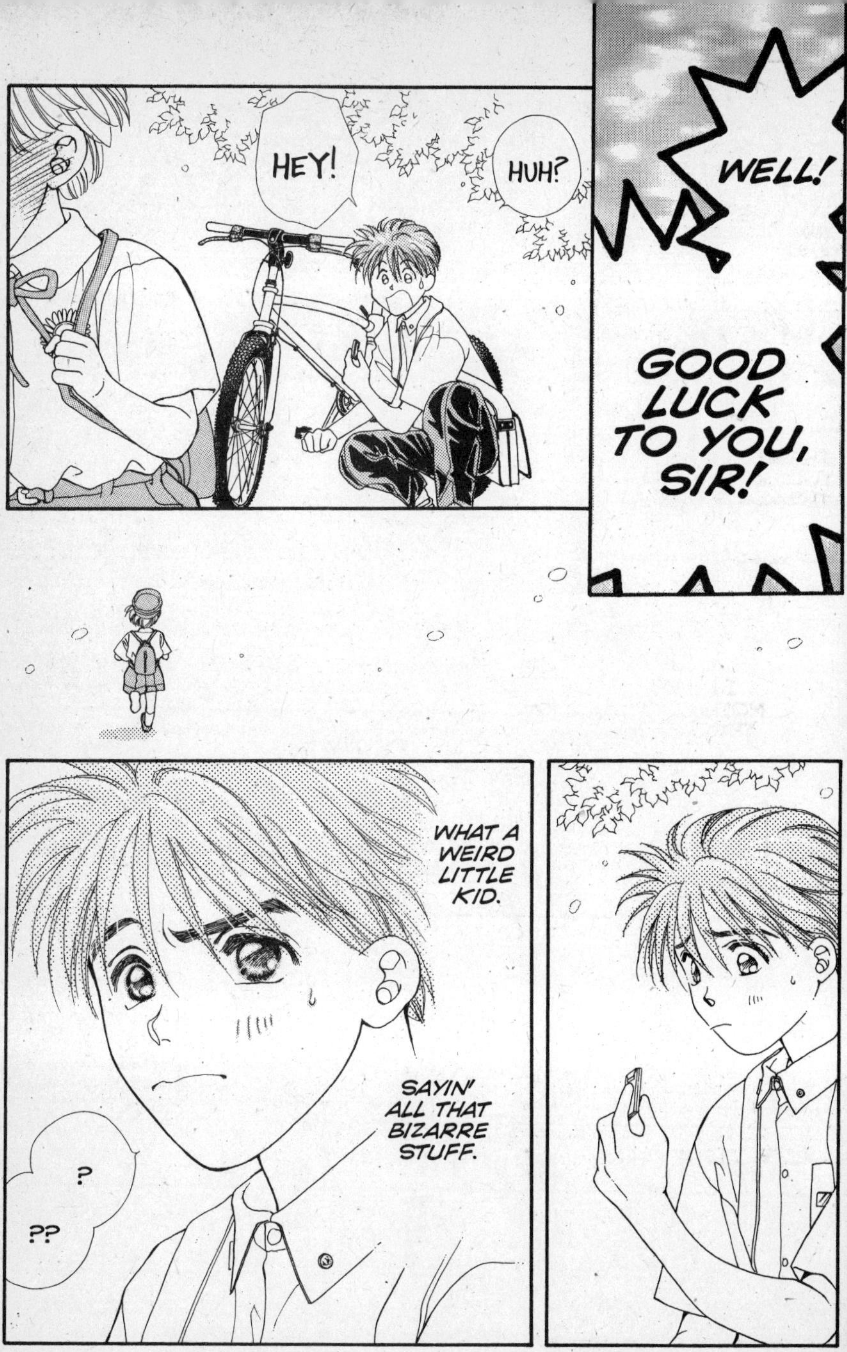
WELL!
GOOD LUCK TO YOU, SIR!
HEY!
HUH?
WHAT A WEIRD LITTLE KID.
SAYIN' ALL THAT BIZARRE STUFF.
?
??

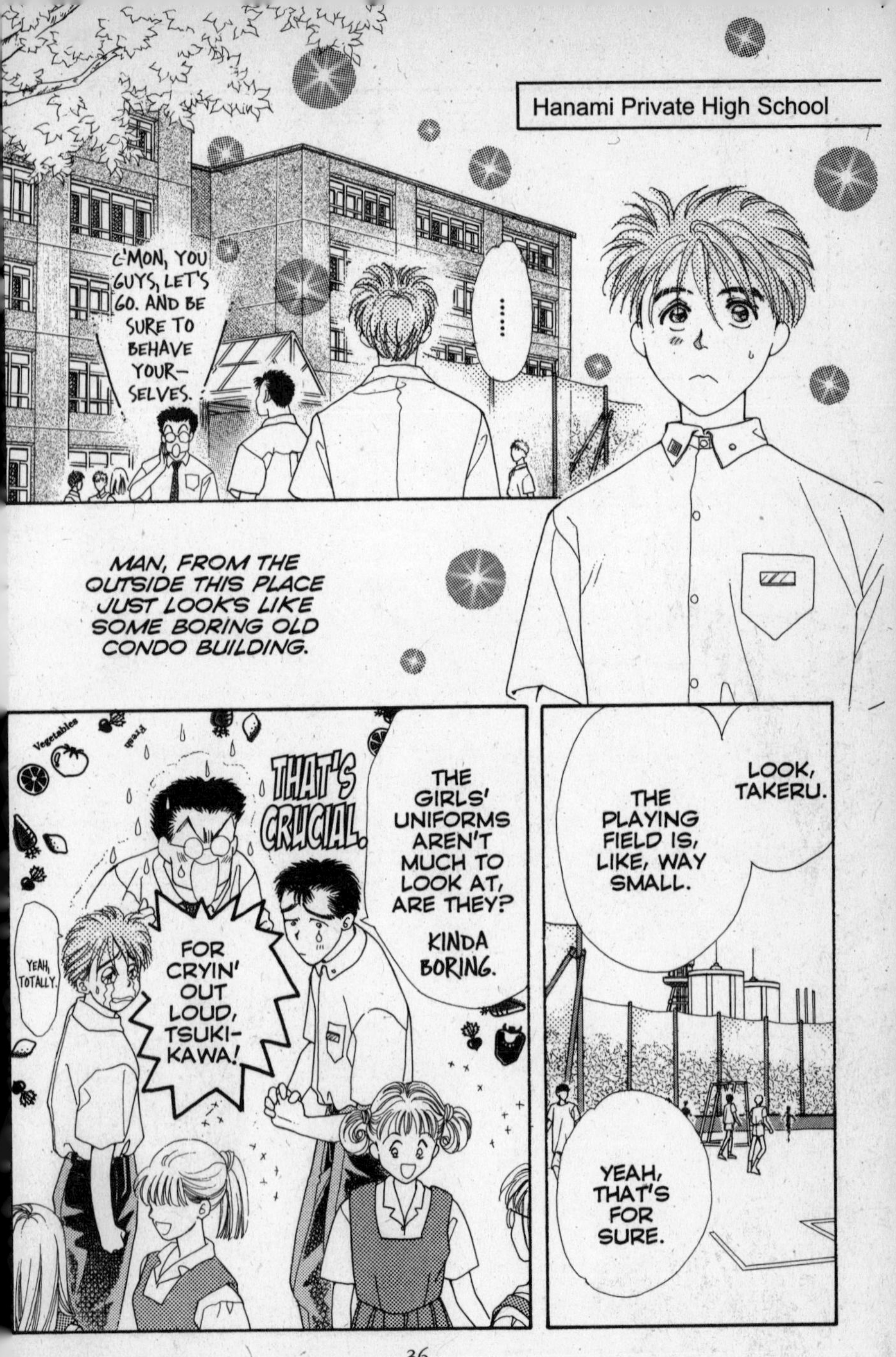
Hanami Private High School
C'MON, YOU GUYS, LET'S GO. AND BE SURE TO BEHAVE YOURSELVES.
......
MAN, FROM THE OUTSIDE THIS PLACE JUST LOOKS LIKE SOME BORING OLD CONDO BUILDING.
LOOK, TAKERU.
THE PLAYING FIELD IS, LIKE, WAY SMALL.
YEAH, THAT'S FOR SURE.
THE GIRLS' UNIFORMS AREN'T MUCH TO LOOK AT, ARE THEY?
KINDA BORING.
THAT'S CRUCIAL.
FOR CRYIN' OUT LOUD, TSUKIKAWA!
YEAH, TOTALLY.

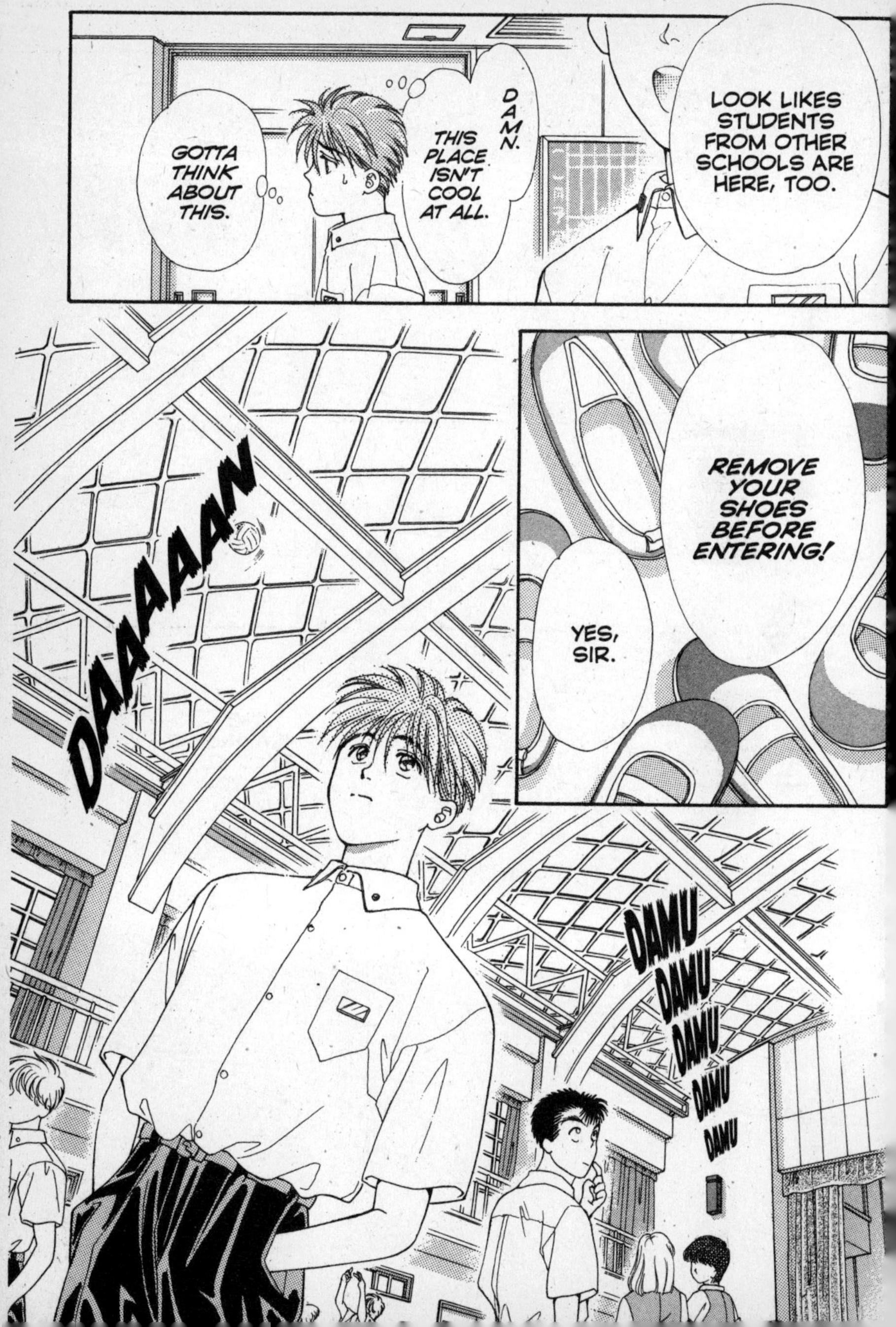
LOOK LIKES STUDENTS FROM OTHER SCHOOLS ARE HERE, TOO.
DAMN.
THIS PLACE ISN'T COOL AT ALL.
GOTTA THINK ABOUT THIS.
REMOVE YOUR SHOES BEFORE ENTERING!
YES, SIR.
DAAAAAN
DAMU DAMU DAMU DAMU DAMU

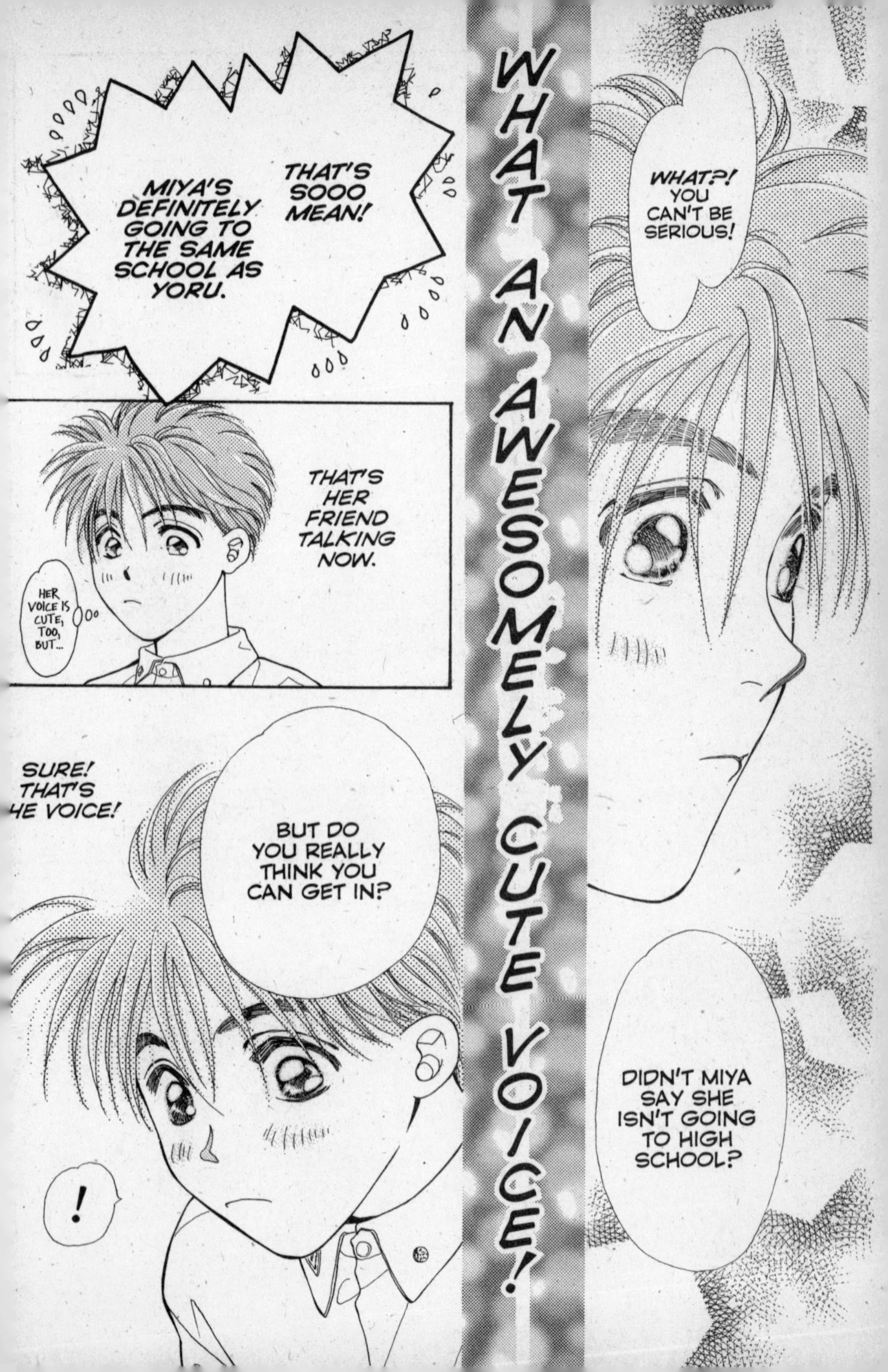
WHAT?! YOU CAN'T BE SERIOUS!
DIDN'T MIYA SAY SHE ISN'T GOING TO HIGH SCHOOL?
WHAT AN AWESOMELY CUTE VOICE!
THAT'S SOOO MEAN!
MIYA'S DEFINITELY GOING TO THE SAME SCHOOL AS YORU.
THAT'S HER FRIEND TALKING NOW.
HER VOICE IS CUTE, TOO, BUT...
BUT DO YOU REALLY THINK YOU CAN GET IN?
SURE! THAT'S HE VOICE!
!

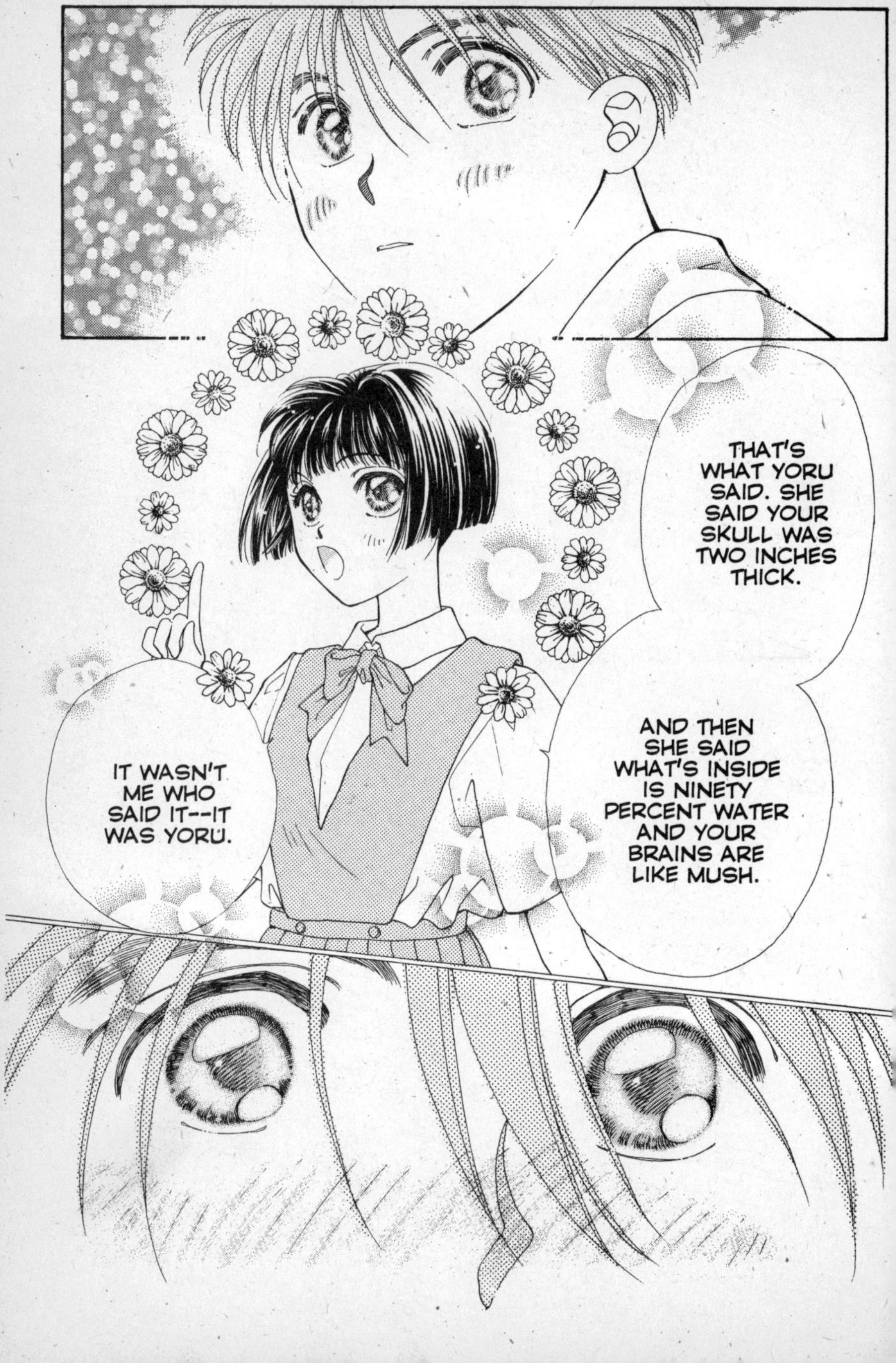
THAT'S WHAT YORU SAID. SHE SAID YOUR SKULL WAS TWO INCHES THICK.
AND THEN SHE SAID WHAT'S INSIDE IS NINETY PERCENT WATER AND YOUR BRAINS ARE LIKE MUSH.
IT WASN'T ME WHO SAID IT--IT WAS YORU.

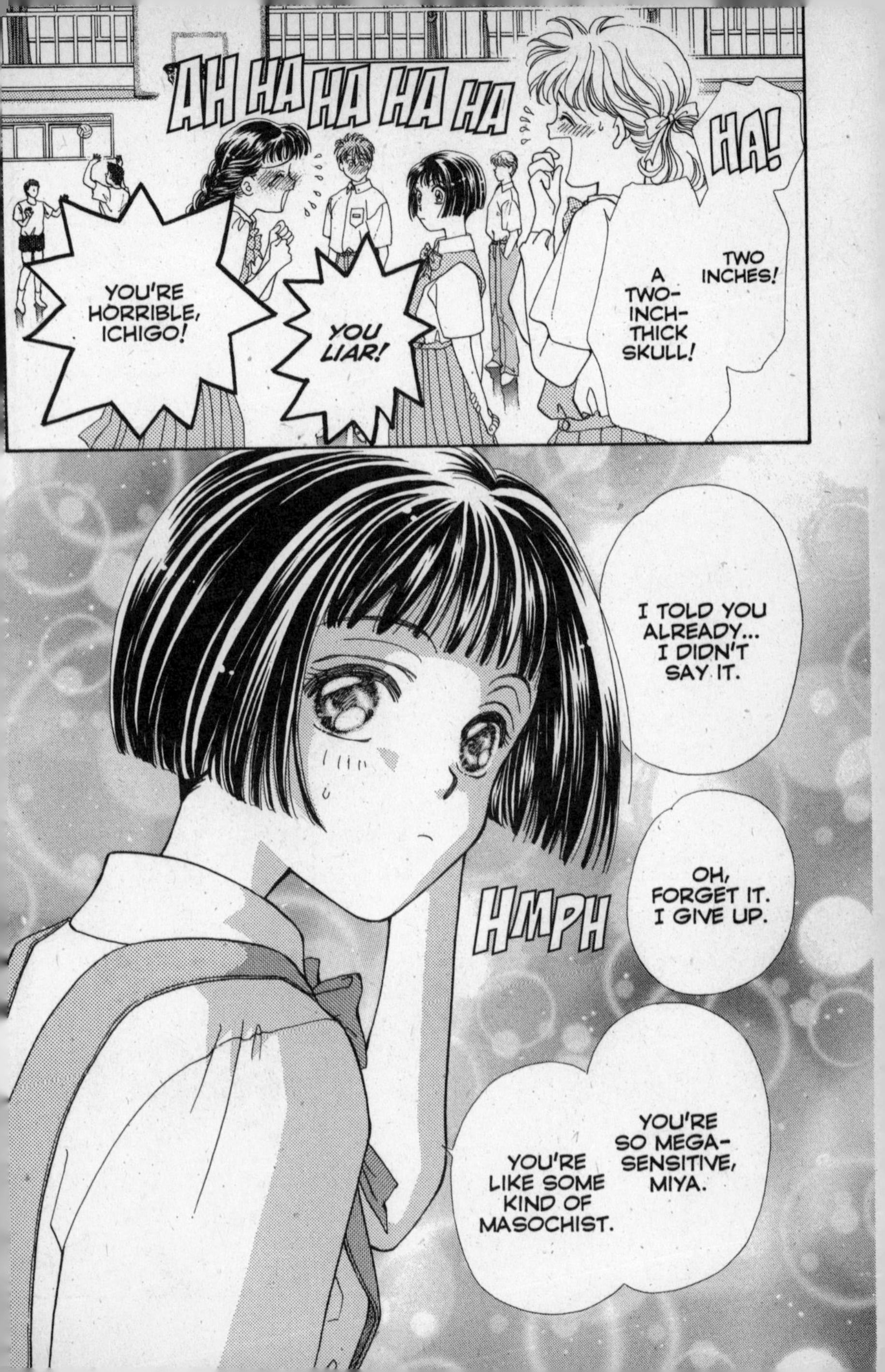
AH HA HA HA HA HA
HA!
TWO INCHES!
A TWO-INCH-THICK SKULL!
YOU LIAR!
YOU'RE HORRIBLE, ICHIGO!
I TOLD YOU ALREADY... I DIDN'T SAY IT.
OH, FORGET IT. I GIVE UP.
HMPH
YOU'RE SO MEGA-SENSITIVE, MIYA.
YOU'RE LIKE SOME KIND OF MASOCHIST.

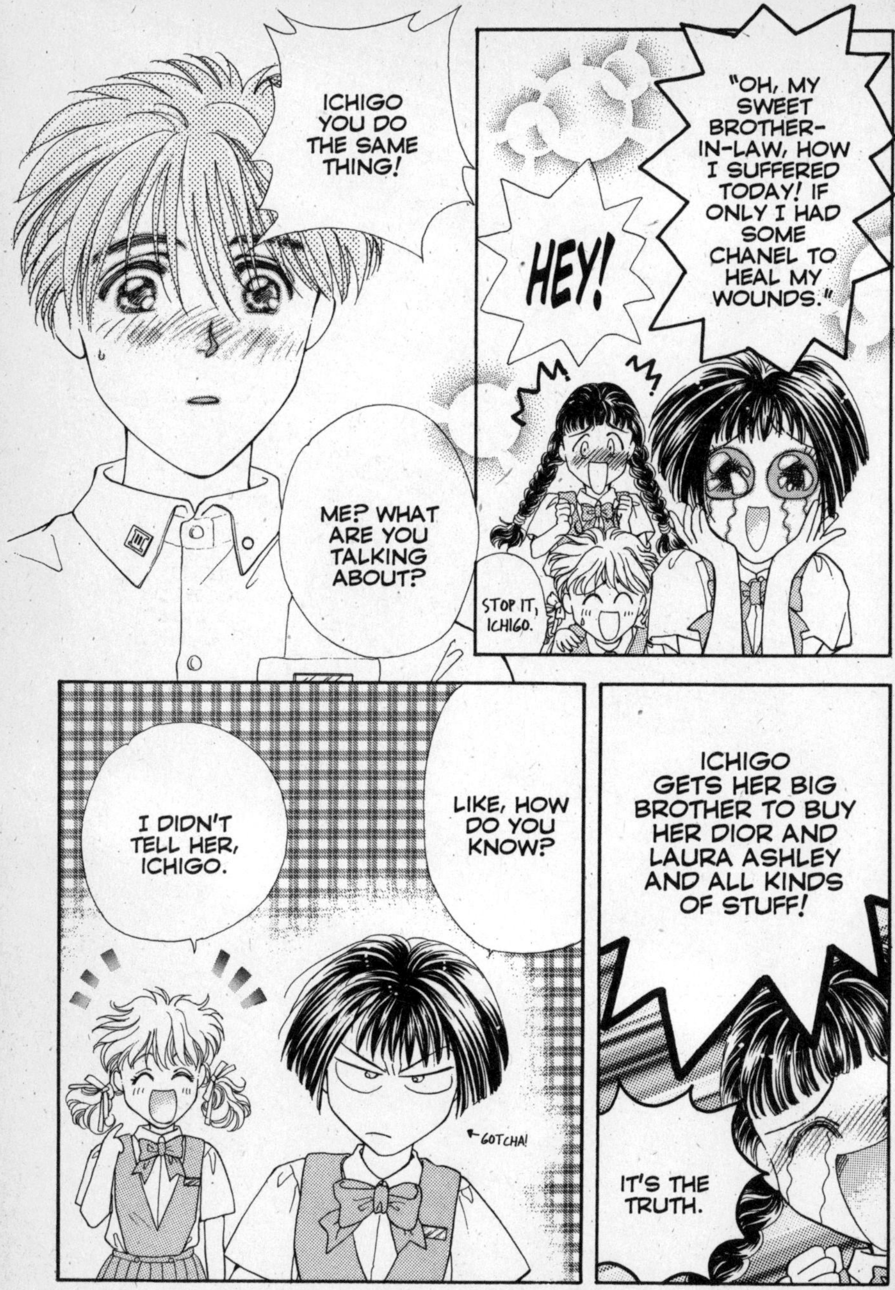
"OH, MY SWEET BROTHER-IN-LAW, HOW I SUFFERED TODAY! IF ONLY I HAD SOME CHANEL TO HEAL MY WOUNDS."
HEY!
STOP IT, ICHIGO.
ICHIGO YOU DO THE SAME THING!
ME? WHAT ARE YOU TALKING ABOUT?
ICHIGO GETS HER BIG BROTHER TO BUY HER DIOR AND LAURA ASHLEY AND ALL KINDS OF STUFF!
IT'S THE TRUTH.
LIKE, HOW DO YOU KNOW?
I DIDN'T TELL HER, ICHIGO.
GOTCHA!

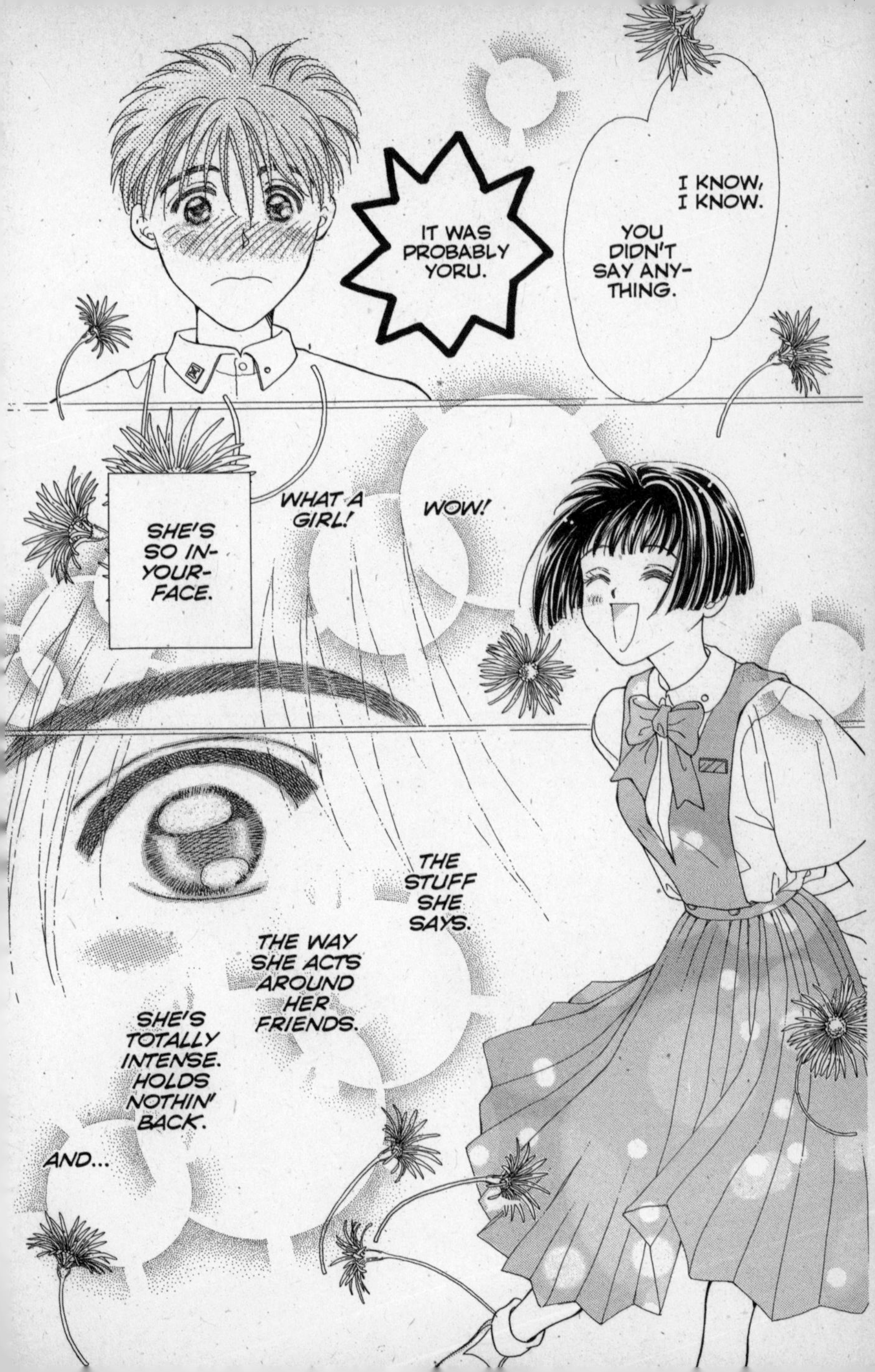
I KNOW, I KNOW.
YOU DIDN'T SAY ANY-THING.
IT WAS PROBABLY YORU.
WOW!
WHAT A GIRL!
SHE'S SO IN-YOUR-FACE.
THE STUFF SHE SAYS.
THE WAY SHE ACTS AROUND HER FRIENDS.
SHE'S TOTALLY INTENSE. HOLDS NOTHIN' BACK.
AND...

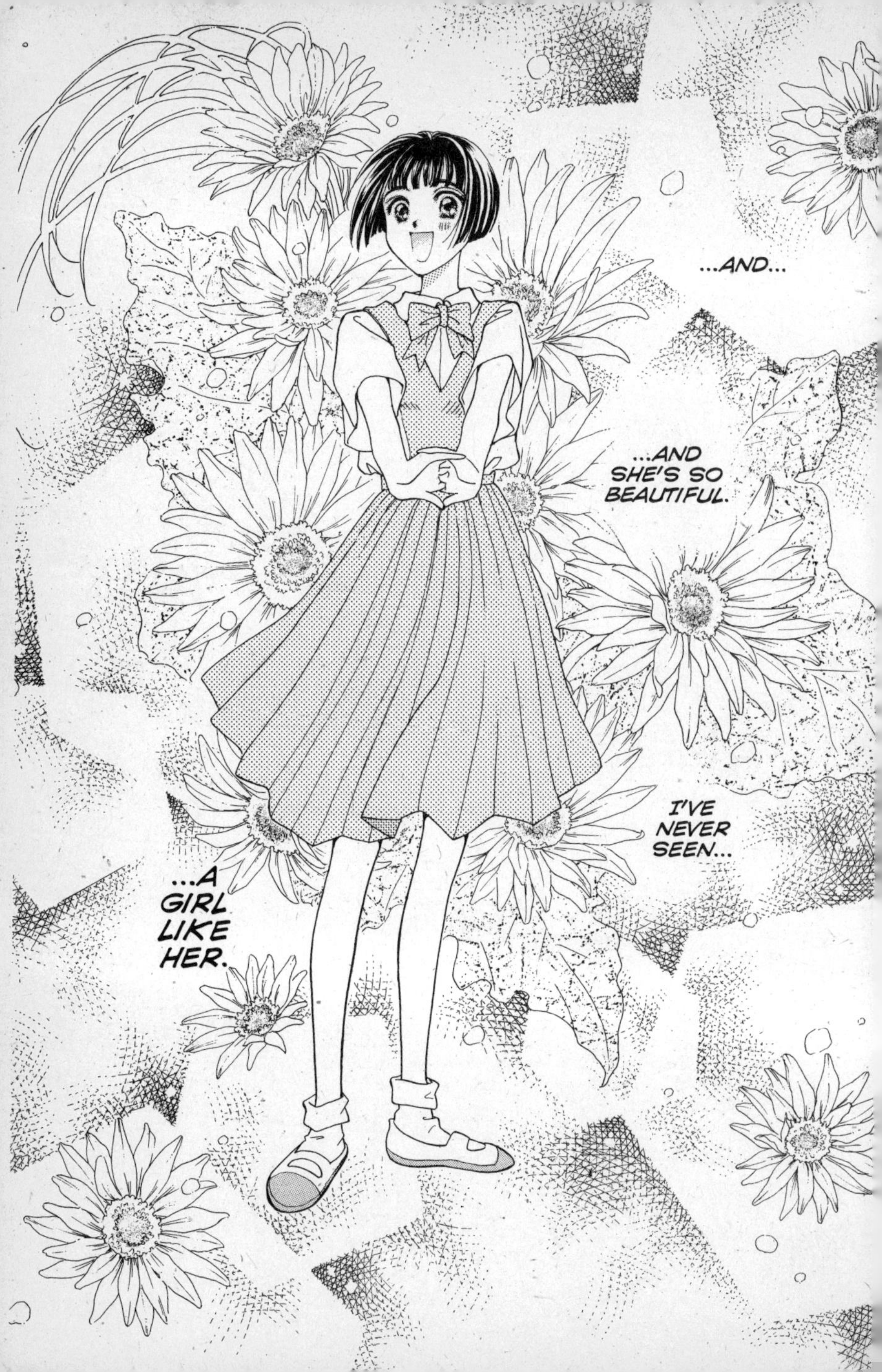
...AND...
...AND SHE'S SO BEAUTIFUL.
I'VE NEVER SEEN...
...A GIRL LIKE HER.

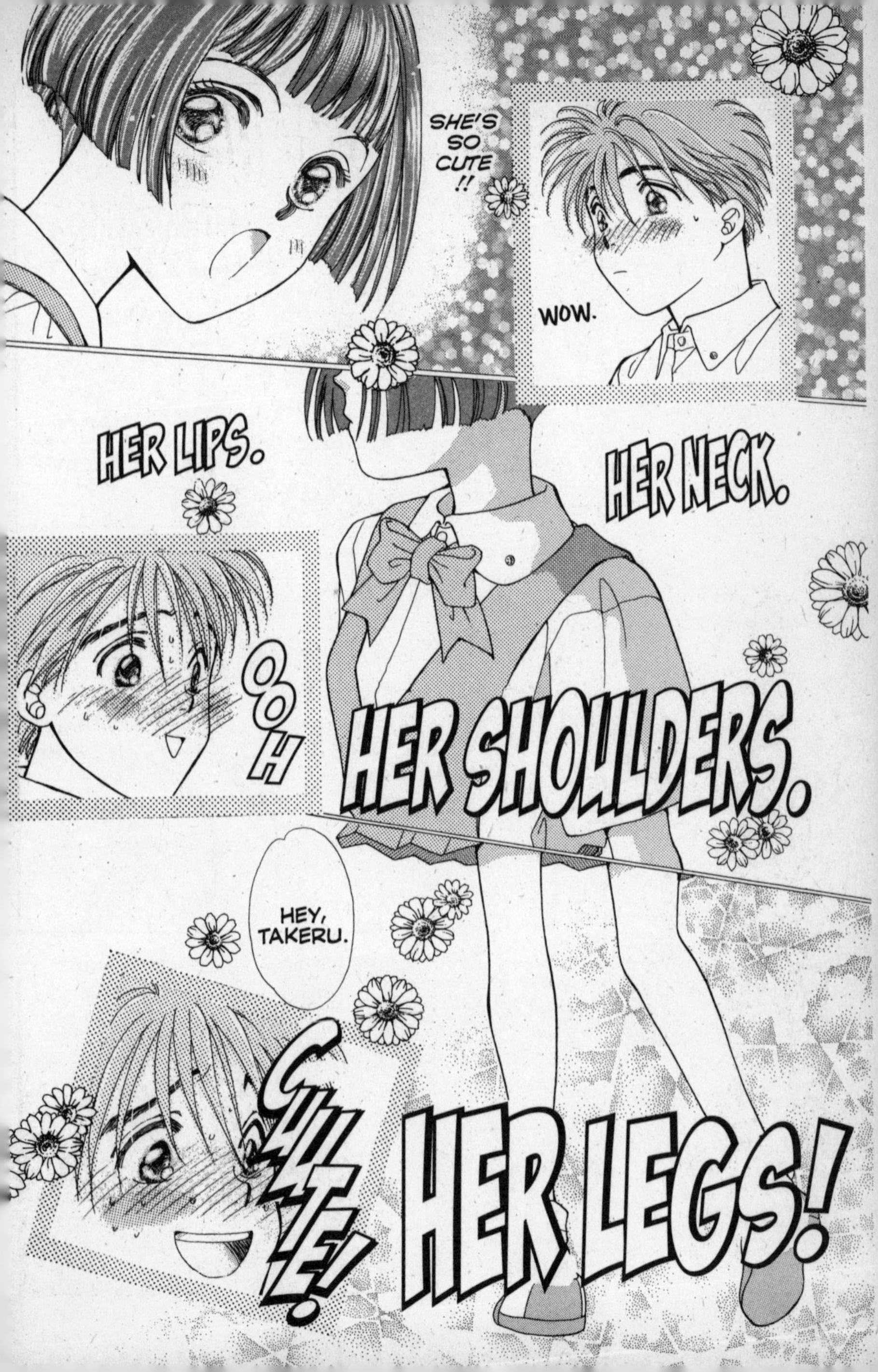
SHE'S SO CUTE !!
WOW.
HER NECK.
HER LIPS.
OOH
HER SHOULDERS.
HEY, TAKERU.
CUUTE!
HER LEGS!

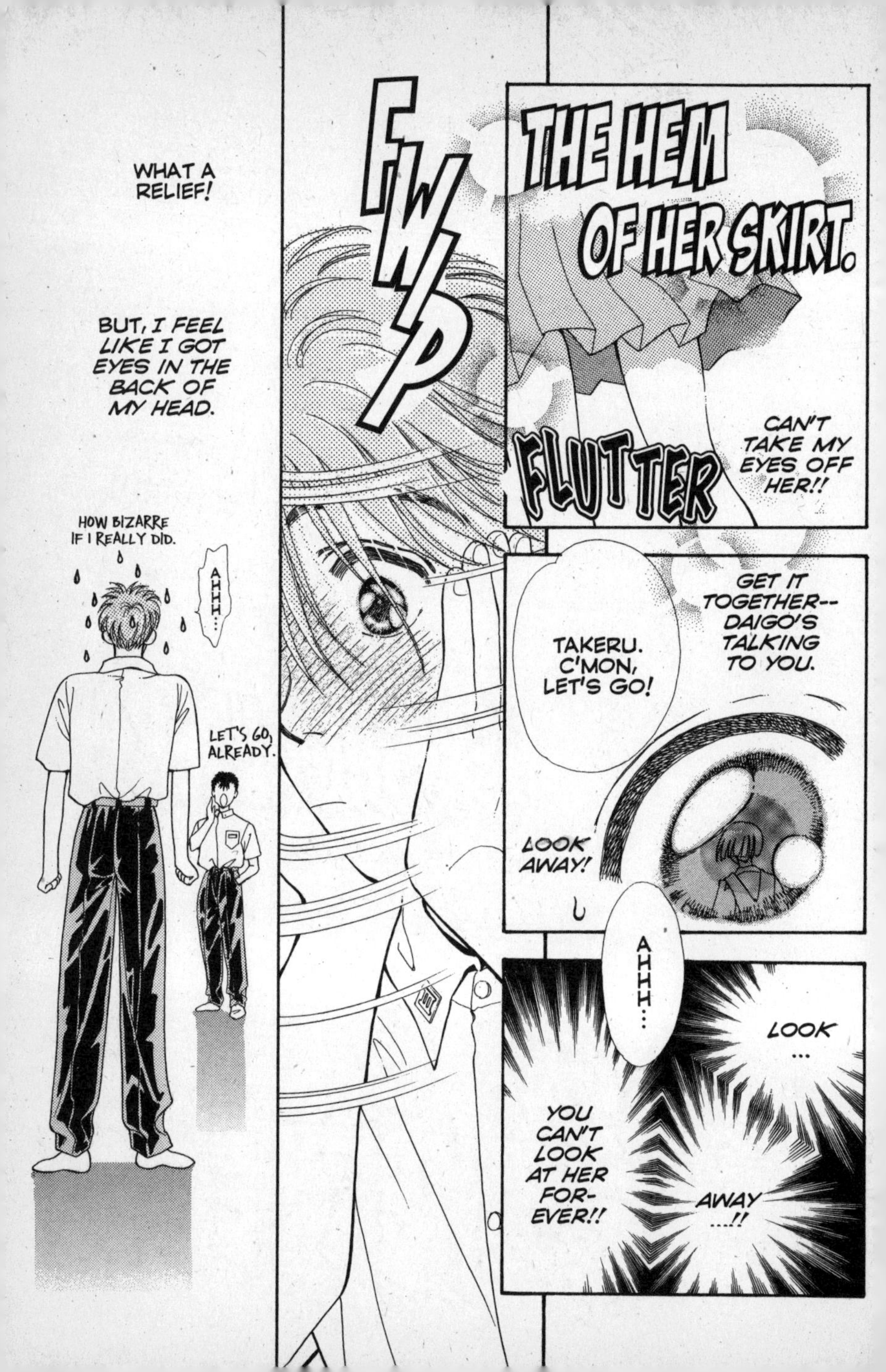
THE HEM OF HER SKIRT.
FLUTTER
CAN'T TAKE MY EYES OFF HER!!
GET IT TOGETHER--DAIGO'S TALKING TO YOU.
TAKERU. C'MON, LET'S GO!
LOOK AWAY!
AHHH...
LOOK ...
AWAY ...!!
YOU CAN'T LOOK AT HER FOR-EVER!!
FWIP
WHAT A RELIEF!
BUT, I FEEL LIKE I GOT EYES IN THE BACK OF MY HEAD.
HOW BIZARRE IF I REALLY DID.
AHHH...
LET'S GO, ALREADY.

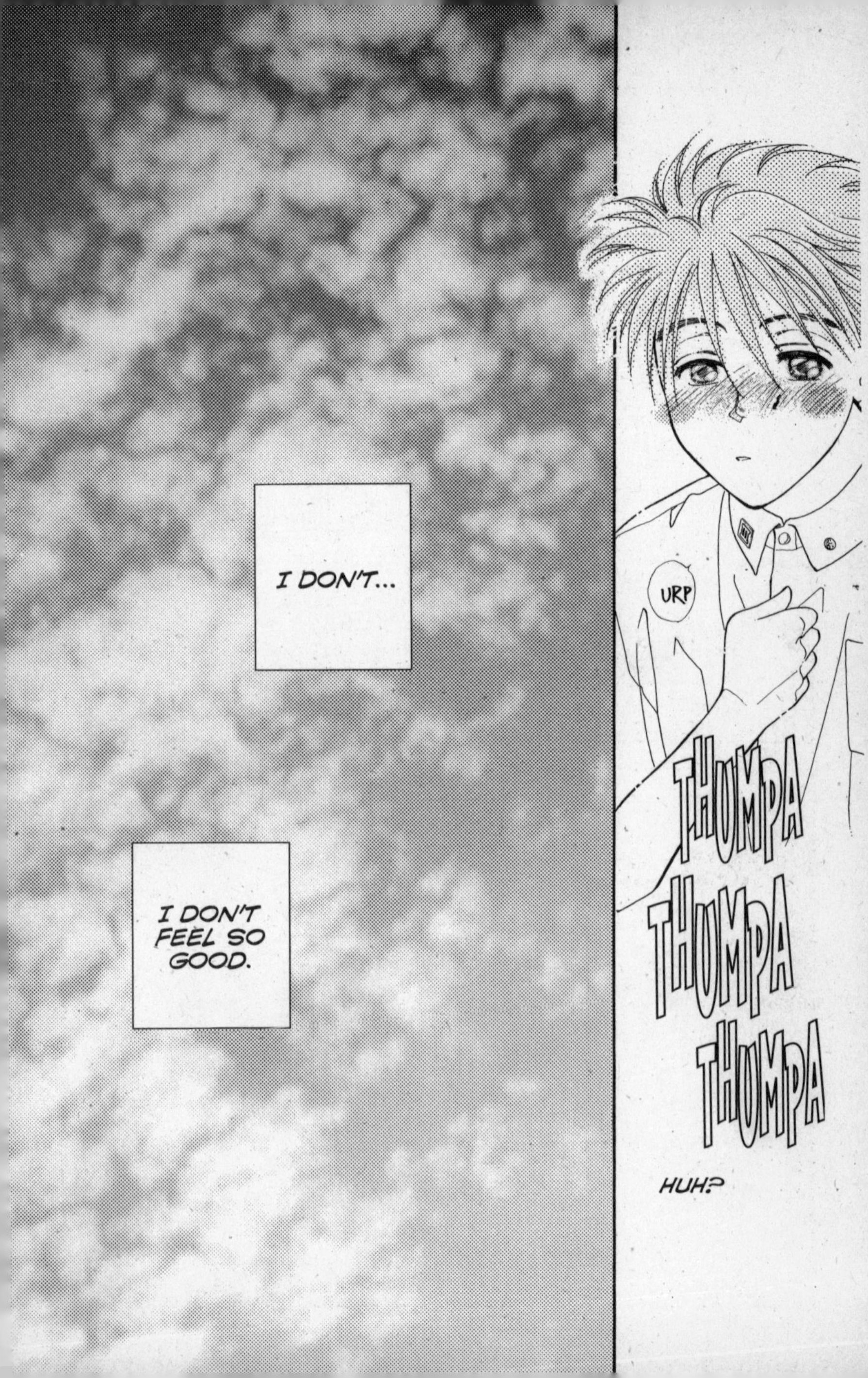
URP
THUMPA
THUMPA
THUMPA
HUH?
I DON'T...
I DON'T FEEL SO GOOD.

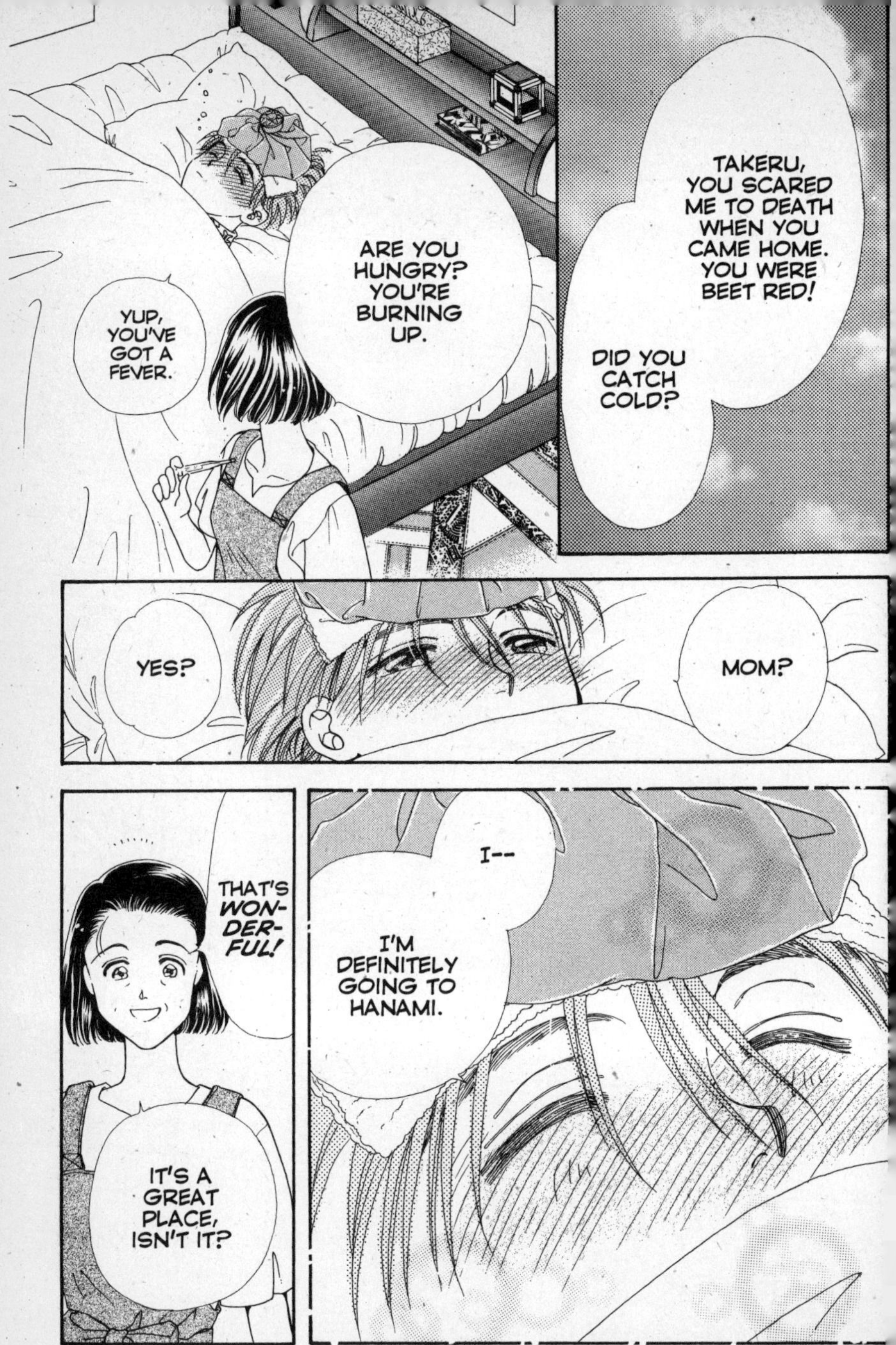
TAKERU, YOU SCARED ME TO DEATH WHEN YOU CAME HOME. YOU WERE BEET RED!
DID YOU CATCH COLD?
ARE YOU HUNGRY? YOU'RE BURNING UP.
YUP, YOU'VE GOT A FEVER.
MOM?
YES?
I--
I'M DEFINITELY GOING TO HANAMI.
THAT'S *WONDERFUL!*
IT'S A GREAT PLACE, ISN'T IT?

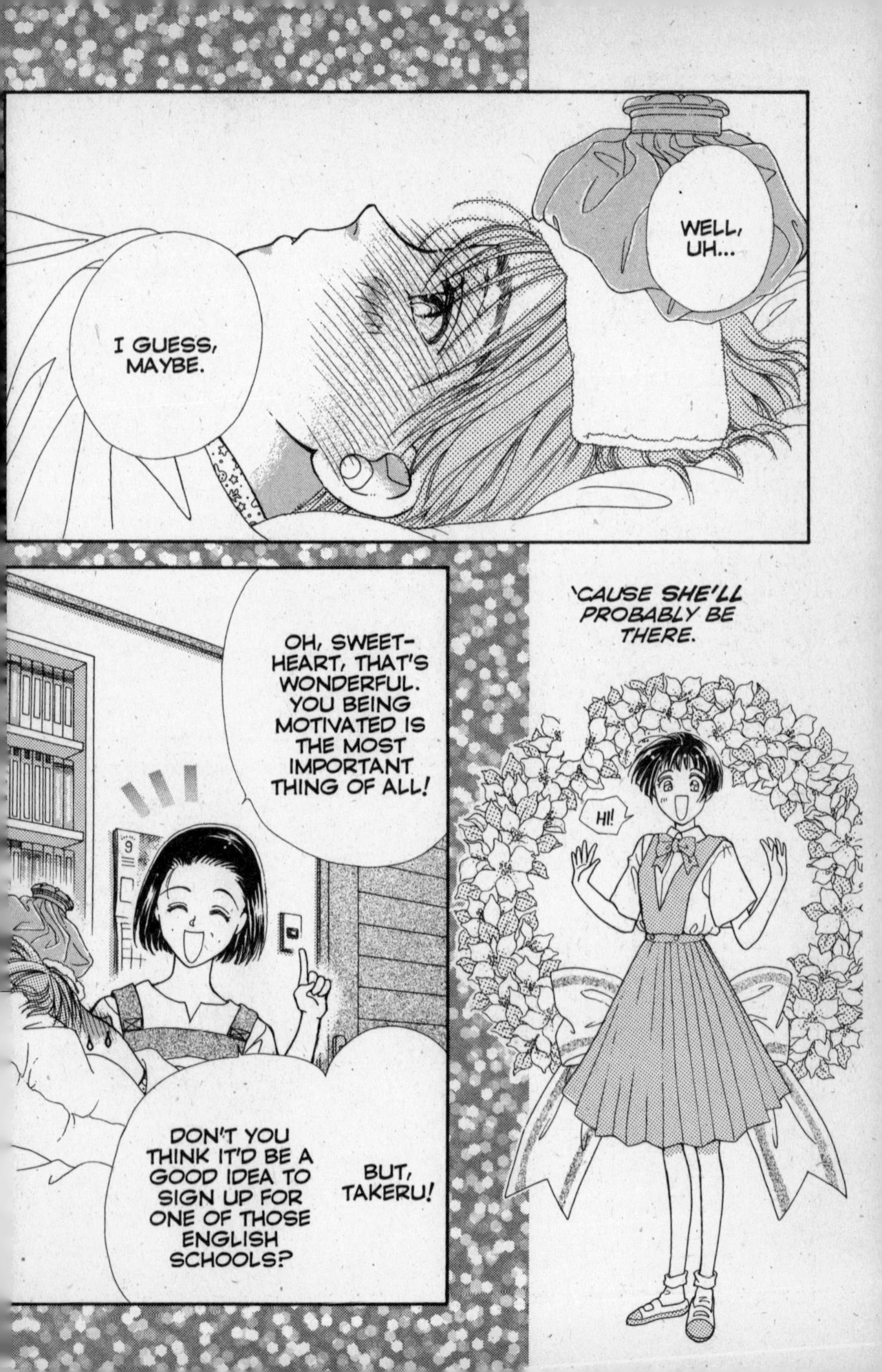
WELL, UH...
I GUESS, MAYBE.
'CAUSE SHE'LL PROBABLY BE THERE.
HI!
OH, SWEET-HEART, THAT'S WONDERFUL. YOU BEING MOTIVATED IS THE MOST IMPORTANT THING OF ALL!
BUT, TAKERU!
DON'T YOU THINK IT'D BE A GOOD IDEA TO SIGN UP FOR ONE OF THOSE ENGLISH SCHOOLS?

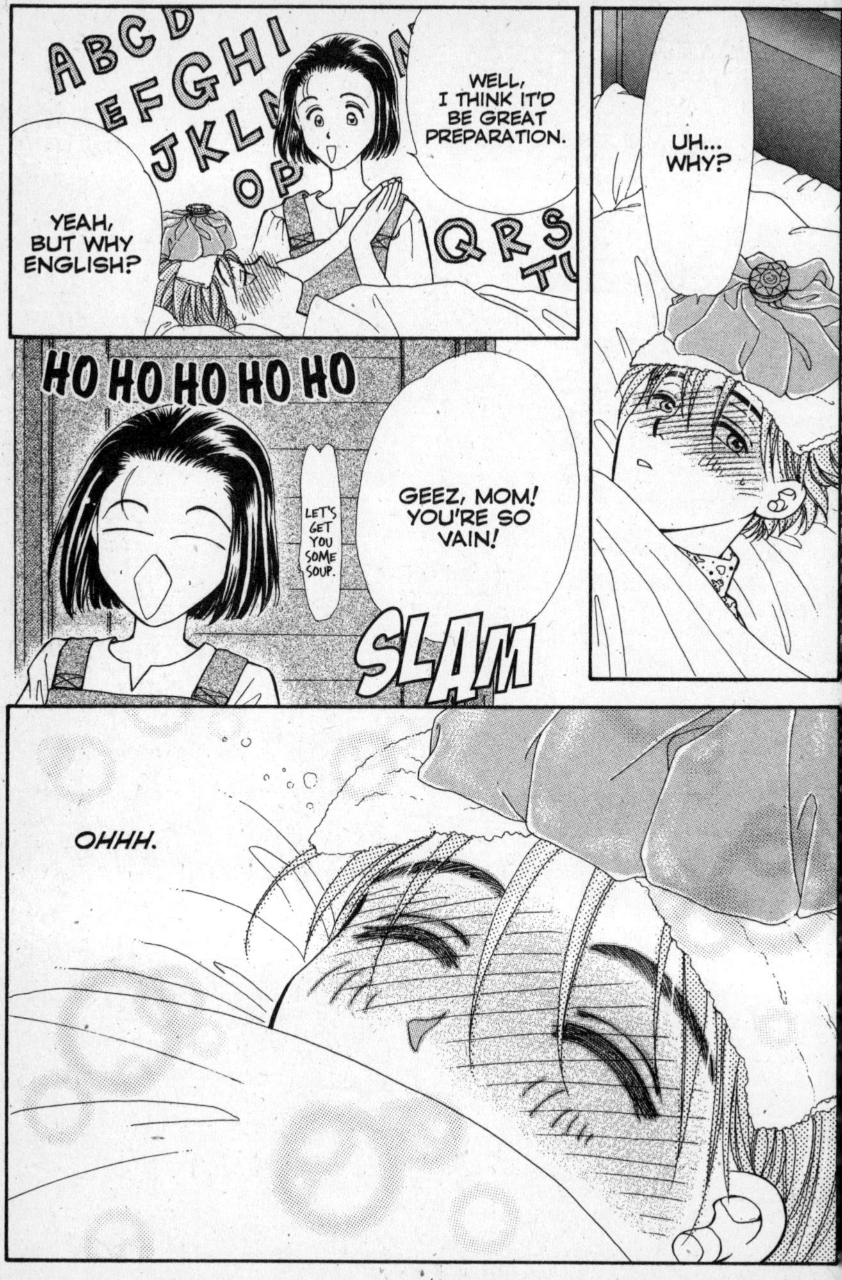
UH... WHY?
WELL, I THINK IT'D BE GREAT PREPARATION.
ABCD
EFGHI
JKL
OP
QRS
TU
YEAH, BUT WHY ENGLISH?
GEEZ, MOM! YOU'RE SO VAIN!
LET'S GET YOU SOME SOUP.
HO HO HO HO HO HO
SLAM
OHHH.

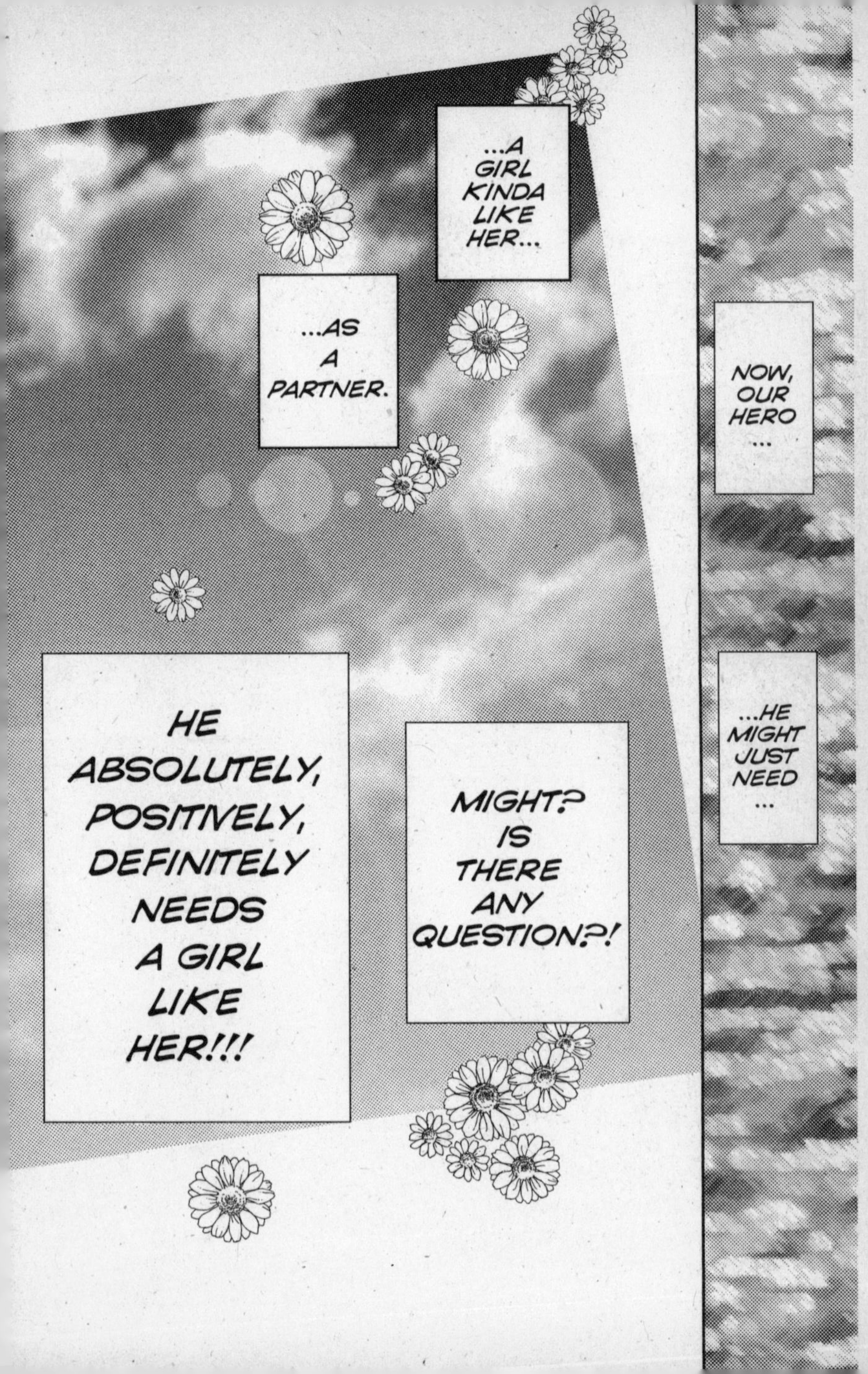
NOW, OUR HERO ...
...HE MIGHT JUST NEED ...
...A GIRL KINDA LIKE HER...
...AS A PARTNER.
MIGHT? IS THERE ANY QUESTION?!
HE ABSOLUTELY, POSITIVELY, DEFINITELY NEEDS A GIRL LIKE HER!!!

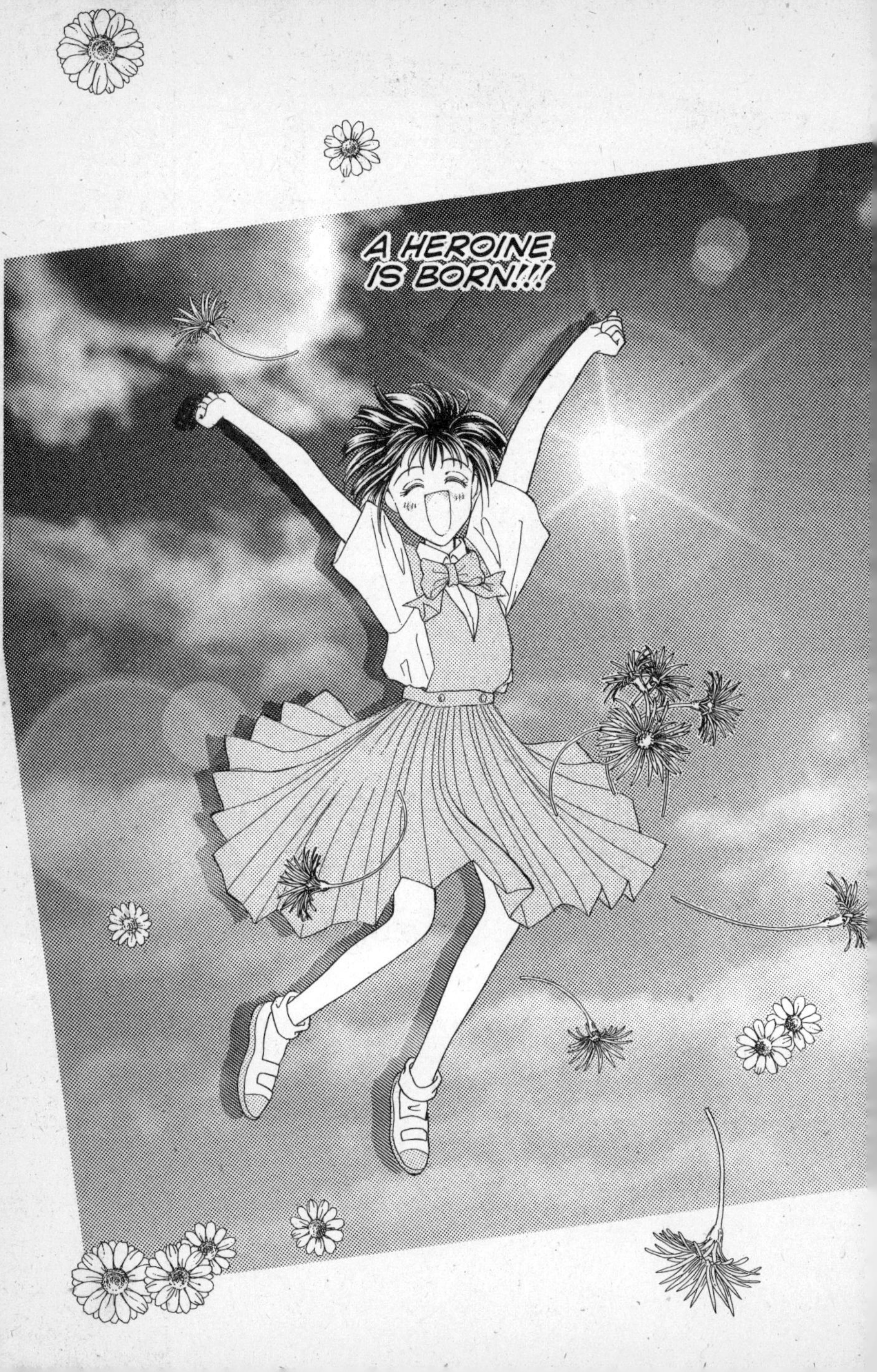
A HEROINE IS BORN!!!

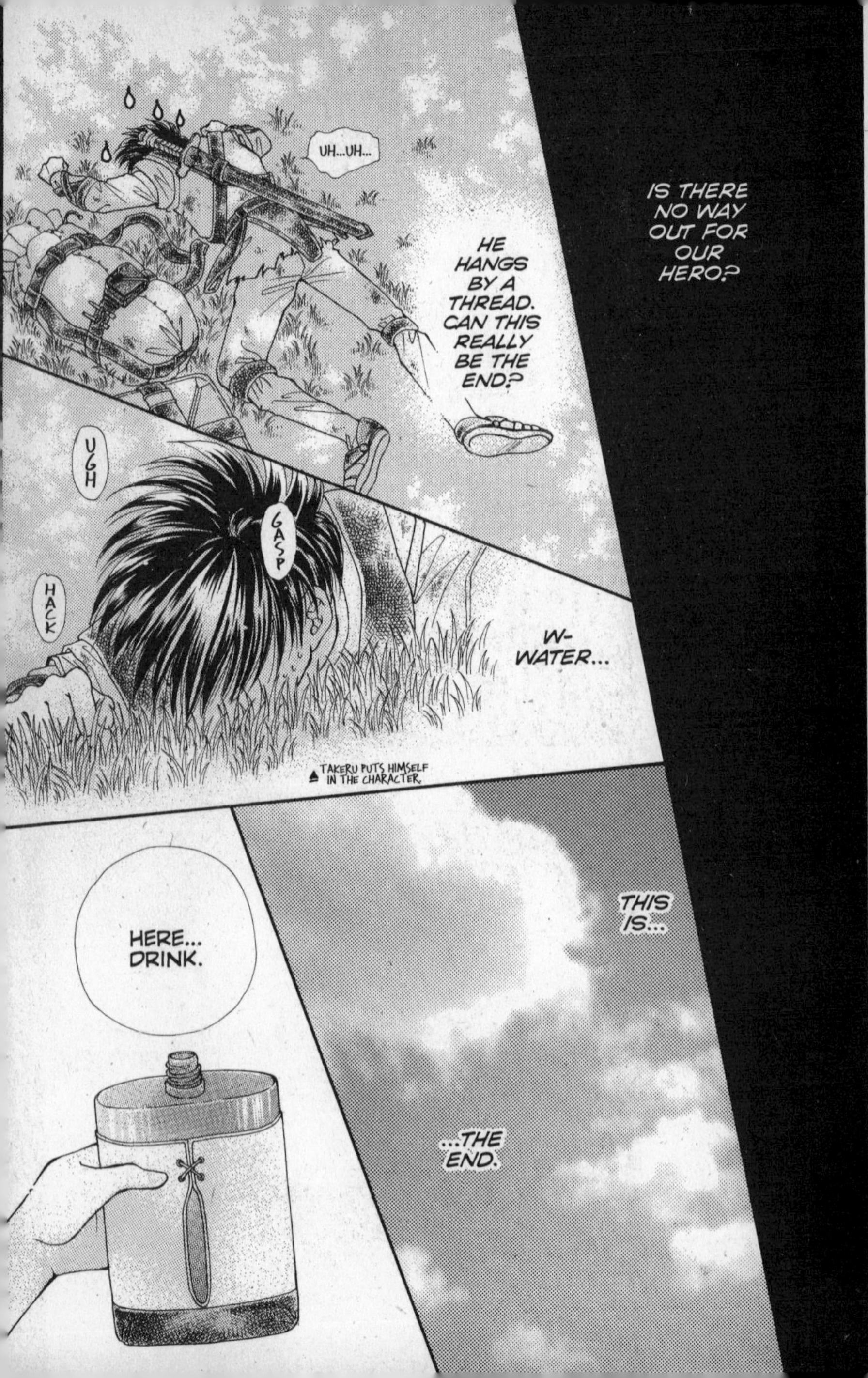

IS THERE NO WAY OUT FOR OUR HERO?
HE HANGS BY A THREAD. CAN THIS REALLY BE THE END?
UH...UH...
W- WATER...
GASP
UGH
HACK
TAKERU PUTS HIMSELF IN THE CHARACTER.
THIS IS...
...THE END.
HERE... DRINK.

1/4 Sidebar No. 2

2

Okay, so here's number 2. By sidebar number 2, we're about a quarter of the way through the new story, now...

So picking up where I left off--I was talking about drawing happier stuff. And the fact is about two years before I finished "Save the World," the characters in that story started to pop up in my head in ways that I thought would be really nice to draw. I mean no matter what it is, drawing the same thing for over seven years can be a grind and I got to where I thought about doing side stories based on the strange little ideas that came to mind under the influence of the Big Project. Perhaps I should explain what I mean in more detail: Let's say "Save the World" is "A." So I was thinking about stories I thought up for "A" and based on the "A" mentality, but...

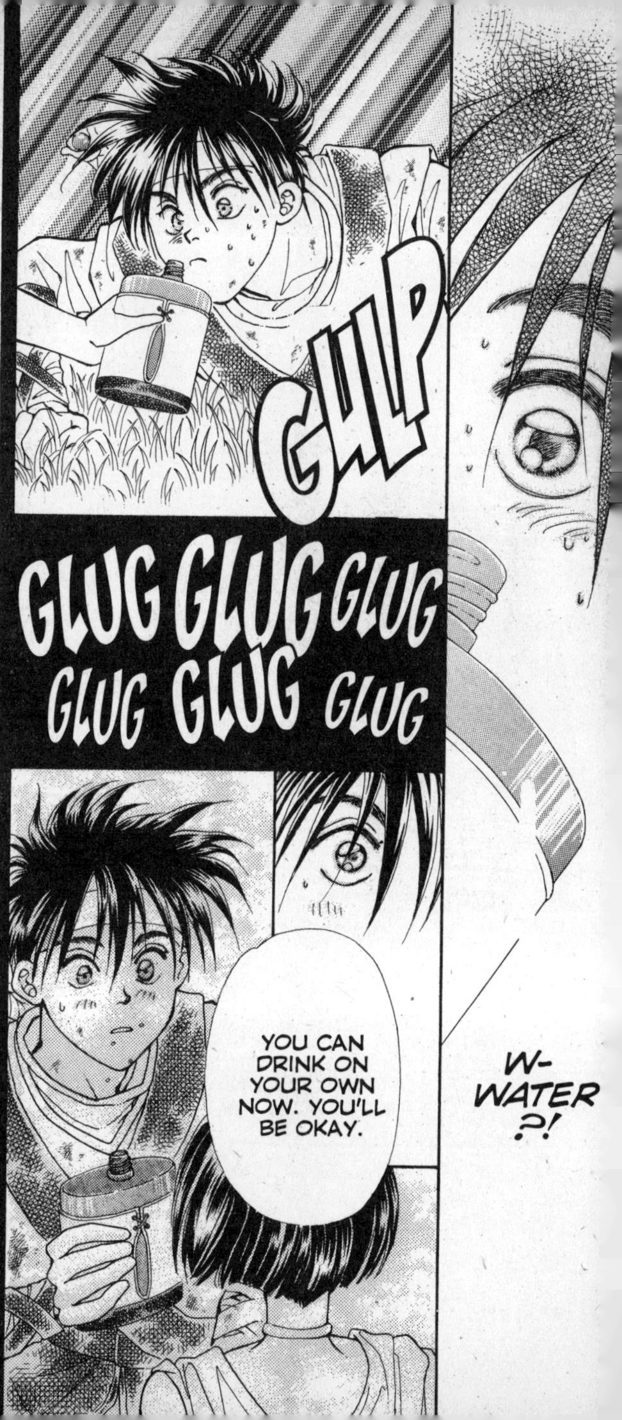
W-WATER?!
GULP
GLUG GLUG GLUG GLUG GLUG GLUG
YOU CAN DRINK ON YOUR OWN NOW. YOU'LL BE OKAY.

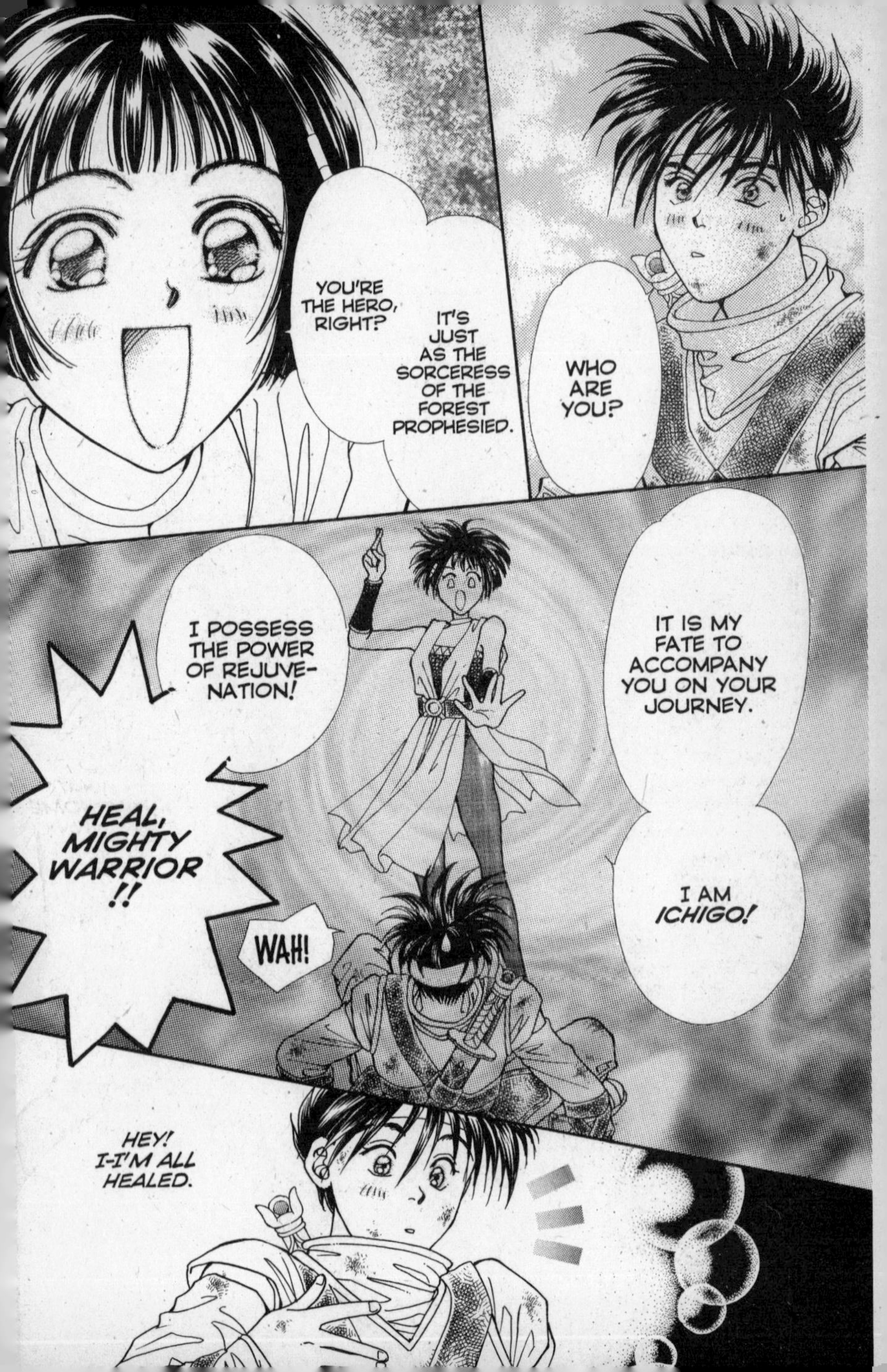
WHO ARE YOU?
YOU'RE THE HERO, RIGHT?
IT'S JUST AS THE SORCERESS OF THE FOREST PROPHESIED.
IT IS MY FATE TO ACCOMPANY YOU ON YOUR JOURNEY.
I AM *ICHIGO!*
I POSSESS THE POWER OF REJUVE-NATION!
HEAL, MIGHTY WARRIOR !!
WAH!
HEY! I-I'M ALL HEALED.

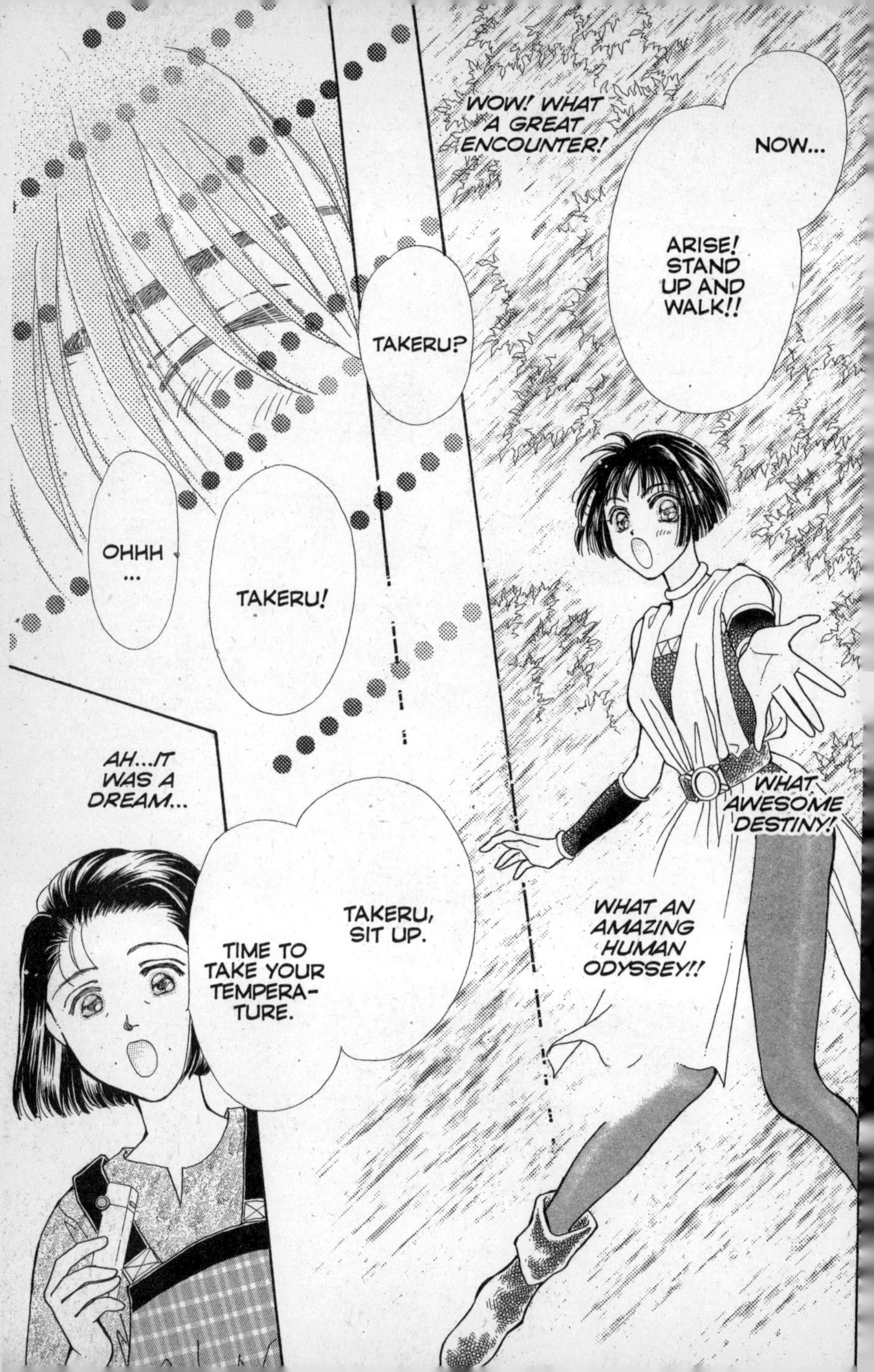
NOW...
ARISE! STAND UP AND WALK!!
WOW! WHAT A GREAT ENCOUNTER!
WHAT AWESOME DESTINY!
WHAT AN AMAZING HUMAN ODYSSEY!!
TAKERU?
TAKERU!
OHHH ...
TAKERU, SIT UP.
TIME TO TAKE YOUR TEMPERA-TURE.
AH...IT WAS A DREAM...

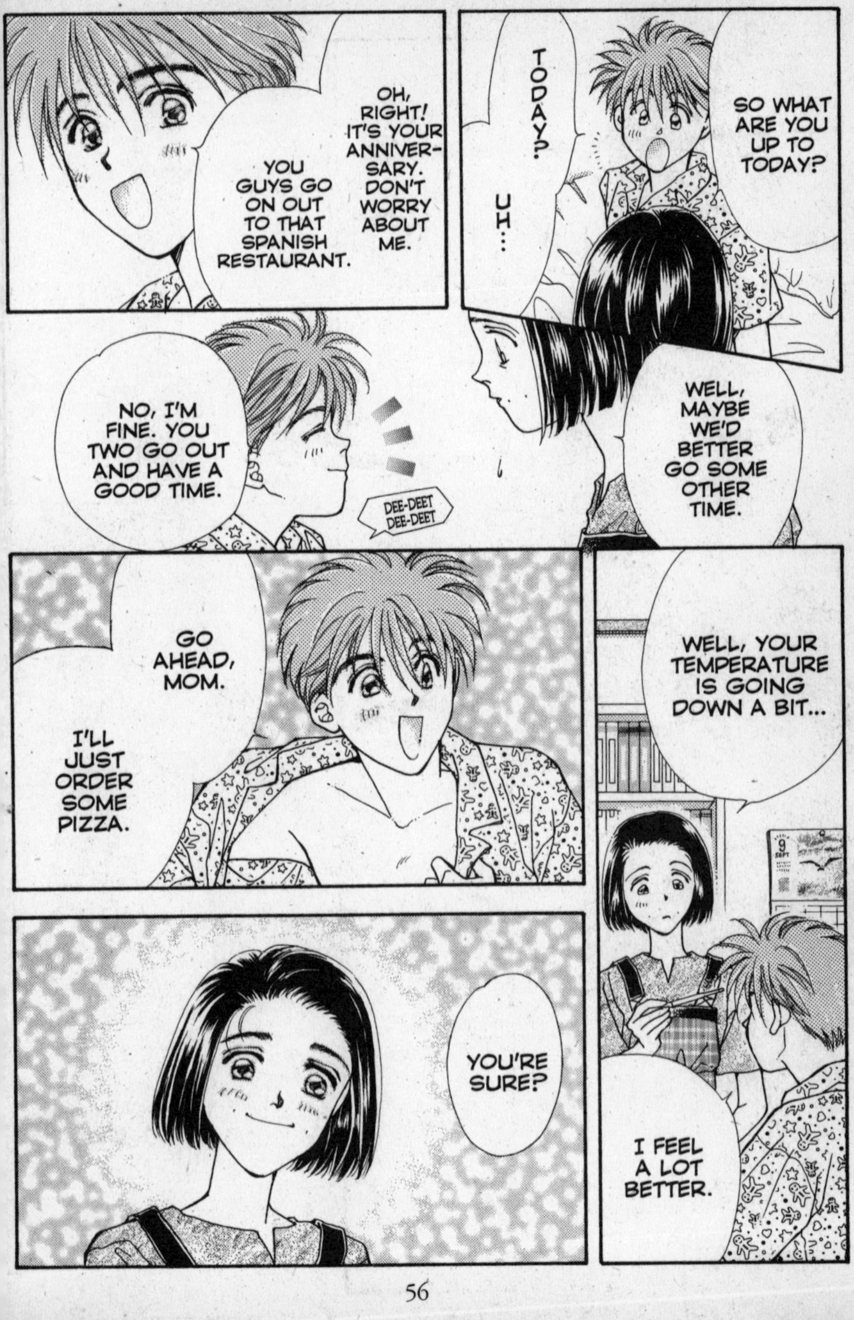
SO WHAT ARE YOU UP TO TODAY?
TODAY?
UH...
OH, RIGHT! IT'S YOUR ANNIVERSARY. DON'T WORRY ABOUT ME.
YOU GUYS GO ON OUT TO THAT SPANISH RESTAURANT.
WELL, MAYBE WE'D BETTER GO SOME OTHER TIME.
DEE-DEET DEE-DEET
NO, I'M FINE. YOU TWO GO OUT AND HAVE A GOOD TIME.
WELL, YOUR TEMPERATURE IS GOING DOWN A BIT...
I FEEL A LOT BETTER.
GO AHEAD, MOM.
I'LL JUST ORDER SOME PIZZA.
YOU'RE SURE?

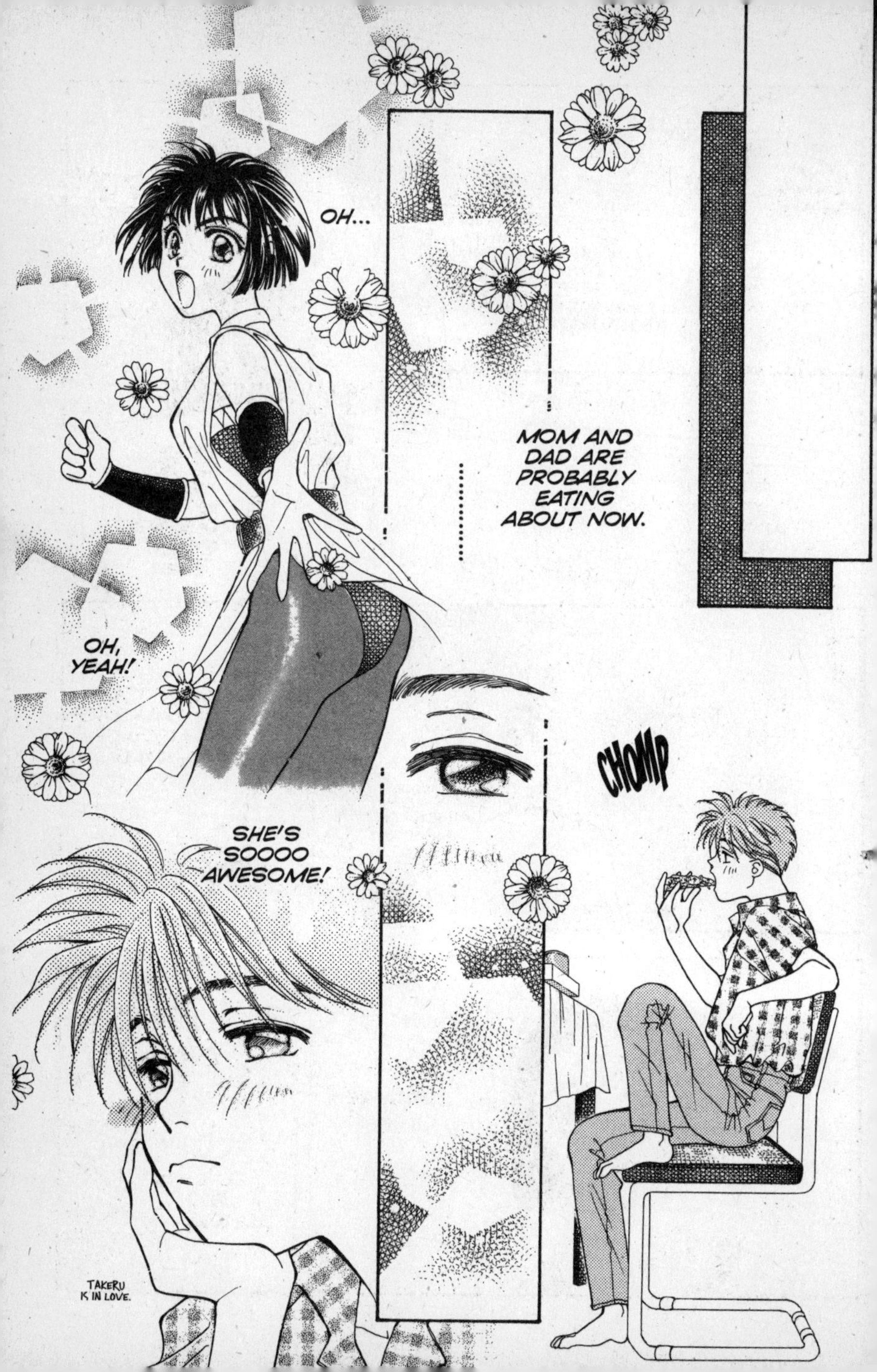
MOM AND DAD ARE PROBABLY EATING ABOUT NOW.
OH...
OH, YEAH!
CHOMP
SHE'S SOOOO AWESOME!
TAKERU IS IN LOVE.

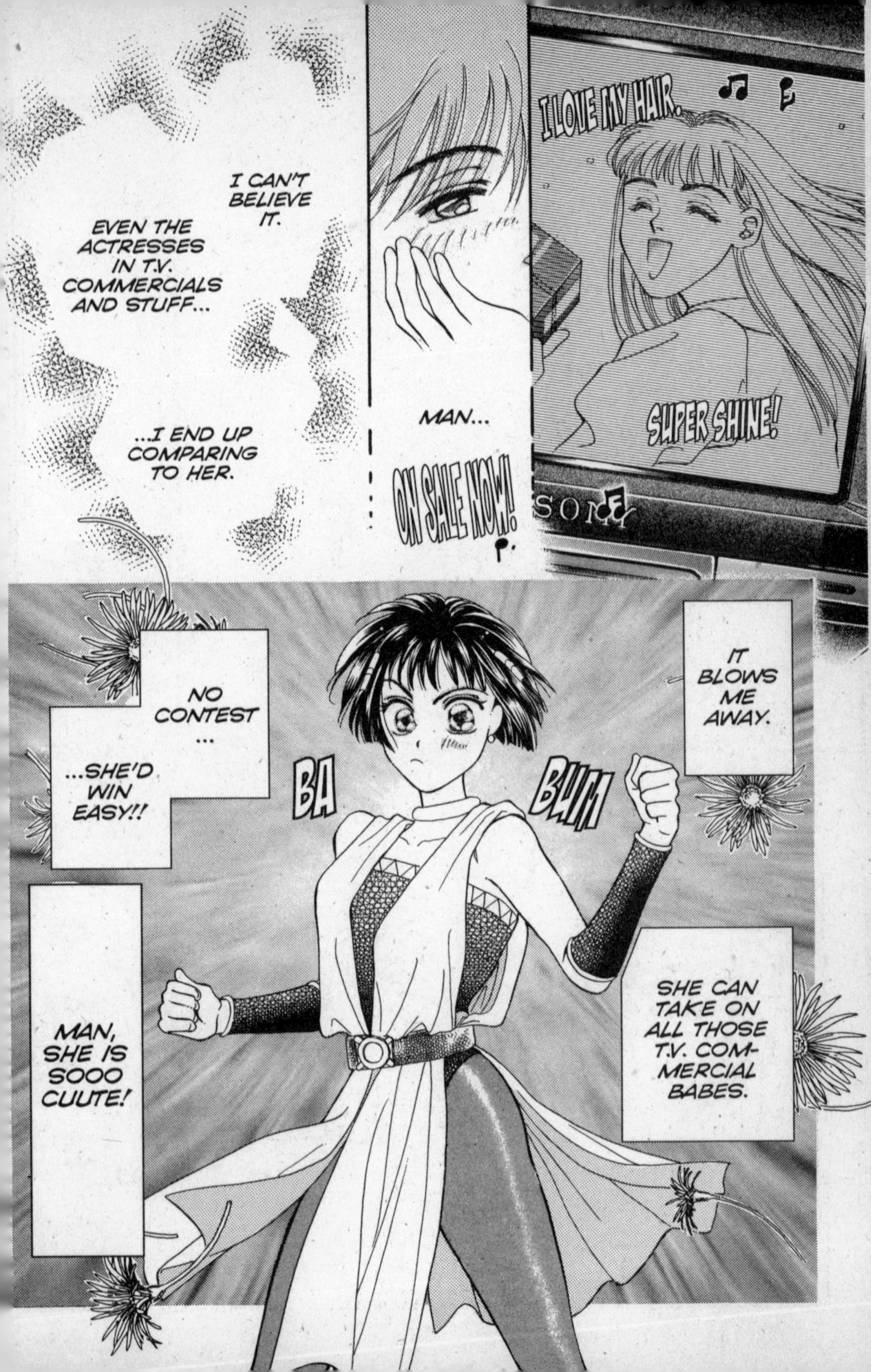
I LOVE MY HAIR.
SUPER SHINE!
ON SALE NOW!
MAN...
I CAN'T BELIEVE IT.
EVEN THE ACTRESSES IN T.V. COMMERCIALS AND STUFF...
...I END UP COMPARING TO HER.
IT BLOWS ME AWAY.
BA
BUM
NO CONTEST ...
...SHE'D WIN EASY!!
SHE CAN TAKE ON ALL THOSE T.V. COM-MERCIAL BABES.
MAN, SHE IS SOOO CUUTE!

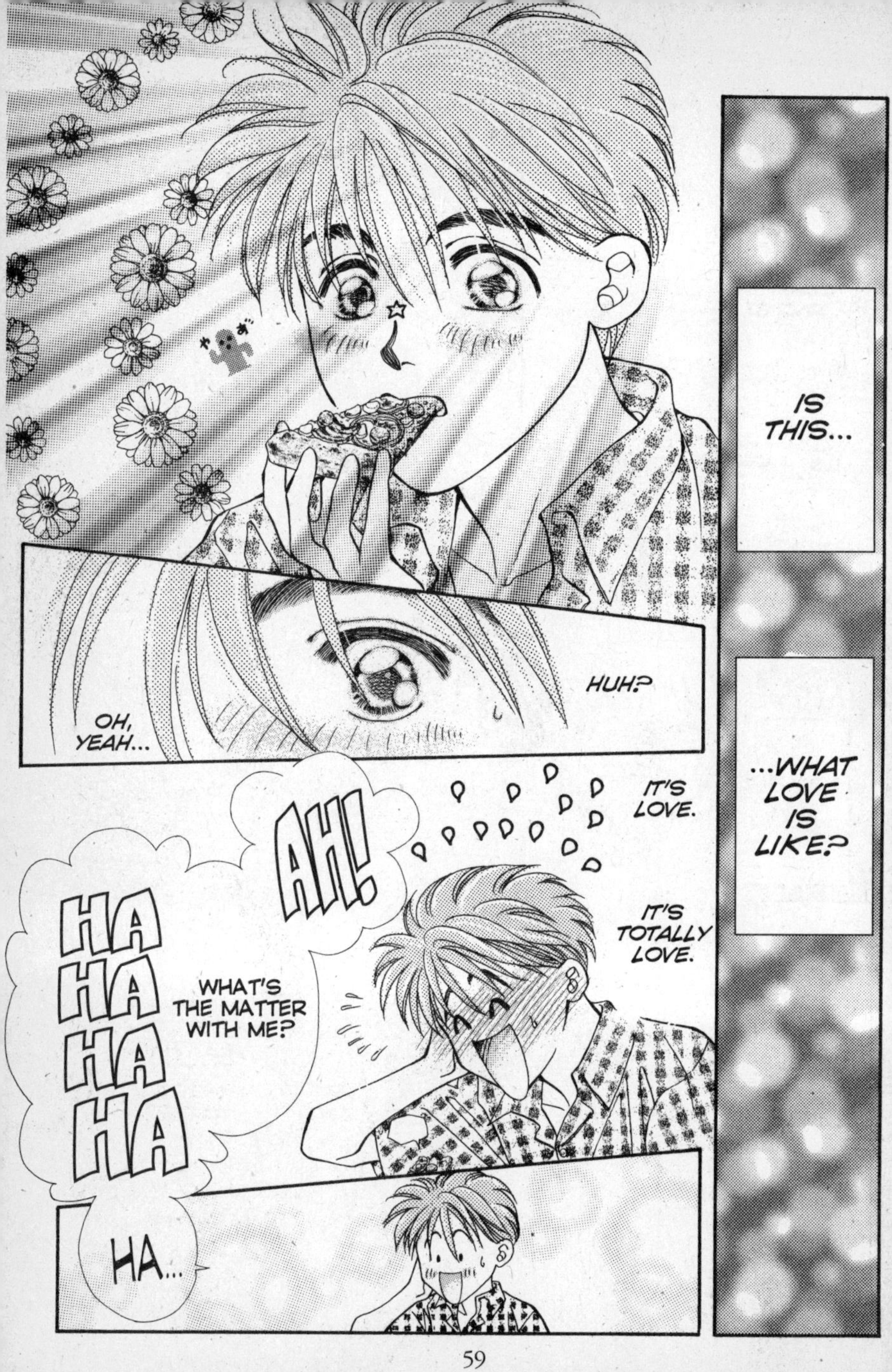
IS THIS...
...WHAT LOVE IS LIKE?
HUH?
OH, YEAH...
IT'S LOVE.
IT'S TOTALLY LOVE.
AH!
WHAT'S THE MATTER WITH ME?
HA HA HA HA HA
HA...

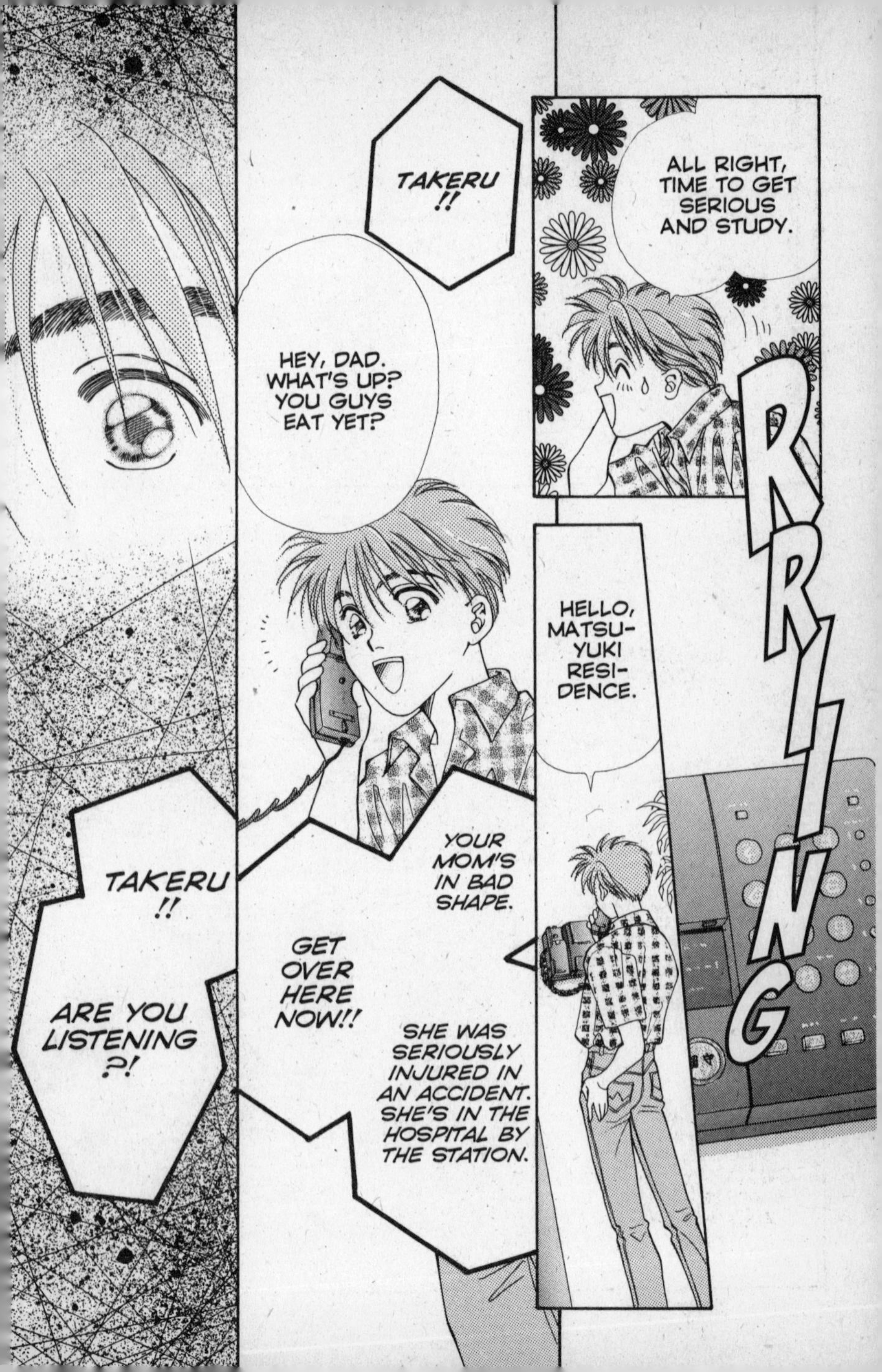
ALL RIGHT, TIME TO GET SERIOUS AND STUDY.
RRIING
HELLO, MATSU-YUKI RESI-DENCE.
TAKERU!!
HEY, DAD. WHAT'S UP? YOU GUYS EAT YET?
YOUR MOM'S IN BAD SHAPE.
SHE WAS SERIOUSLY INJURED IN AN ACCIDENT. SHE'S IN THE HOSPITAL BY THE STATION.
GET OVER HERE NOW!!
TAKERU!!
ARE YOU LISTENING?!

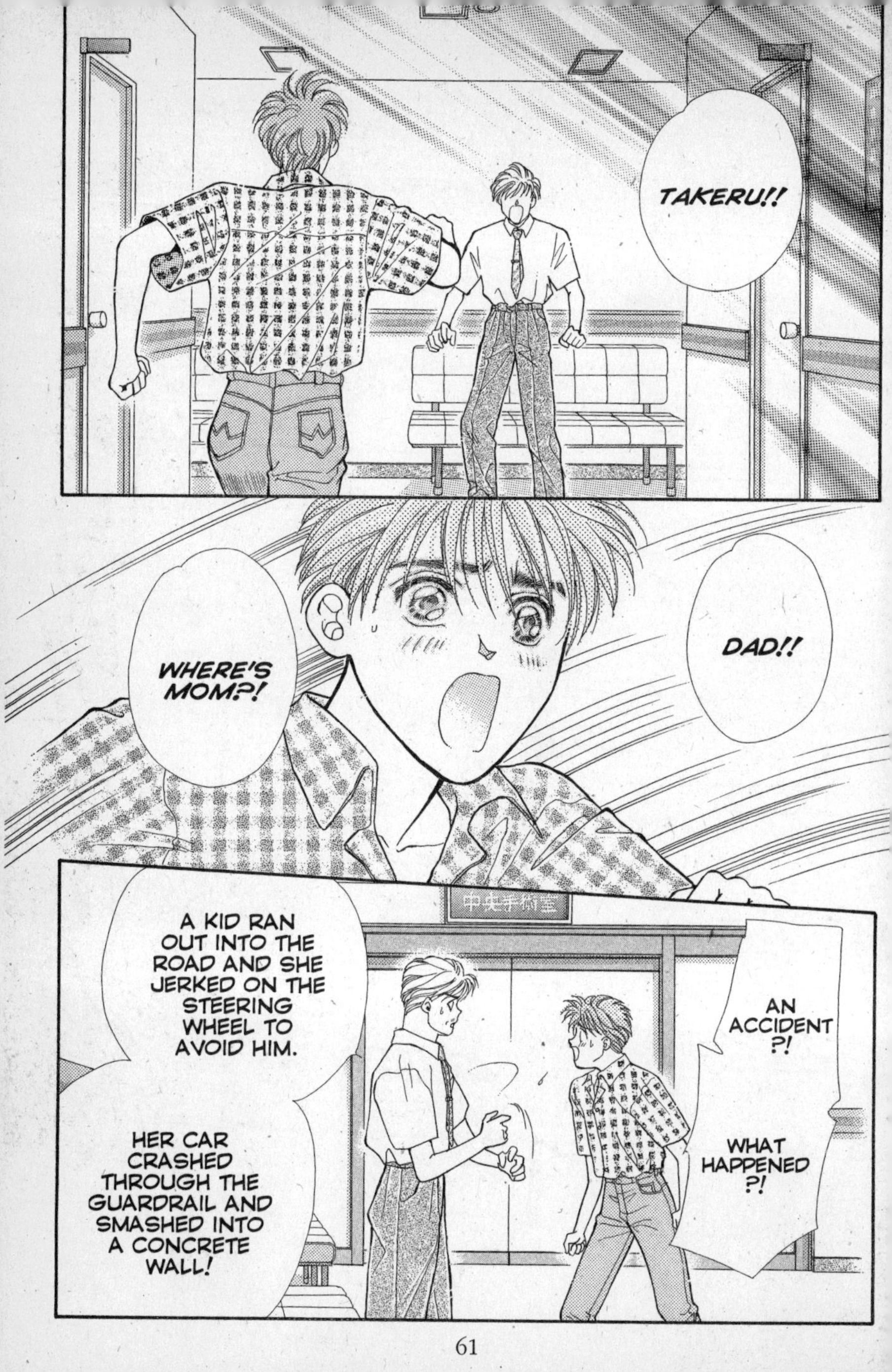
TAKERU!!
DAD!!
WHERE'S MOM?!
AN ACCIDENT ?!
WHAT HAPPENED ?!
A KID RAN OUT INTO THE ROAD AND SHE JERKED ON THE STEERING WHEEL TO AVOID HIM.
HER CAR CRASHED THROUGH THE GUARDRAIL AND SMASHED INTO A CONCRETE WALL!

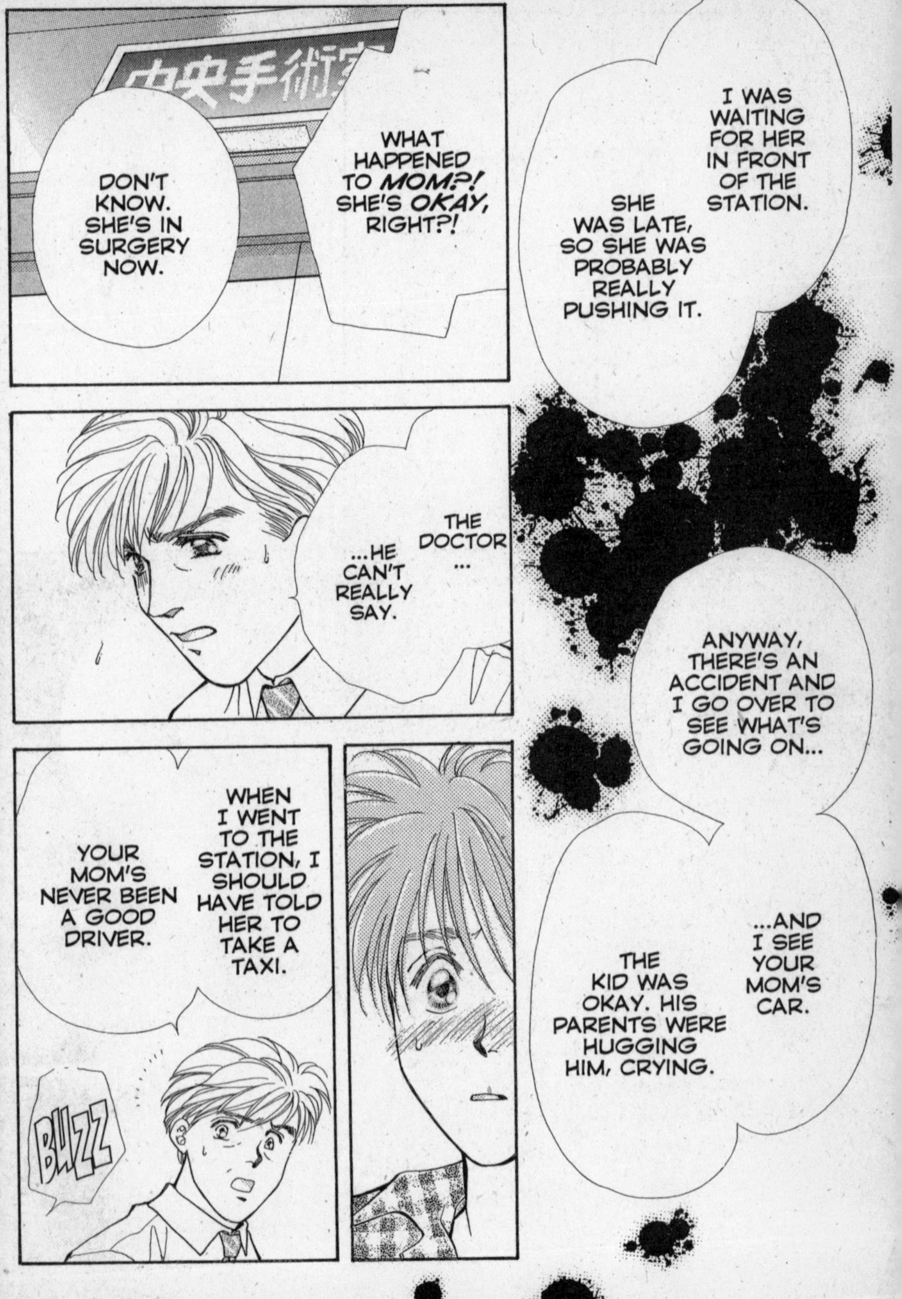
I WAS WAITING FOR HER IN FRONT OF THE STATION.
SHE WAS LATE, SO SHE WAS PROBABLY REALLY PUSHING IT.
ANYWAY, THERE'S AN ACCIDENT AND I GO OVER TO SEE WHAT'S GOING ON...
...AND I SEE YOUR MOM'S CAR.
THE KID WAS OKAY. HIS PARENTS WERE HUGGING HIM, CRYING.
中央手術
WHAT HAPPENED TO ***MOM?!*** SHE'S ***OKAY,*** RIGHT?!
DON'T KNOW. SHE'S IN SURGERY NOW.
THE DOCTOR ...
...HE CAN'T REALLY SAY.
WHEN I WENT TO THE STATION, I SHOULD HAVE TOLD HER TO TAKE A TAXI.
YOUR MOM'S NEVER BEEN A GOOD DRIVER.
BUZZ

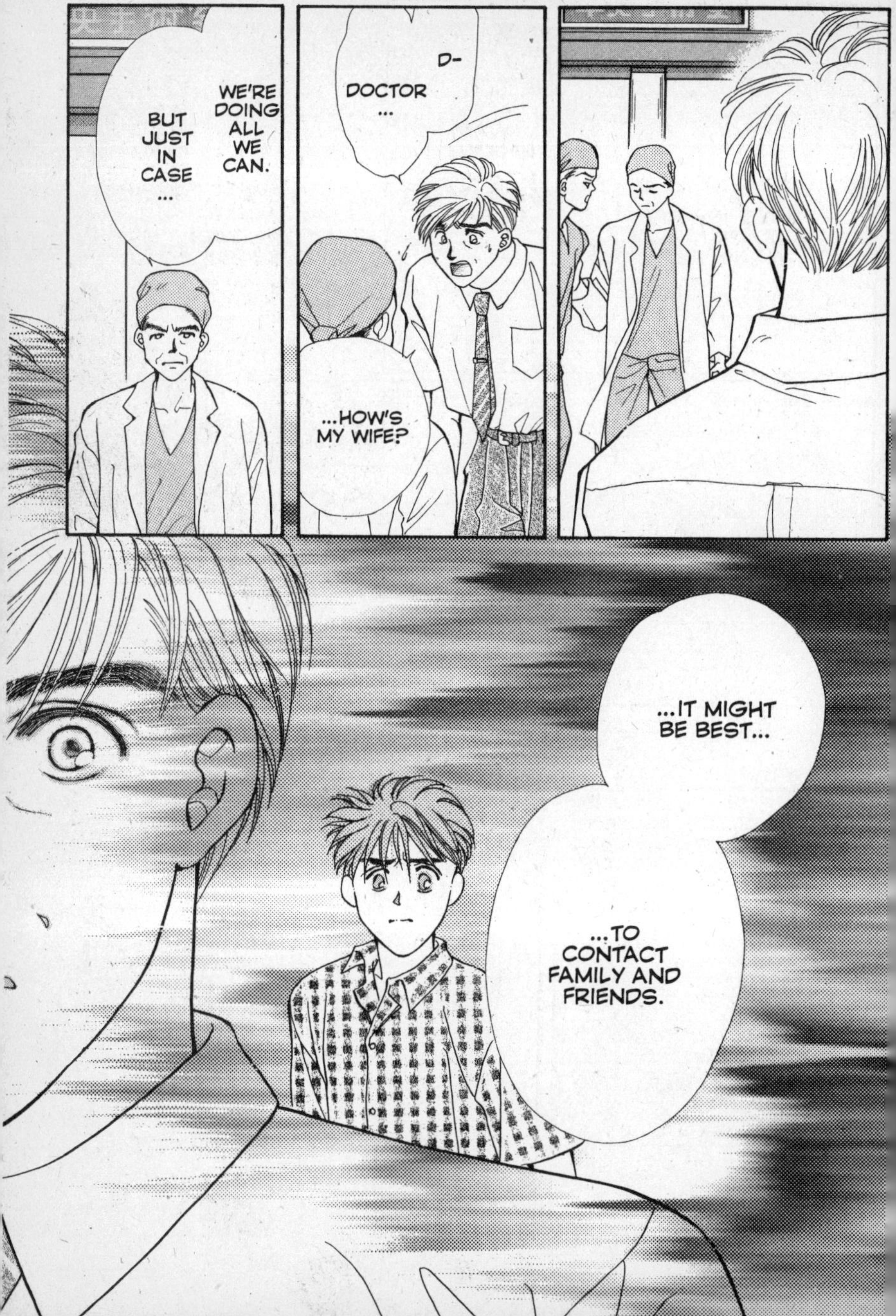
D- DOCTOR ...
...HOW'S MY WIFE?
WE'RE DOING ALL WE CAN.
BUT JUST IN CASE ...
...IT MIGHT BE BEST...
...TO CONTACT FAMILY AND FRIENDS.

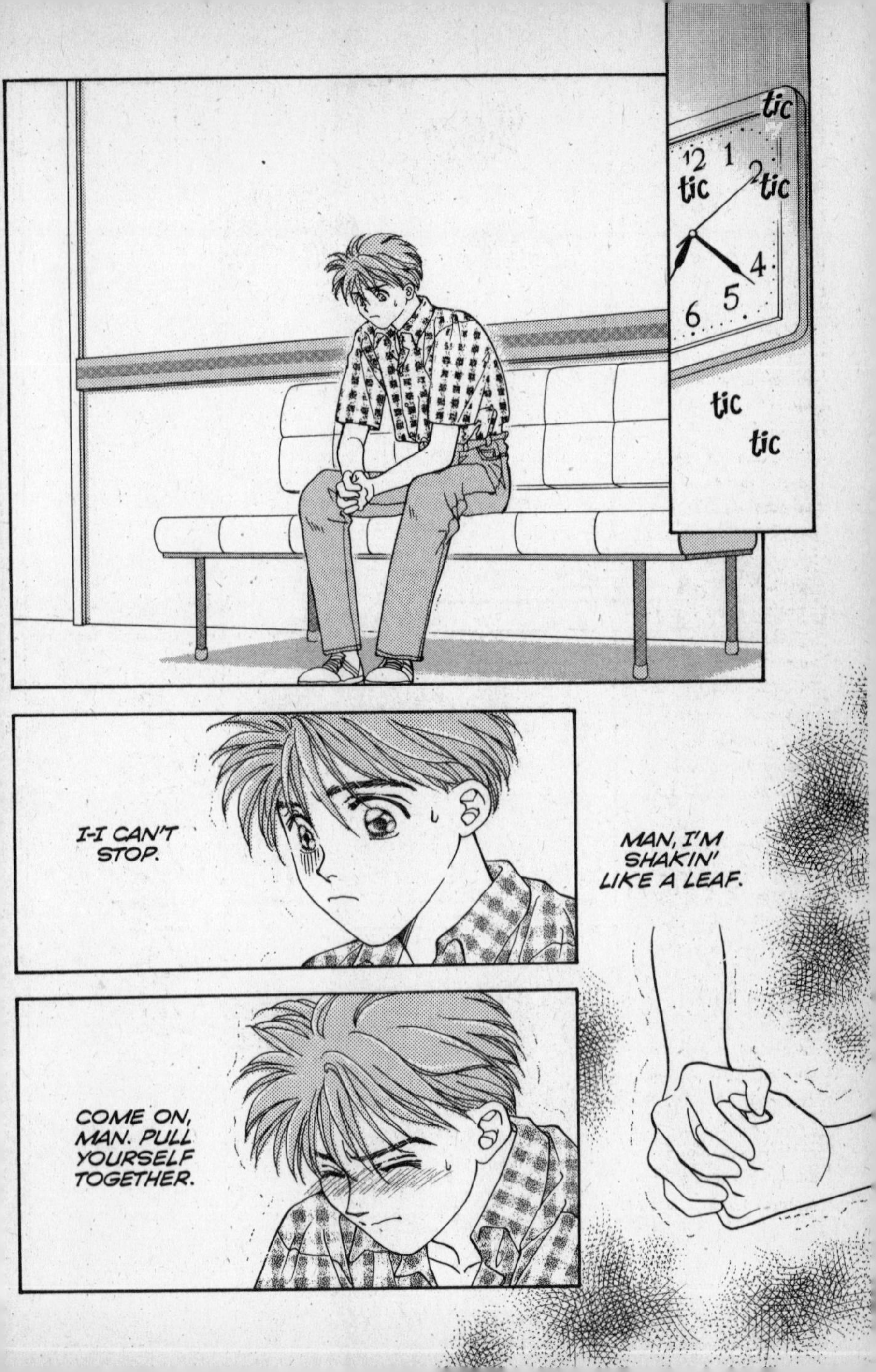
tic
tic
tic
tic
tic
MAN, I'M SHAKIN' LIKE A LEAF.
I-I CAN'T STOP.
COME ON, MAN. PULL YOURSELF TOGETHER.

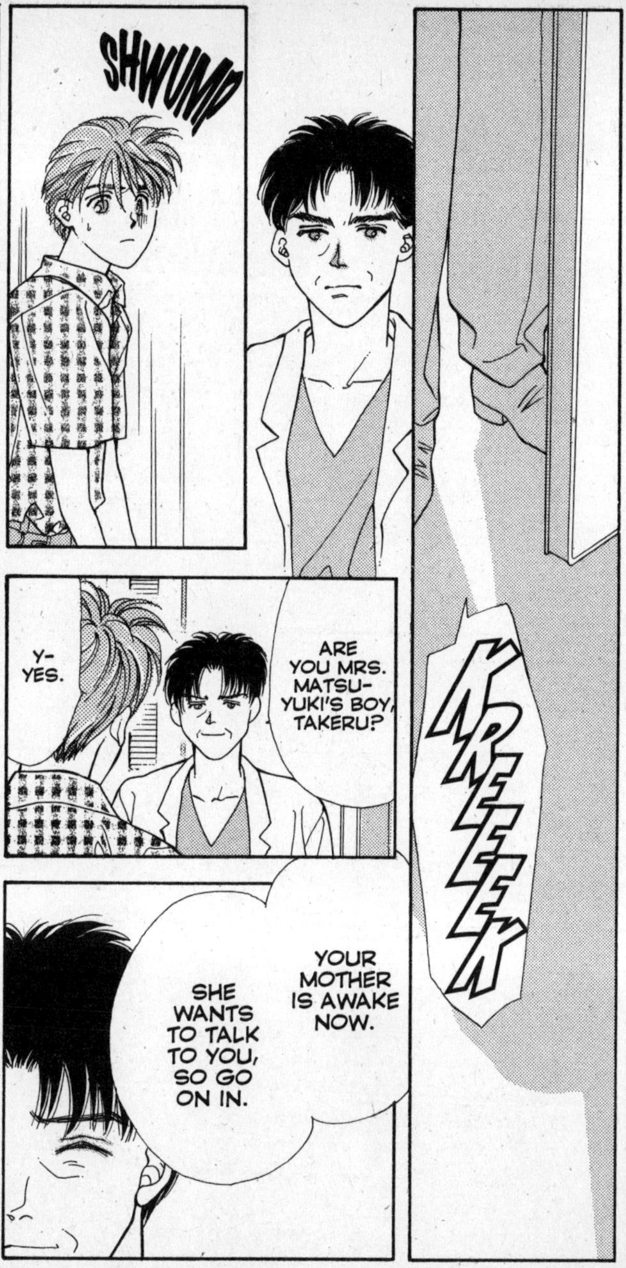
KREEEK
SHWUMP
ARE YOU MRS. MATSU-YUKI'S BOY, TAKERU?
Y-YES.
YOUR MOTHER IS AWAKE NOW.
SHE WANTS TO TALK TO YOU, SO GO ON IN.

1/4 Sidebar No. 3

3

...But I always looked at all of "A" from kind of a detached perspective and played with different ideas. For example, I might think, "this is a good storyline but what would happen if I brought in different elements, put it in a completely different setting?" Anyway, that's what I'd end up thinking (hee hee). But sometimes bringing in different elements meant I'd have to change around the scene to make things fit and that would change the scene so much that it ended up as a different story altogether. So even though an idea is based on "A" it's not really A-1 or whatever, it's "B" or "Z"--it's a whole new story. And even though it's something I consciously did, I can't really explain how these ideas ended up that way.

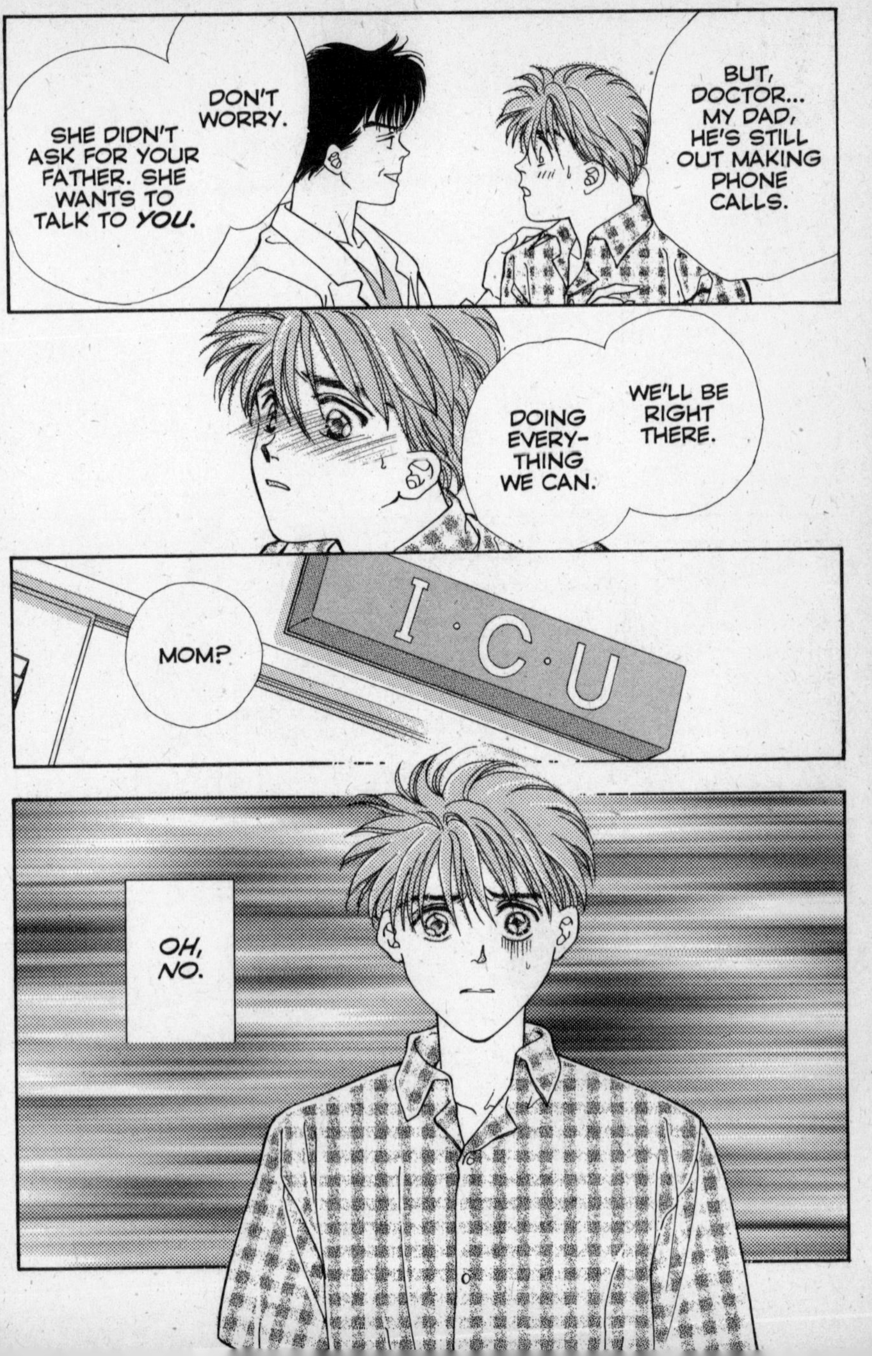
BUT, DOCTOR... MY DAD, HE'S STILL OUT MAKING PHONE CALLS.
DON'T WORRY.
SHE DIDN'T ASK FOR YOUR FATHER. SHE WANTS TO TALK TO *YOU*.
WE'LL BE RIGHT THERE.
DOING EVERY-THING WE CAN.
I·C·U
MOM?
OH, NO.

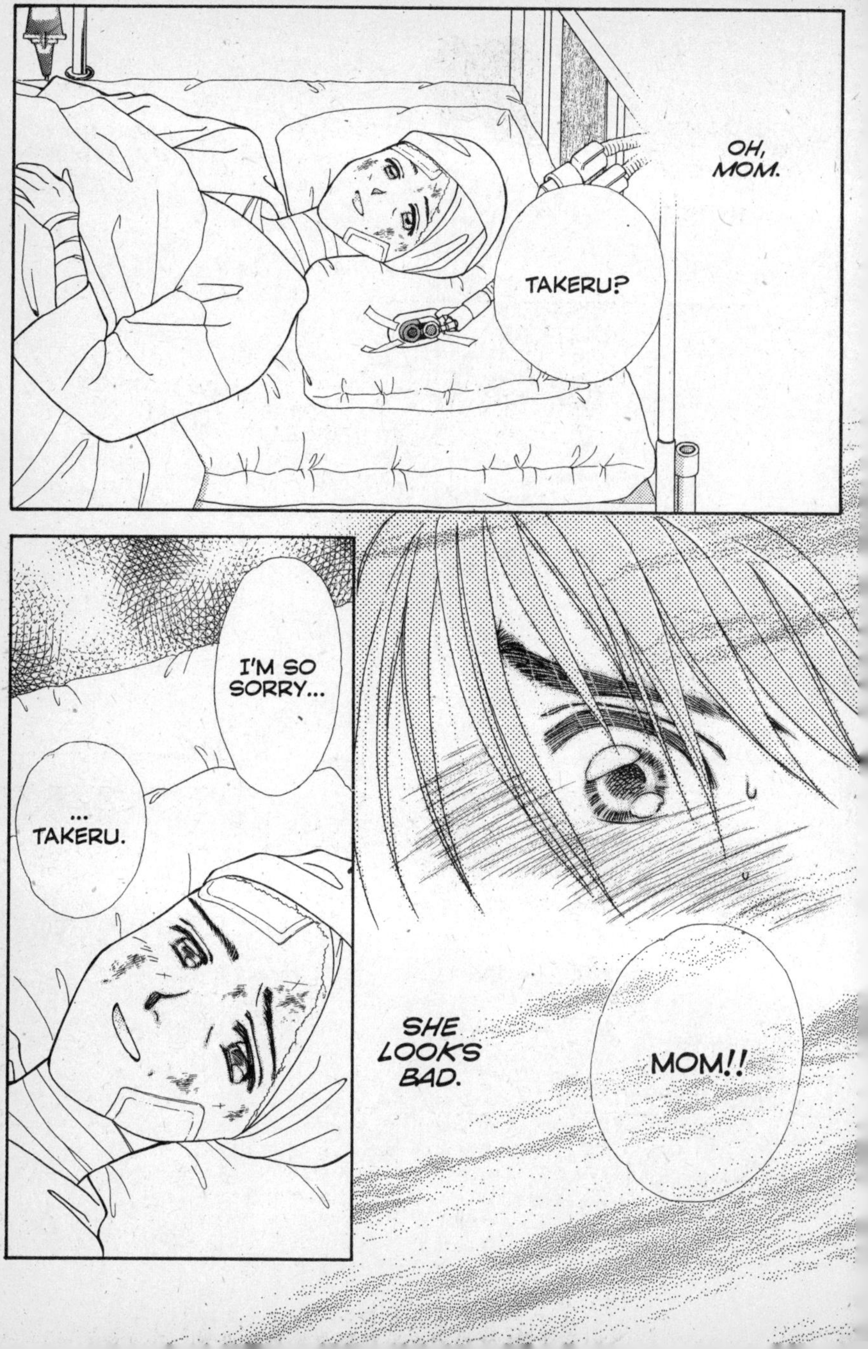
OH, MOM.
TAKERU?
MOM!!
SHE LOOKS BAD.
I'M SO SORRY...
...TAKERU.

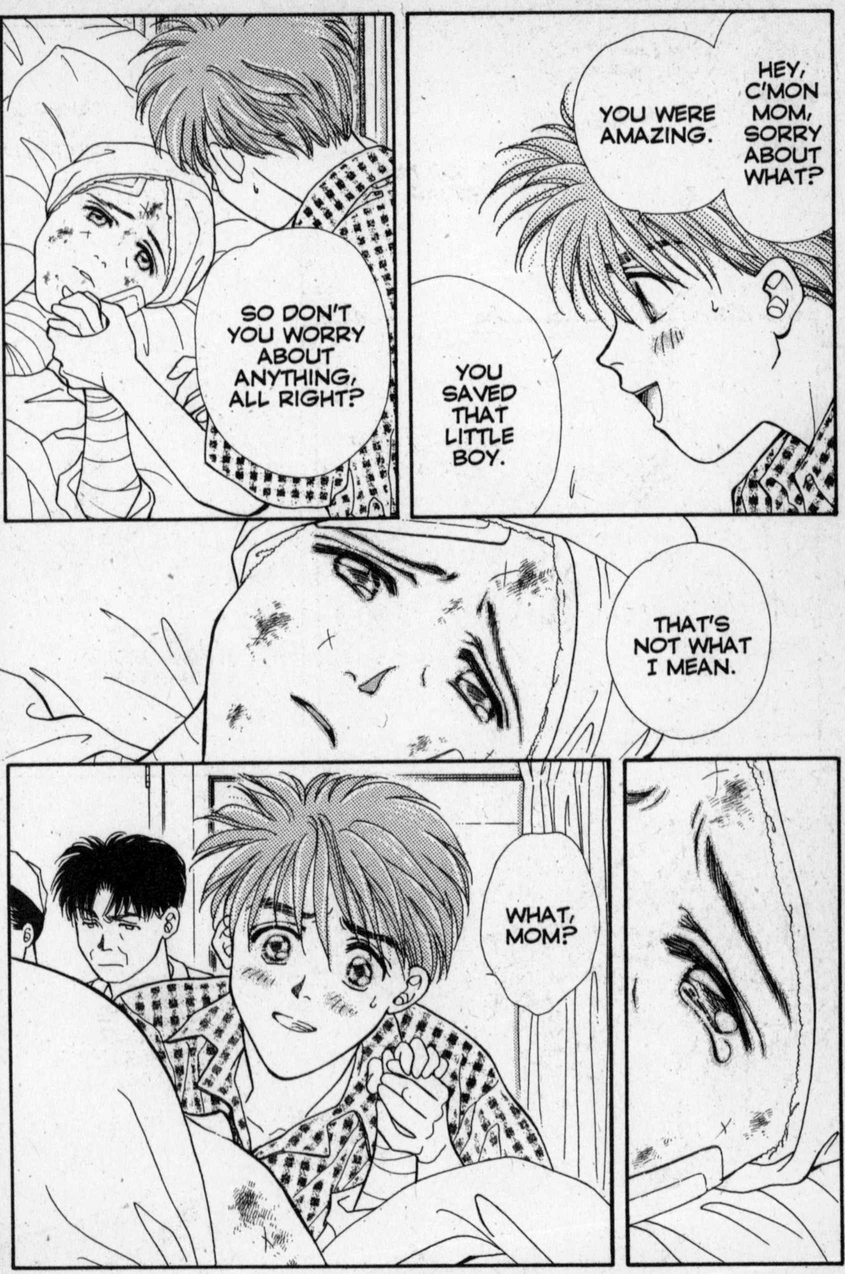
HEY, C'MON MOM, SORRY ABOUT WHAT?
YOU WERE AMAZING.
YOU SAVED THAT LITTLE BOY.
SO DON'T YOU WORRY ABOUT ANYTHING, ALL RIGHT?
THAT'S NOT WHAT I MEAN.
WHAT, MOM?

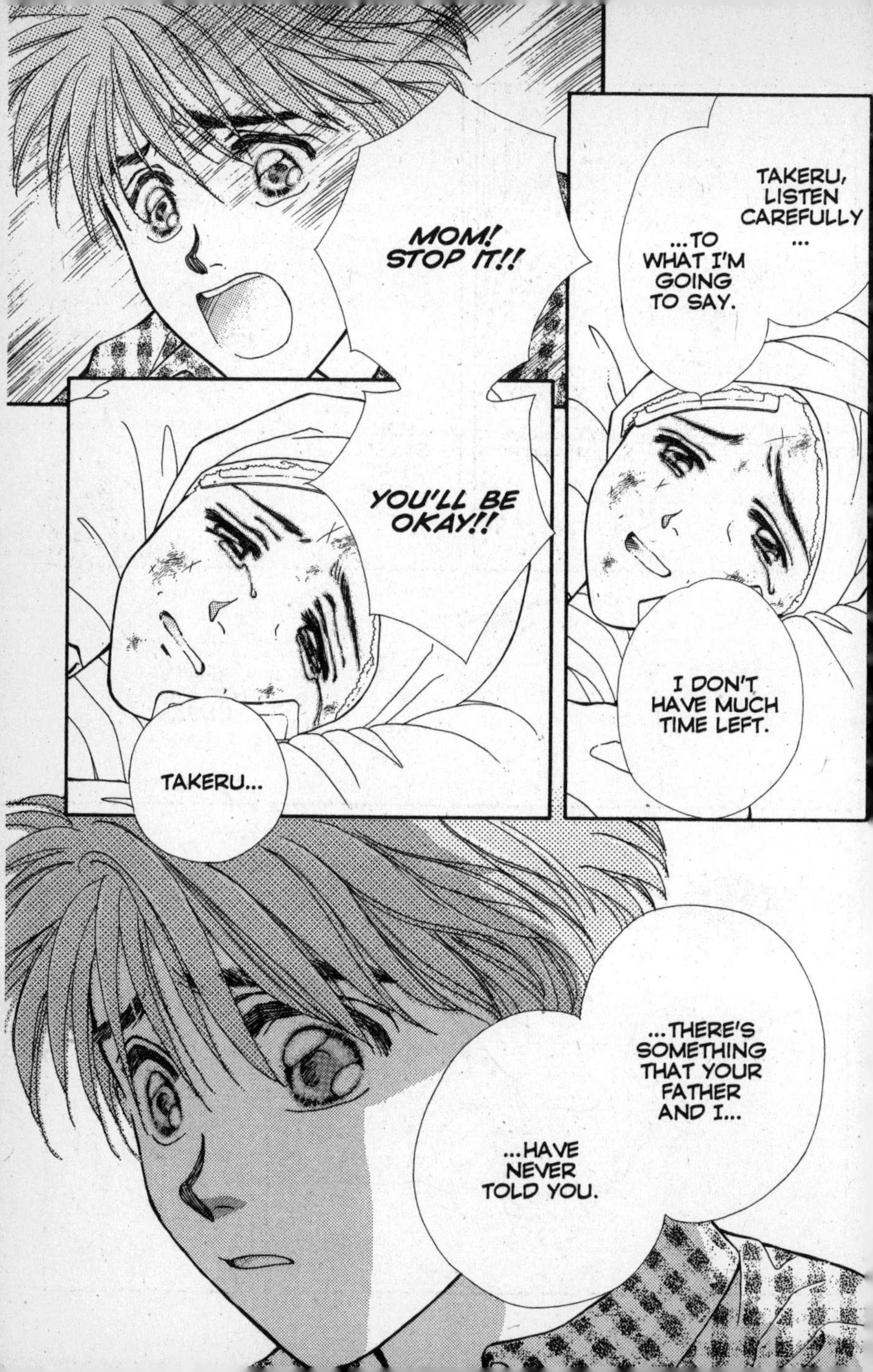
MOM! STOP IT!!
YOU'LL BE OKAY!!
TAKERU...
TAKERU, LISTEN CAREFULLY ...
...TO WHAT I'M GOING TO SAY.
I DON'T HAVE MUCH TIME LEFT.
...THERE'S SOMETHING THAT YOUR FATHER AND I...
...HAVE NEVER TOLD YOU.

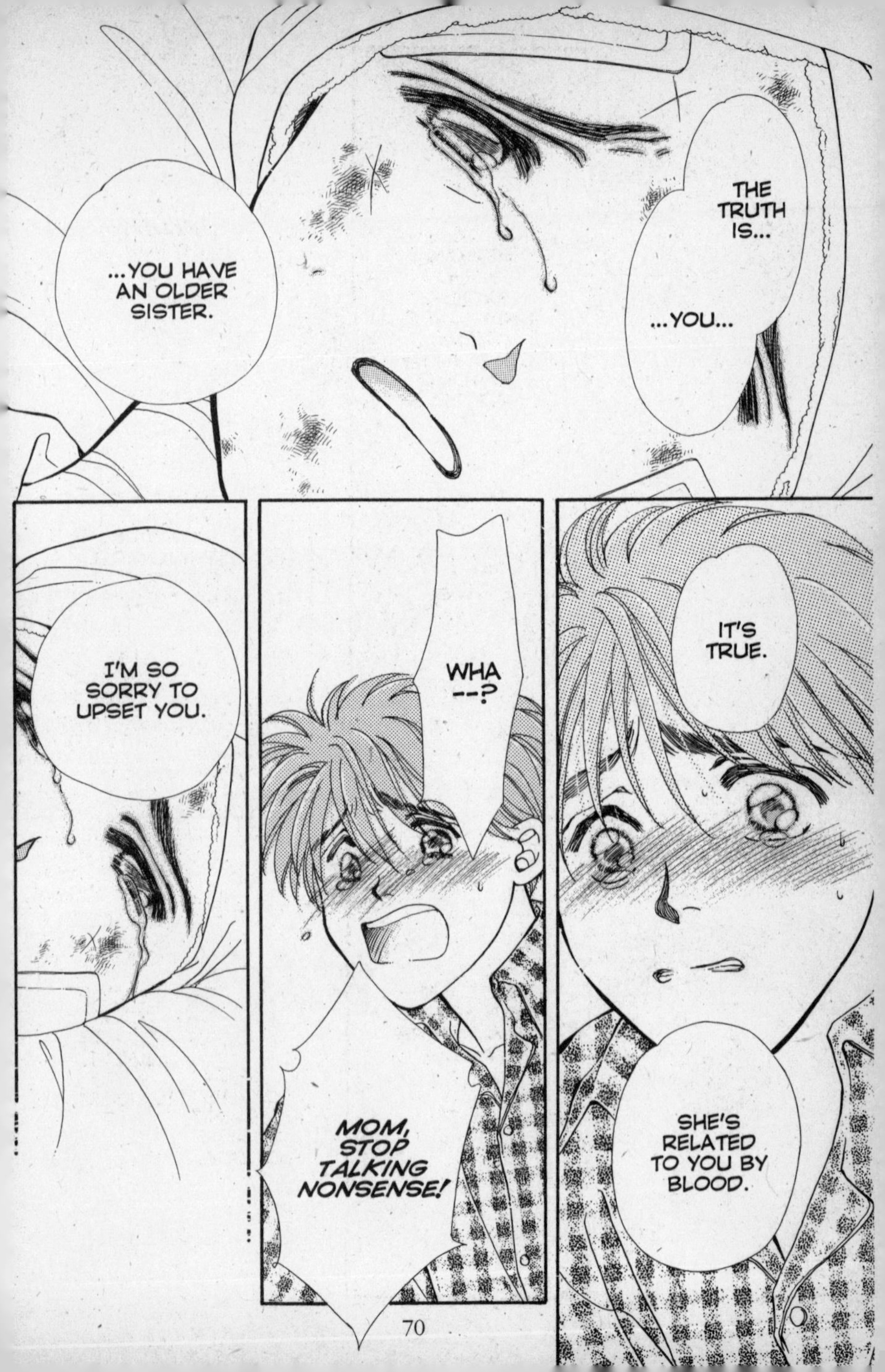
THE TRUTH IS...
...YOU...
...YOU HAVE AN OLDER SISTER.
IT'S TRUE.
SHE'S RELATED TO YOU BY BLOOD.
WHA--?
MOM, STOP TALKING NONSENSE!
I'M SO SORRY TO UPSET YOU.

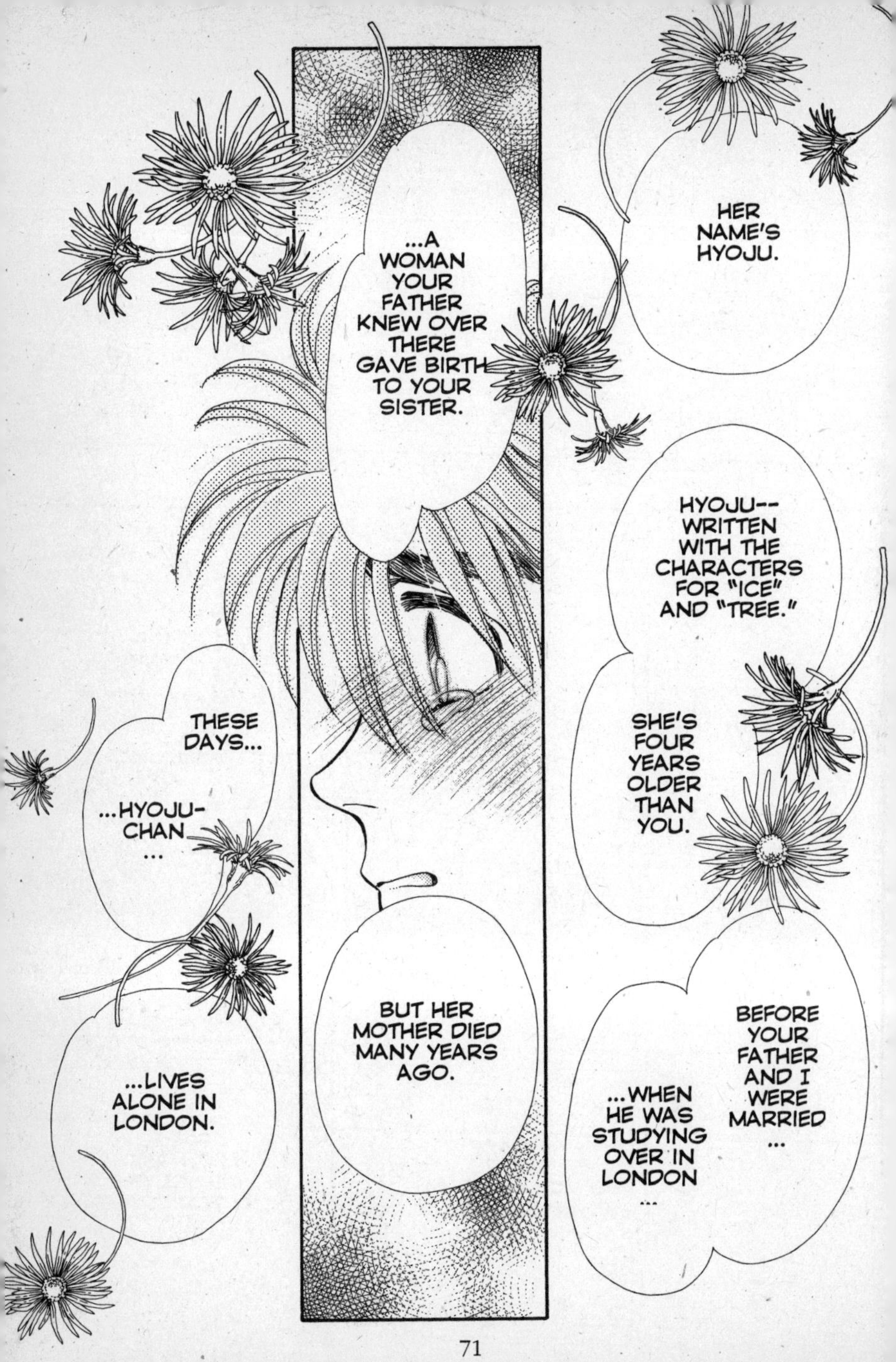
BEFORE YOUR FATHER AND I WERE MARRIED ...
...WHEN HE WAS STUDYING OVER IN LONDON ...
...A WOMAN YOUR FATHER KNEW OVER THERE GAVE BIRTH TO YOUR SISTER.
HER NAME'S HYOJU.
HYOJU--WRITTEN WITH THE CHARACTERS FOR "ICE" AND "TREE."
SHE'S FOUR YEARS OLDER THAN YOU.
BUT HER MOTHER DIED MANY YEARS AGO.
THESE DAYS...
...HYOJU-CHAN ...
...LIVES ALONE IN LONDON.

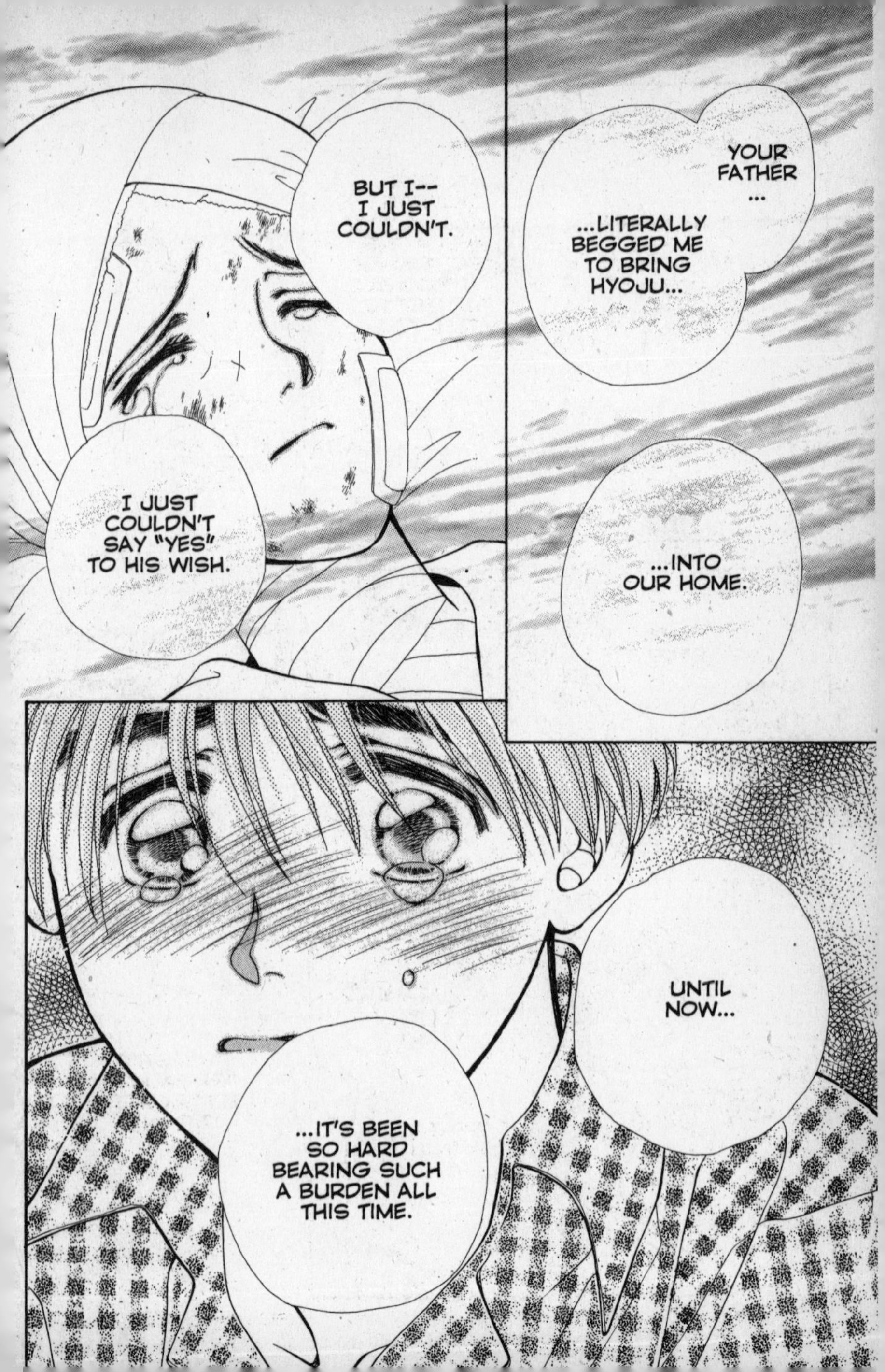
YOUR FATHER ...
...LITERALLY BEGGED ME TO BRING HYOJU...
...INTO OUR HOME.
BUT I-- I JUST COULDN'T.
I JUST COULDN'T SAY "YES" TO HIS WISH.
UNTIL NOW...
...IT'S BEEN SO HARD BEARING SUCH A BURDEN ALL THIS TIME.

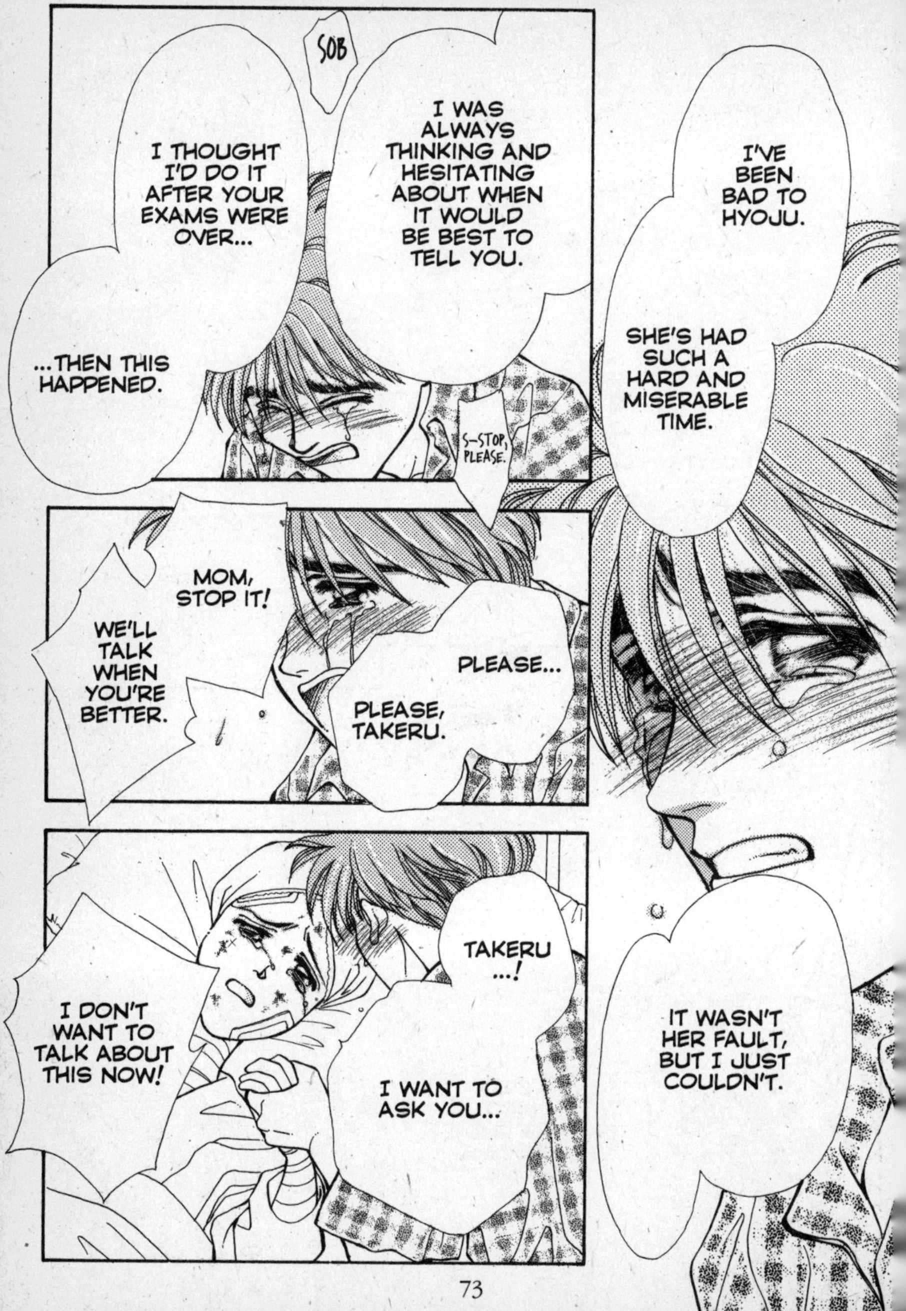
I'VE BEEN BAD TO HYOJU.
SHE'S HAD SUCH A HARD AND MISERABLE TIME.
IT WASN'T HER FAULT, BUT I JUST COULDN'T.
SOB
I WAS ALWAYS THINKING AND HESITATING ABOUT WHEN IT WOULD BE BEST TO TELL YOU.
I THOUGHT I'D DO IT AFTER YOUR EXAMS WERE OVER...
...THEN THIS HAPPENED.
S-STOP, PLEASE.
PLEASE...
PLEASE, TAKERU.
MOM, STOP IT!
WE'LL TALK WHEN YOU'RE BETTER.
TAKERU ...!
I WANT TO ASK YOU...
I DON'T WANT TO TALK ABOUT THIS NOW!

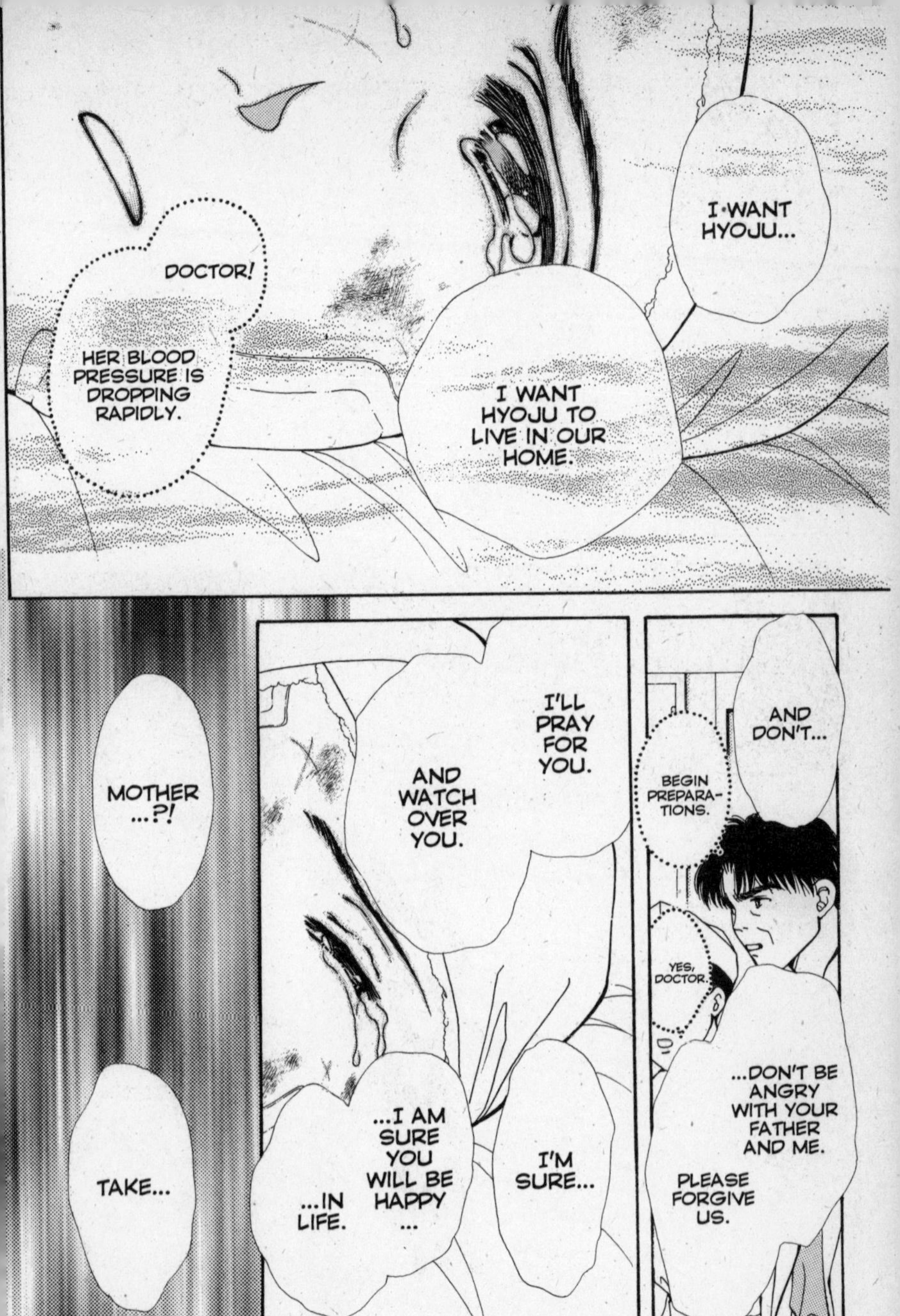
I WANT HYOJU...
I WANT HYOJU TO LIVE IN OUR HOME.
DOCTOR!
HER BLOOD PRESSURE IS DROPPING RAPIDLY.
AND DON'T...
BEGIN PREPARATIONS.
YES, DOCTOR.
...DON'T BE ANGRY WITH YOUR FATHER AND ME.
PLEASE FORGIVE US.
I'LL PRAY FOR YOU.
AND WATCH OVER YOU.
I'M SURE...
...I AM SURE YOU WILL BE HAPPY ...
...IN LIFE.
MOTHER ...?!
TAKE...

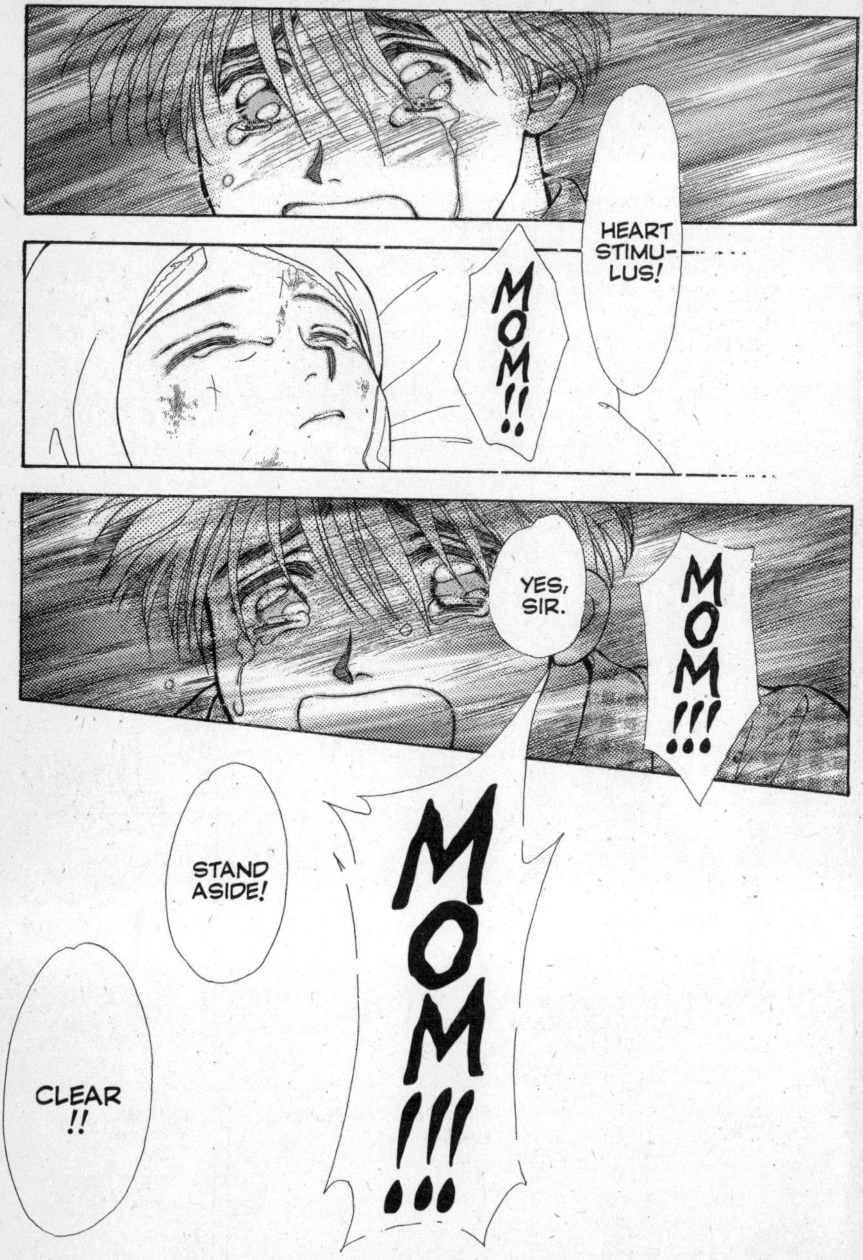
HEART STIMU-LUS!
MOM!!
MOM!!!
YES, SIR.
MOM!!!
STAND ASIDE!
CLEAR!!

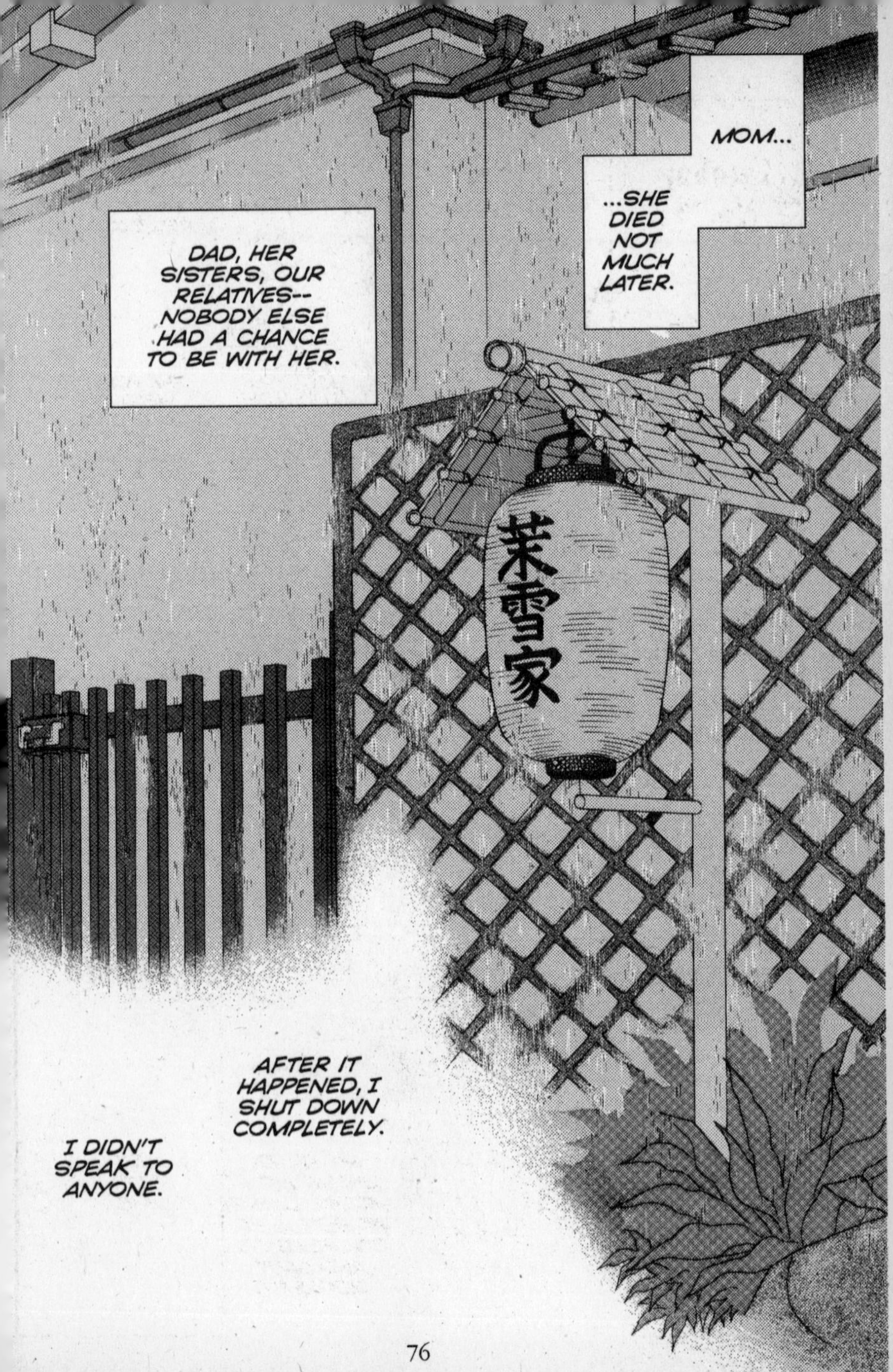
MOM...
...SHE DIED NOT MUCH LATER.
DAD, HER SISTERS, OUR RELATIVES-- NOBODY ELSE HAD A CHANCE TO BE WITH HER.
茉雪家
AFTER IT HAPPENED, I SHUT DOWN COMPLETELY.
I DIDN'T SPEAK TO ANYONE.

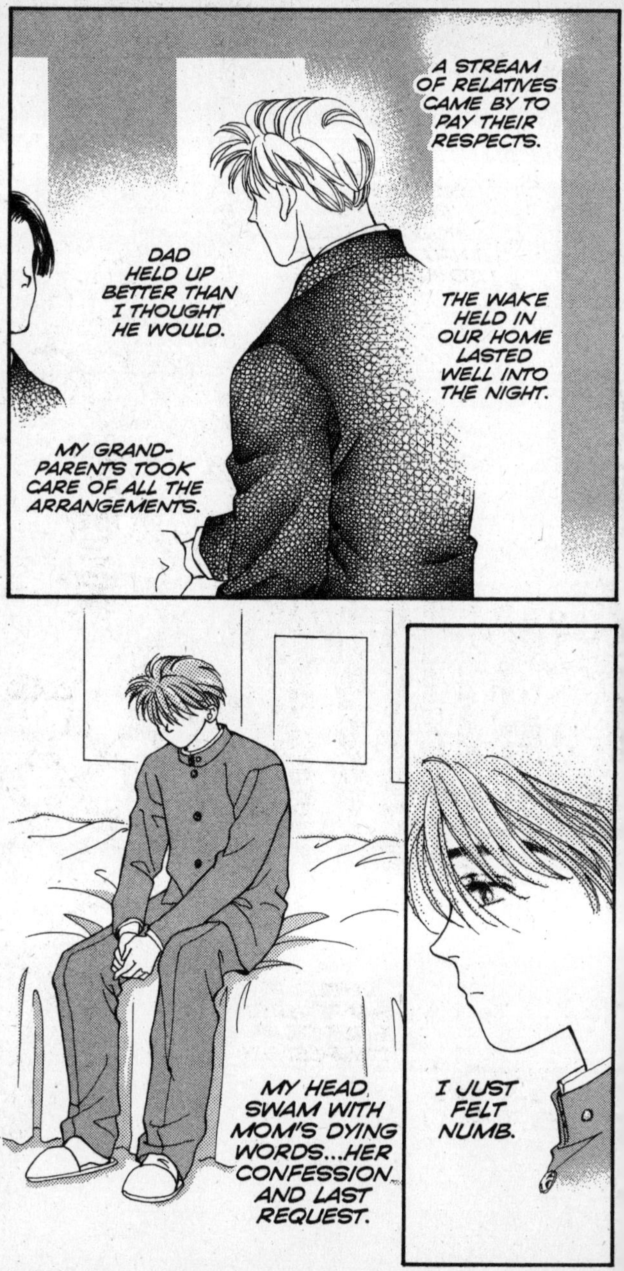
A STREAM OF RELATIVES CAME BY TO PAY THEIR RESPECTS.
THE WAKE HELD IN OUR HOME LASTED WELL INTO THE NIGHT.
DAD HELD UP BETTER THAN I THOUGHT HE WOULD.
MY GRAND-PARENTS TOOK CARE OF ALL THE ARRANGEMENTS.
I JUST FELT NUMB.
MY HEAD SWAM WITH MOM'S DYING WORDS...HER CONFESSION AND LAST REQUEST.

1/4 Sidebar No. 4

4

So that's how I started work on "Tower of the future." I wanted it to have a bright mood, but the first volume is really, really sad. For the second volume, I had planned to really get into meat of the story but the mood took a completely different turn.
As I wrote in the sidebars for the last volume of "Save the World," I'm really fascinated by the notion of "time." And just as the past was a central theme of "Save the World," the future is a central theme of "Tower of the Future"--as its title suggests. We don't know from where the future will come, but aren't the "past," "present," and "future" all just words applied to the slippery notion of change we call "time"? We start with the "past," then the "present," and after that the "future."

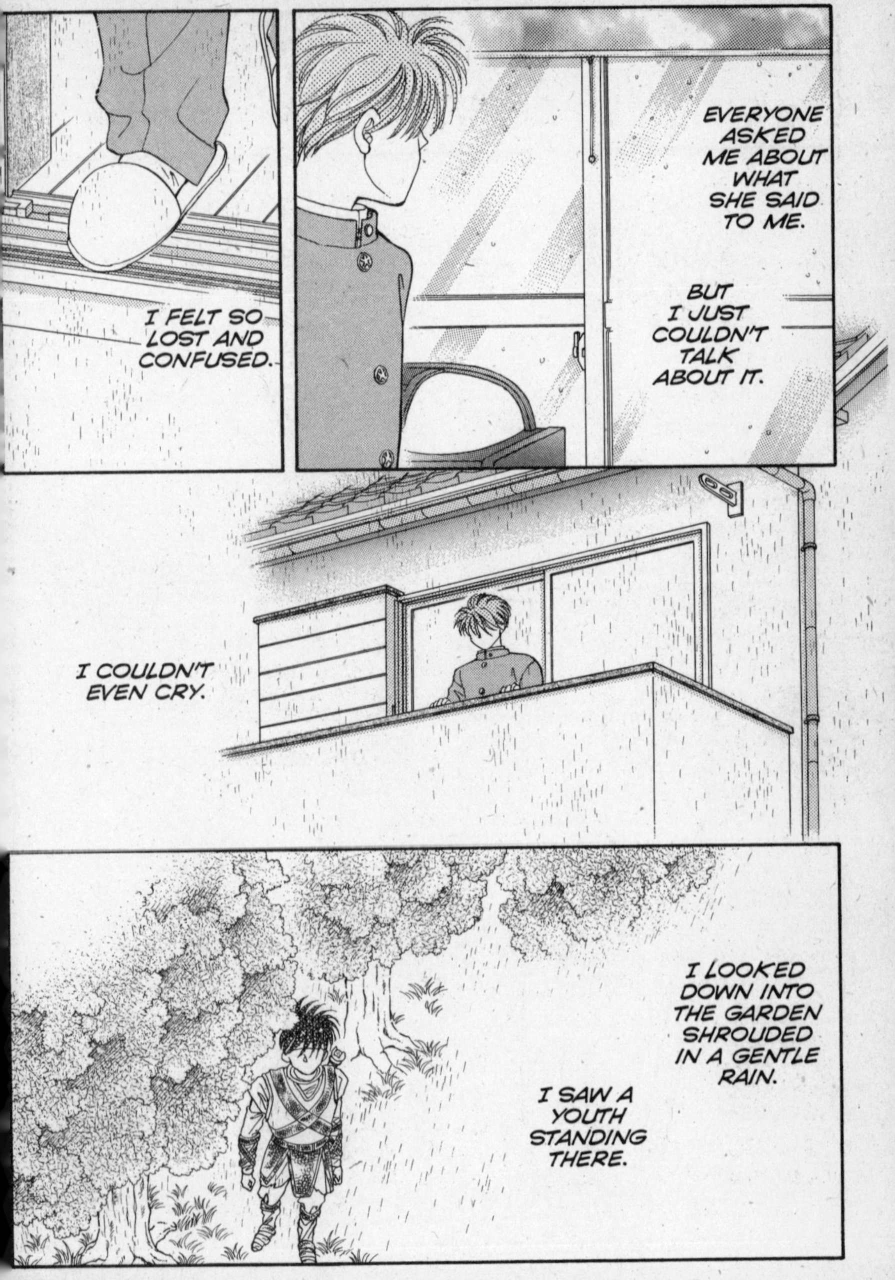
EVERYONE ASKED ME ABOUT WHAT SHE SAID TO ME.
BUT I JUST COULDN'T TALK ABOUT IT.
I FELT SO LOST AND CONFUSED.
I COULDN'T EVEN CRY.
I LOOKED DOWN INTO THE GARDEN SHROUDED IN A GENTLE RAIN.
I SAW A YOUTH STANDING THERE.

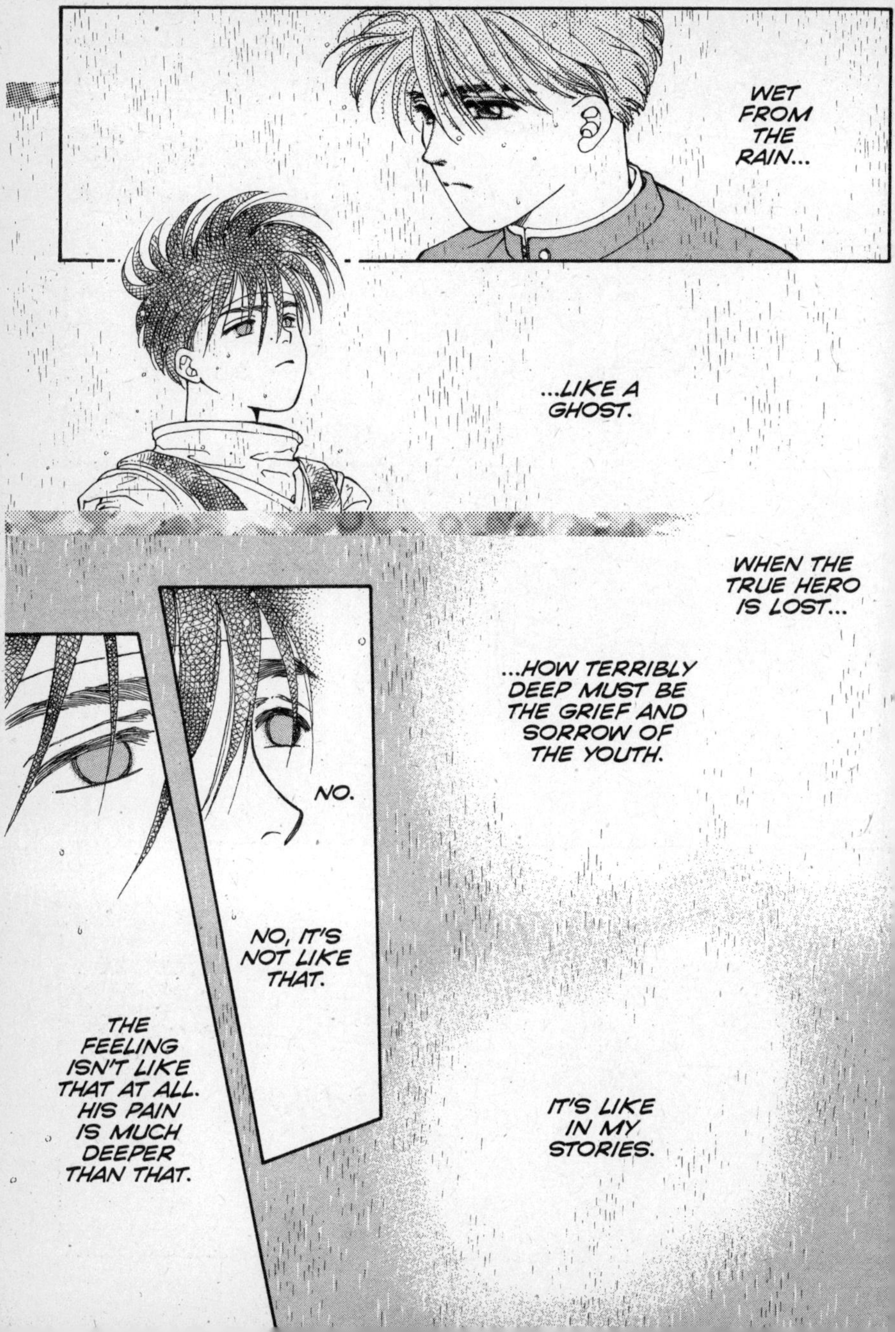
WET FROM THE RAIN...
...LIKE A GHOST.
WHEN THE TRUE HERO IS LOST...
...HOW TERRIBLY DEEP MUST BE THE GRIEF AND SORROW OF THE YOUTH.
IT'S LIKE IN MY STORIES.
NO.
NO, IT'S NOT LIKE THAT.
THE FEELING ISN'T LIKE THAT AT ALL. HIS PAIN IS MUCH DEEPER THAN THAT.

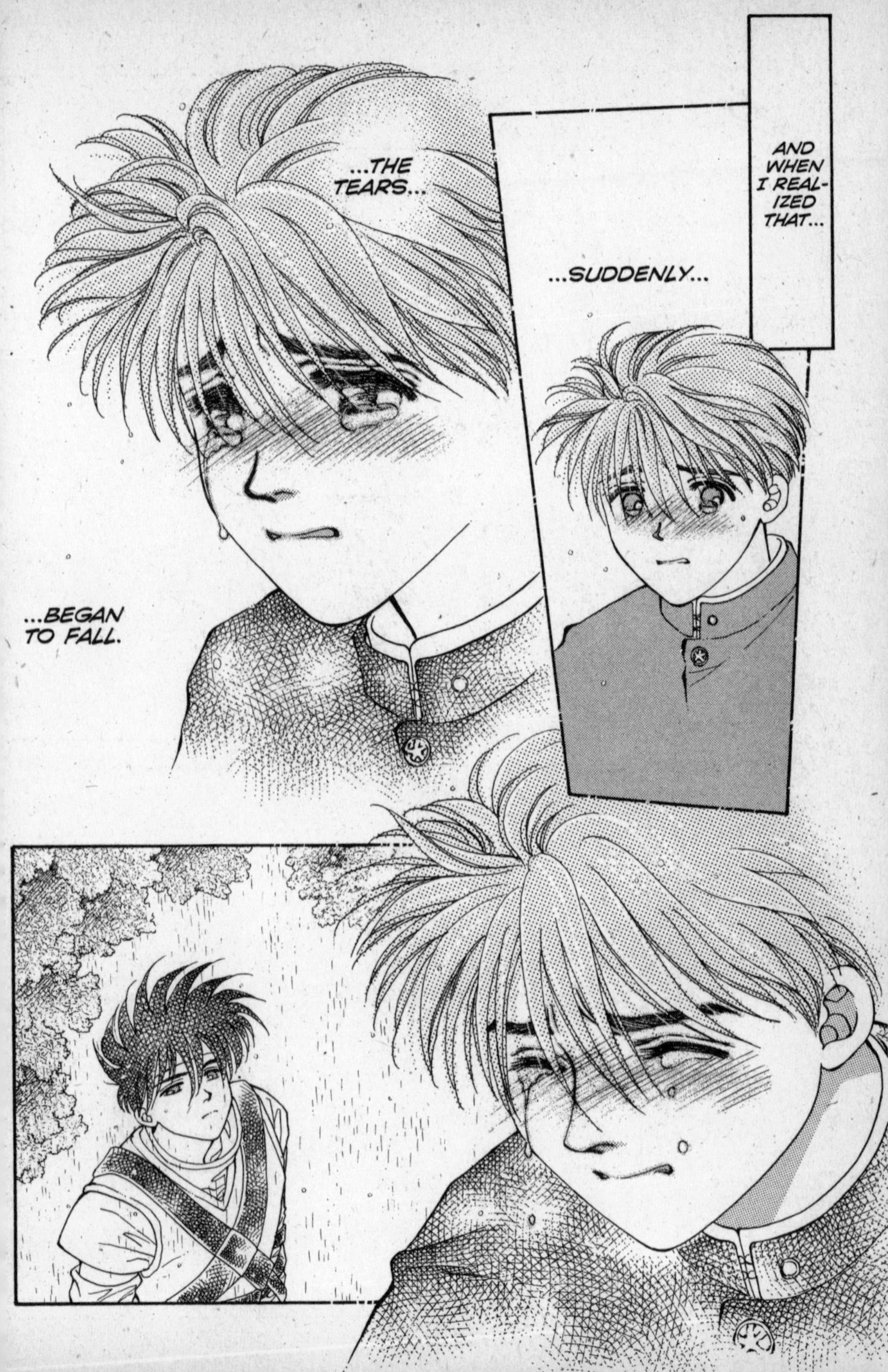
AND WHEN I REAL-IZED THAT...
...SUDDENLY...
...THE TEARS...
...BEGAN TO FALL.

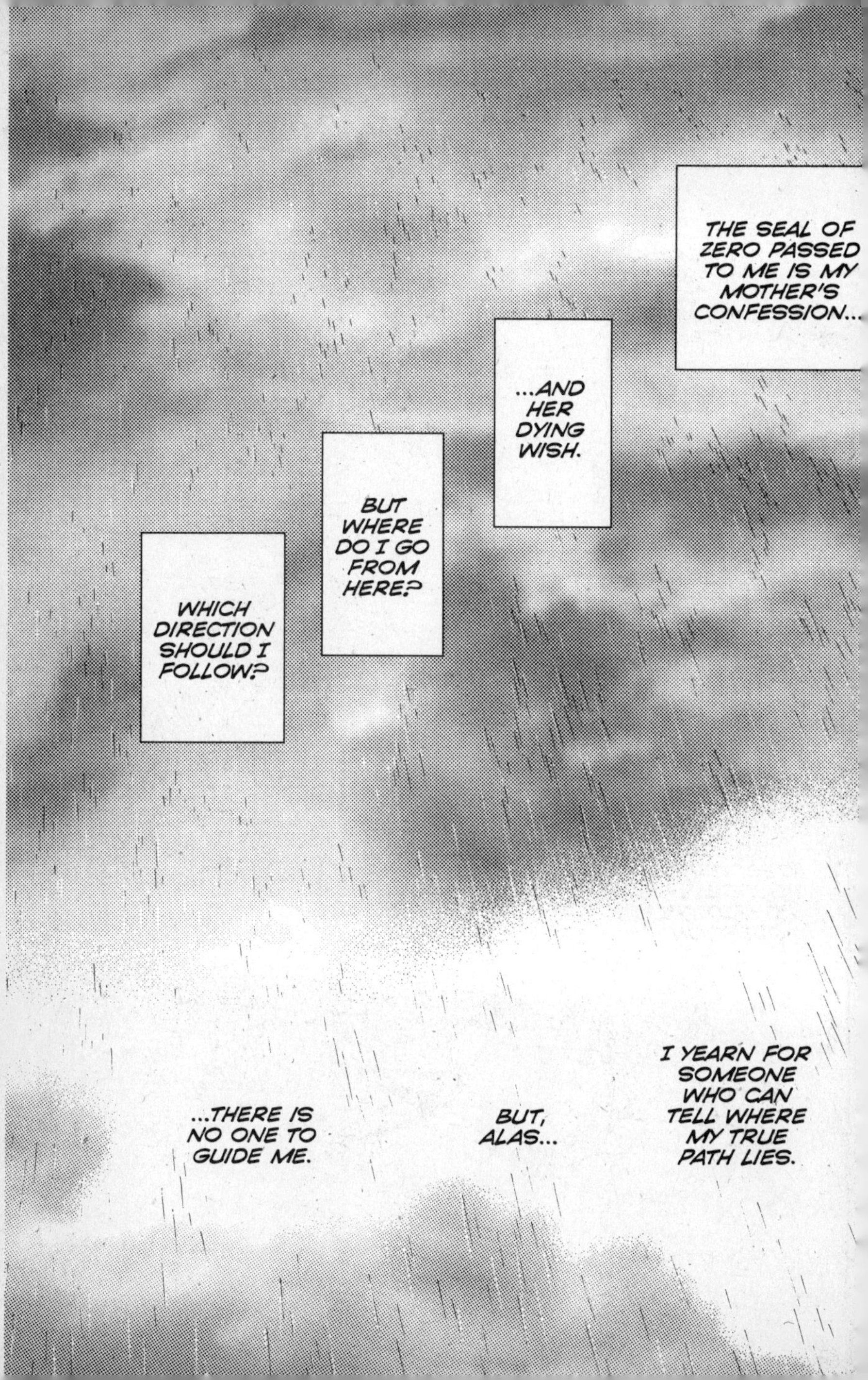
THE SEAL OF ZERO PASSED TO ME IS MY MOTHER'S CONFESSION...
...AND HER DYING WISH.
BUT WHERE DO I GO FROM HERE?
WHICH DIRECTION SHOULD I FOLLOW?
I YEARN FOR SOMEONE WHO CAN TELL WHERE MY TRUE PATH LIES.
BUT, ALAS...
...THERE IS NO ONE TO GUIDE ME.

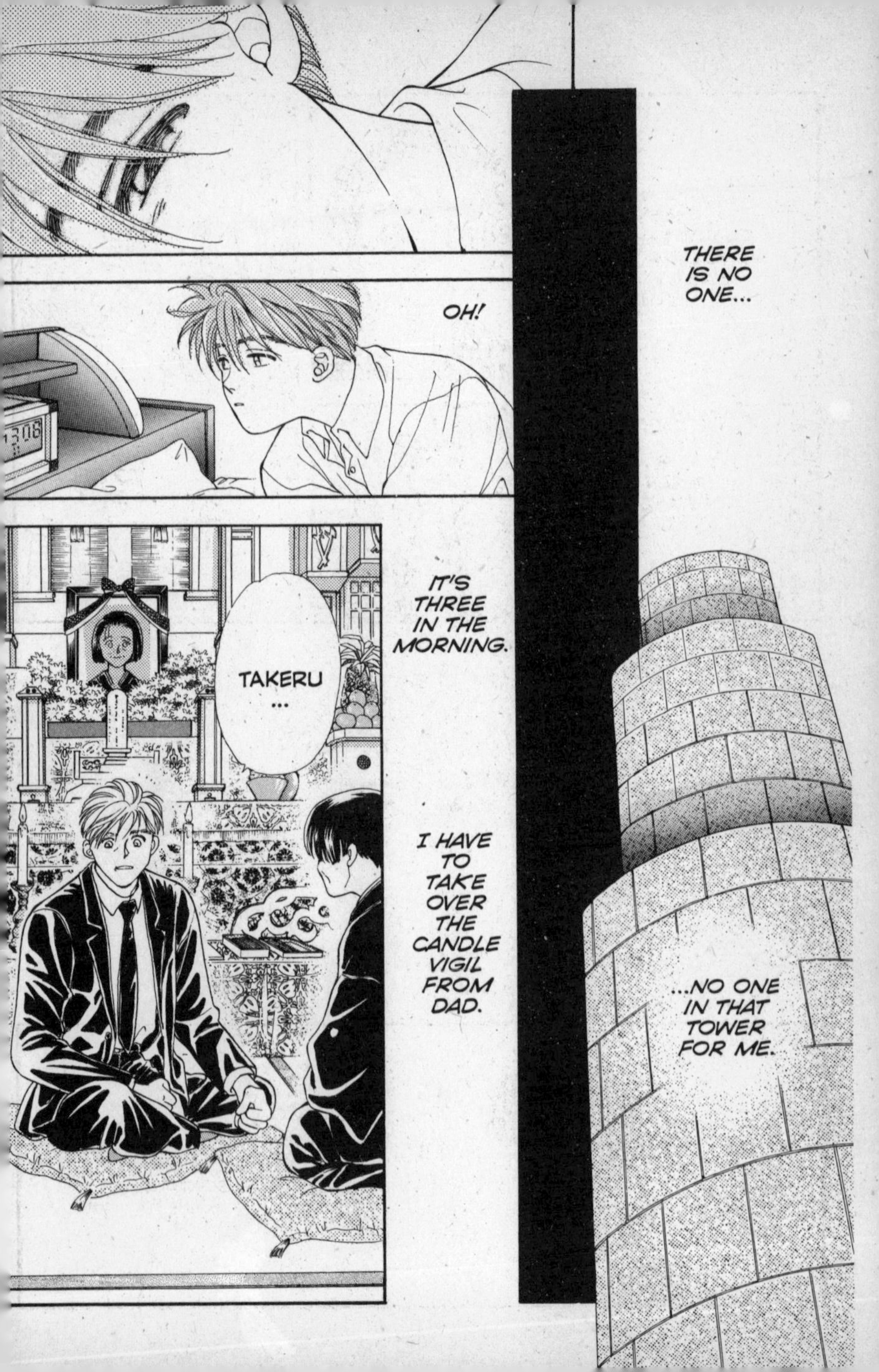
THERE IS NO ONE...
...NO ONE IN THAT TOWER FOR ME.
OH!
IT'S THREE IN THE MORNING.
TAKERU ...
I HAVE TO TAKE OVER THE CANDLE VIGIL FROM DAD.

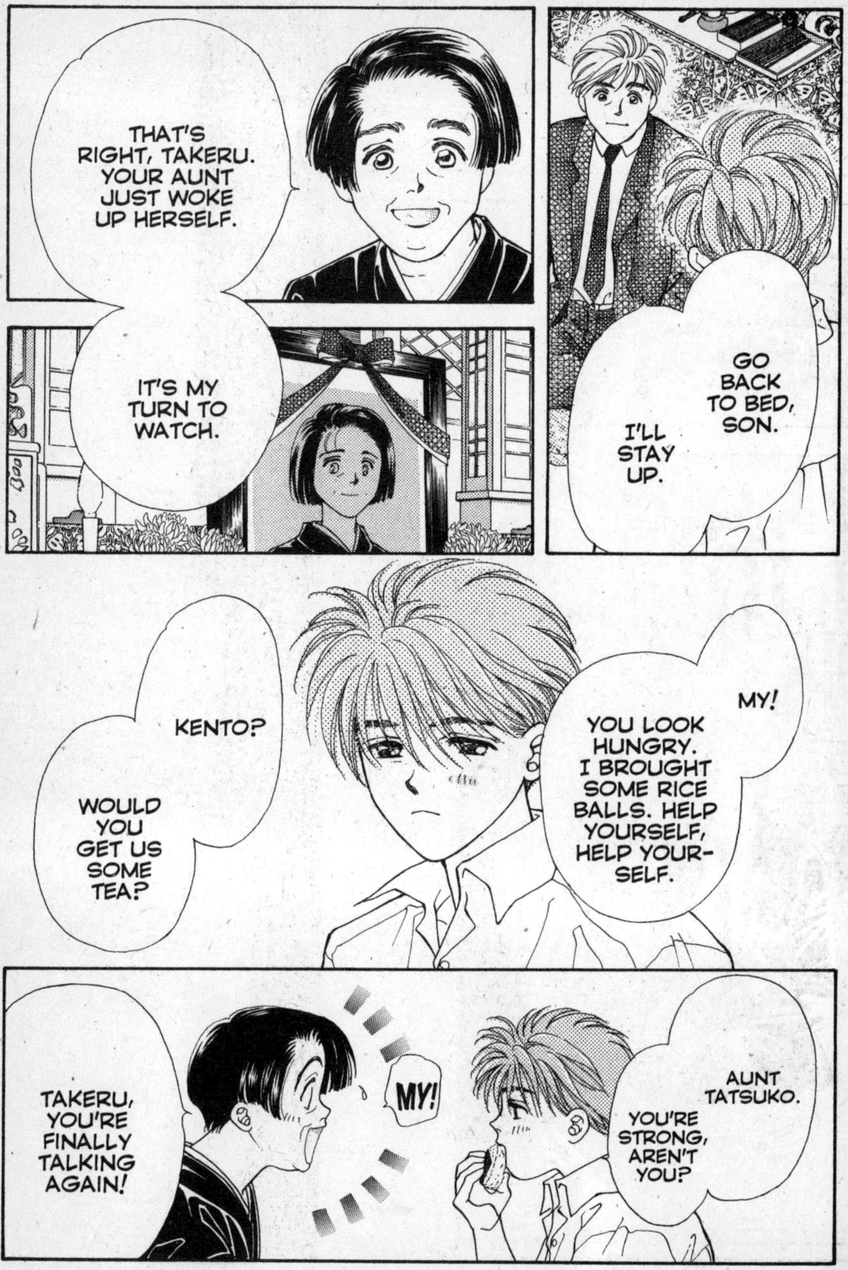
GO BACK TO BED, SON.
I'LL STAY UP.
THAT'S RIGHT, TAKERU. YOUR AUNT JUST WOKE UP HERSELF.
IT'S MY TURN TO WATCH.
MY!
YOU LOOK HUNGRY. I BROUGHT SOME RICE BALLS. HELP YOURSELF, HELP YOUR-SELF.
KENTO?
WOULD YOU GET US SOME TEA?
AUNT TATSUKO.
YOU'RE STRONG, AREN'T YOU?
MY!
TAKERU, YOU'RE FINALLY TALKING AGAIN!

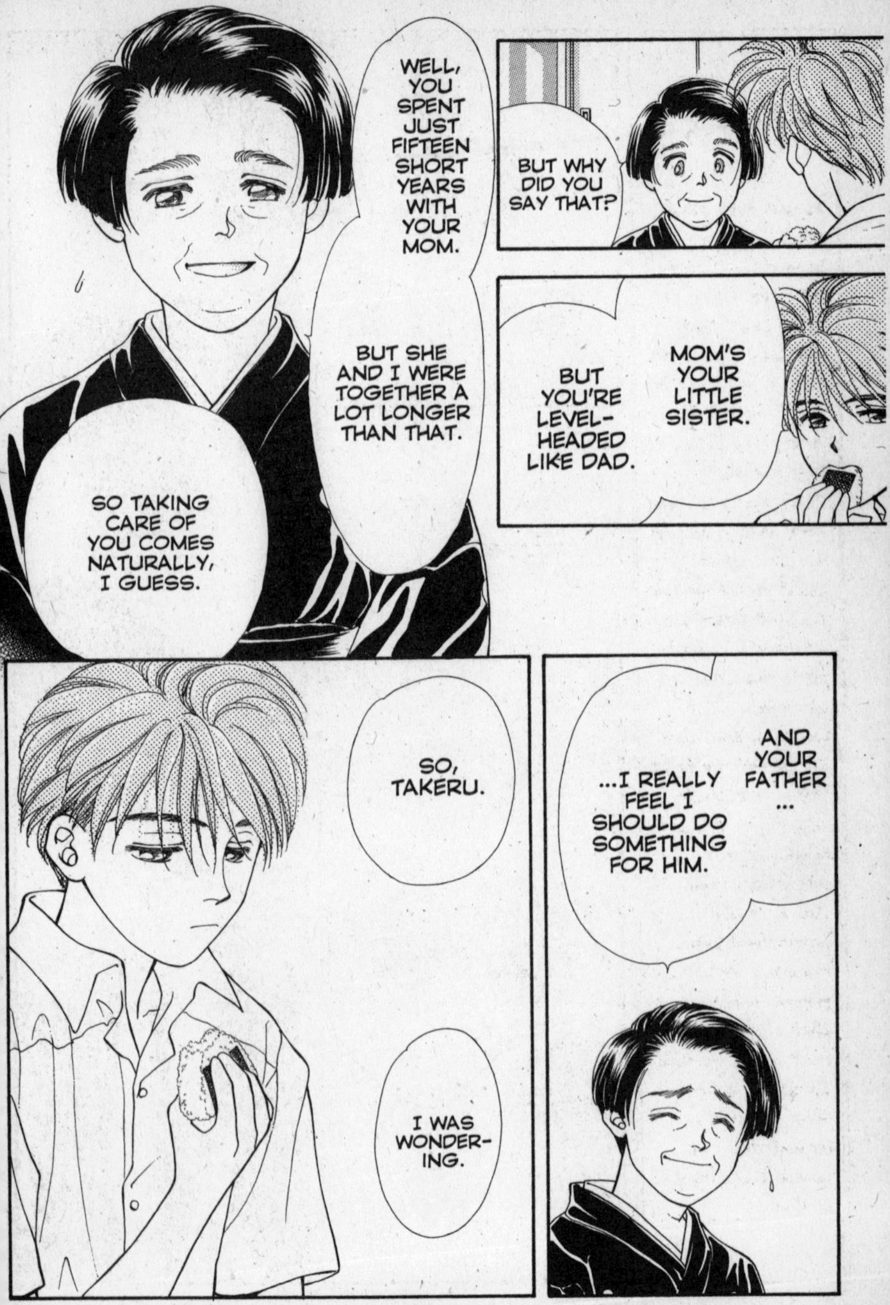
BUT WHY DID YOU SAY THAT?
MOM'S YOUR LITTLE SISTER.
BUT YOU'RE LEVEL-HEADED LIKE DAD.
WELL, YOU SPENT JUST FIFTEEN SHORT YEARS WITH YOUR MOM.
BUT SHE AND I WERE TOGETHER A LOT LONGER THAN THAT.
SO TAKING CARE OF YOU COMES NATURALLY, I GUESS.
AND YOUR FATHER ...
...I REALLY FEEL I SHOULD DO SOMETHING FOR HIM.
SO, TAKERU.
I WAS WONDER-ING.

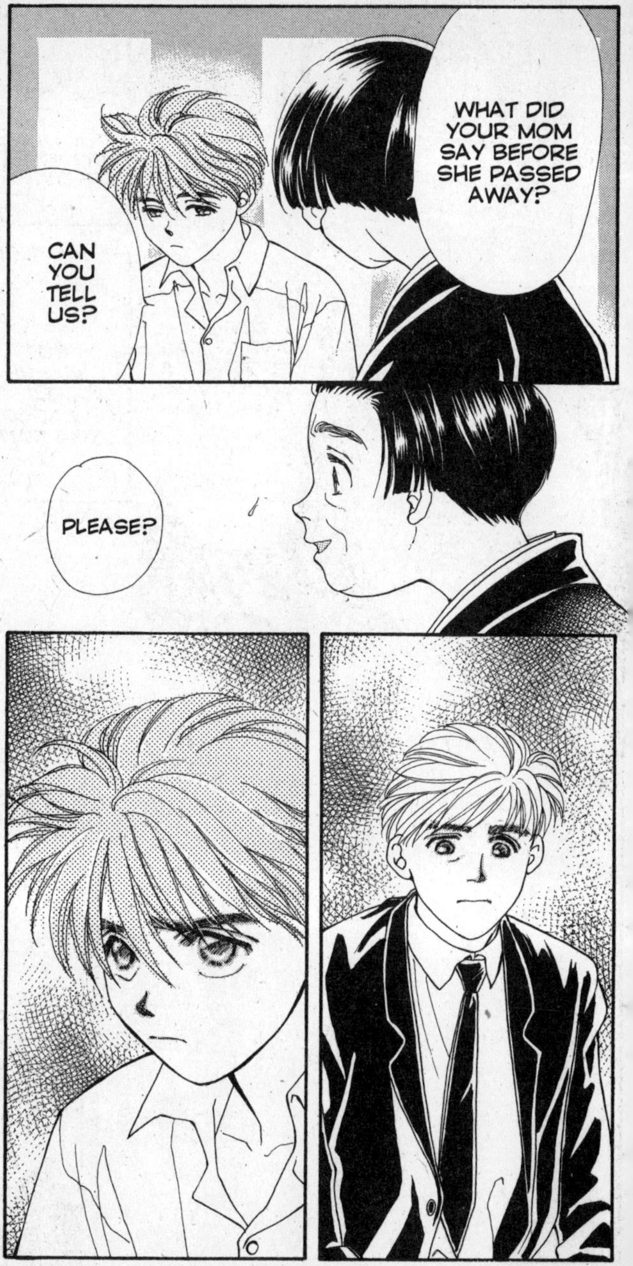
WHAT DID YOUR MOM SAY BEFORE SHE PASSED AWAY?
CAN YOU TELL US?
PLEASE?

1/4 Sidebar No. 5

5

Do you ever think about what comes before the future? Isn't the future the thing that points the way for time? What I mean is that time's birthplace is really the future (not the past). Think about all the time that makes up our lives. When we count back from our twilight years we ultimately come to zero, the year we were born. And what happens when we arrive? We're at zero--so a whole new thing is sure to begin. Ha! No, seriously, I think this is really interesting! Time revolves, time is reborn. The thing that created time must surely be God. They say that in India there is a legend that this world is a dream of God's.

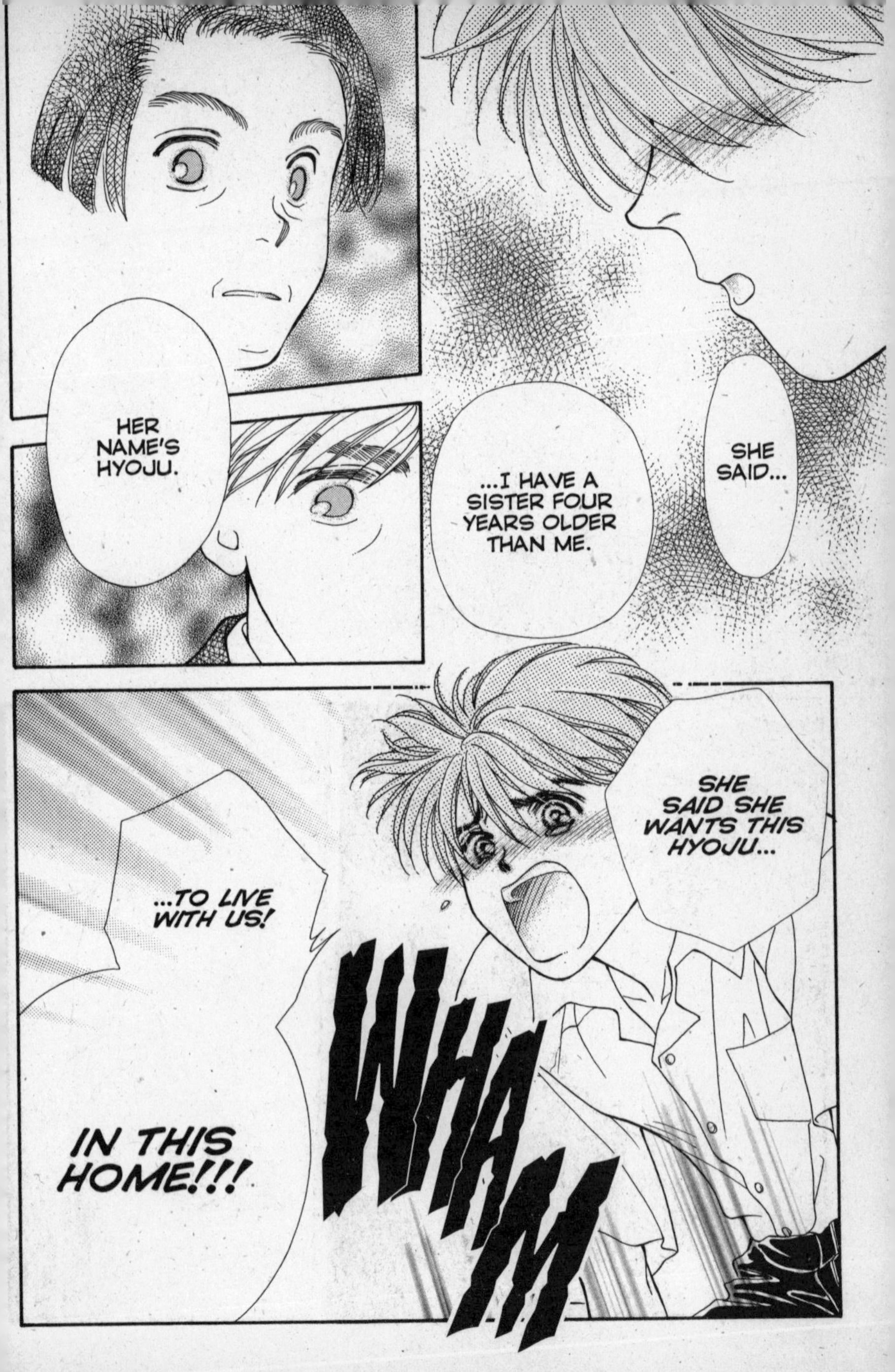
SHE SAID...
...I HAVE A SISTER FOUR YEARS OLDER THAN ME.
HER NAME'S HYOJU.
SHE SAID SHE WANTS THIS HYOJU...
WHAM
...TO LIVE WITH US!
IN THIS HOME!!!

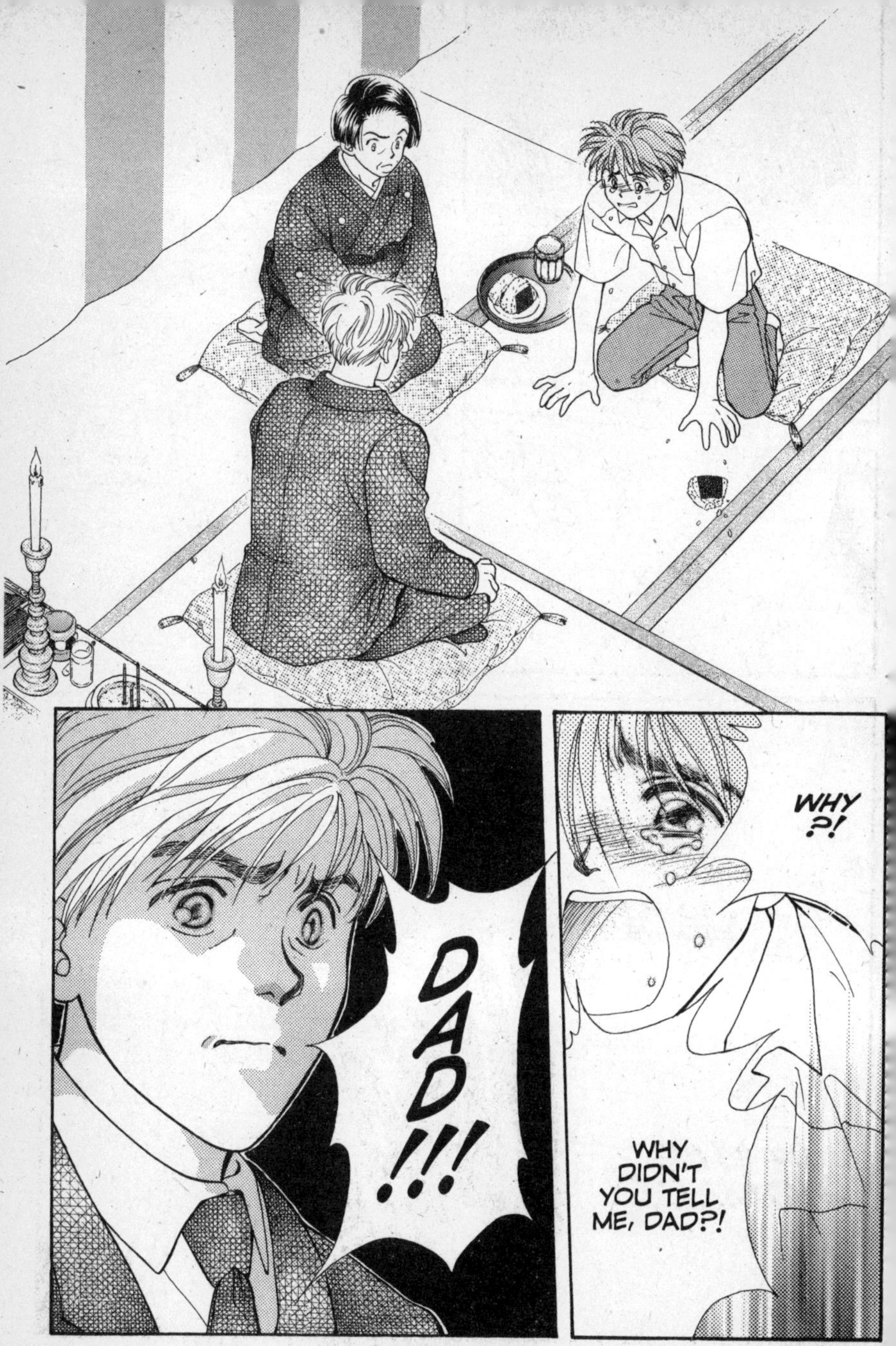
WHY?!
WHY DIDN'T YOU TELL ME, DAD?!
DAD!!!

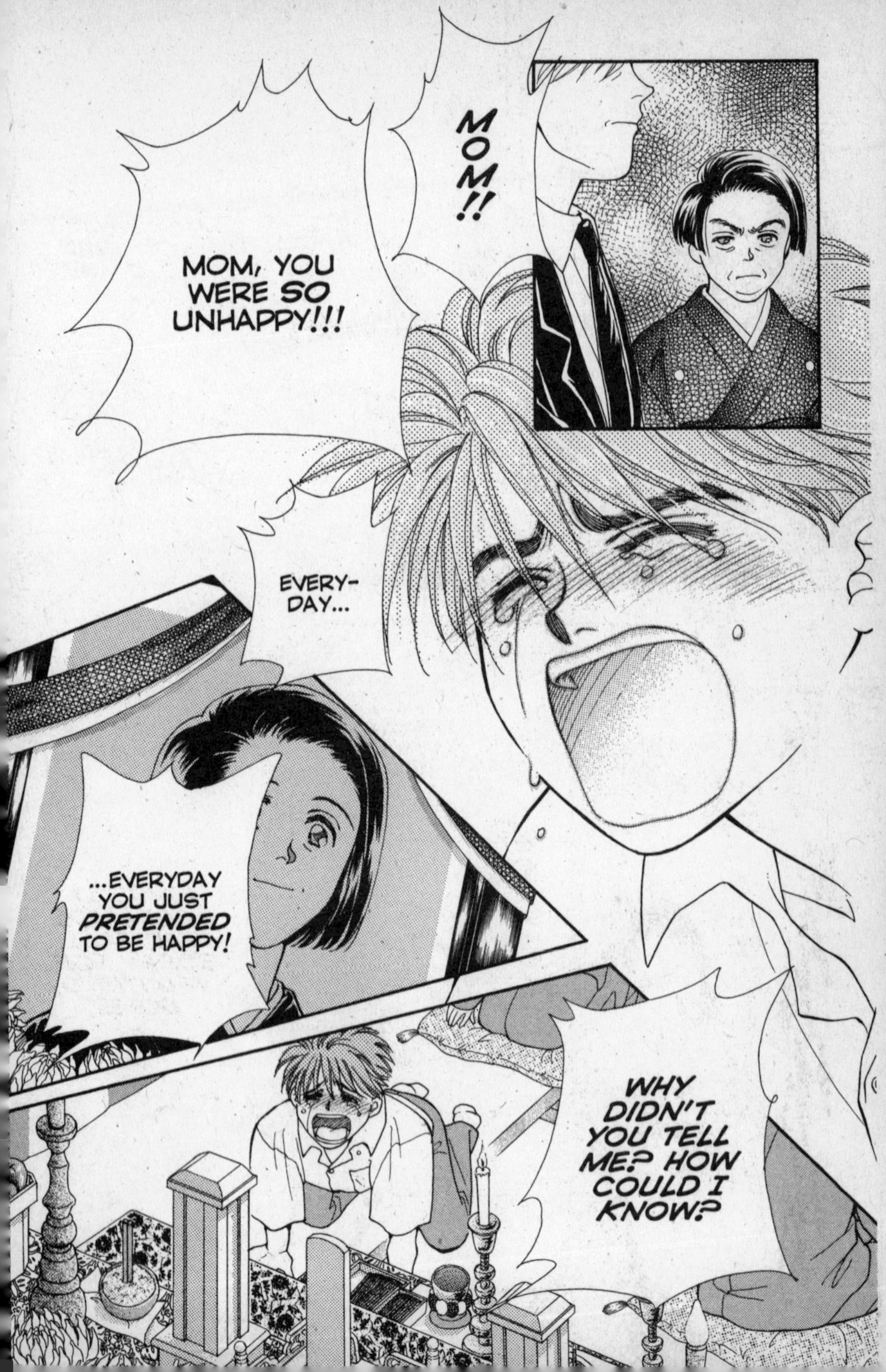
MOM!!
MOM, YOU WERE SO UNHAPPY!!!
EVERY-DAY...
...EVERYDAY YOU JUST PRETENDED TO BE HAPPY!
WHY DIDN'T YOU TELL ME? HOW COULD I KNOW?

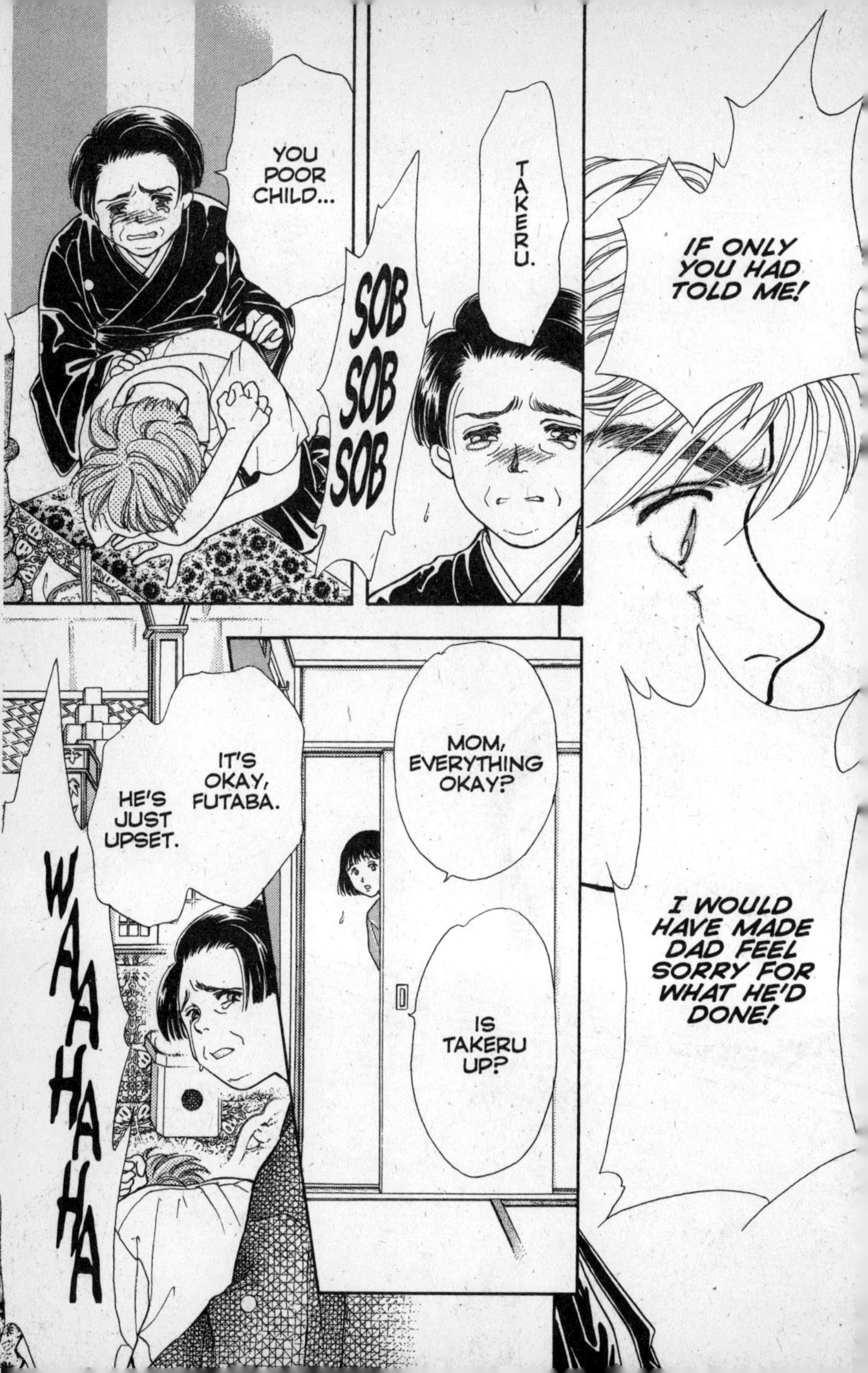
IF ONLY YOU HAD TOLD ME!
I WOULD HAVE MADE DAD FEEL SORRY FOR WHAT HE'D DONE!
TAKERU.
SOB SOB SOB
YOU POOR CHILD...
MOM, EVERYTHING OKAY?
IS TAKERU UP?
IT'S OKAY, FUTABA.
HE'S JUST UPSET.
WAAAHAHAHA

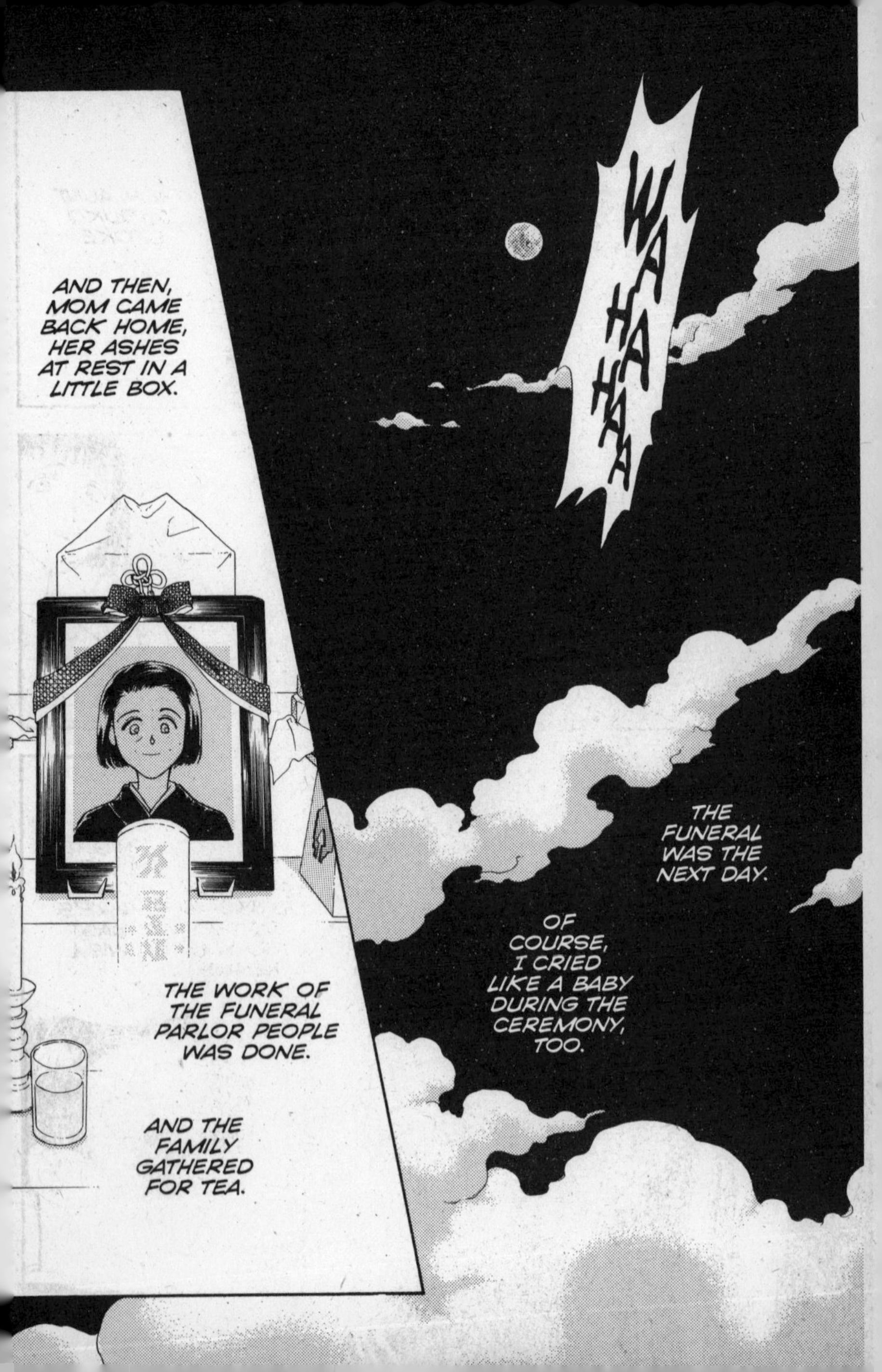
WAHAHAHAA
THE FUNERAL WAS THE NEXT DAY.
OF COURSE, I CRIED LIKE A BABY DURING THE CEREMONY, TOO.
AND THEN, MOM CAME BACK HOME, HER ASHES AT REST IN A LITTLE BOX.
THE WORK OF THE FUNERAL PARLOR PEOPLE WAS DONE.
AND THE FAMILY GATHERED FOR TEA.

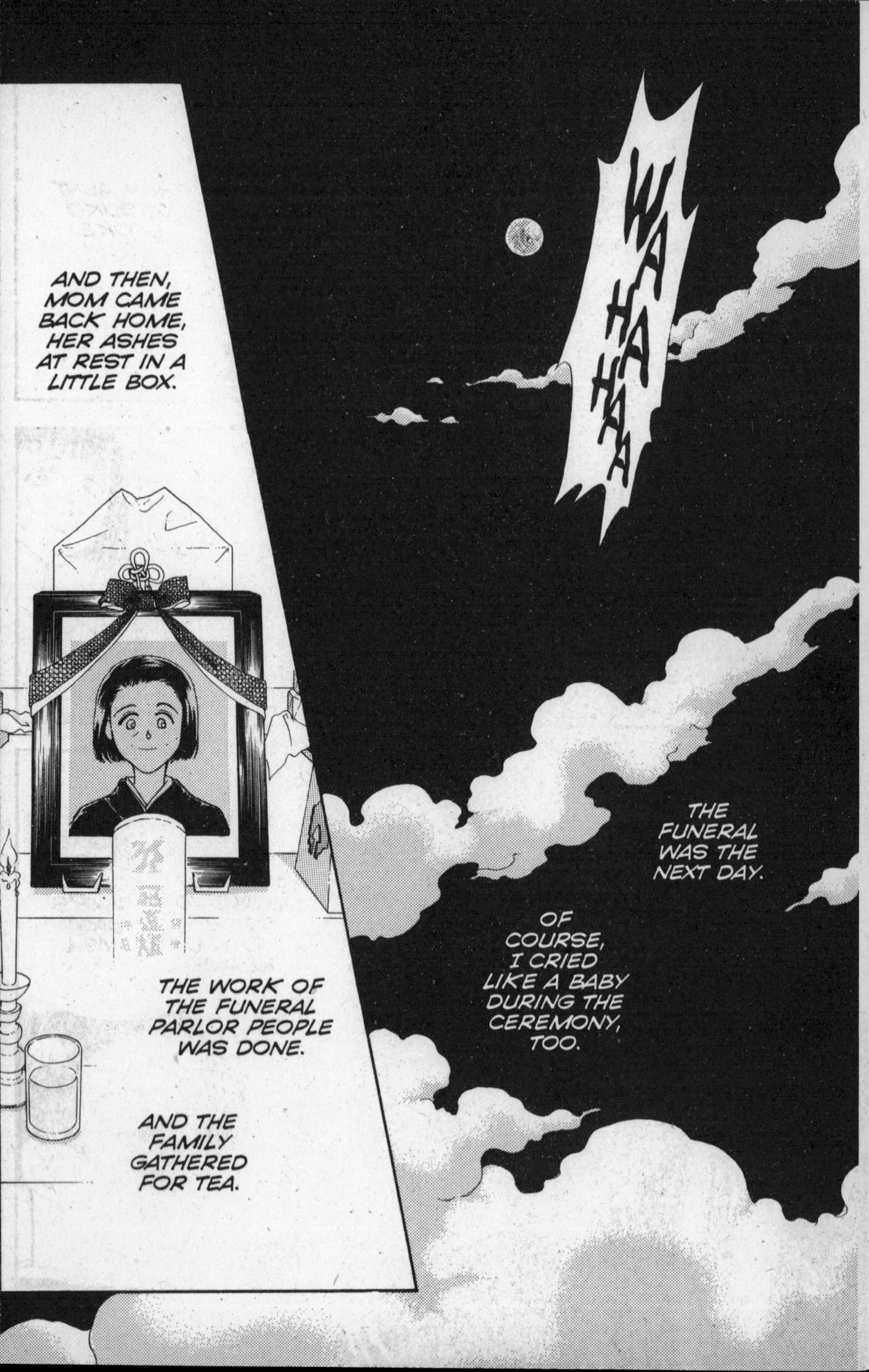
WAHAHAHAA
THE FUNERAL WAS THE NEXT DAY.
OF COURSE, I CRIED LIKE A BABY DURING THE CEREMONY, TOO.
AND THEN, MOM CAME BACK HOME, HER ASHES AT REST IN A LITTLE BOX.
THE WORK OF THE FUNERAL PARLOR PEOPLE WAS DONE.
AND THE FAMILY GATHERED FOR TEA.

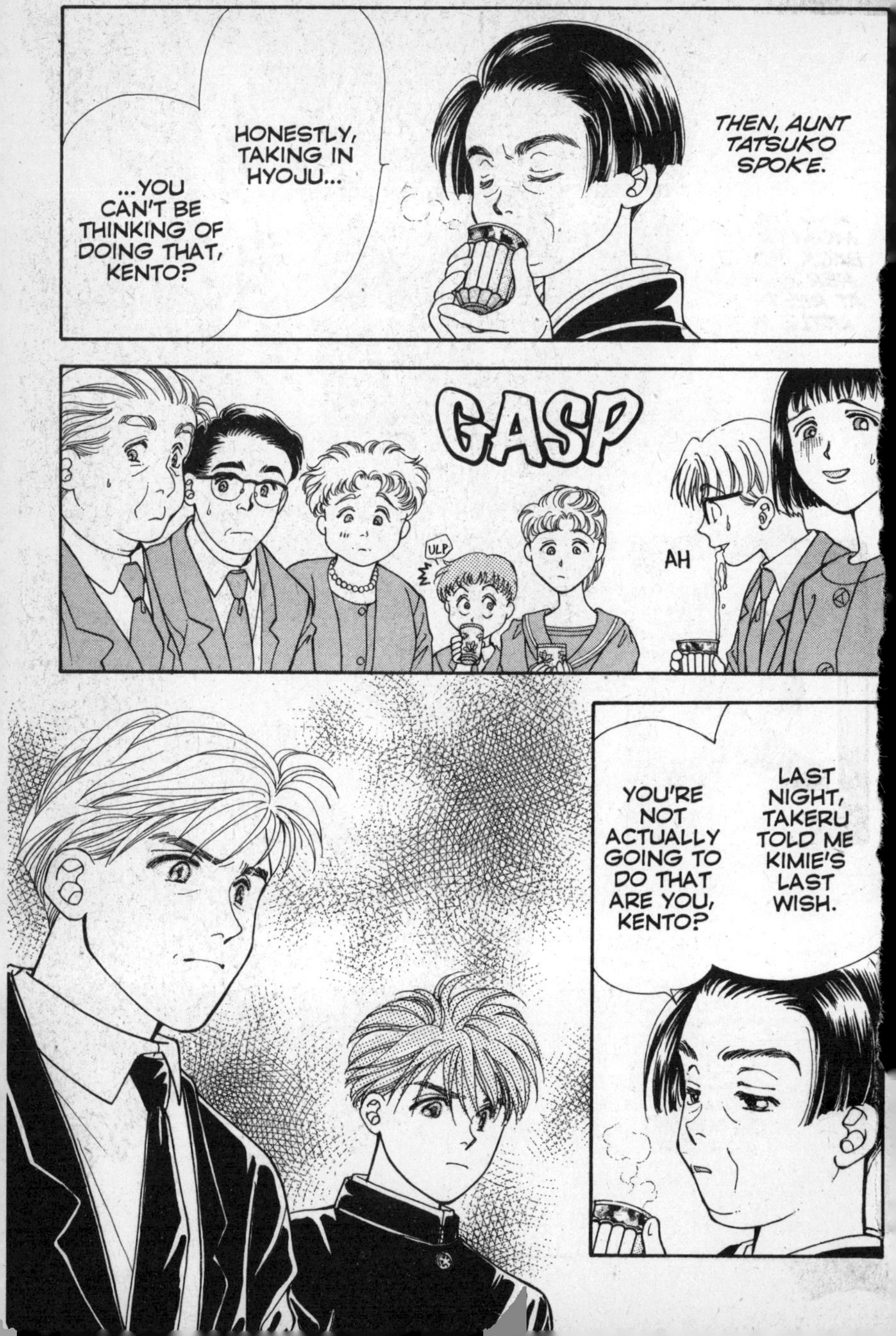
THEN, AUNT TATSUKO SPOKE.
HONESTLY, TAKING IN HYOJU...
...YOU CAN'T BE THINKING OF DOING THAT, KENTO?
GASP
AH
ULP
LAST NIGHT, TAKERU TOLD ME KIMIE'S LAST WISH.
YOU'RE NOT ACTUALLY GOING TO DO THAT ARE YOU, KENTO?

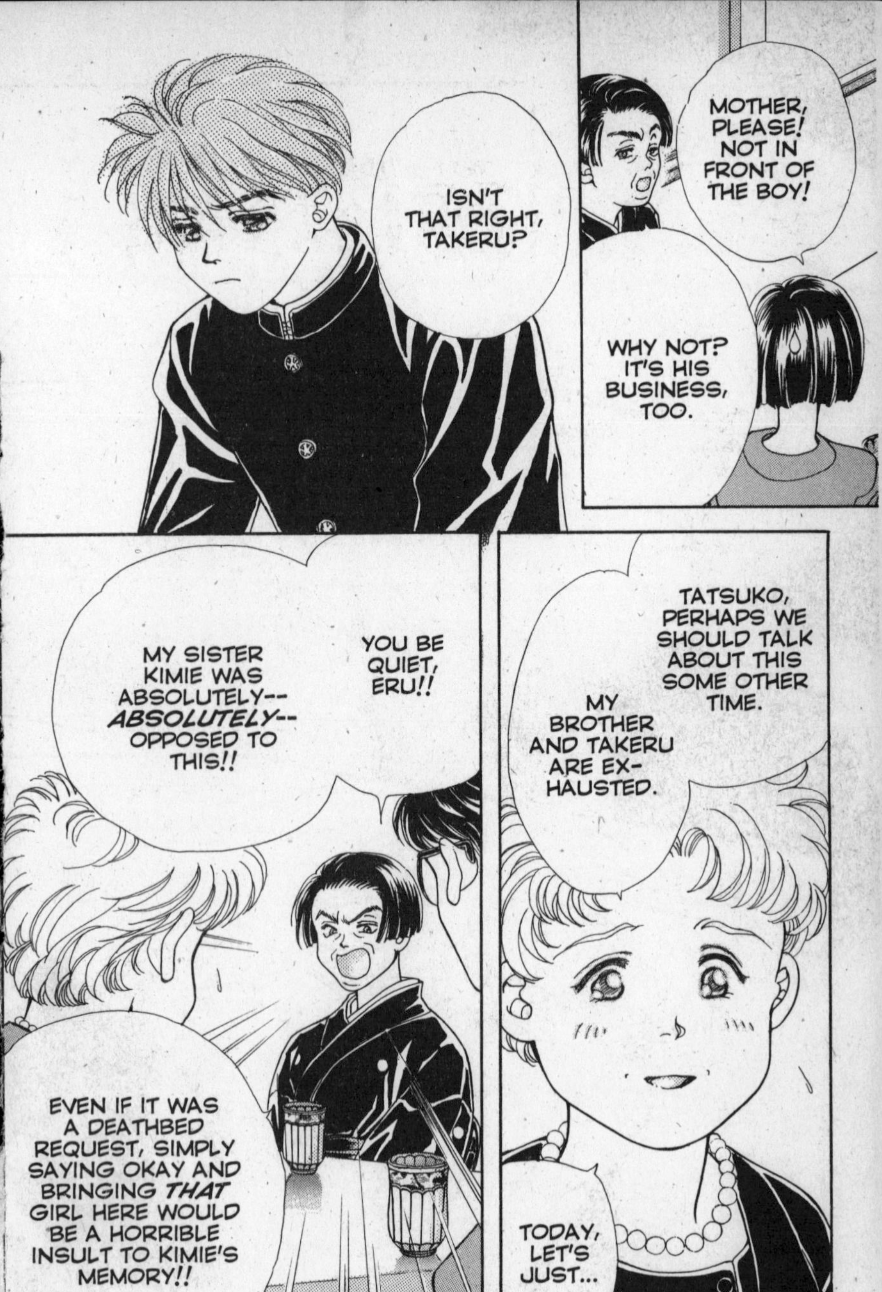
MOTHER, PLEASE! NOT IN FRONT OF THE BOY!
WHY NOT? IT'S HIS BUSINESS, TOO.
ISN'T THAT RIGHT, TAKERU?
TATSUKO, PERHAPS WE SHOULD TALK ABOUT THIS SOME OTHER TIME.
MY BROTHER AND TAKERU ARE EX-HAUSTED.
TODAY, LET'S JUST...
YOU BE QUIET, ERU!!
MY SISTER KIMIE WAS ABSOLUTELY-- *ABSOLUTELY*-- OPPOSED TO THIS!!
EVEN IF IT WAS A DEATHBED REQUEST, SIMPLY SAYING OKAY AND BRINGING *THAT* GIRL HERE WOULD BE A HORRIBLE INSULT TO KIMIE'S MEMORY!!

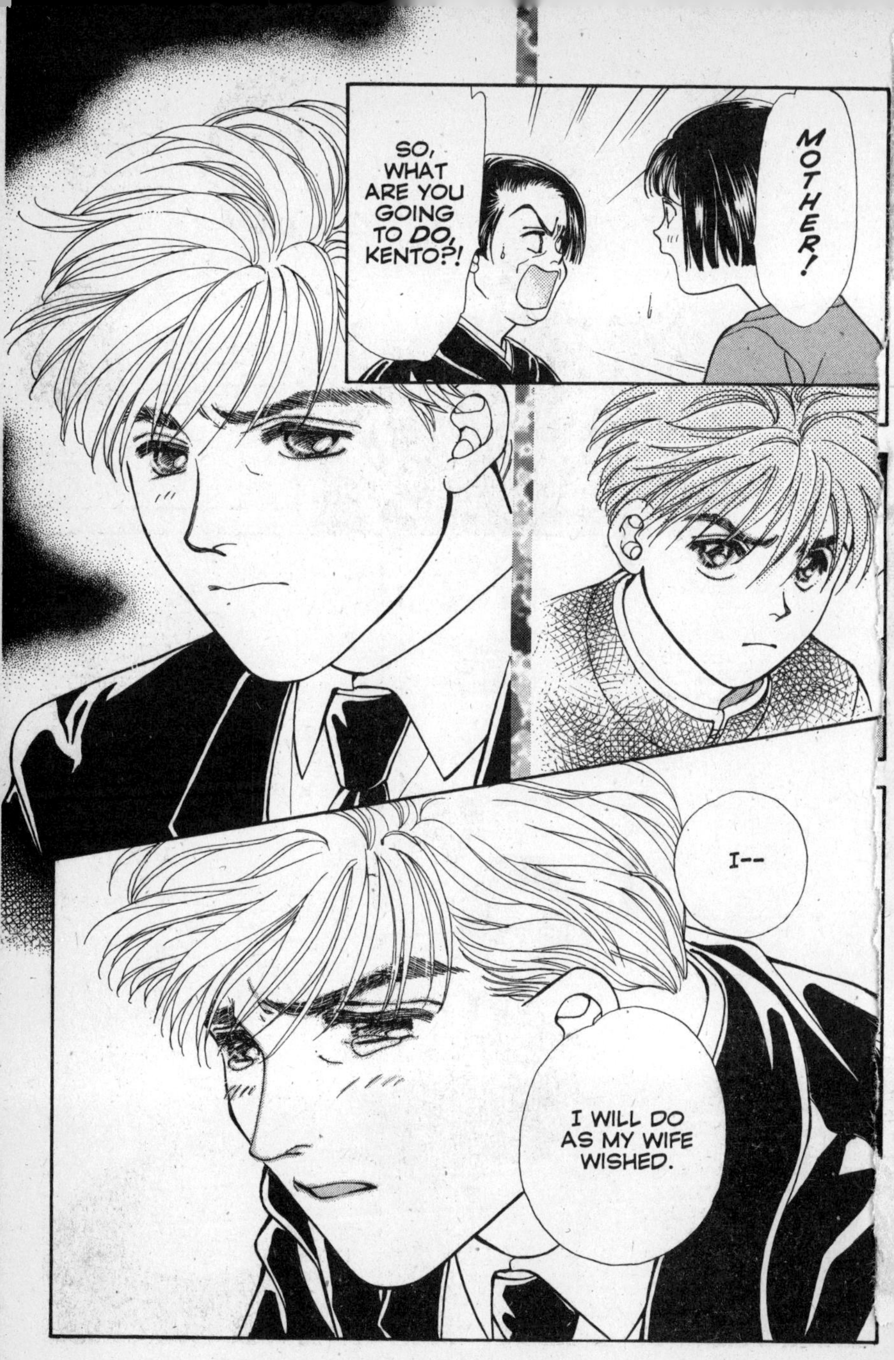
MOTHER!
SO, WHAT ARE YOU GOING TO DO, KENTO?!
I--
I WILL DO AS MY WIFE WISHED.

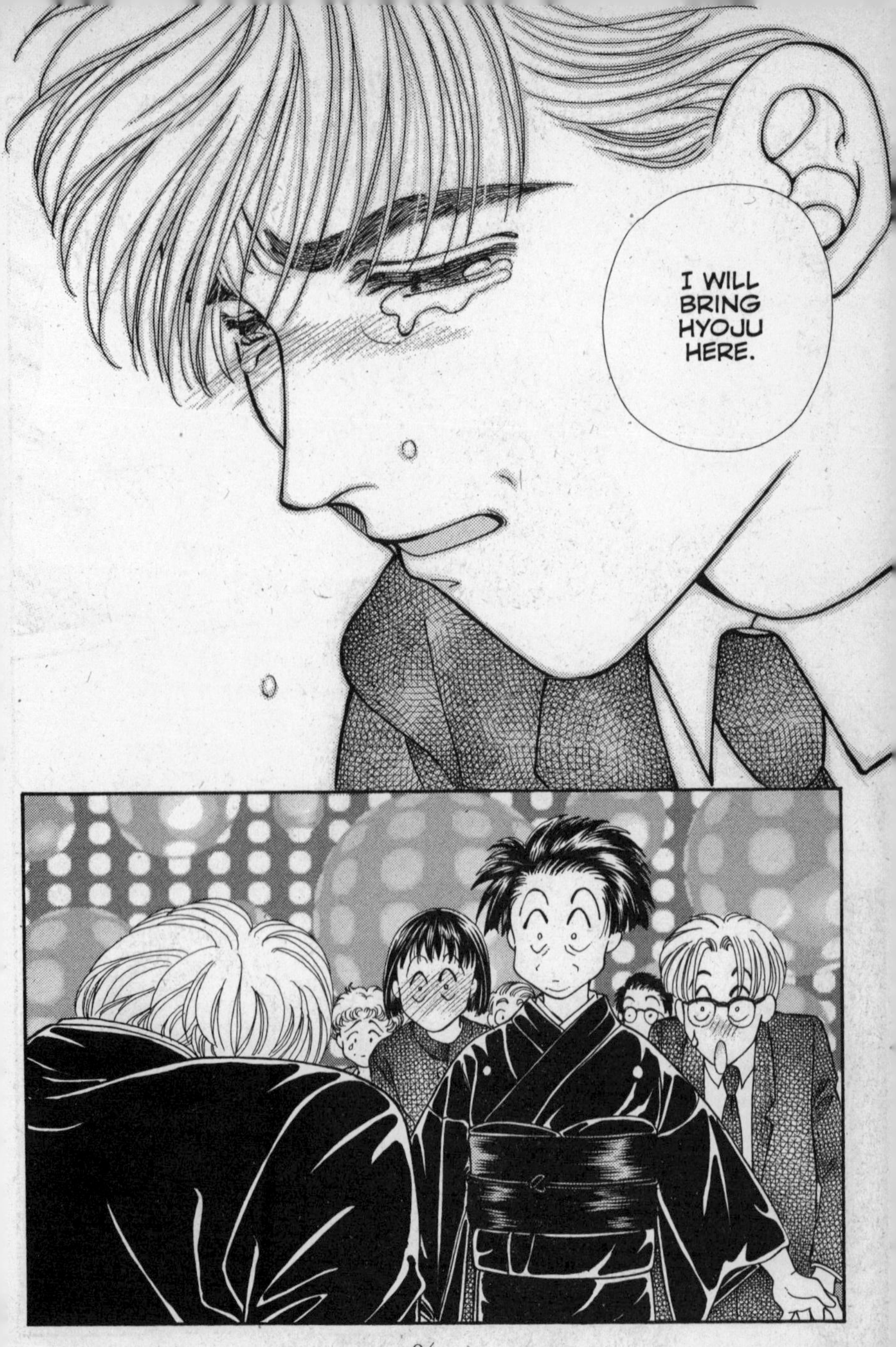
I WILL BRING HYOJU HERE.

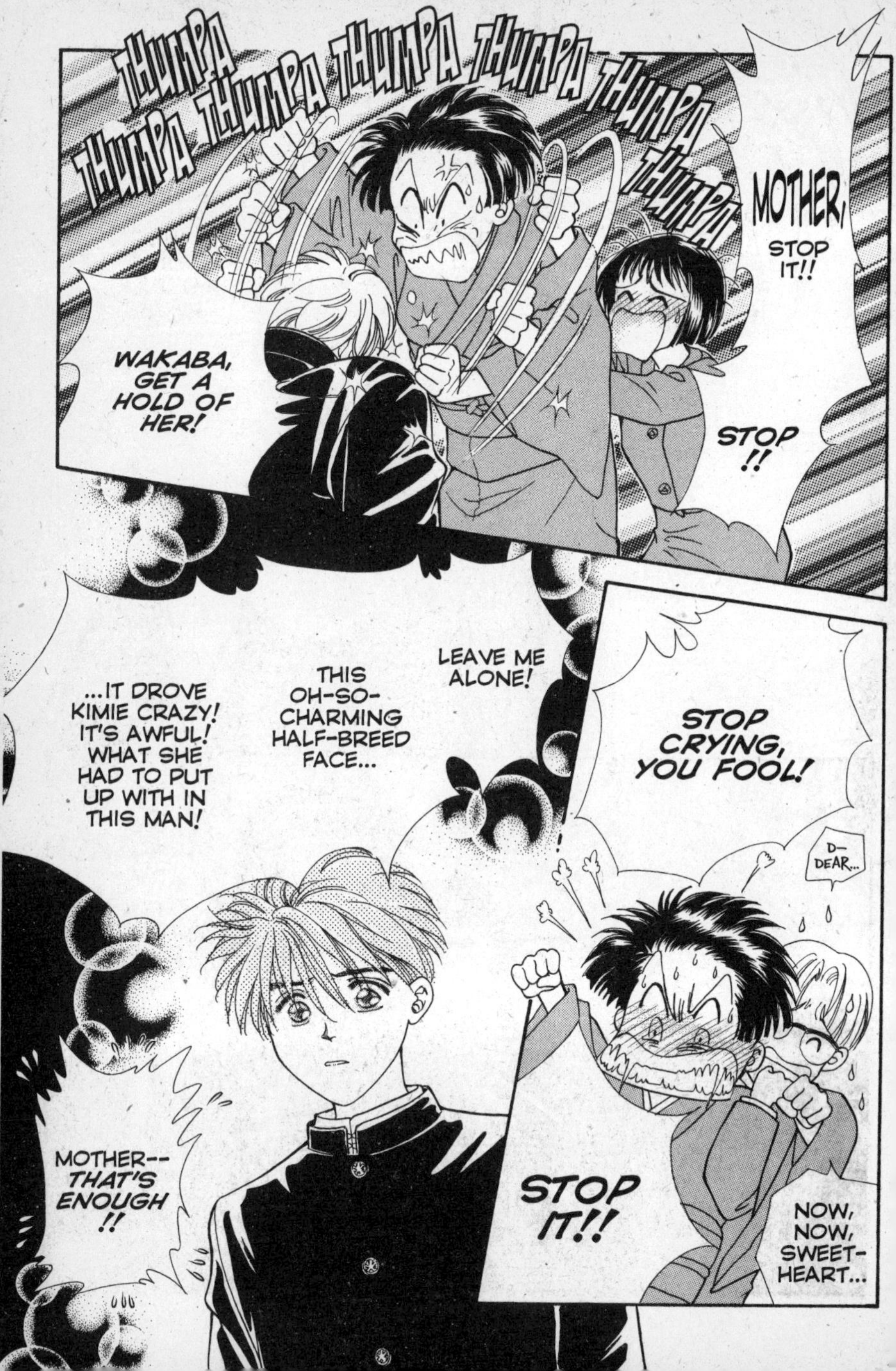
MOTHER, STOP IT!!
THUMPA THUMPA THUMPA THUMPA THUMPA THUMPA THUMPA THUMPA
STOP !!
WAKABA, GET A HOLD OF HER!
STOP CRYING, YOU FOOL!
LEAVE ME ALONE!
THIS OH-SO-CHARMING HALF-BREED FACE...
...IT DROVE KIMIE CRAZY! IT'S AWFUL! WHAT SHE HAD TO PUT UP WITH IN THIS MAN!
D-DEAR...
NOW, NOW, SWEET-HEART...
STOP IT!!
MOTHER-- THAT'S ENOUGH !!

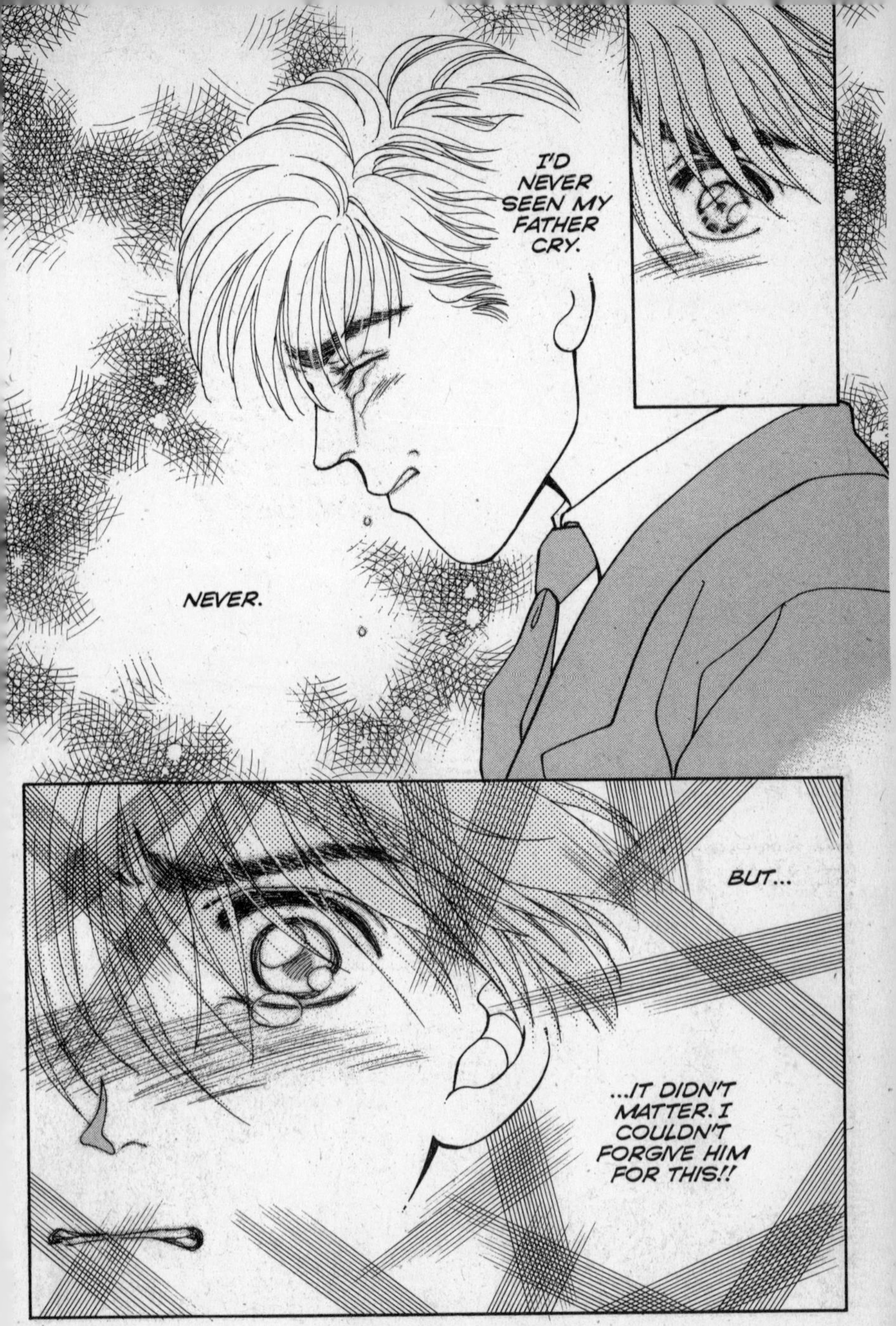
I'D NEVER SEEN MY FATHER CRY.
NEVER.
BUT...
...IT DIDN'T MATTER. I COULDN'T FORGIVE HIM FOR THIS!!

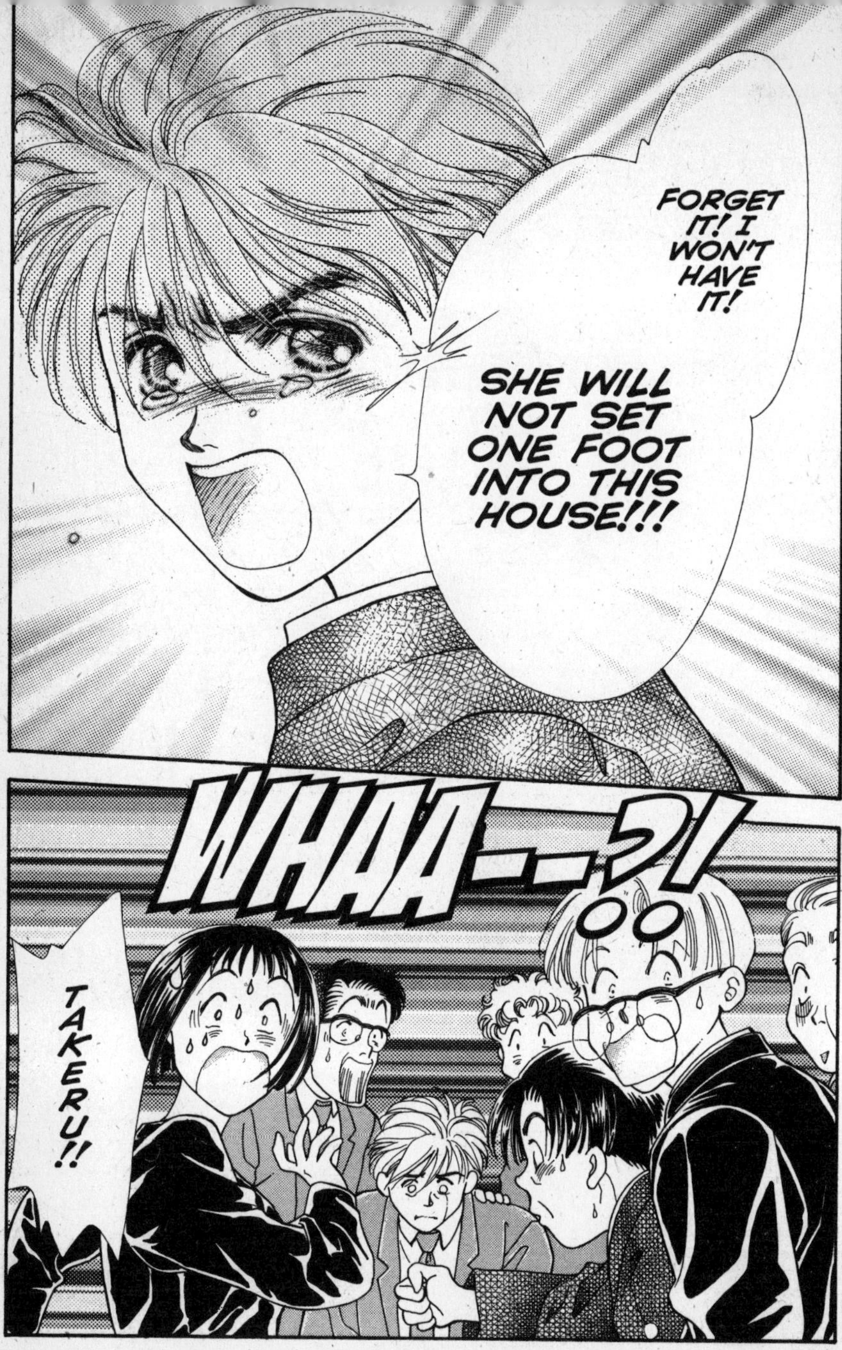
FORGET IT! I WON'T HAVE IT!
SHE WILL NOT SET ONE FOOT INTO THIS HOUSE!!!
WHAA--?!
TAKERU!!

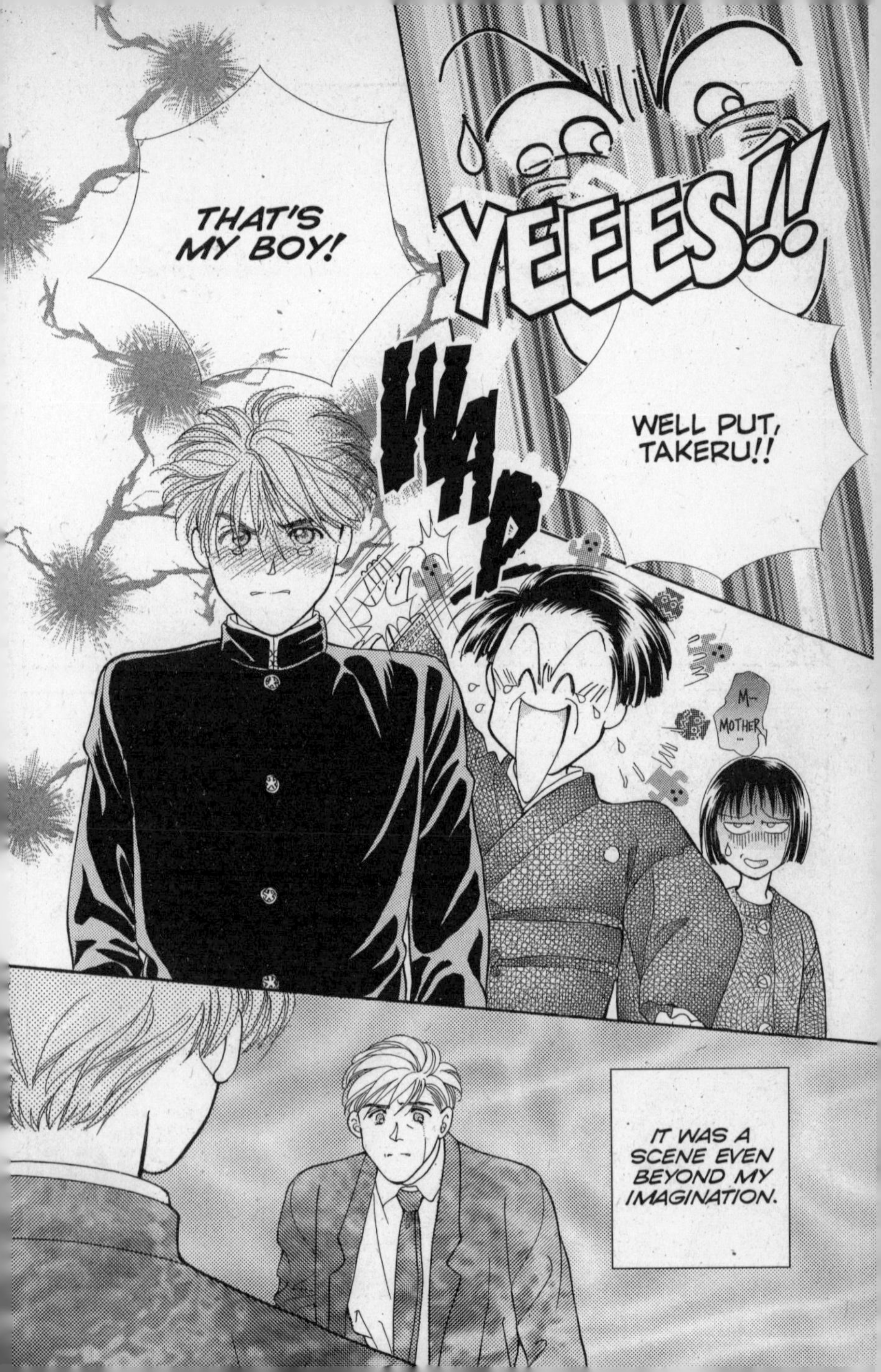
YEEES!!
WELL PUT, TAKERU!!
WAP
THAT'S MY BOY!
M-- MOTHER ...
IT WAS A SCENE EVEN BEYOND MY IMAGINATION.

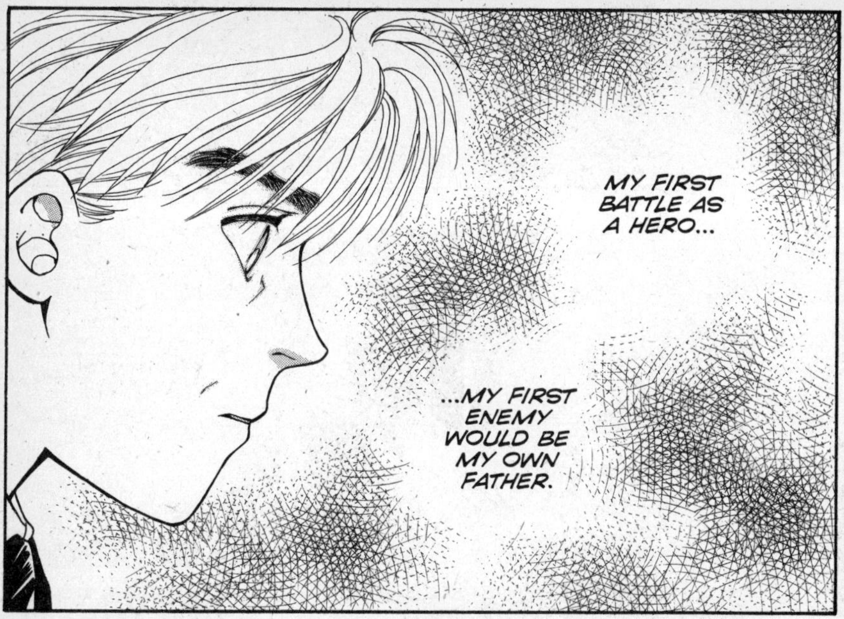
MY FIRST BATTLE AS A HERO...
...MY FIRST ENEMY WOULD BE MY OWN FATHER.
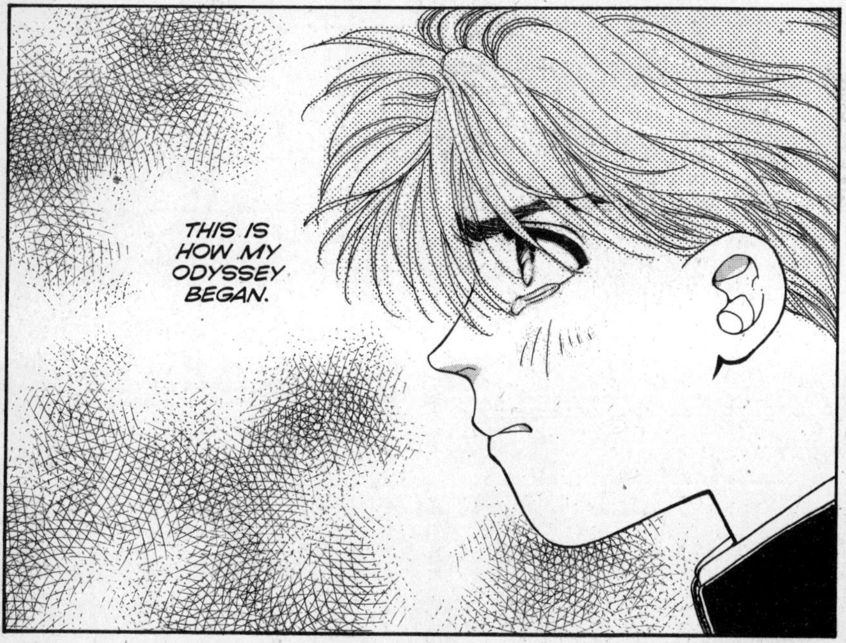
THIS IS HOW MY ODYSSEY BEGAN.

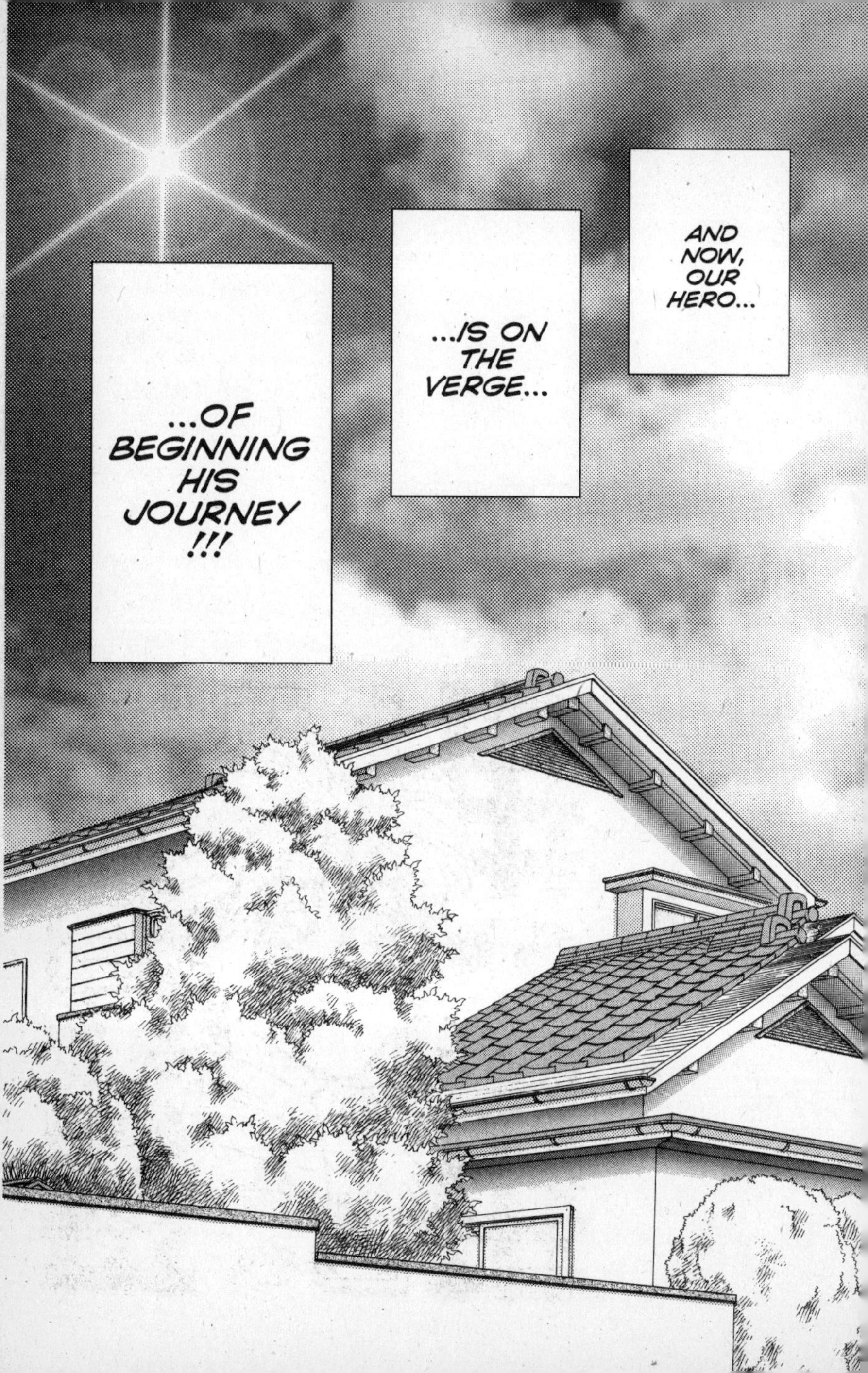
AND NOW, OUR HERO...
...IS ON THE VERGE...
...OF BEGINNING HIS JOURNEY !!!

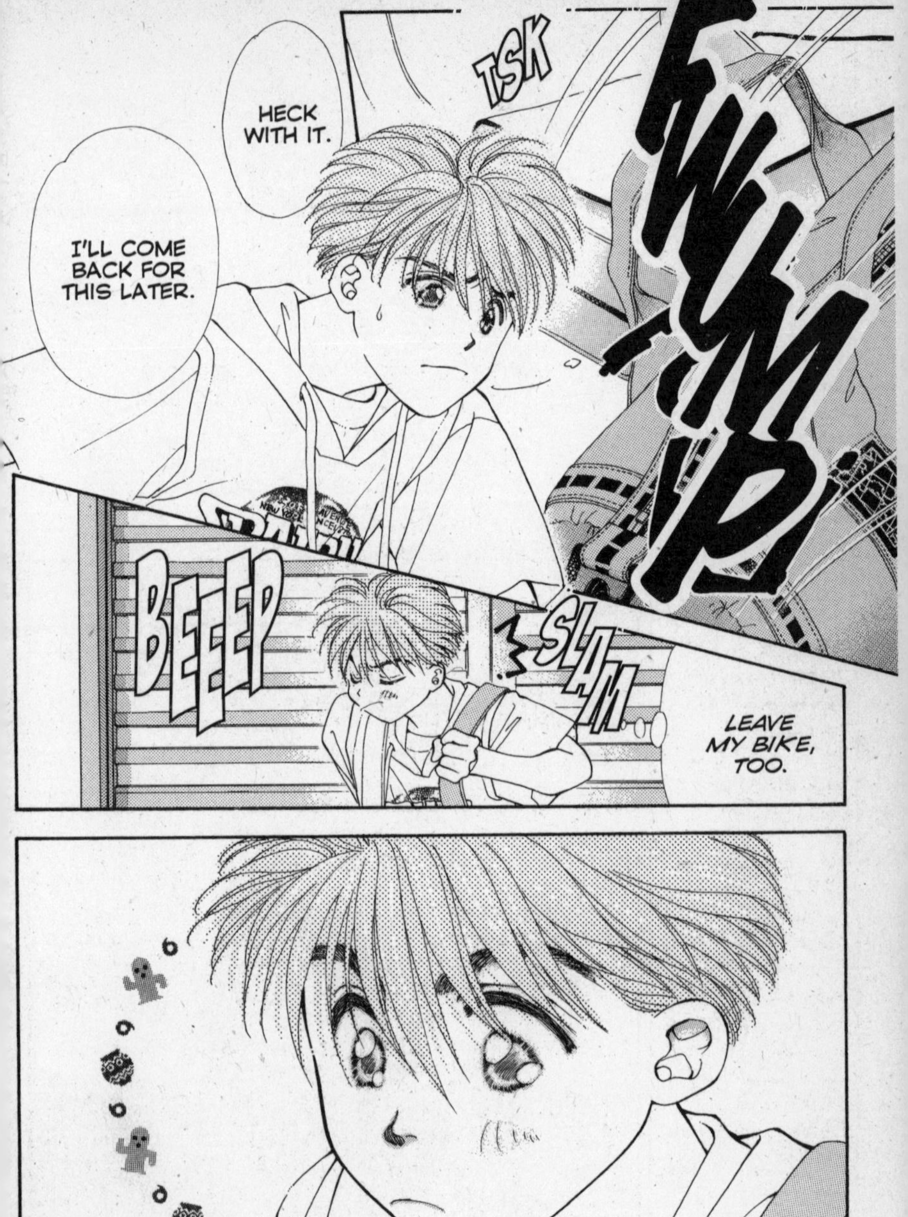
FWUMP
TSK
HECK WITH IT.
I'LL COME BACK FOR THIS LATER.
SLAM
LEAVE MY BIKE, TOO.
BEEP

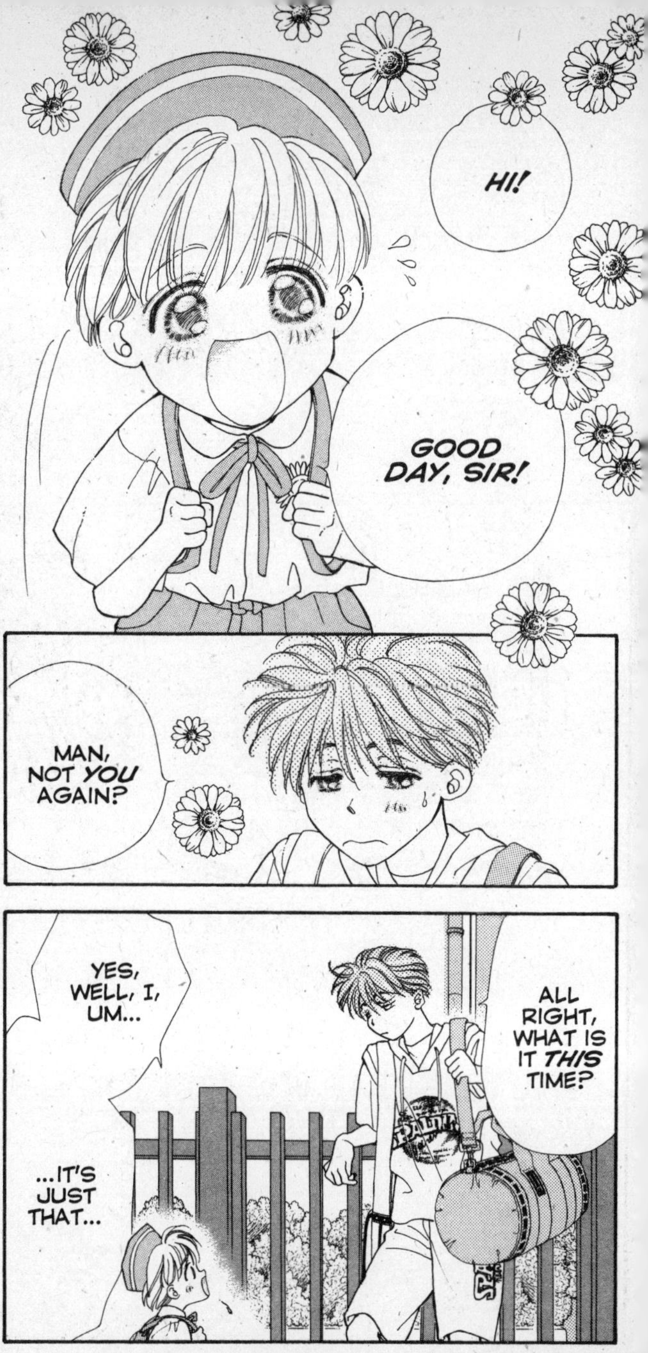
HI!
GOOD DAY, SIR!
MAN, NOT *YOU* AGAIN?
ALL RIGHT, WHAT IS IT *THIS* TIME?
YES, WELL, I, UM...
...IT'S JUST THAT...

1/4 Sidebar No. 6

6

So zero is when God awakens. That means that time might be just another aspect of God's existence. And maybe this world is a dream in the mind of God. And maybe even God goes through rebirth. And, who knows, maybe there's even more than one God and maybe they have conversations like this:
"Man, I had a weird dream last night."
"Yeah? Me, too."
And if it should happen to be the same dream...
"It seems, we know each other from a past life..."
Hmm....
Well, enough of my simple philosophizing. We could go on forever, so let's leave it at that.
The main point is that this was my state of mind when I started on "Tower of the Future."
Pretty weird--that's for sure!

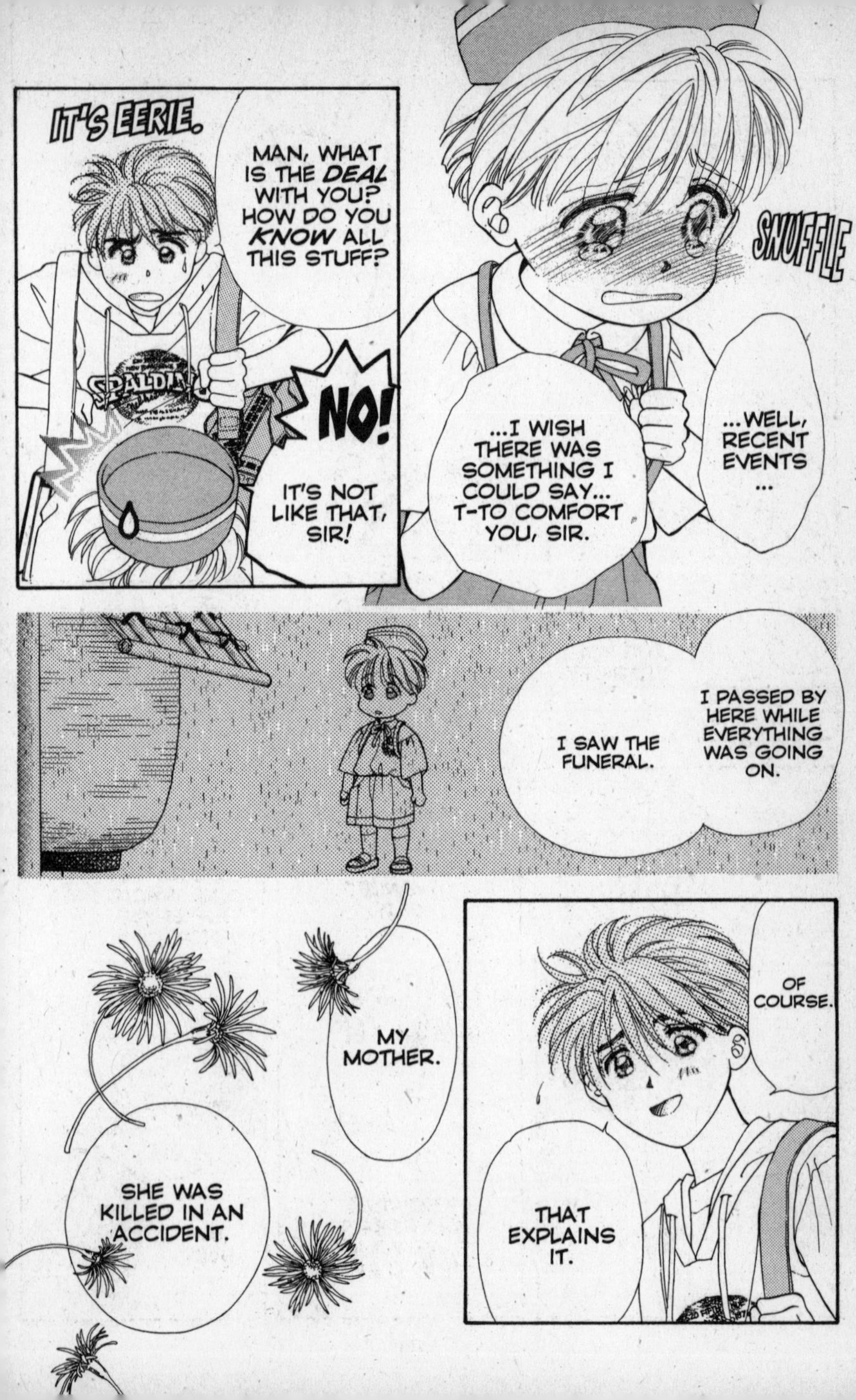
SNUFFLE
...WELL, RECENT EVENTS ...
...I WISH THERE WAS SOMETHING I COULD SAY... T-TO COMFORT YOU, SIR.
IT'S EERIE.
MAN, WHAT IS THE *DEAL* WITH YOU? HOW DO YOU *KNOW* ALL THIS STUFF?
NO!
IT'S NOT LIKE THAT, SIR!
I PASSED BY HERE WHILE EVERYTHING WAS GOING ON.
I SAW THE FUNERAL.
OF COURSE.
THAT EXPLAINS IT.
MY MOTHER.
SHE WAS KILLED IN AN ACCIDENT.

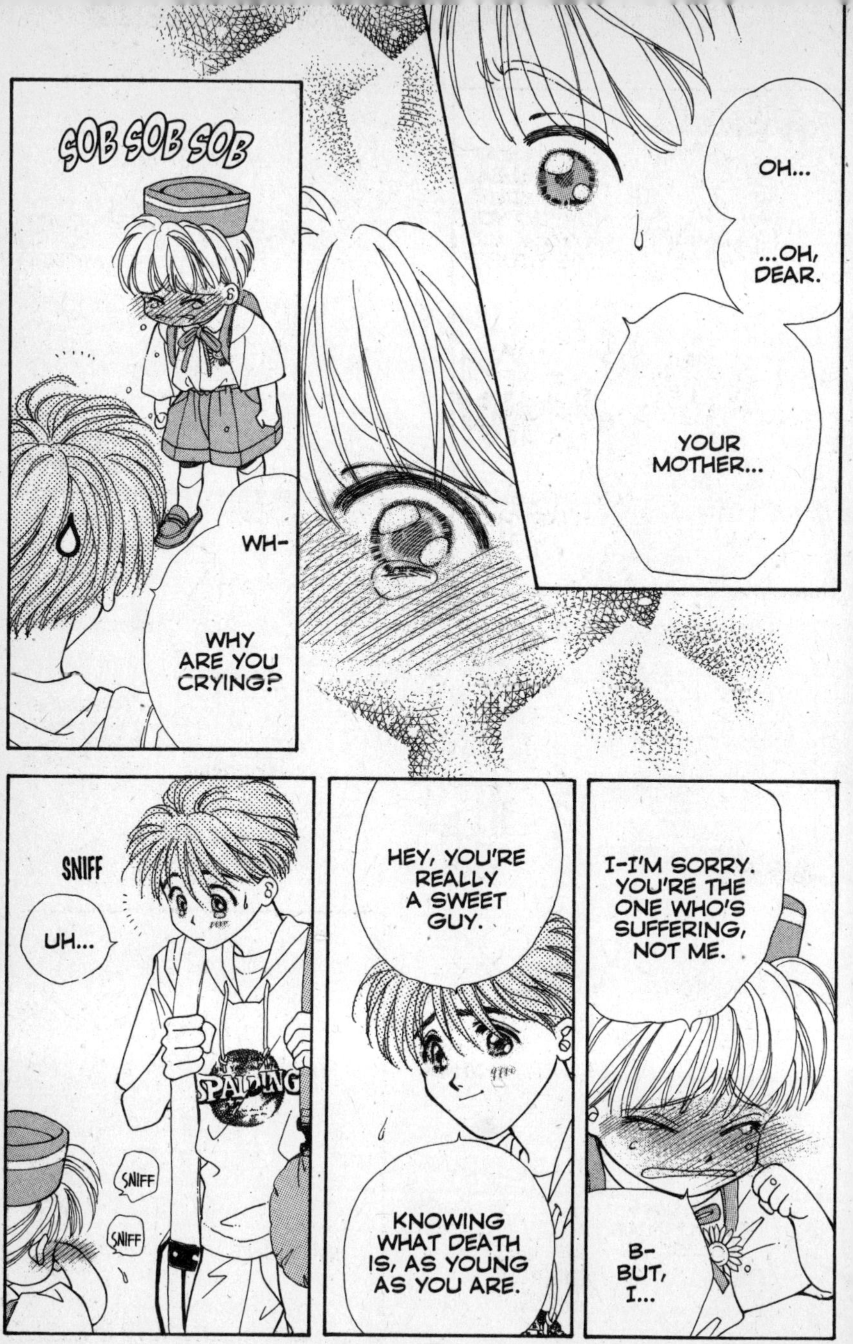
OH...
...OH, DEAR.
YOUR MOTHER...
SOB SOB SOB
WH-
WHY ARE YOU CRYING?
I-I'M SORRY. YOU'RE THE ONE WHO'S SUFFERING, NOT ME.
B-BUT, I...
HEY, YOU'RE REALLY A SWEET GUY.
KNOWING WHAT DEATH IS, AS YOUNG AS YOU ARE.
SNIFF
UH...
SPALDING
SNIFF
SNIFF

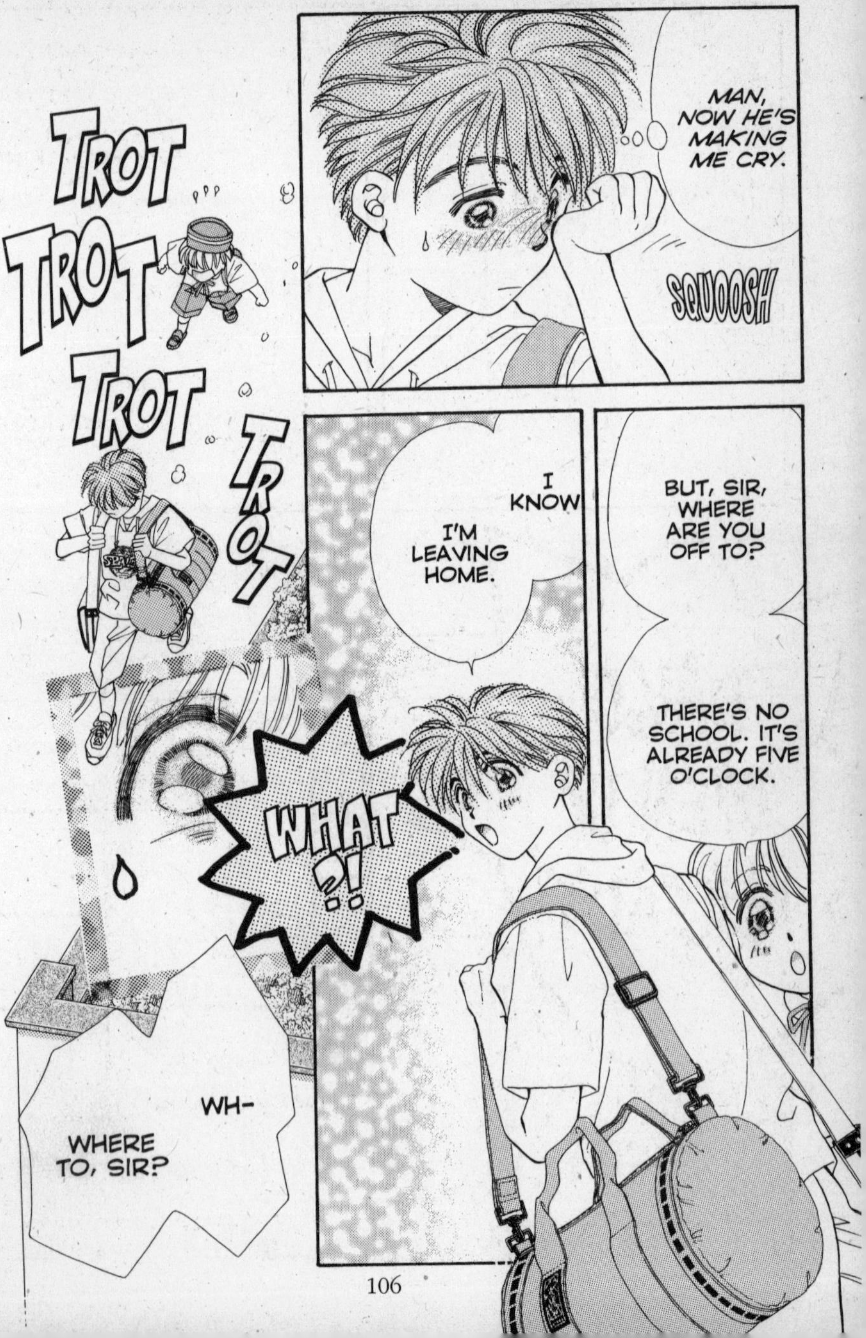
MAN, NOW HE'S MAKING ME CRY.
SQUOOSH
TROT TROT TROT TROT
BUT, SIR, WHERE ARE YOU OFF TO?
THERE'S NO SCHOOL. IT'S ALREADY FIVE O'CLOCK.
I KNOW
I'M LEAVING HOME.
WHAT?!
WH-
WHERE TO, SIR?

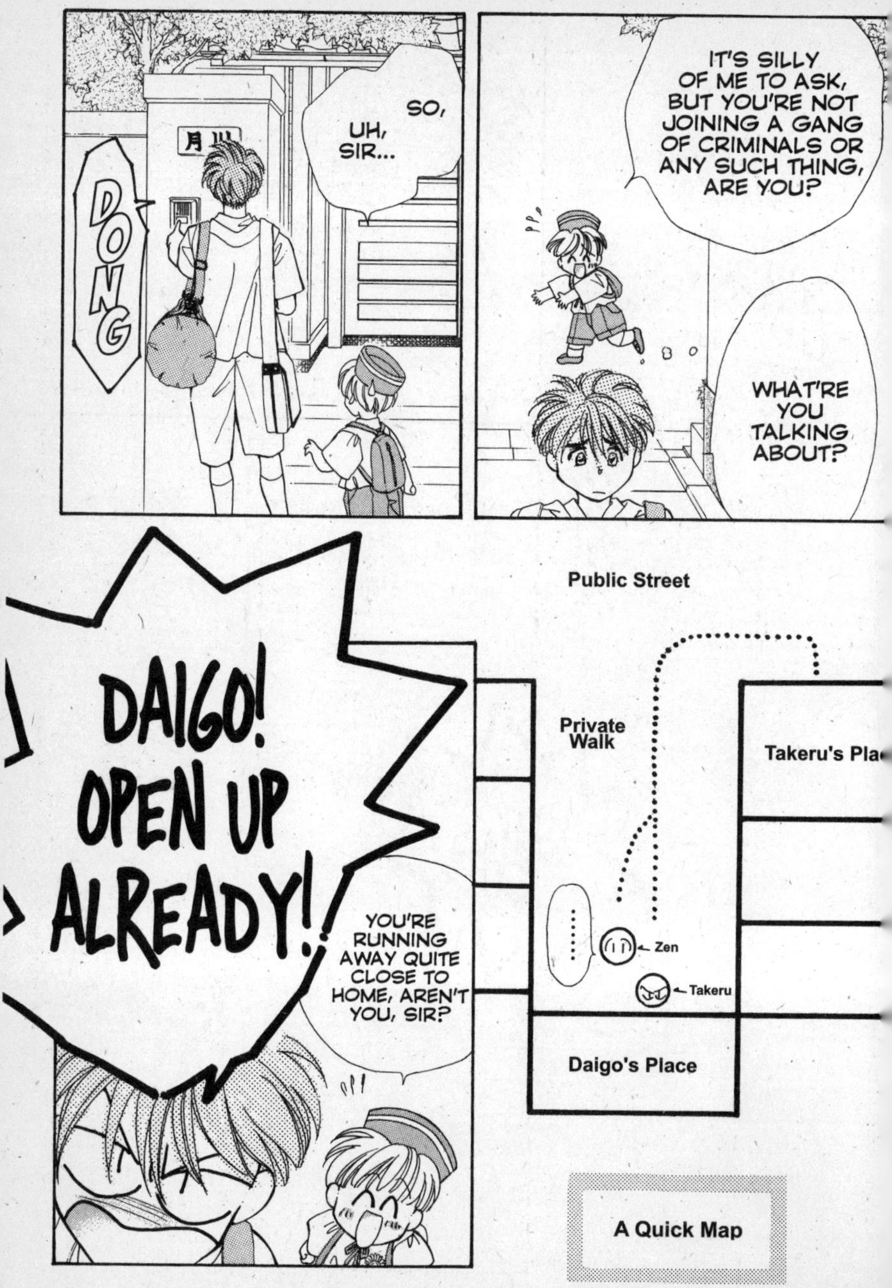
IT'S SILLY OF ME TO ASK, BUT YOU'RE NOT JOINING A GANG OF CRIMINALS OR ANY SUCH THING, ARE YOU?
WHAT'RE YOU TALKING ABOUT?
SO, UH, SIR...
DONG
A Quick Map
Public Street
Private Walk
Takeru's Pla
Zen
Takeru
Daigo's Place
DAIGO! OPEN UP ALREADY!
YOU'RE RUNNING AWAY QUITE CLOSE TO HOME, AREN'T YOU, SIR?

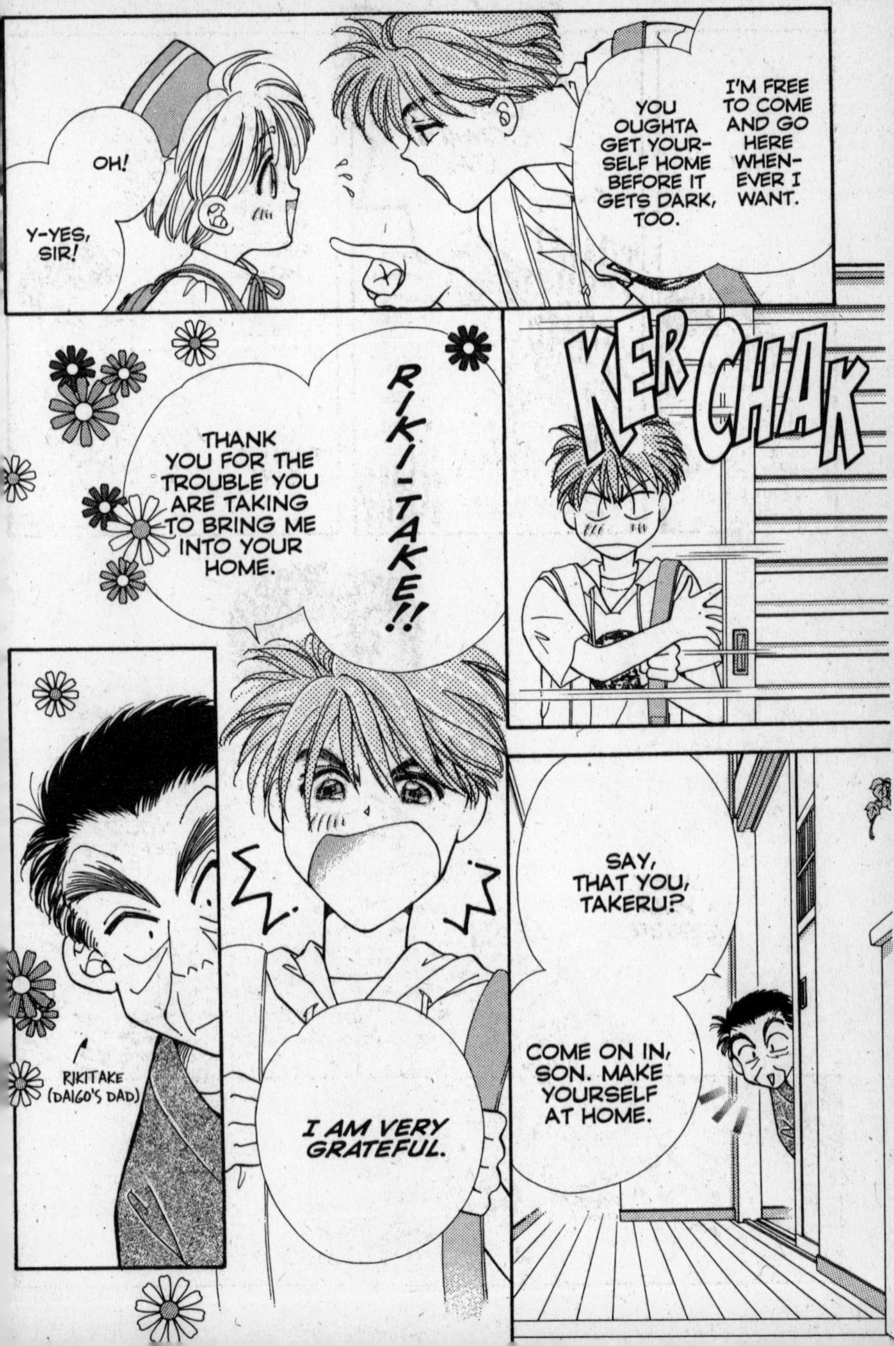
I'M FREE TO COME AND GO HERE WHENEVER I WANT.
YOU OUGHTA GET YOURSELF HOME BEFORE IT GETS DARK, TOO.
OH!
Y-YES, SIR!
KERCHAK
SAY, THAT YOU, TAKERU?
COME ON IN, SON. MAKE YOURSELF AT HOME.
THANK YOU FOR THE TROUBLE YOU ARE TAKING TO BRING ME INTO YOUR HOME.
RIKI-TAKE!!
I AM VERY GRATEFUL.
RIKITAKE (DAIGO'S DAD)

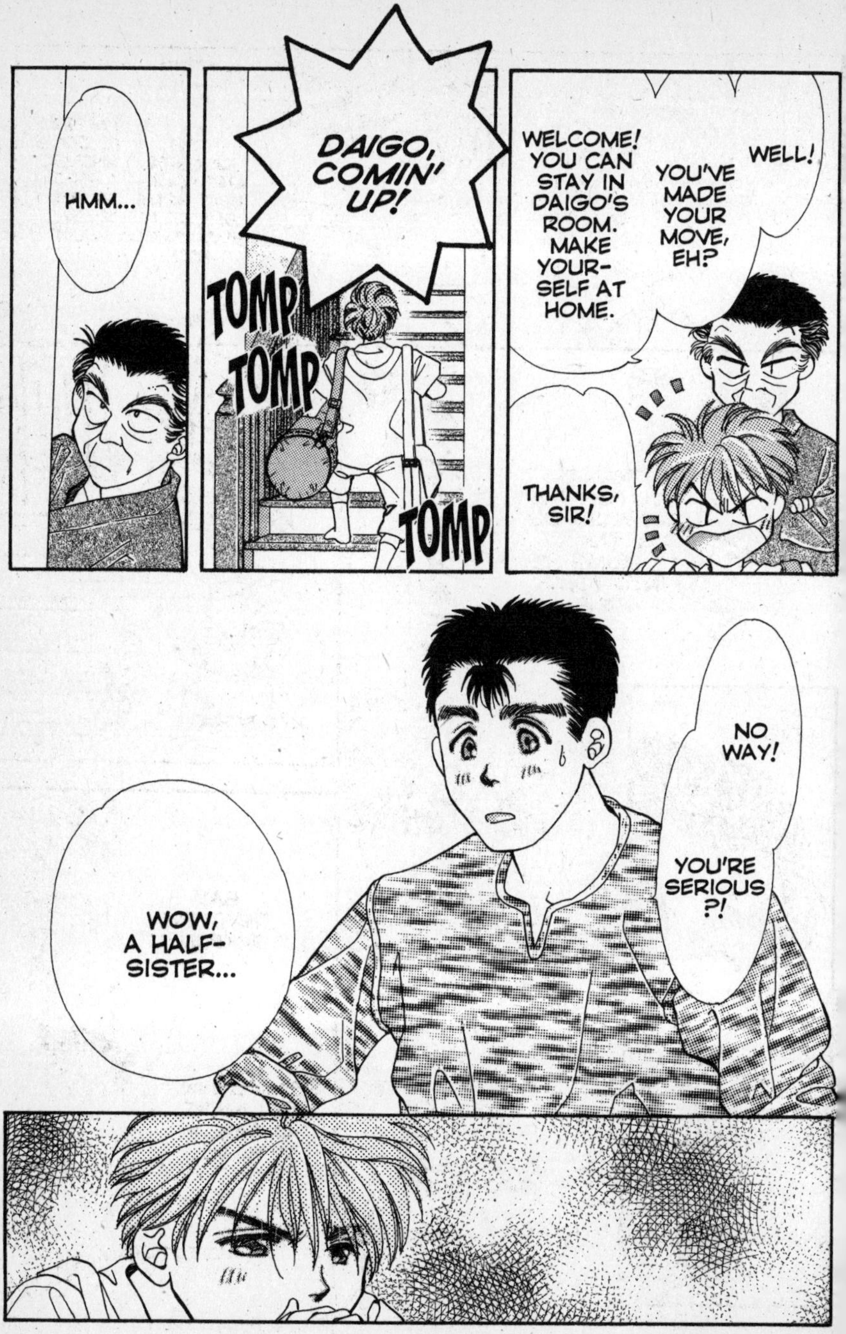
WELL!
YOU'VE MADE YOUR MOVE, EH?
WELCOME! YOU CAN STAY IN DAIGO'S ROOM. MAKE YOUR-SELF AT HOME.
THANKS, SIR!
DAIGO, COMIN' UP!
TOMP
TOMP
TOMP
HMM...
NO WAY!
YOU'RE SERIOUS ?!
WOW, A HALF-SISTER...

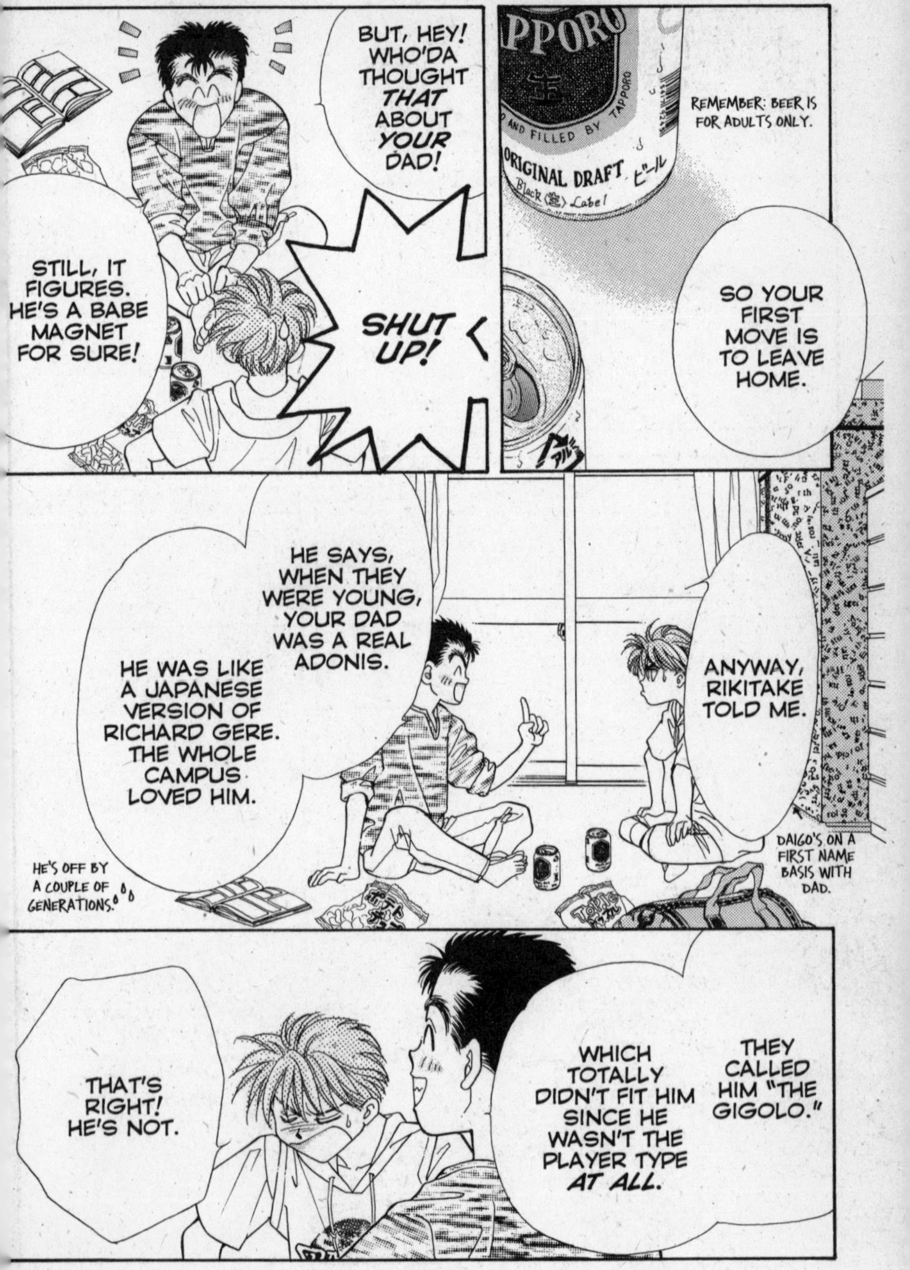
REMEMBER: BEER IS FOR ADULTS ONLY.
SO YOUR FIRST MOVE IS TO LEAVE HOME.
BUT, HEY! WHO'DA THOUGHT *THAT* ABOUT *YOUR* DAD!
SHUT UP!
STILL, IT FIGURES. HE'S A BABE MAGNET FOR SURE!
ANYWAY, RIKITAKE TOLD ME.
DAIGO'S ON A FIRST NAME BASIS WITH DAD.
HE SAYS, WHEN THEY WERE YOUNG, YOUR DAD WAS A REAL ADONIS.
HE WAS LIKE A JAPANESE VERSION OF RICHARD GERE. THE WHOLE CAMPUS LOVED HIM.
HE'S OFF BY A COUPLE OF GENERATIONS.
THEY CALLED HIM "THE GIGOLO."
WHICH TOTALLY DIDN'T FIT HIM SINCE HE WASN'T THE PLAYER TYPE *AT ALL*.
THAT'S RIGHT! HE'S NOT.

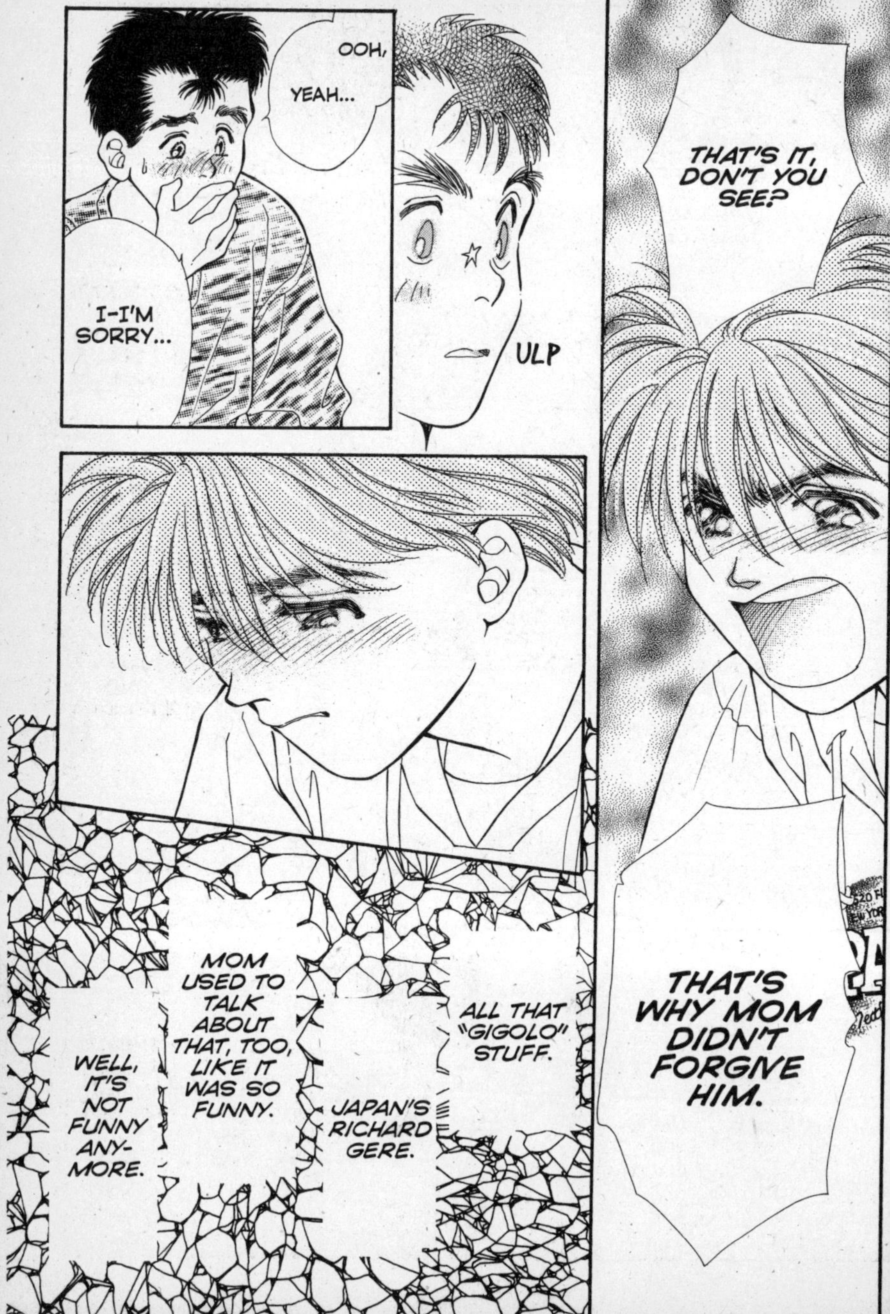
THAT'S IT, DON'T YOU SEE?
THAT'S WHY MOM DIDN'T FORGIVE HIM.
OOH, YEAH...
ULP
I-I'M SORRY...
ALL THAT "GIGOLO" STUFF.
JAPAN'S RICHARD GERE.
MOM USED TO TALK ABOUT THAT, TOO, LIKE IT WAS SO FUNNY.
WELL, IT'S NOT FUNNY ANY-MORE.

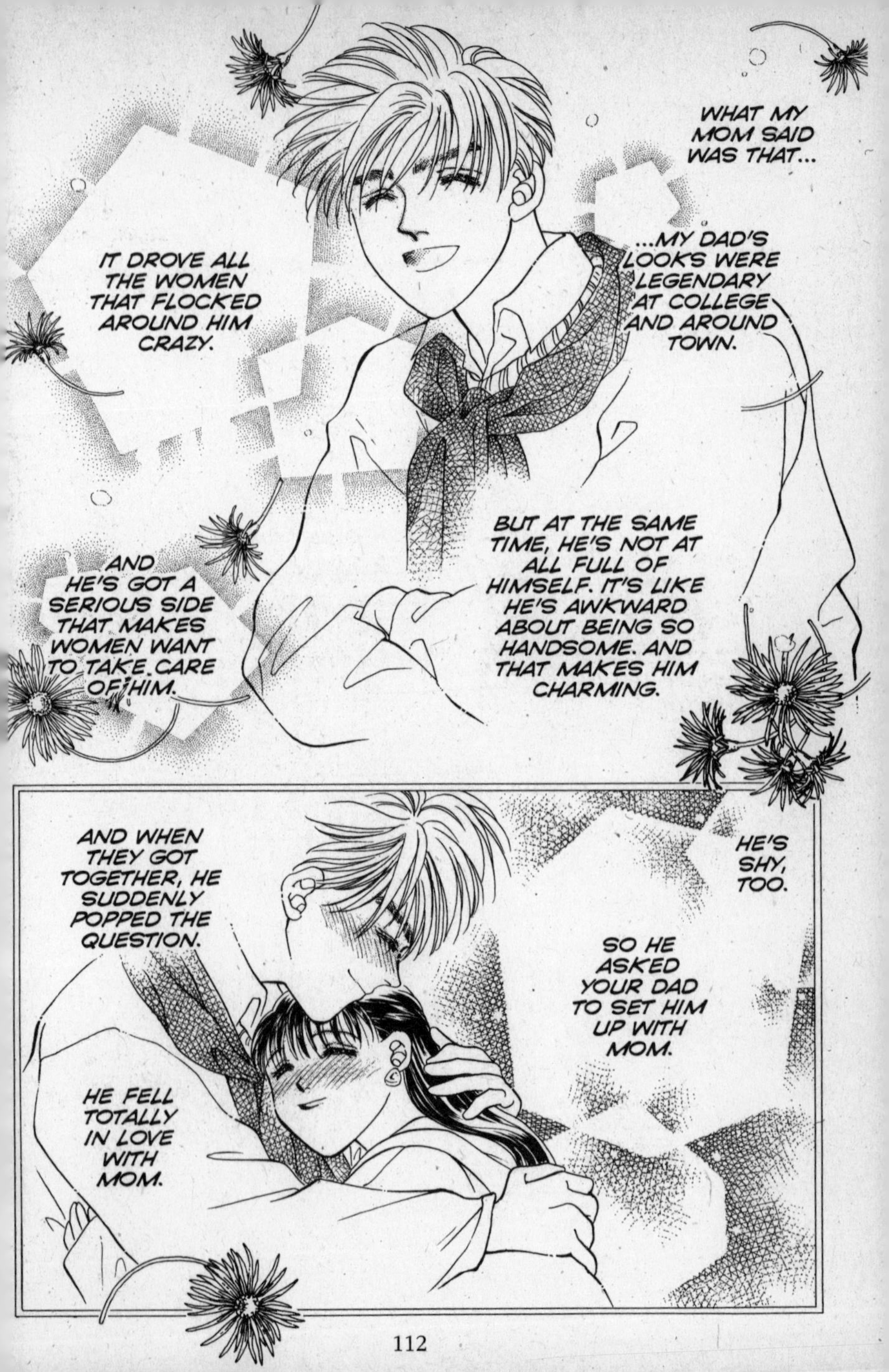
WHAT MY MOM SAID WAS THAT...
...MY DAD'S LOOKS WERE LEGENDARY AT COLLEGE AND AROUND TOWN.
IT DROVE ALL THE WOMEN THAT FLOCKED AROUND HIM CRAZY.
BUT AT THE SAME TIME, HE'S NOT AT ALL FULL OF HIMSELF. IT'S LIKE HE'S AWKWARD ABOUT BEING SO HANDSOME. AND THAT MAKES HIM CHARMING.
AND HE'S GOT A SERIOUS SIDE THAT MAKES WOMEN WANT TO TAKE CARE OF HIM.
HE'S SHY, TOO.
SO HE ASKED YOUR DAD TO SET HIM UP WITH MOM.
AND WHEN THEY GOT TOGETHER, HE SUDDENLY POPPED THE QUESTION.
HE FELL TOTALLY IN LOVE WITH MOM.

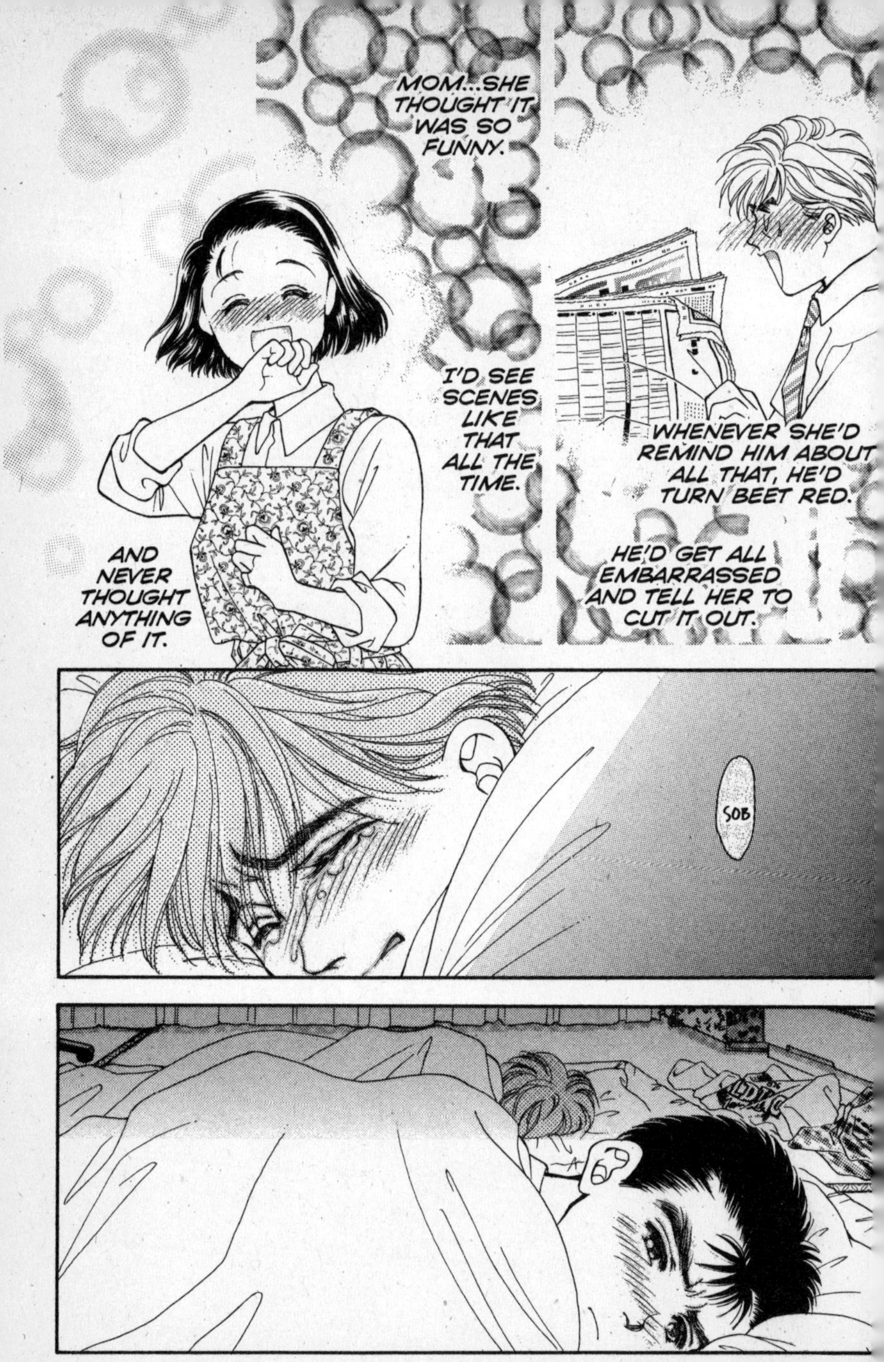
WHENEVER SHE'D REMIND HIM ABOUT ALL THAT, HE'D TURN BEET RED.
HE'D GET ALL EMBARRASSED AND TELL HER TO CUT IT OUT.
MOM...SHE THOUGHT IT WAS SO FUNNY.
I'D SEE SCENES LIKE THAT ALL THE TIME.
AND NEVER THOUGHT ANYTHING OF IT.
SOB

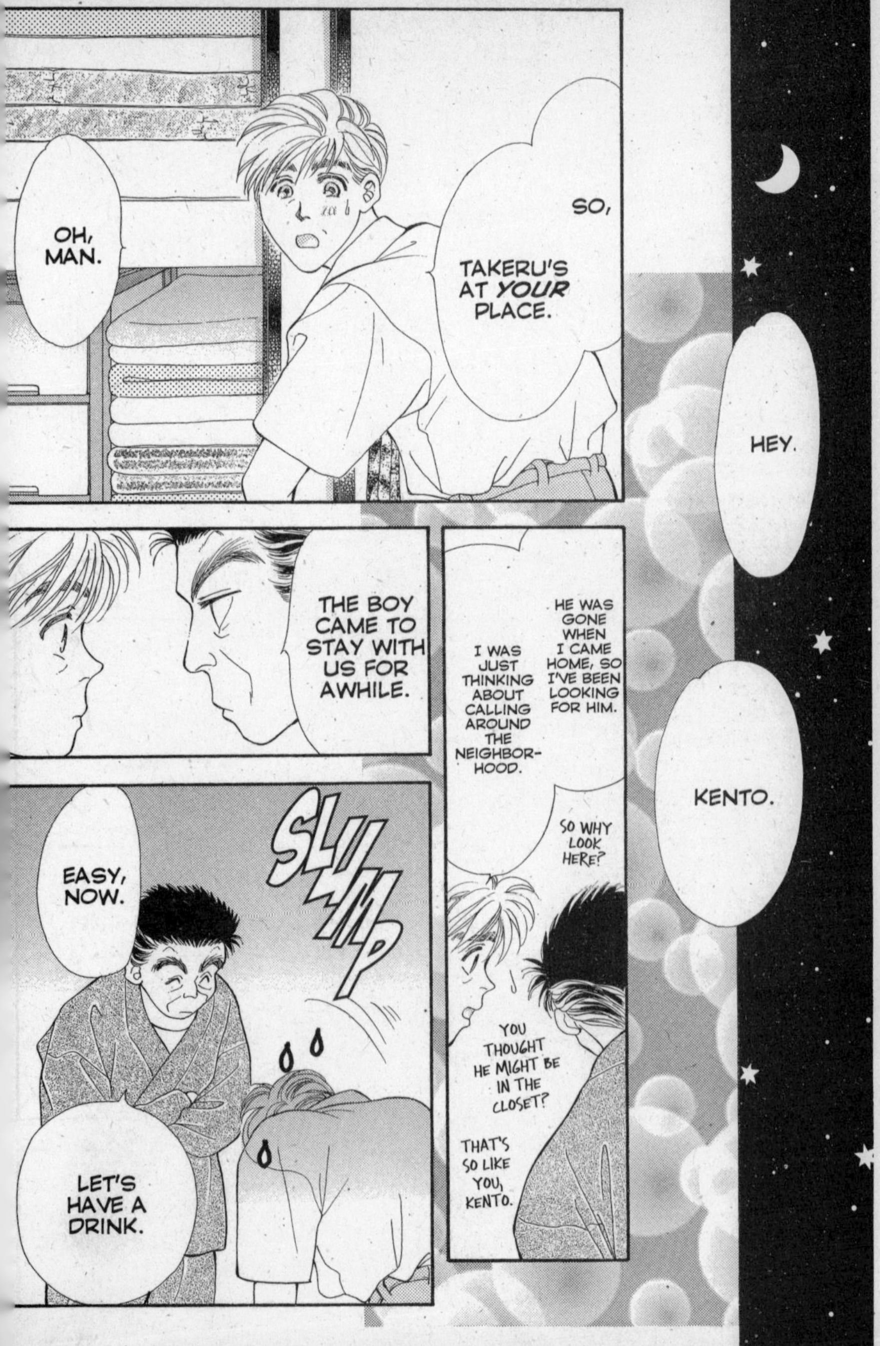
HEY.
KENTO.
SO,
TAKERU'S AT *YOUR* PLACE.
OH, MAN.
HE WAS GONE WHEN I CAME HOME, SO I'VE BEEN LOOKING FOR HIM.
I WAS JUST THINKING ABOUT CALLING AROUND THE NEIGHBOR-HOOD.
SO WHY LOOK HERE?
YOU THOUGHT HE MIGHT BE IN THE CLOSET?
THAT'S SO LIKE YOU, KENTO.
THE BOY CAME TO STAY WITH US FOR AWHILE.
SLUMP
EASY, NOW.
LET'S HAVE A DRINK.

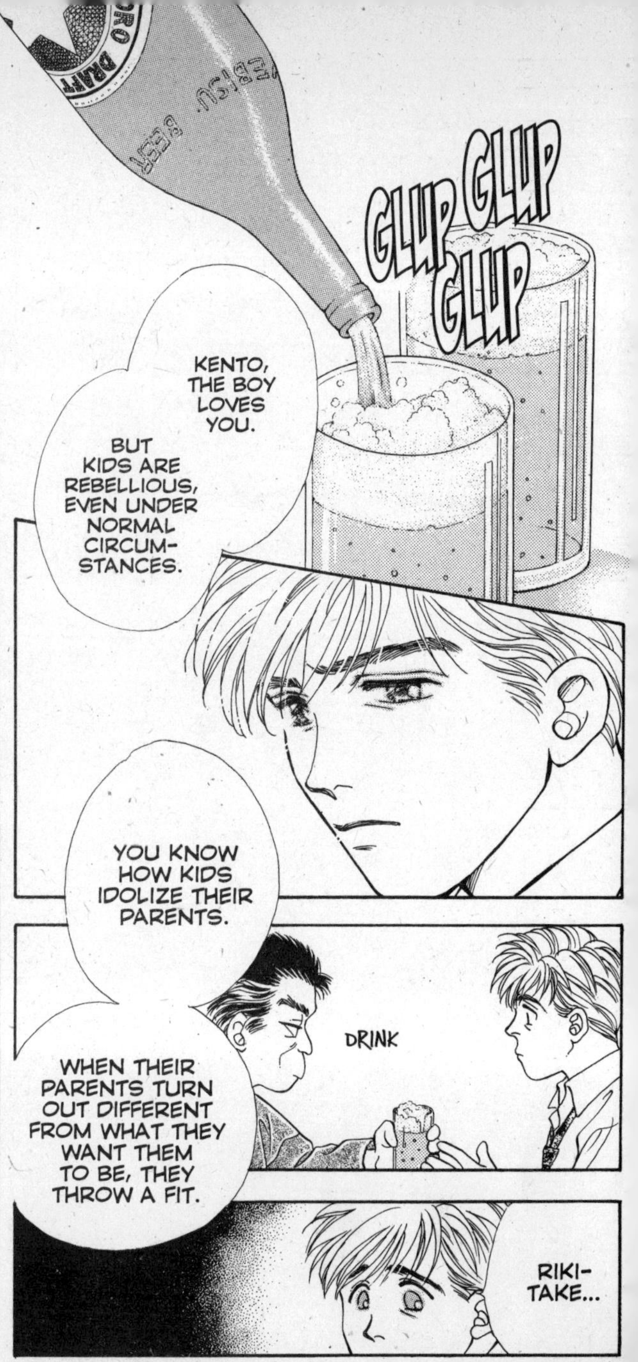
GLUP GLUP GLUP
KENTO, THE BOY LOVES YOU.
BUT KIDS ARE REBELLIOUS, EVEN UNDER NORMAL CIRCUM-STANCES.
YOU KNOW HOW KIDS IDOLIZE THEIR PARENTS.
DRINK
WHEN THEIR PARENTS TURN OUT DIFFERENT FROM WHAT THEY WANT THEM TO BE, THEY THROW A FIT.
RIKI-TAKE...

1/4 Sidebar No. 7

≡7≡

The fact is, I couldn't decide whether to make the main character Takeru or Ichigo. Either one would've worked, but Takeru was a better fit for a personality that reacts to the strange twists and turns of life. If a character doesn't react with amazement at life's mysteries, there's nothing to build the story on. Now if it were Ichigo, she probably just say something like:

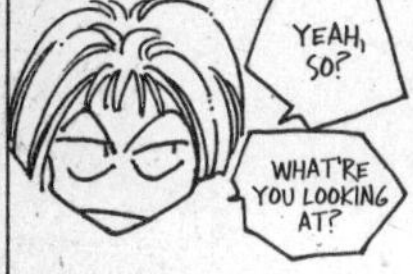
YEAH, SO?
WHAT'RE YOU LOOKING AT?

The story unfolds so that she doesn't show up much in the first volume, but I'm really looking forward to getting into her character and developing her off-the-wall personality.

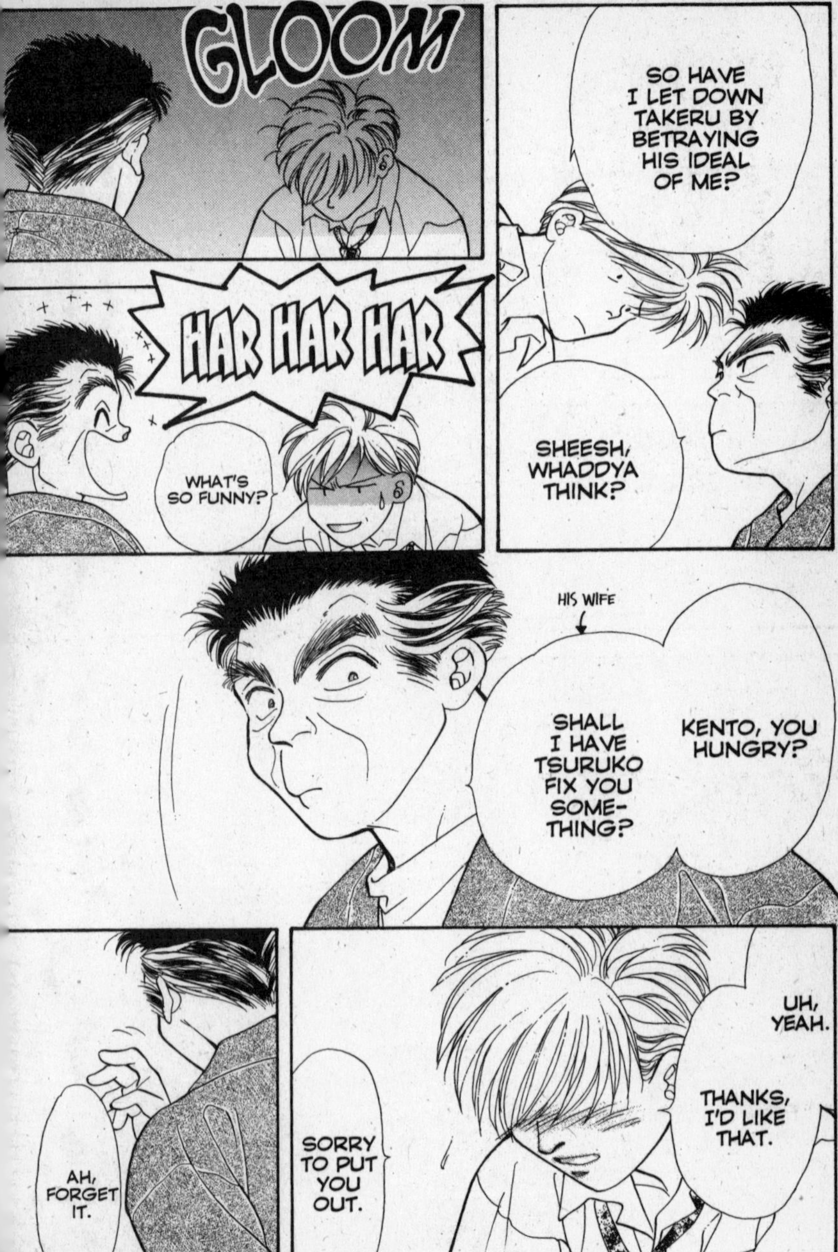
SO HAVE I LET DOWN TAKERU BY BETRAYING HIS IDEAL OF ME?
SHEESH, WHADDYA THINK?
GLOOM
HAR HAR HAR
WHAT'S SO FUNNY?
KENTO, YOU HUNGRY?
SHALL I HAVE TSURUKO FIX YOU SOME-THING?
HIS WIFE
UH, YEAH.
THANKS, I'D LIKE THAT.
SORRY TO PUT YOU OUT.
AH, FORGET IT.

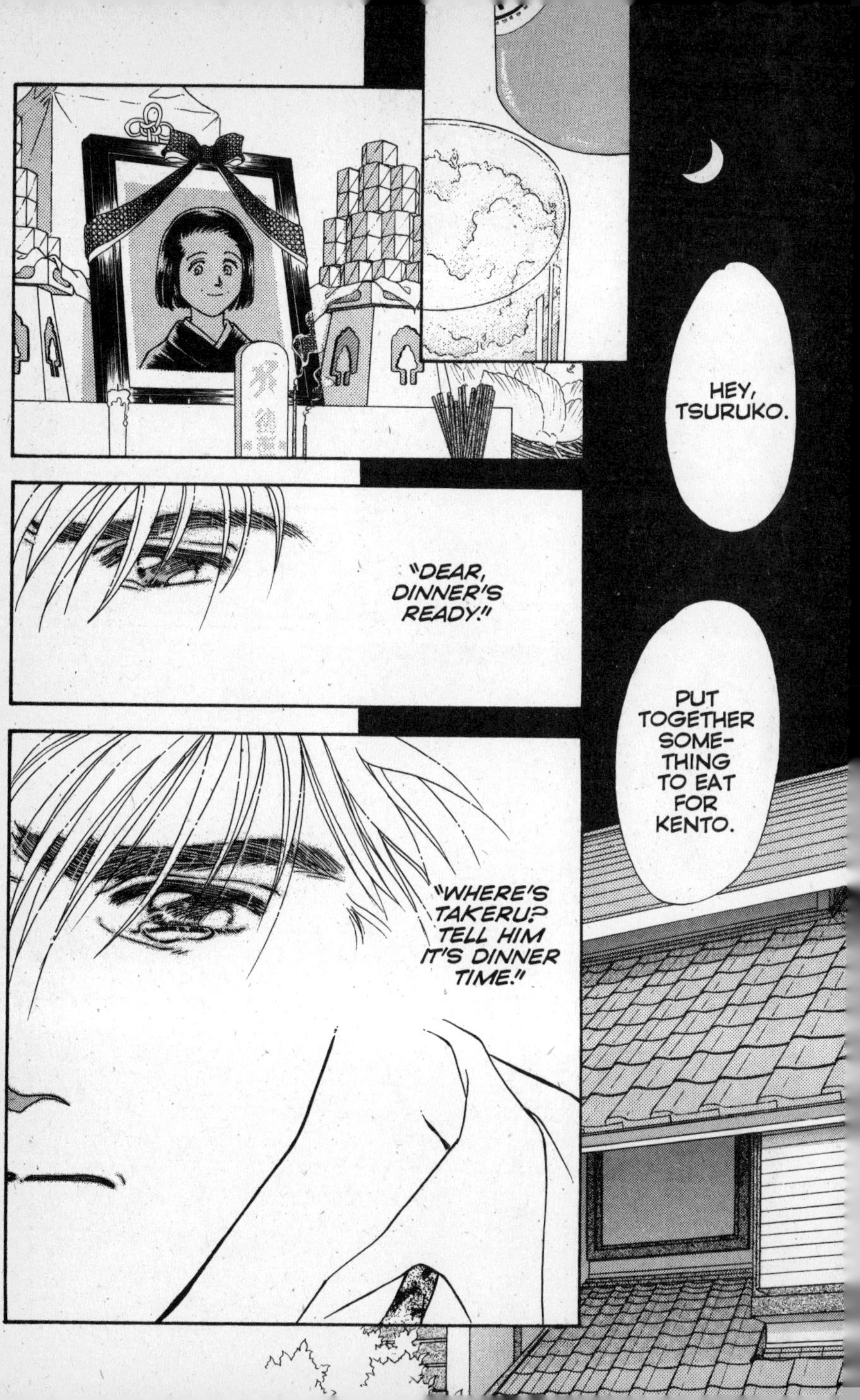
HEY, TSURUKO.
PUT TOGETHER SOME-THING TO EAT FOR KENTO.
"DEAR, DINNER'S READY!"
"WHERE'S TAKERU? TELL HIM IT'S DINNER TIME."

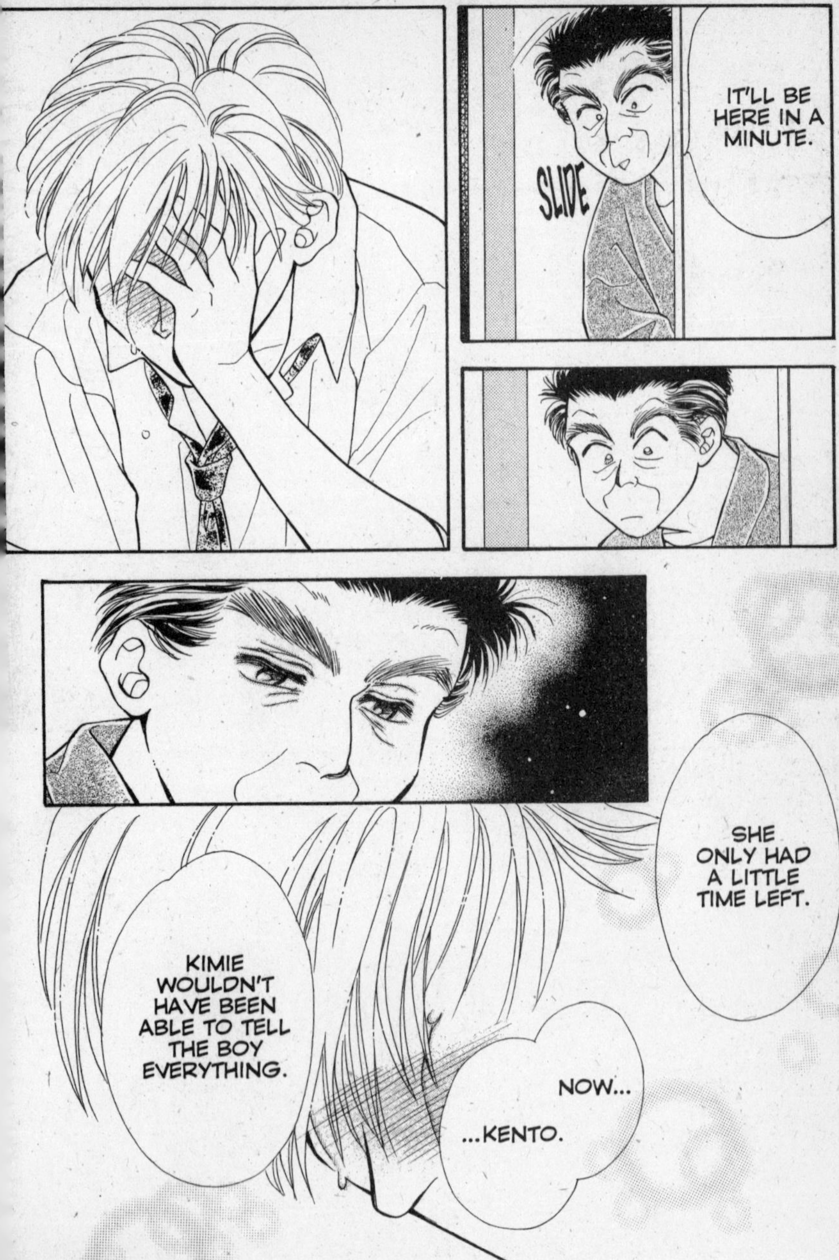
IT'LL BE HERE IN A MINUTE.
SLIDE
SHE ONLY HAD A LITTLE TIME LEFT.
KIMIE WOULDN'T HAVE BEEN ABLE TO TELL THE BOY EVERYTHING.
NOW...
...KENTO.

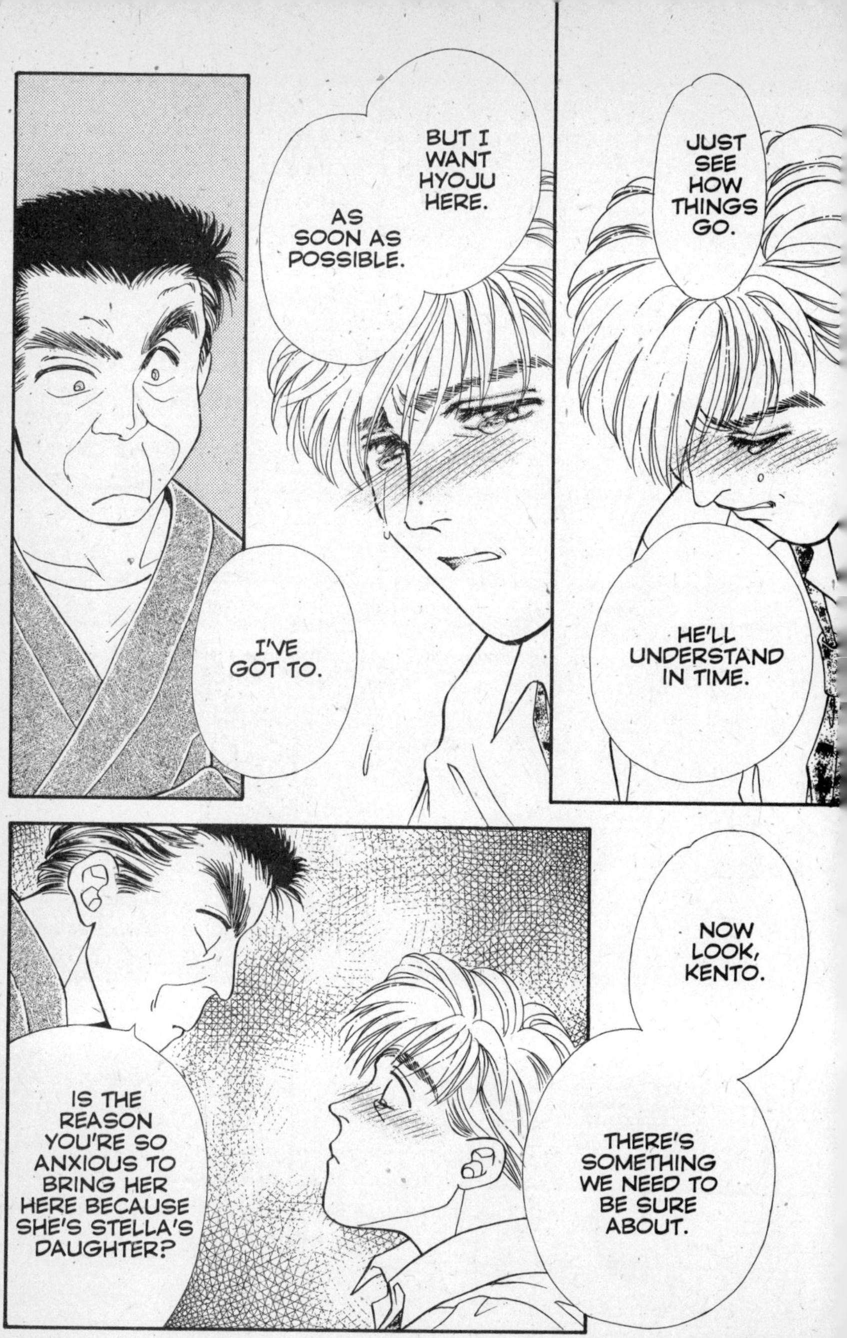
JUST SEE HOW THINGS GO.
HE'LL UNDERSTAND IN TIME.
BUT I WANT HYOJU HERE.
AS SOON AS POSSIBLE.
I'VE GOT TO.
NOW LOOK, KENTO.
THERE'S SOMETHING WE NEED TO BE SURE ABOUT.
IS THE REASON YOU'RE SO ANXIOUS TO BRING HER HERE BECAUSE SHE'S STELLA'S DAUGHTER?

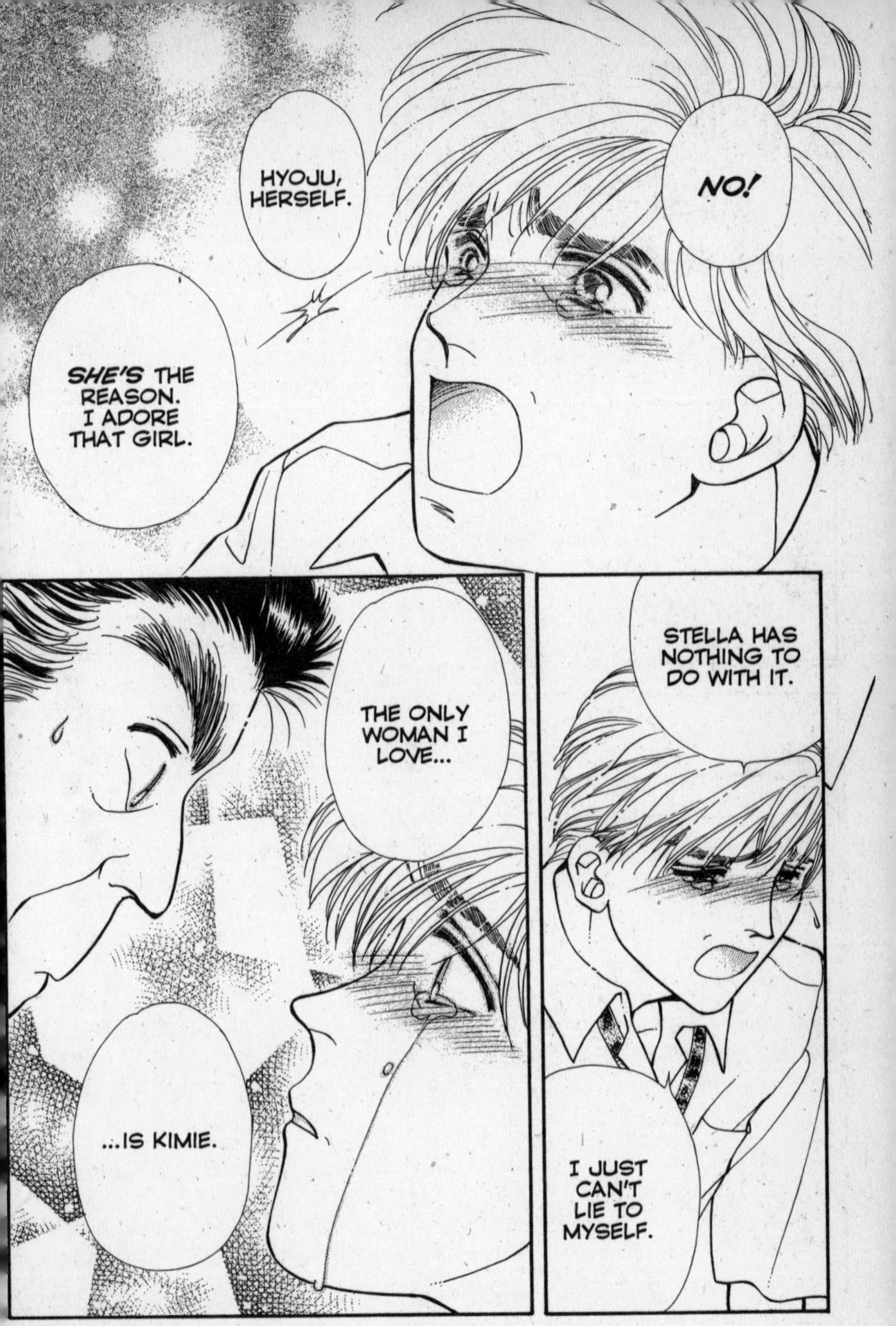
NO!
HYOJU, HERSELF.
SHE'S THE REASON. I ADORE THAT GIRL.
STELLA HAS NOTHING TO DO WITH IT.
I JUST CAN'T LIE TO MYSELF.
THE ONLY WOMAN I LOVE...
...IS KIMIE.

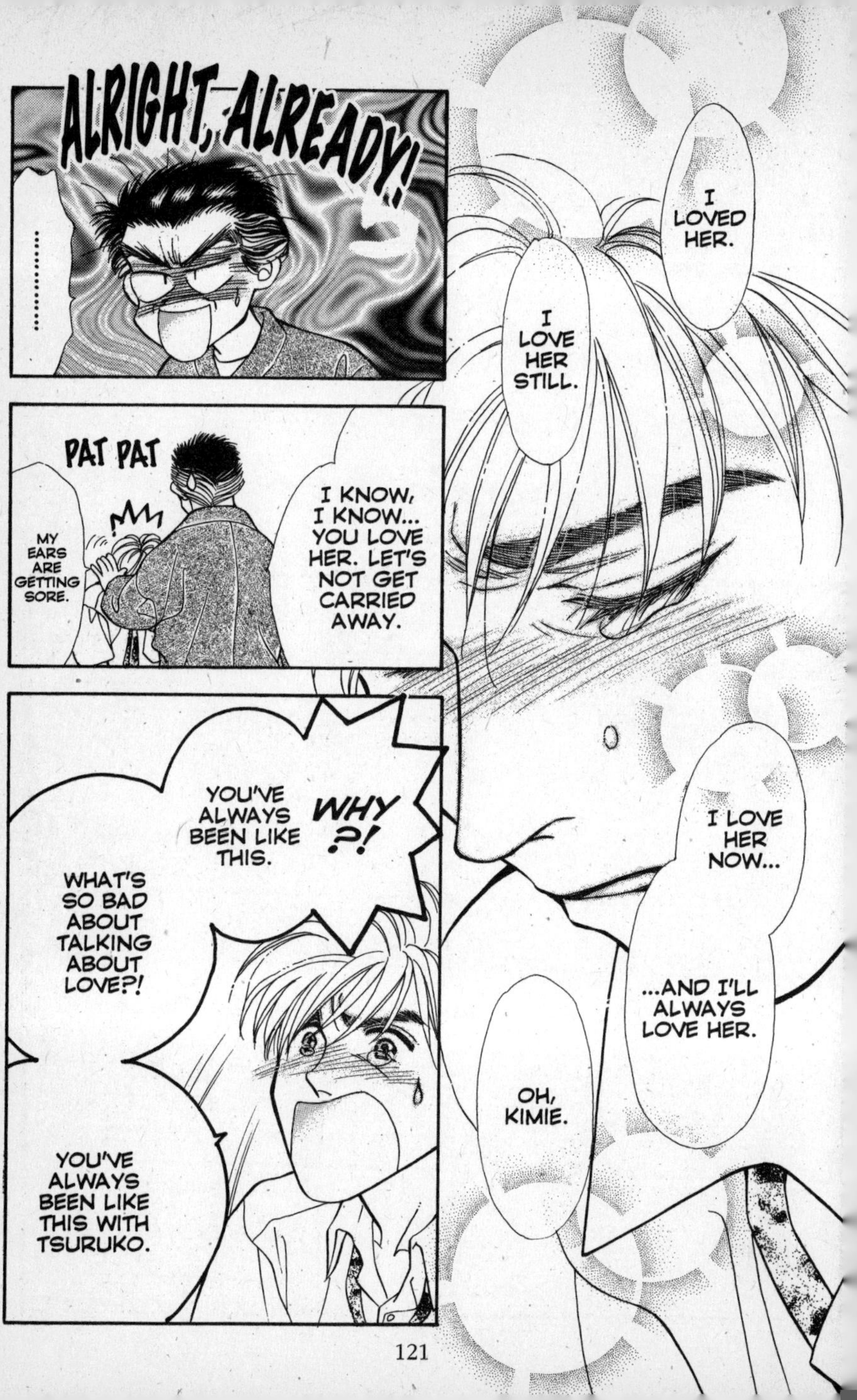

I LOVED HER.
I LOVE HER STILL.
I LOVE HER NOW...
...AND I'LL ALWAYS LOVE HER.
OH, KIMIE.
ALRIGHT, ALREADY!
....
I KNOW, I KNOW... YOU LOVE HER. LET'S NOT GET CARRIED AWAY.
PAT PAT
MY EARS ARE GETTING SORE.
WHY?!
YOU'VE ALWAYS BEEN LIKE THIS.
WHAT'S SO BAD ABOUT TALKING ABOUT LOVE?!
YOU'VE ALWAYS BEEN LIKE THIS WITH TSURUKO.

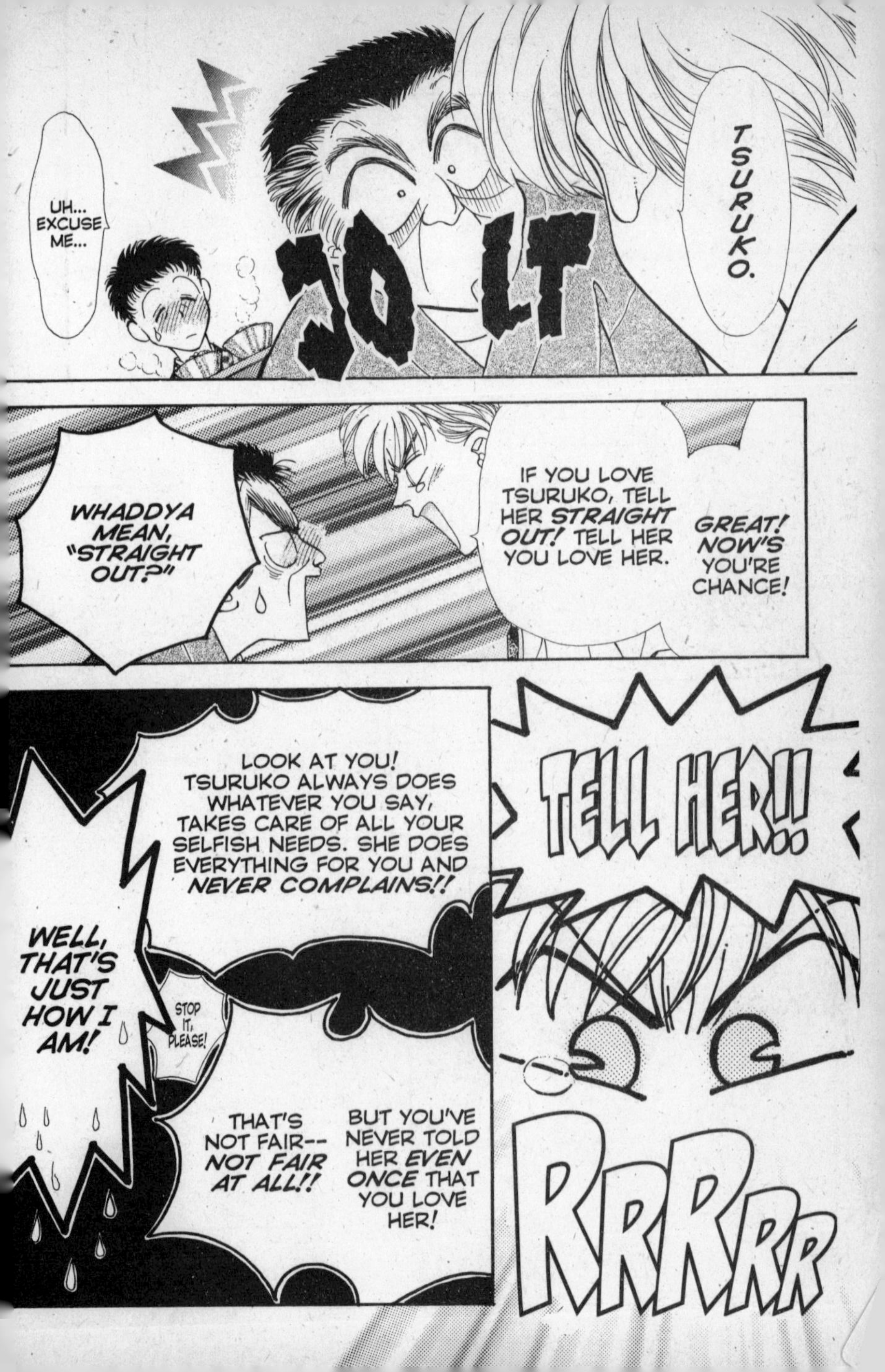
TSURUKO.
JOLT
UH... EXCUSE ME...
GREAT! NOW'S YOU'RE CHANCE!
IF YOU LOVE TSURUKO, TELL HER STRAIGHT OUT! TELL HER YOU LOVE HER.
WHADDYA MEAN, "STRAIGHT OUT?"
TELL HER!!
RRRRR
LOOK AT YOU! TSURUKO ALWAYS DOES WHATEVER YOU SAY, TAKES CARE OF ALL YOUR SELFISH NEEDS. SHE DOES EVERYTHING FOR YOU AND NEVER COMPLAINS!!
WELL, THAT'S JUST HOW I AM!
STOP IT, PLEASE!
BUT YOU'VE NEVER TOLD HER EVEN ONCE THAT YOU LOVE HER!
THAT'S NOT FAIR-- NOT FAIR AT ALL!!

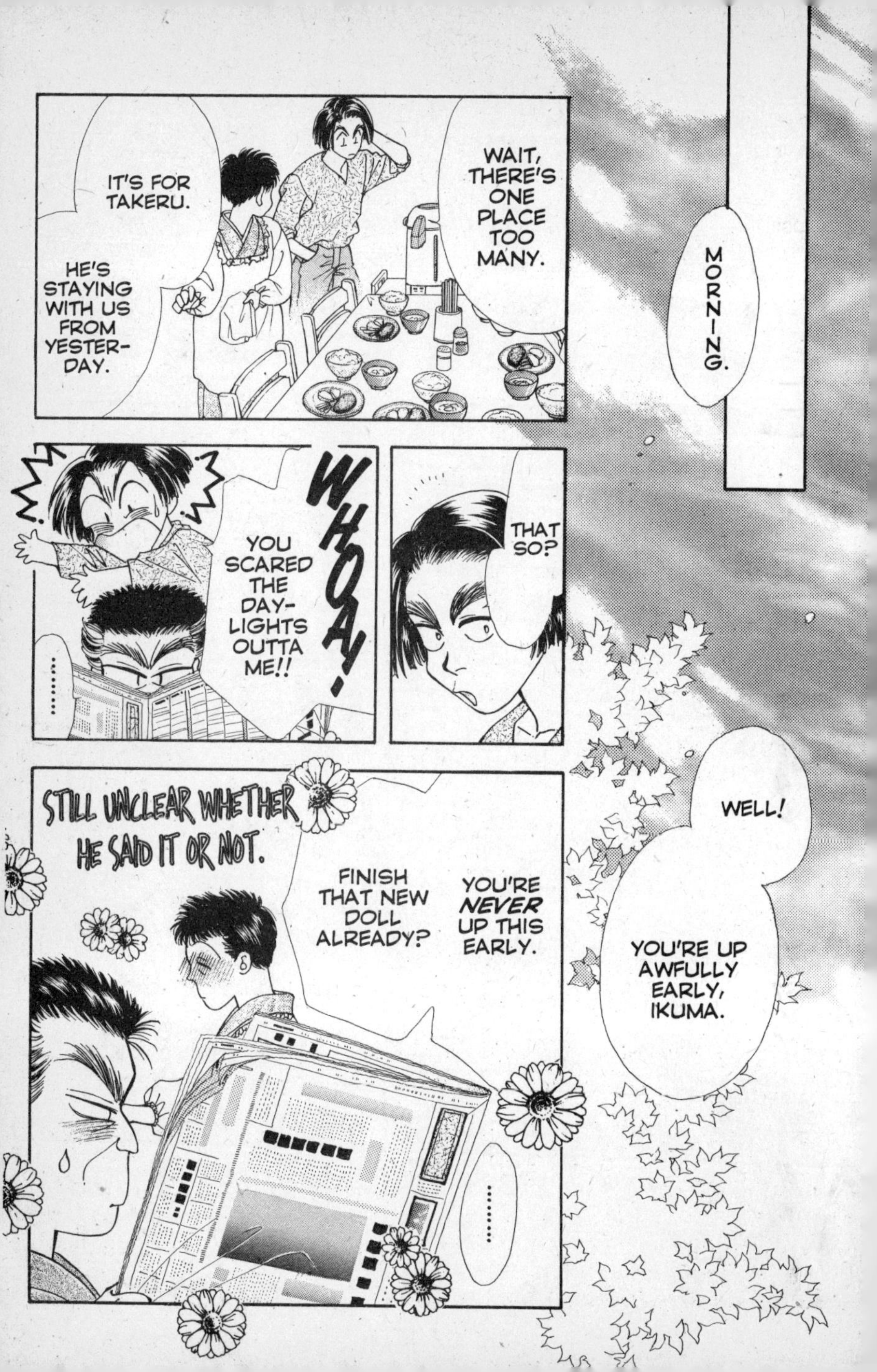
MORNING.
WELL!
YOU'RE UP AWFULLY EARLY, IKUMA.
WAIT, THERE'S ONE PLACE TOO MANY.
IT'S FOR TAKERU.
HE'S STAYING WITH US FROM YESTERDAY.
THAT SO?
WHOA!
YOU SCARED THE DAYLIGHTS OUTTA ME!!
......
YOU'RE *NEVER* UP THIS EARLY.
FINISH THAT NEW DOLL ALREADY?
STILL UNCLEAR WHETHER HE SAID IT OR NOT.
......

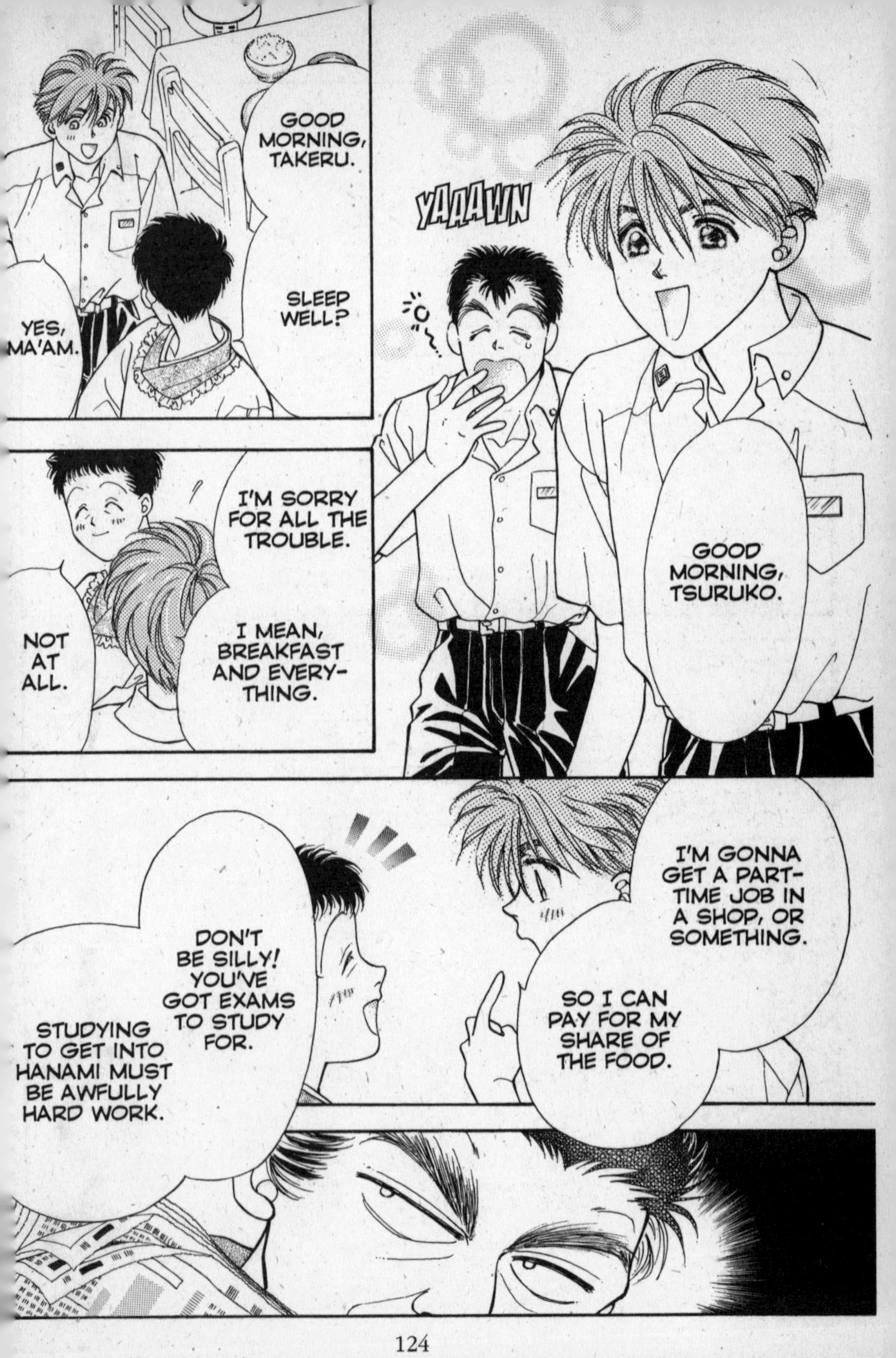
YAAAWN
GOOD MORNING, TSURUKO.
GOOD MORNING, TAKERU.
SLEEP WELL?
YES, MA'AM.
I'M SORRY FOR ALL THE TROUBLE.
I MEAN, BREAKFAST AND EVERY-THING.
NOT AT ALL.
I'M GONNA GET A PART-TIME JOB IN A SHOP, OR SOMETHING.
SO I CAN PAY FOR MY SHARE OF THE FOOD.
DON'T BE SILLY! YOU'VE GOT EXAMS TO STUDY FOR.
STUDYING TO GET INTO HANAMI MUST BE AWFULLY HARD WORK.

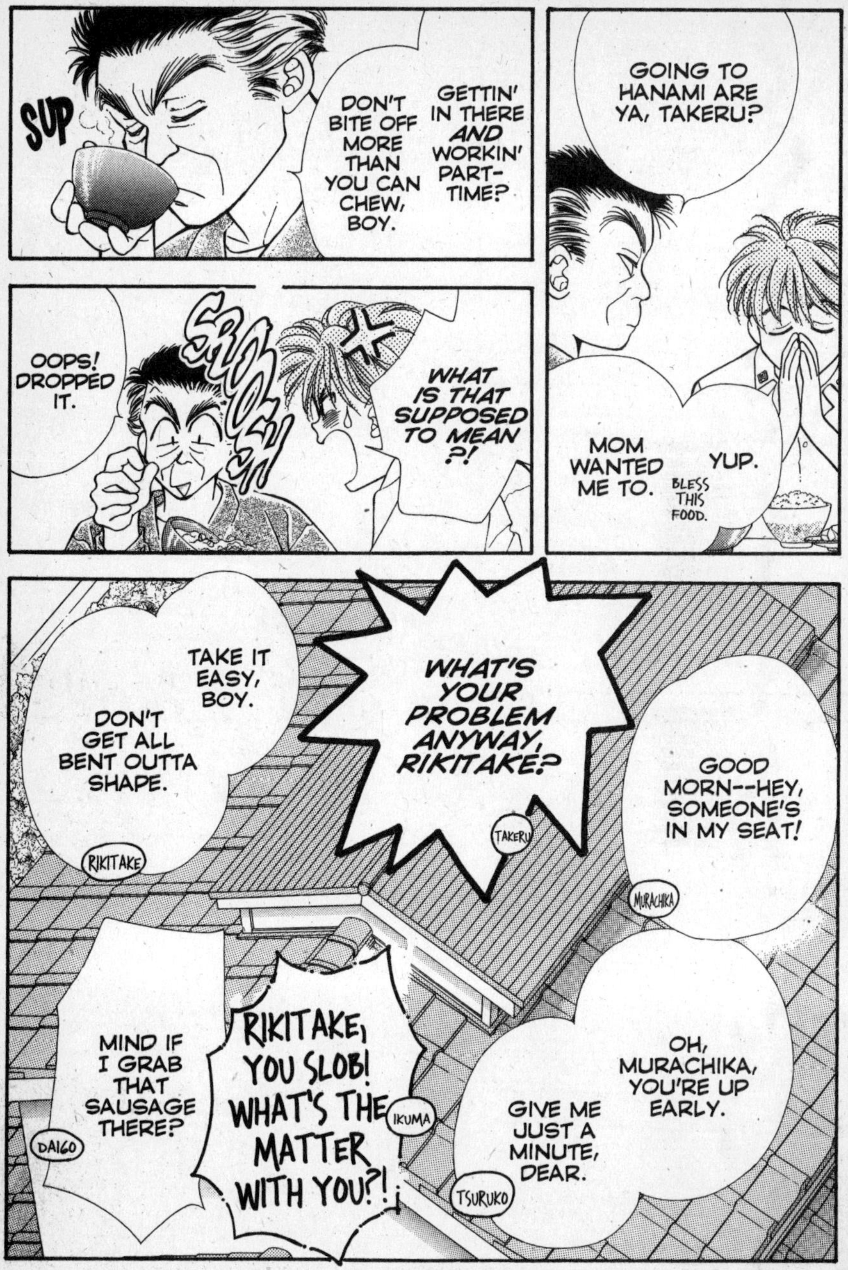
GOING TO HANAMI ARE YA, TAKERU?
YUP.
MOM WANTED ME TO.
BLESS THIS FOOD.
GETTIN' IN THERE AND WORKIN' PART-TIME?
DON'T BITE OFF MORE THAN YOU CAN CHEW, BOY.
SUP
WHAT IS THAT SUPPOSED TO MEAN?!
OOPS! DROPPED IT.
GOOD MORN--HEY, SOMEONE'S IN MY SEAT!
MURACHIKA
WHAT'S YOUR PROBLEM ANYWAY, RIKITAKE?
TAKERU
TAKE IT EASY, BOY.
DON'T GET ALL BENT OUTTA SHAPE.
RIKITAKE
OH, MURACHIKA, YOU'RE UP EARLY.
GIVE ME JUST A MINUTE, DEAR.
TSURUKO
RIKITAKE, YOU SLOB! WHAT'S THE MATTER WITH YOU?!
IKUMA
MIND IF I GRAB THAT SAUSAGE THERE?
DAIGO

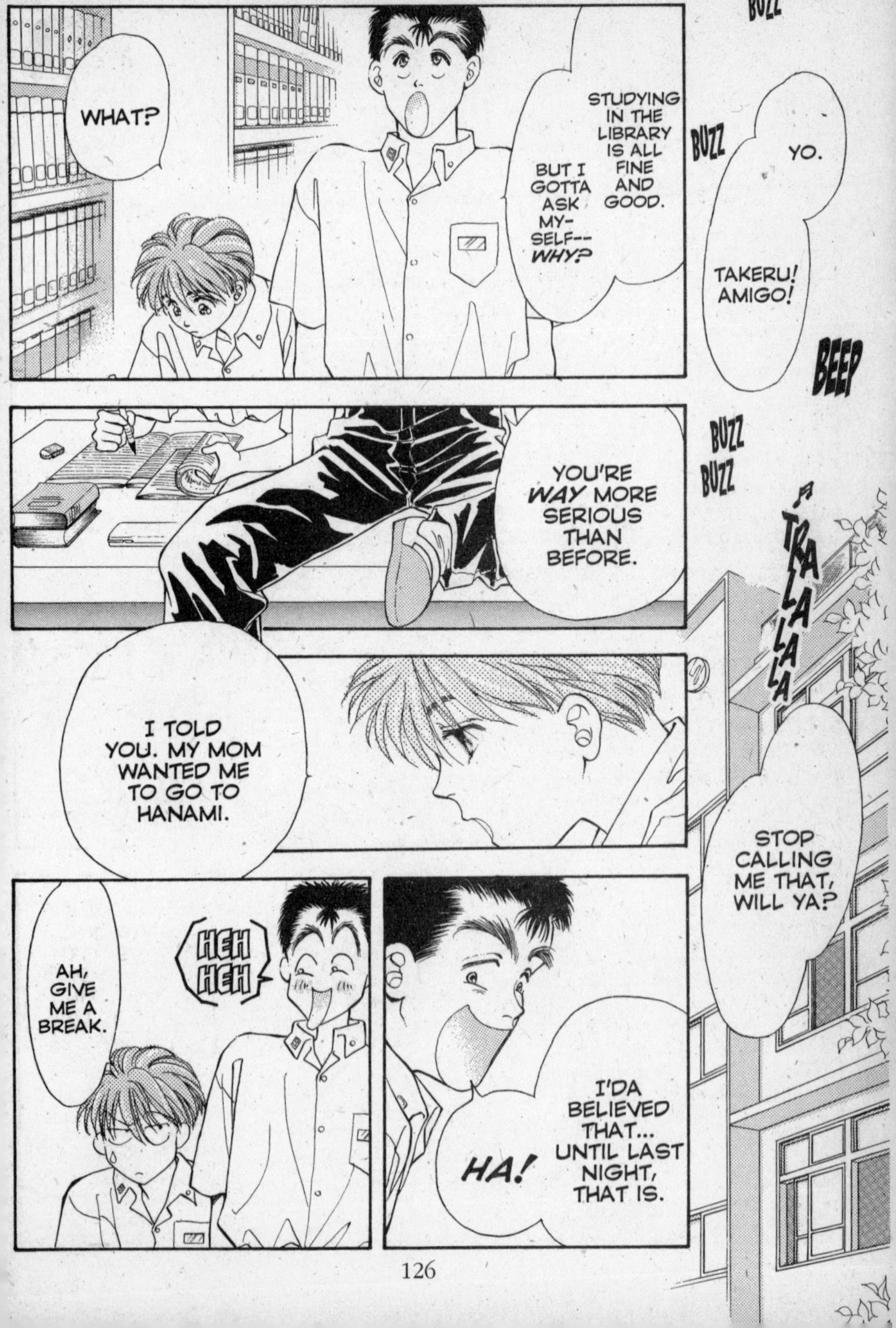
BUZZ
BUZZ
YO.
TAKERU! AMIGO!
BEEP
BUZZ BUZZ
♪ TRA LA LA LA LA
STOP CALLING ME THAT, WILL YA?
STUDYING IN THE LIBRARY IS ALL FINE AND GOOD.
BUT I GOTTA ASK MYSELF-- *WHY?*
WHAT?
YOU'RE *WAY* MORE SERIOUS THAN BEFORE.
I TOLD YOU. MY MOM WANTED ME TO GO TO HANAMI.
I'DA BELIEVED THAT... UNTIL LAST NIGHT, THAT IS.
HA!
HEH HEH
AH, GIVE ME A BREAK.

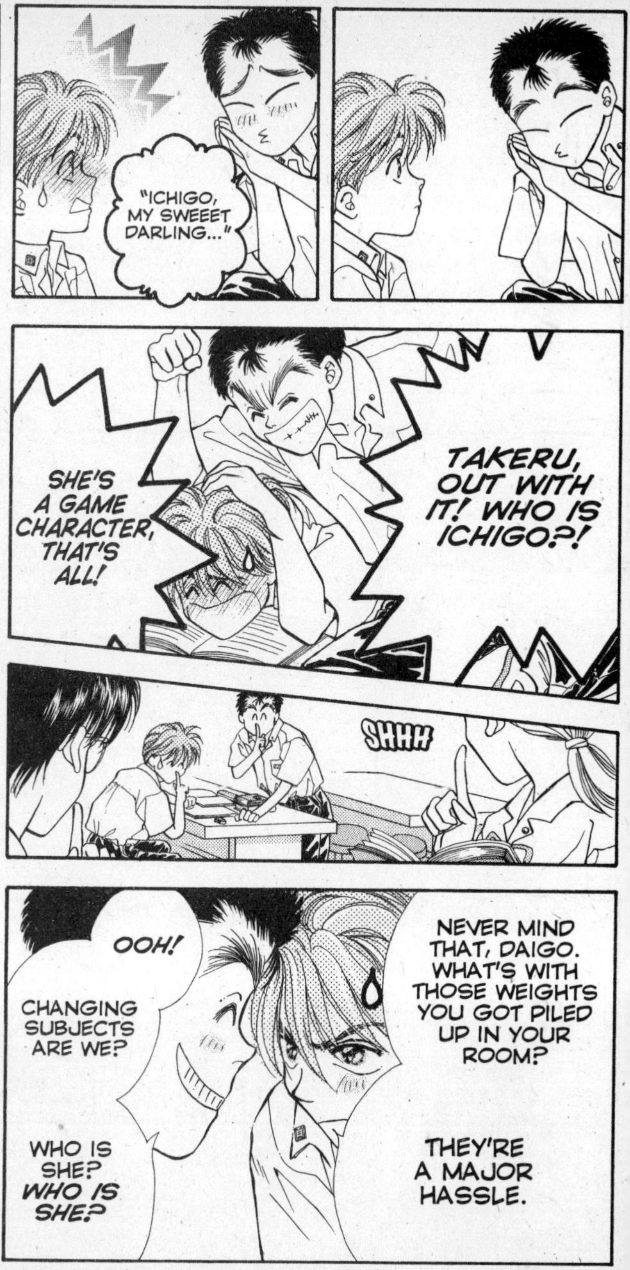
"ICHIGO, MY SWEEET DARLING..."
TAKERU, OUT WITH IT! WHO IS ICHIGO?!
SHE'S A GAME CHARACTER, THAT'S ALL!
SHHH
NEVER MIND THAT, DAIGO. WHAT'S WITH THOSE WEIGHTS YOU GOT PILED UP IN YOUR ROOM?
THEY'RE A MAJOR HASSLE.
OOH!
CHANGING SUBJECTS ARE WE?
WHO IS SHE? *WHO IS SHE?*

1/4 Sidebar No. 8

8

I have to confess that I haven't thought through at all the force of Zero, the story that Takeru's writing at his computer. That's because rather than me write the story, I want it to be something that Takeru does on his own. That is, I want to make it so that my central character grows and develops. He has to develop both experience and ability. You all probably think that by groping around like this right from the start, I'm just making the job harder on myself. But I think knowing this side of things makes reading the story all the more fun.

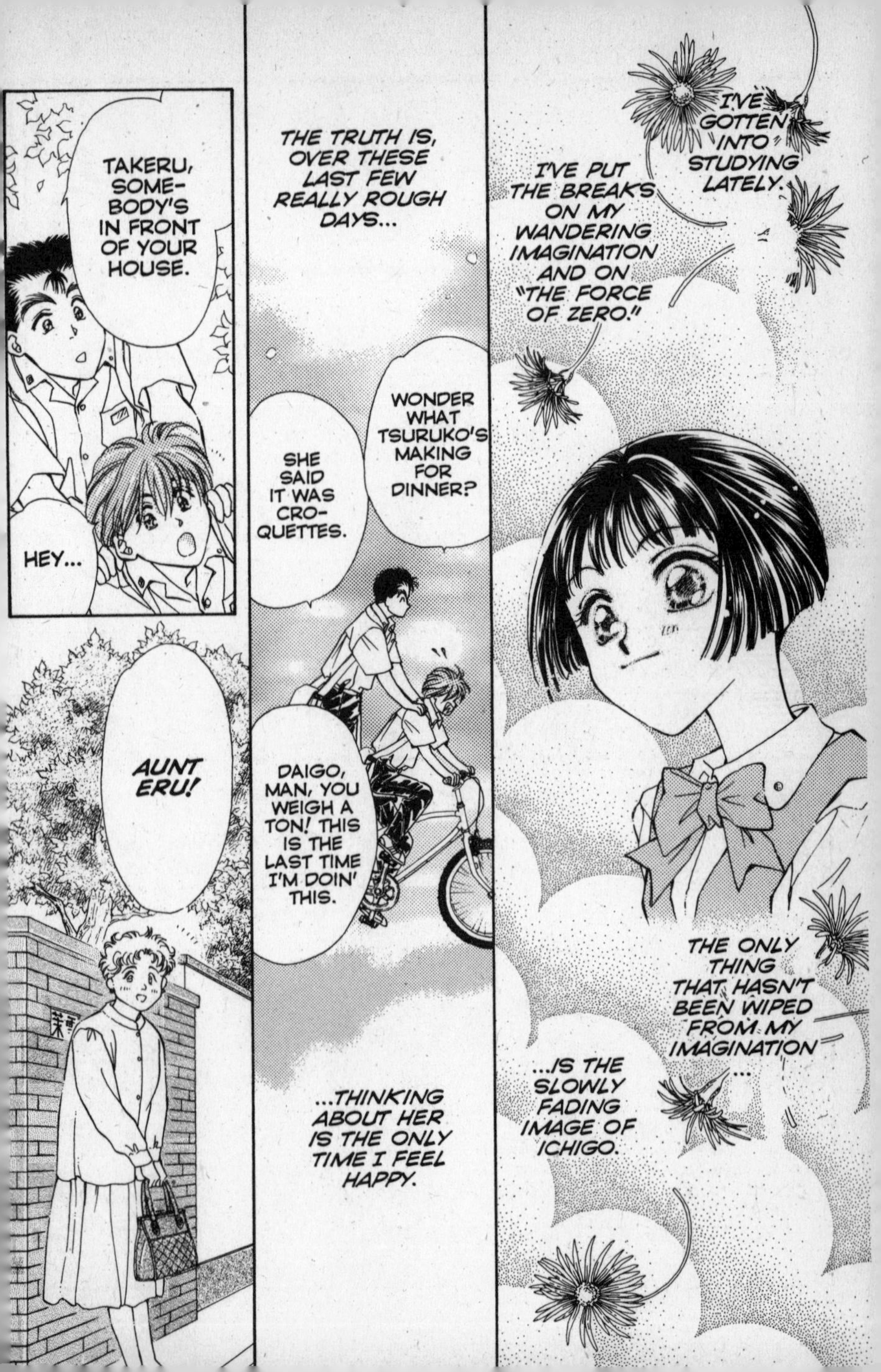
I'VE GOTTEN INTO STUDYING LATELY.
I'VE PUT THE BREAKS ON MY WANDERING IMAGINATION AND ON "THE FORCE OF ZERO."
THE ONLY THING THAT HASN'T BEEN WIPED FROM MY IMAGINATION...
...IS THE SLOWLY FADING IMAGE OF ICHIGO.
THE TRUTH IS, OVER THESE LAST FEW REALLY ROUGH DAYS...
WONDER WHAT TSURUKO'S MAKING FOR DINNER?
SHE SAID IT WAS CRO-QUETTES.
DAIGO, MAN, YOU WEIGH A TON! THIS IS THE LAST TIME I'M DOIN' THIS.
...THINKING ABOUT HER IS THE ONLY TIME I FEEL HAPPY.
TAKERU, SOME-BODY'S IN FRONT OF YOUR HOUSE.
HEY...
AUNT ERU!

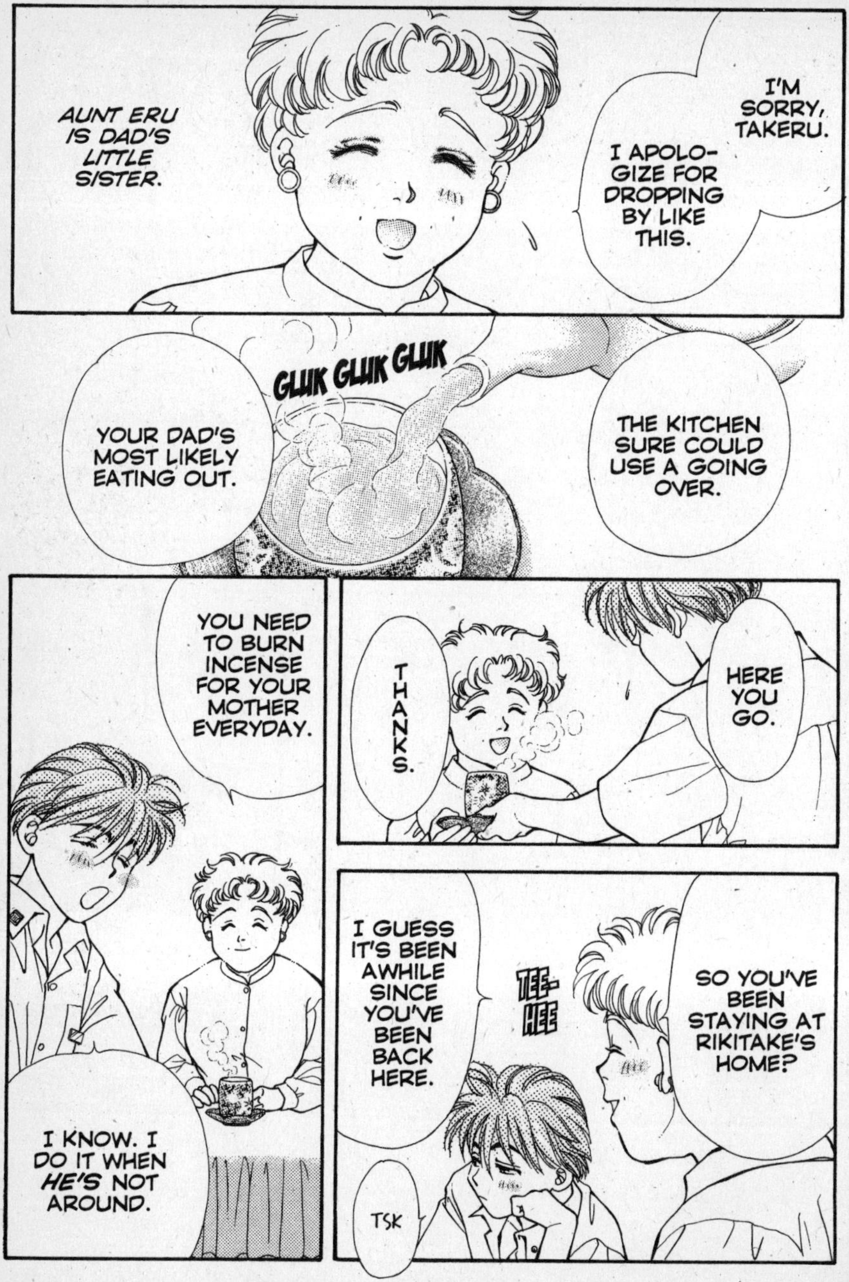
I'M SORRY, TAKERU.
I APOLO-GIZE FOR DROPPING BY LIKE THIS.
AUNT ERU IS DAD'S LITTLE SISTER.
THE KITCHEN SURE COULD USE A GOING OVER.
GLUK GLUK GLUK
YOUR DAD'S MOST LIKELY EATING OUT.
HERE YOU GO.
THANKS.
SO YOU'VE BEEN STAYING AT RIKITAKE'S HOME?
TEE-HEE
I GUESS IT'S BEEN AWHILE SINCE YOU'VE BEEN BACK HERE.
TSK
YOU NEED TO BURN INCENSE FOR YOUR MOTHER EVERYDAY.
I KNOW. I DO IT WHEN *HE'S* NOT AROUND.

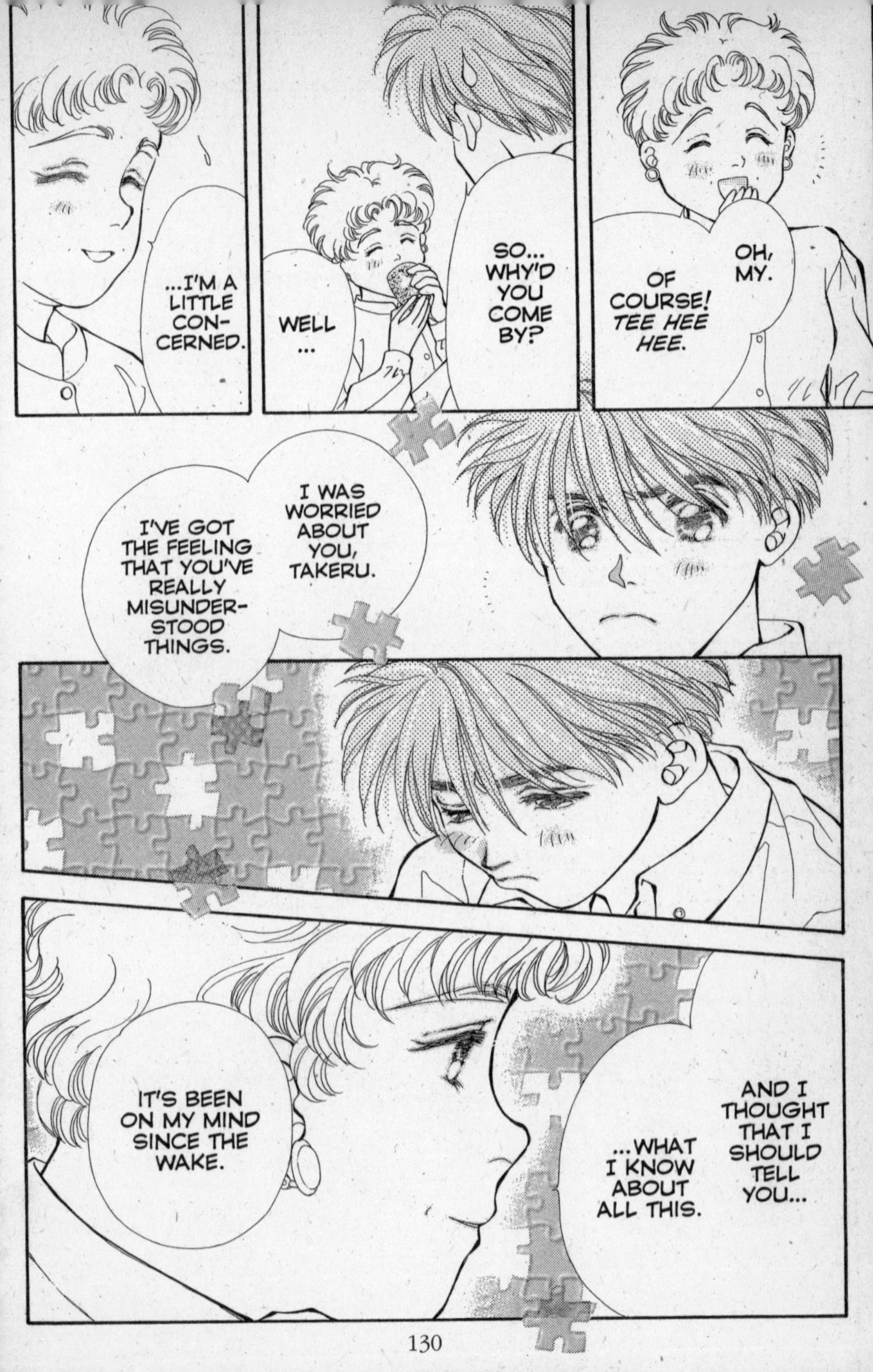
OH, MY.
OF COURSE! *TEE HEE HEE.*
SO... WHY'D YOU COME BY?
WELL ...
...I'M A LITTLE CON-CERNED.
I WAS WORRIED ABOUT YOU, TAKERU.
I'VE GOT THE FEELING THAT YOU'VE REALLY MISUNDER-STOOD THINGS.
AND I THOUGHT THAT I SHOULD TELL YOU...
...WHAT I KNOW ABOUT ALL THIS.
IT'S BEEN ON MY MIND SINCE THE WAKE.

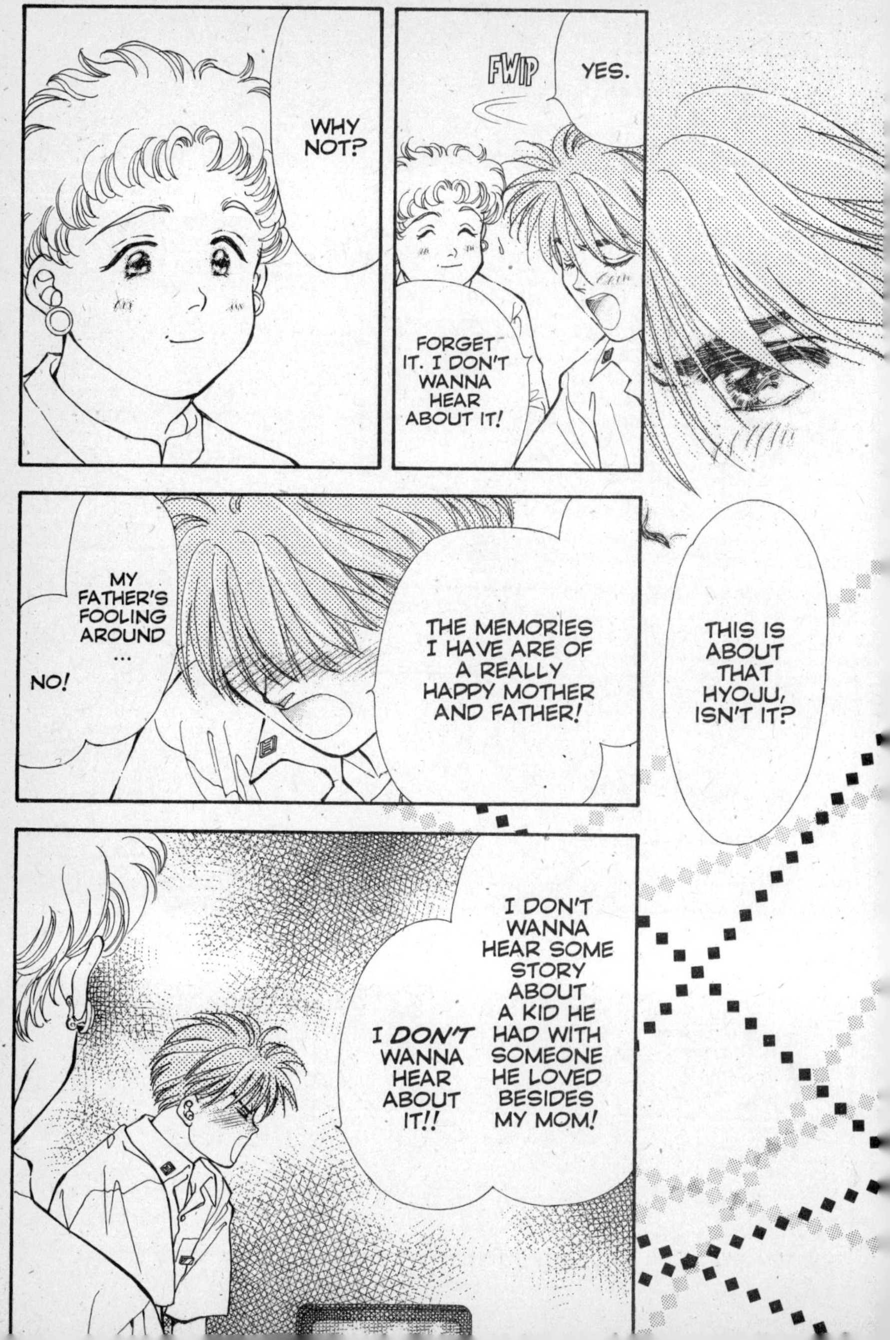
YES.
FWIP
FORGET IT. I DON'T WANNA HEAR ABOUT IT!
WHY NOT?
THIS IS ABOUT THAT HYOJU, ISN'T IT?
THE MEMORIES I HAVE ARE OF A REALLY HAPPY MOTHER AND FATHER!
MY FATHER'S FOOLING AROUND ...
NO!
I DON'T WANNA HEAR SOME STORY ABOUT A KID HE HAD WITH SOMEONE HE LOVED BESIDES MY MOM!
I *DON'T* WANNA HEAR ABOUT IT!!

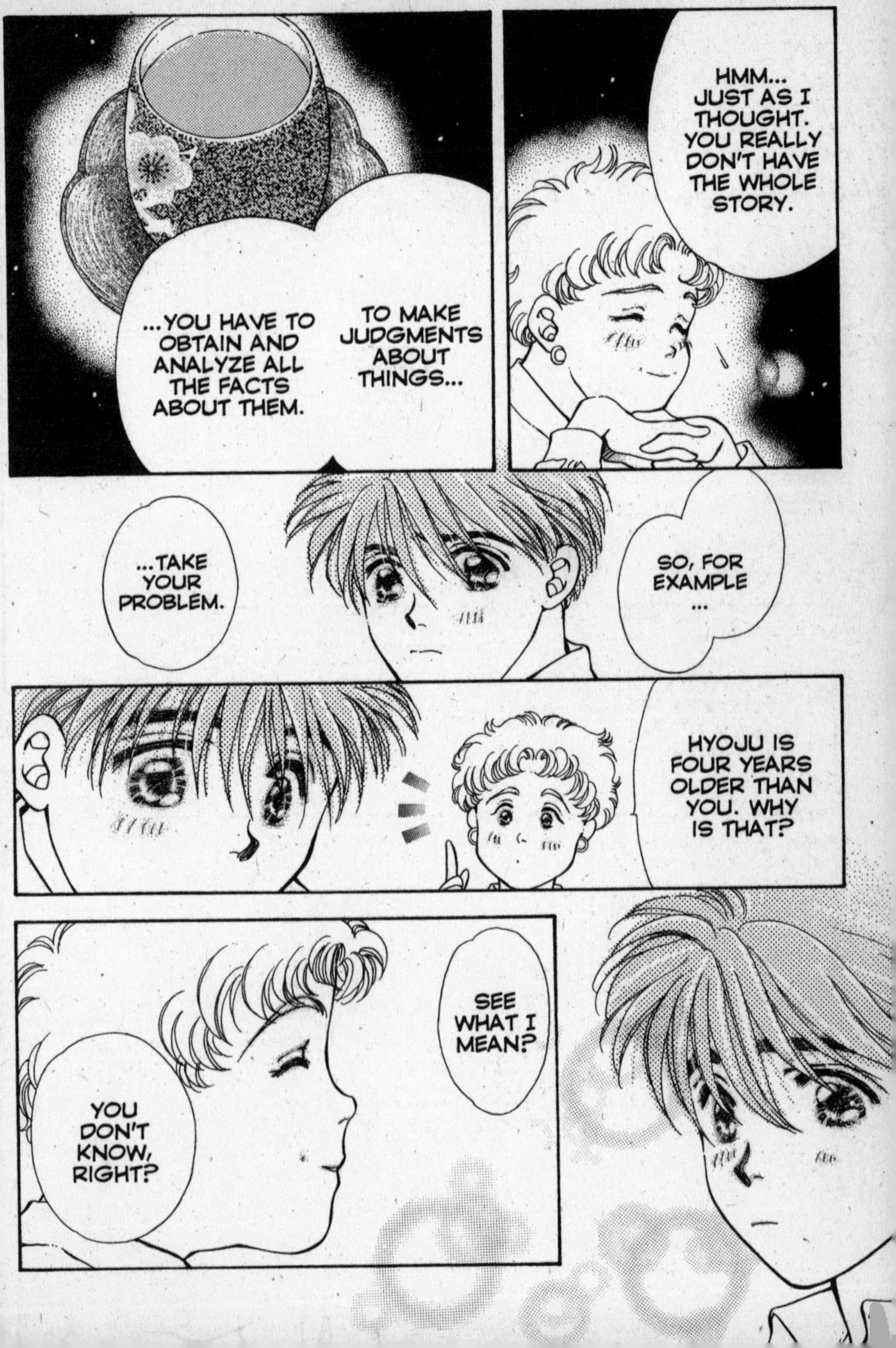
HMM... JUST AS I THOUGHT. YOU REALLY DON'T HAVE THE WHOLE STORY.
TO MAKE JUDGMENTS ABOUT THINGS...
...YOU HAVE TO OBTAIN AND ANALYZE ALL THE FACTS ABOUT THEM.
SO, FOR EXAMPLE ...
...TAKE YOUR PROBLEM.
HYOJU IS FOUR YEARS OLDER THAN YOU. WHY IS THAT?
SEE WHAT I MEAN?
YOU DON'T KNOW, RIGHT?

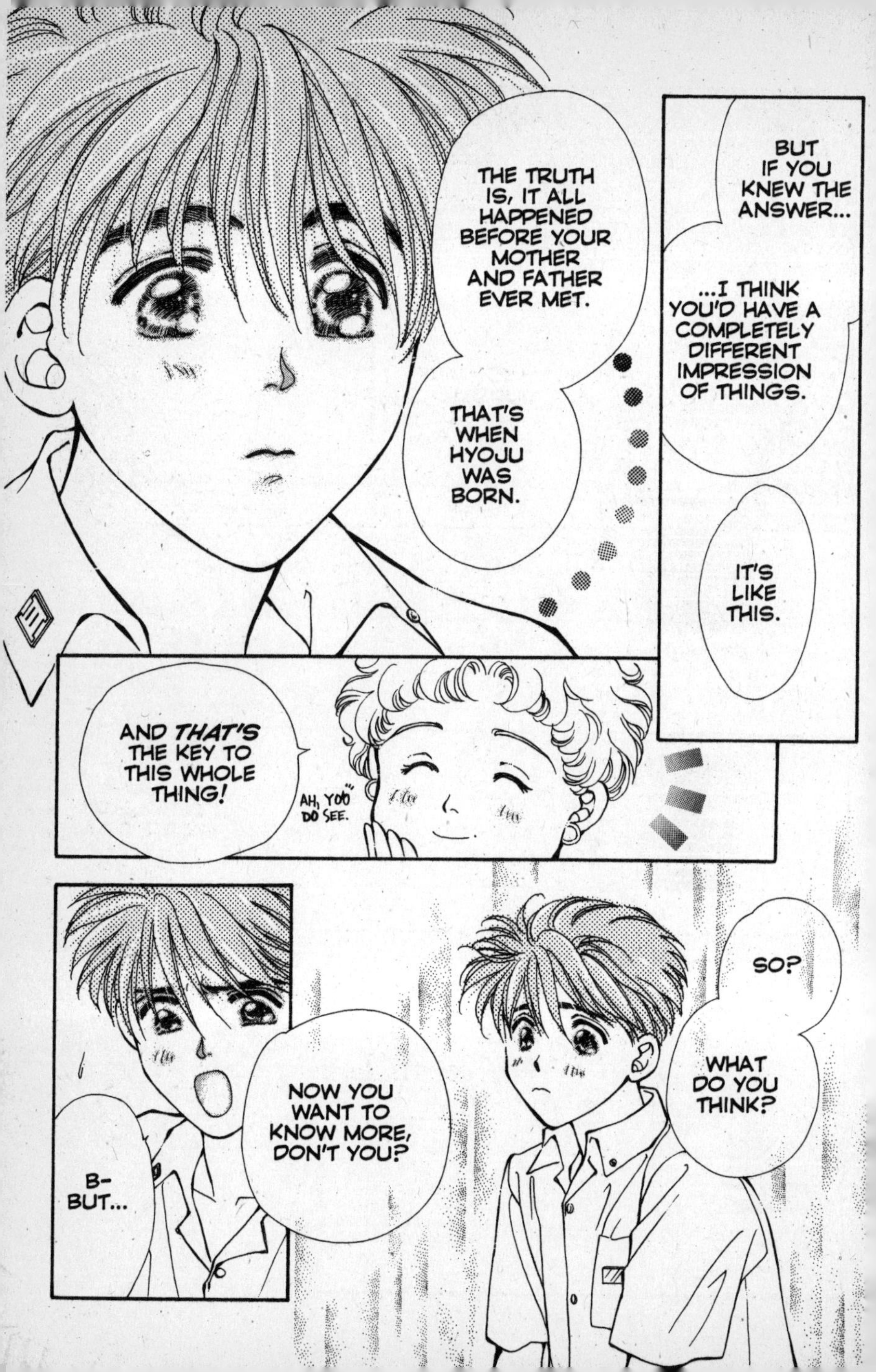
BUT IF YOU KNEW THE ANSWER...
...I THINK YOU'D HAVE A COMPLETELY DIFFERENT IMPRESSION OF THINGS.
IT'S LIKE THIS.
THE TRUTH IS, IT ALL HAPPENED BEFORE YOUR MOTHER AND FATHER EVER MET.
THAT'S WHEN HYOJU WAS BORN.
AH, YOU DO SEE.
AND *THAT'S* THE KEY TO THIS WHOLE THING!
SO?
WHAT DO YOU THINK?
NOW YOU WANT TO KNOW MORE, DON'T YOU?
B- BUT...

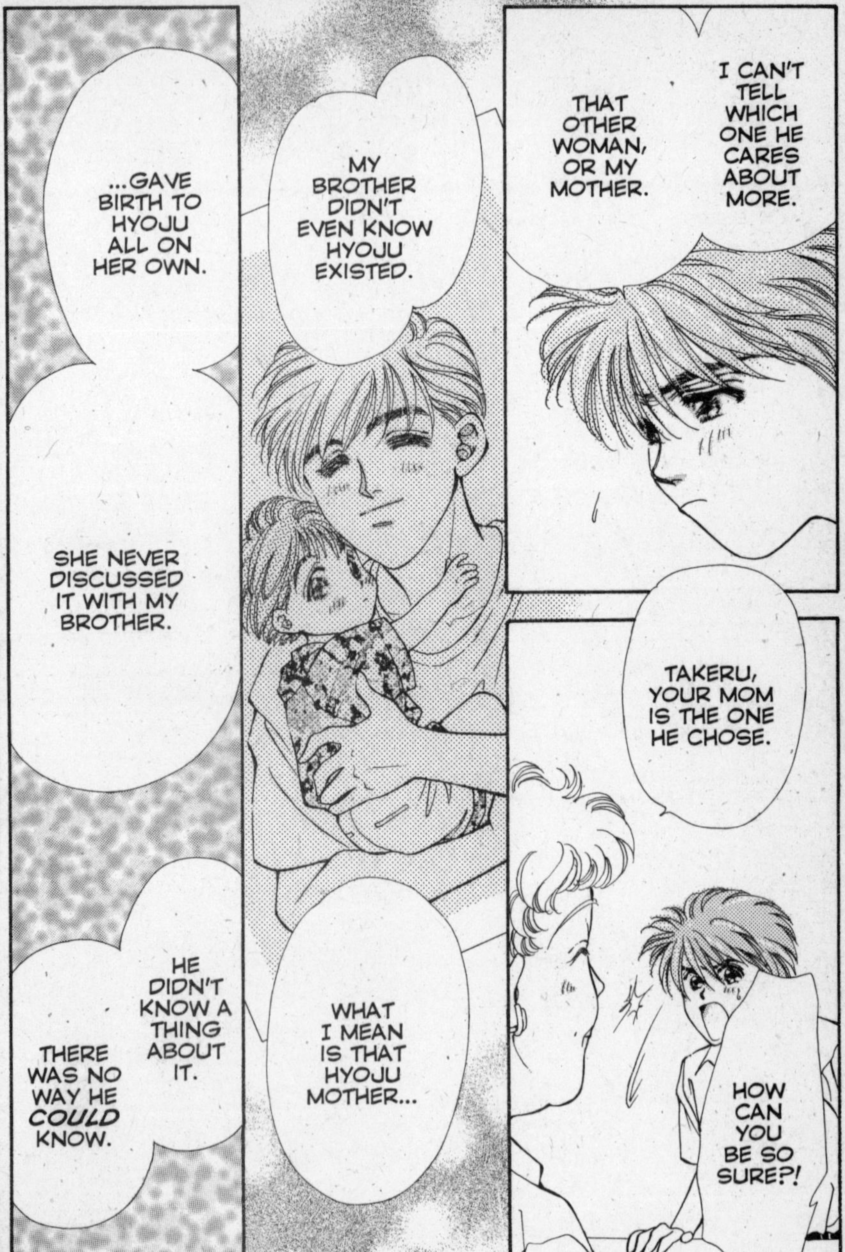
I CAN'T TELL WHICH ONE HE CARES ABOUT MORE.
THAT OTHER WOMAN, OR MY MOTHER.
TAKERU, YOUR MOM IS THE ONE HE CHOSE.
HOW CAN YOU BE SO SURE?!
MY BROTHER DIDN'T EVEN KNOW HYOJU EXISTED.
WHAT I MEAN IS THAT HYOJU MOTHER...
...GAVE BIRTH TO HYOJU ALL ON HER OWN.
SHE NEVER DISCUSSED IT WITH MY BROTHER.
HE DIDN'T KNOW A THING ABOUT IT.
THERE WAS NO WAY HE *COULD* KNOW.

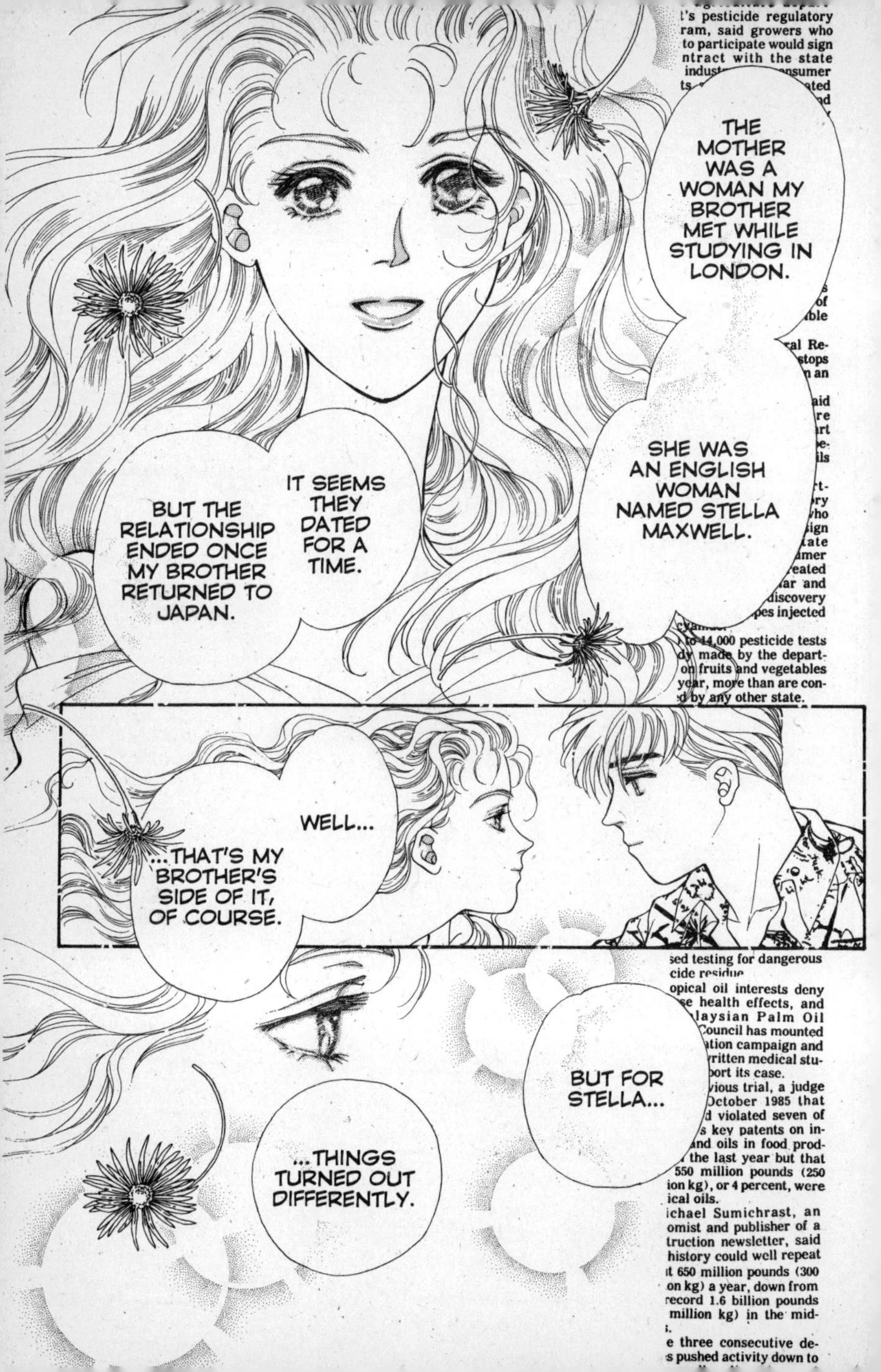
THE MOTHER WAS A WOMAN MY BROTHER MET WHILE STUDYING IN LONDON.
SHE WAS AN ENGLISH WOMAN NAMED STELLA MAXWELL.
IT SEEMS THEY DATED FOR A TIME.
BUT THE RELATIONSHIP ENDED ONCE MY BROTHER RETURNED TO JAPAN.
WELL...
...THAT'S MY BROTHER'S SIDE OF IT, OF COURSE.
BUT FOR STELLA...
...THINGS TURNED OUT DIFFERENTLY.

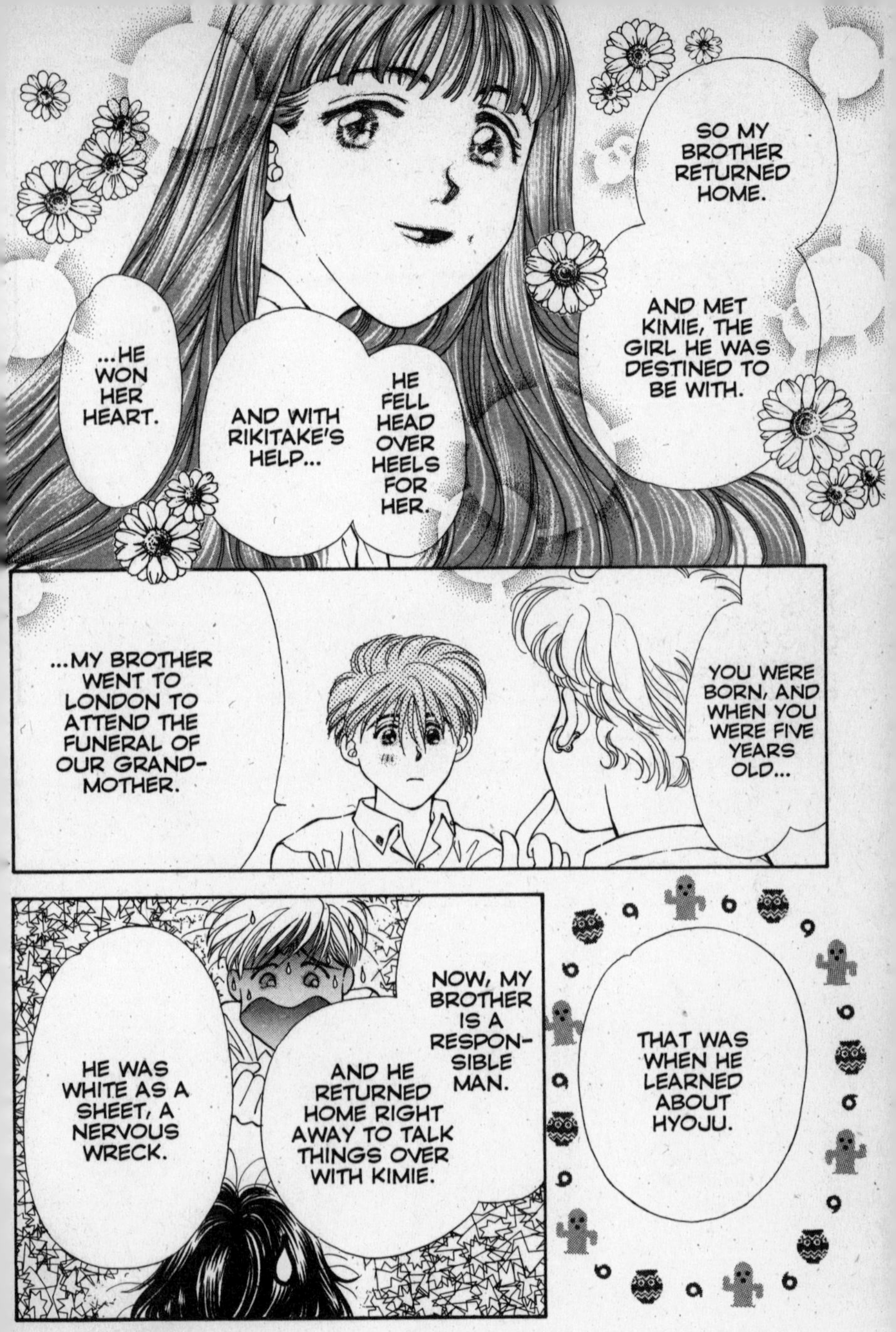
SO MY BROTHER RETURNED HOME.
AND MET KIMIE, THE GIRL HE WAS DESTINED TO BE WITH.
HE FELL HEAD OVER HEELS FOR HER.
AND WITH RIKITAKE'S HELP...
...HE WON HER HEART.
YOU WERE BORN, AND WHEN YOU WERE FIVE YEARS OLD...
...MY BROTHER WENT TO LONDON TO ATTEND THE FUNERAL OF OUR GRAND-MOTHER.
THAT WAS WHEN HE LEARNED ABOUT HYOJU.
NOW, MY BROTHER IS A RESPONSIBLE MAN.
AND HE RETURNED HOME RIGHT AWAY TO TALK THINGS OVER WITH KIMIE.
HE WAS WHITE AS A SHEET, A NERVOUS WRECK.

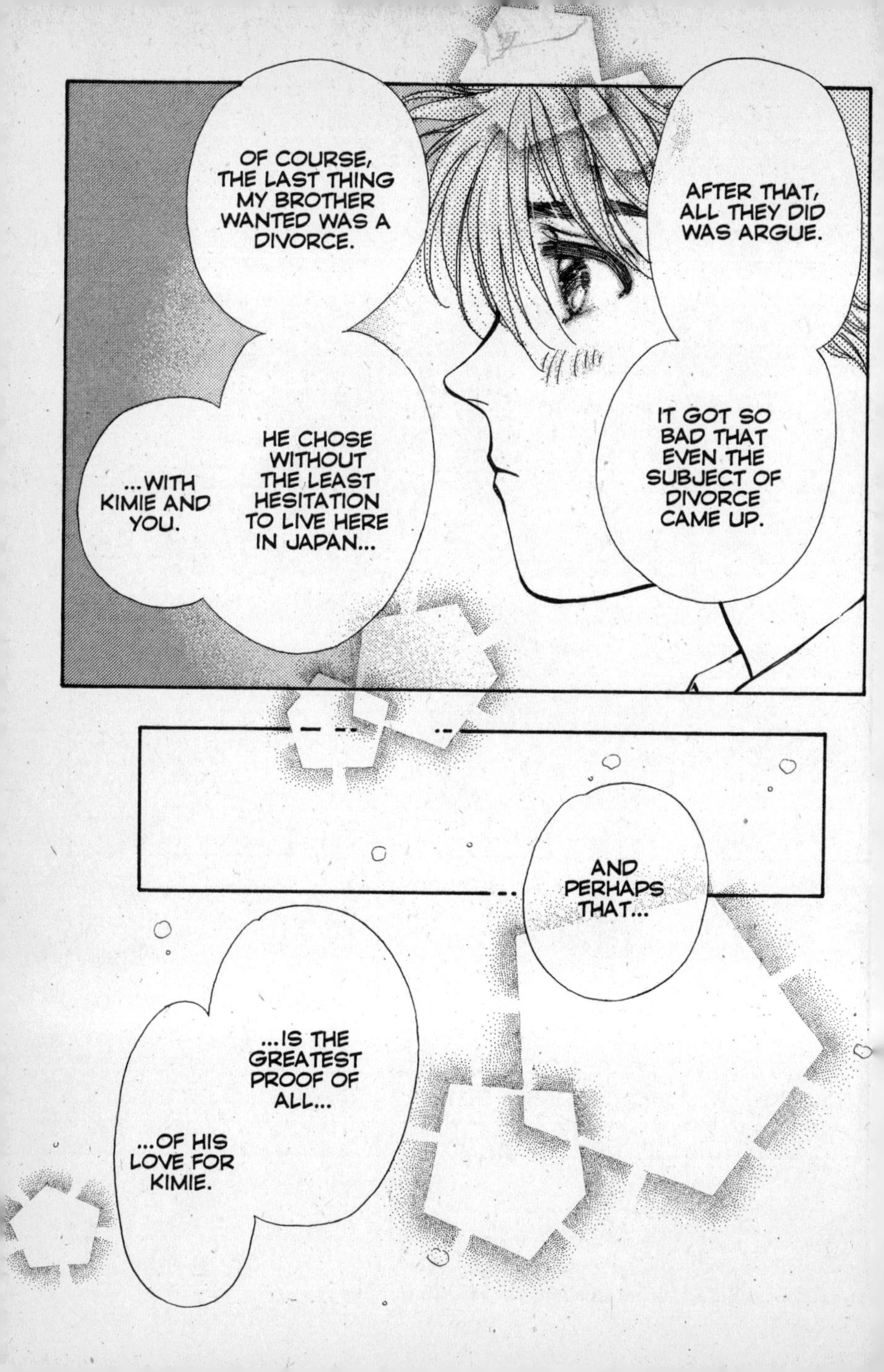
AFTER THAT, ALL THEY DID WAS ARGUE.
IT GOT SO BAD THAT EVEN THE SUBJECT OF DIVORCE CAME UP.
OF COURSE, THE LAST THING MY BROTHER WANTED WAS A DIVORCE.
HE CHOSE WITHOUT THE LEAST HESITATION TO LIVE HERE IN JAPAN...
...WITH KIMIE AND YOU.
AND PERHAPS THAT...
...IS THE GREATEST PROOF OF ALL...
...OF HIS LOVE FOR KIMIE.

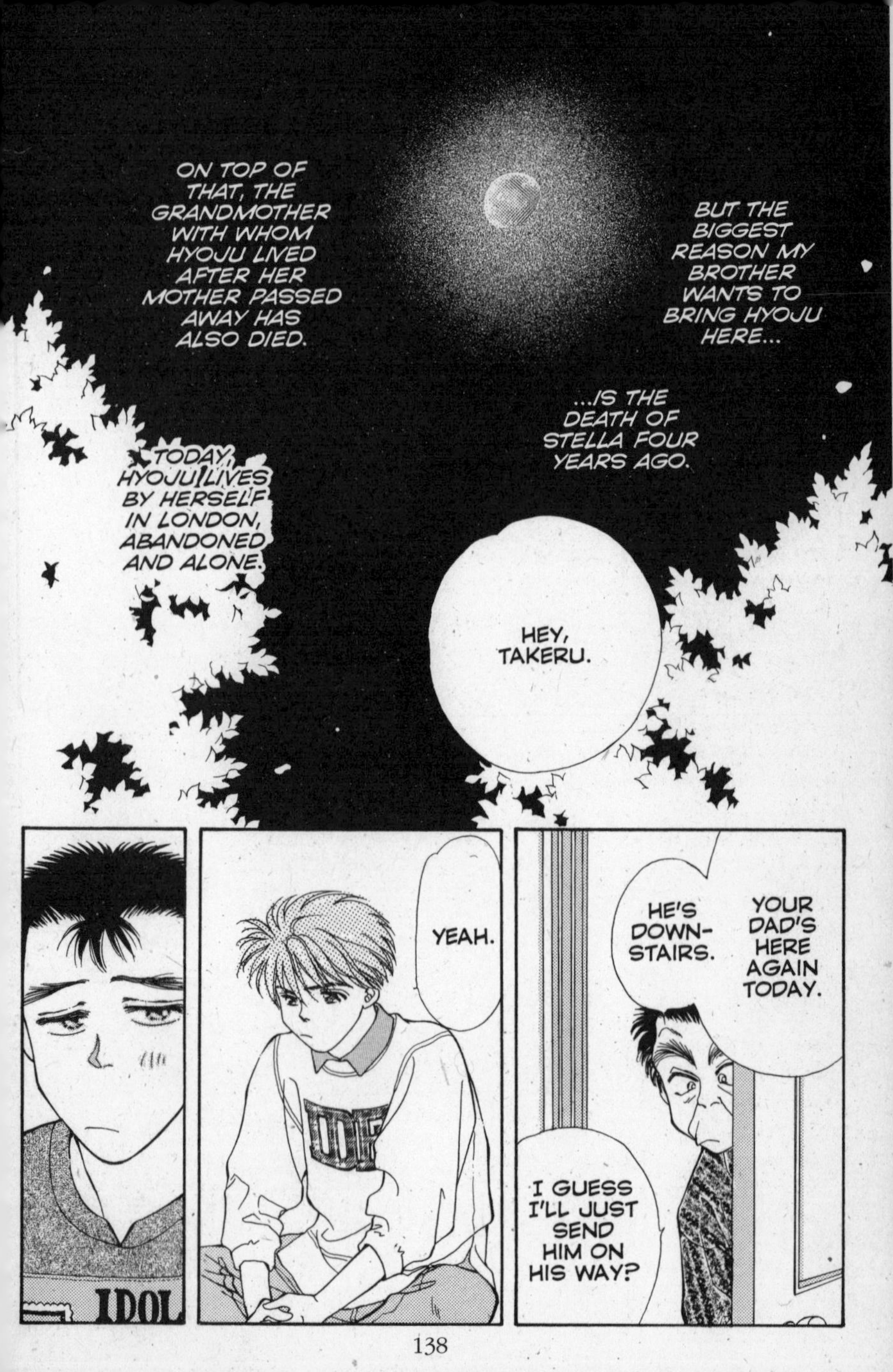

ON TOP OF THAT, THE GRANDMOTHER WITH WHOM HYOJU LIVED AFTER HER MOTHER PASSED AWAY HAS ALSO DIED.
TODAY, HYOJU LIVES BY HERSELF IN LONDON, ABANDONED AND ALONE.
BUT THE BIGGEST REASON MY BROTHER WANTS TO BRING HYOJU HERE...
...IS THE DEATH OF STELLA FOUR YEARS AGO.
HEY, TAKERU.
YOUR DAD'S HERE AGAIN TODAY.
HE'S DOWN-STAIRS.
I GUESS I'LL JUST SEND HIM ON HIS WAY?
YEAH.
IDOL

1/4 Sidebar No. 9

9

This sort of by-the-seat-of-the-pants approach makes things pretty rough for Takada-kun, my editor. Forgive me, Takada-kun! But it's too late for me to change an old habit. And anyway, doing so would take the fun out of drawing. Still, Takada's a strict but just editor!! Whether he's praising or condemning he's right on the mark. When I watch him work I think editing must be really interesting work --but I don't have the patience for it. Editing is hard work. You have to have the stamina for it. Still, it's really interesting to watch the editorial staff at work, how they go about making a manga take shape.

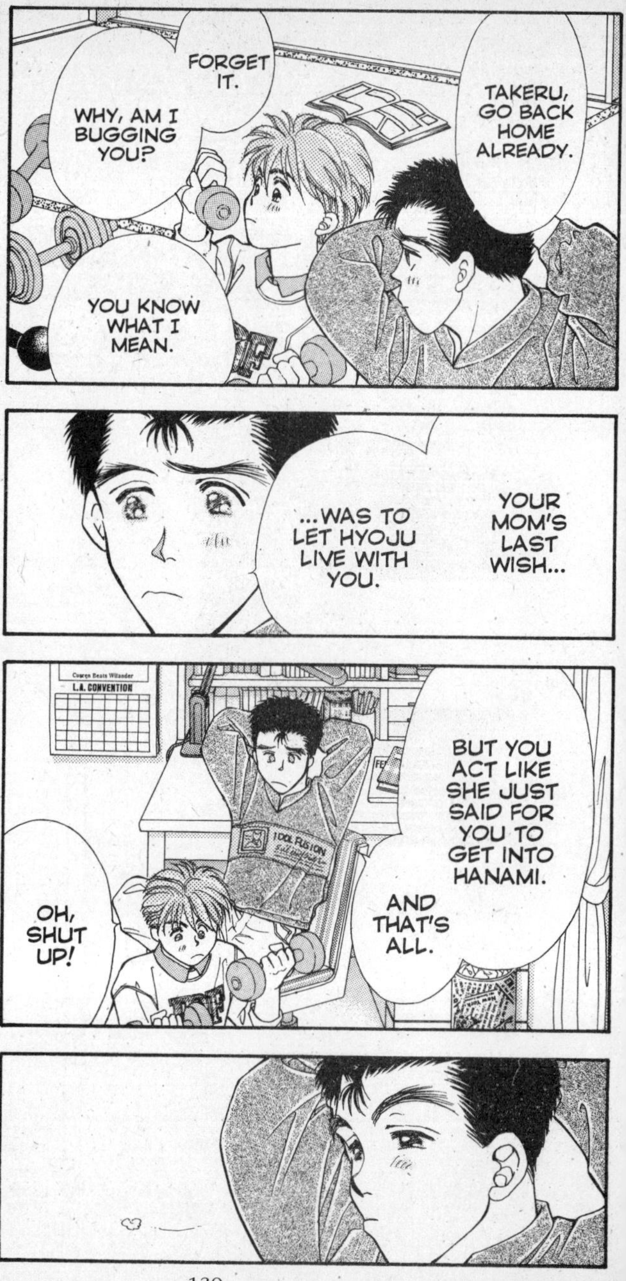

TAKERU, GO BACK HOME ALREADY.
FORGET IT.
WHY, AM I BUGGING YOU?
YOU KNOW WHAT I MEAN.
YOUR MOM'S LAST WISH...
...WAS TO LET HYOJU LIVE WITH YOU.
BUT YOU ACT LIKE SHE JUST SAID FOR YOU TO GET INTO HANAMI.
AND THAT'S ALL.
OH, SHUT UP!

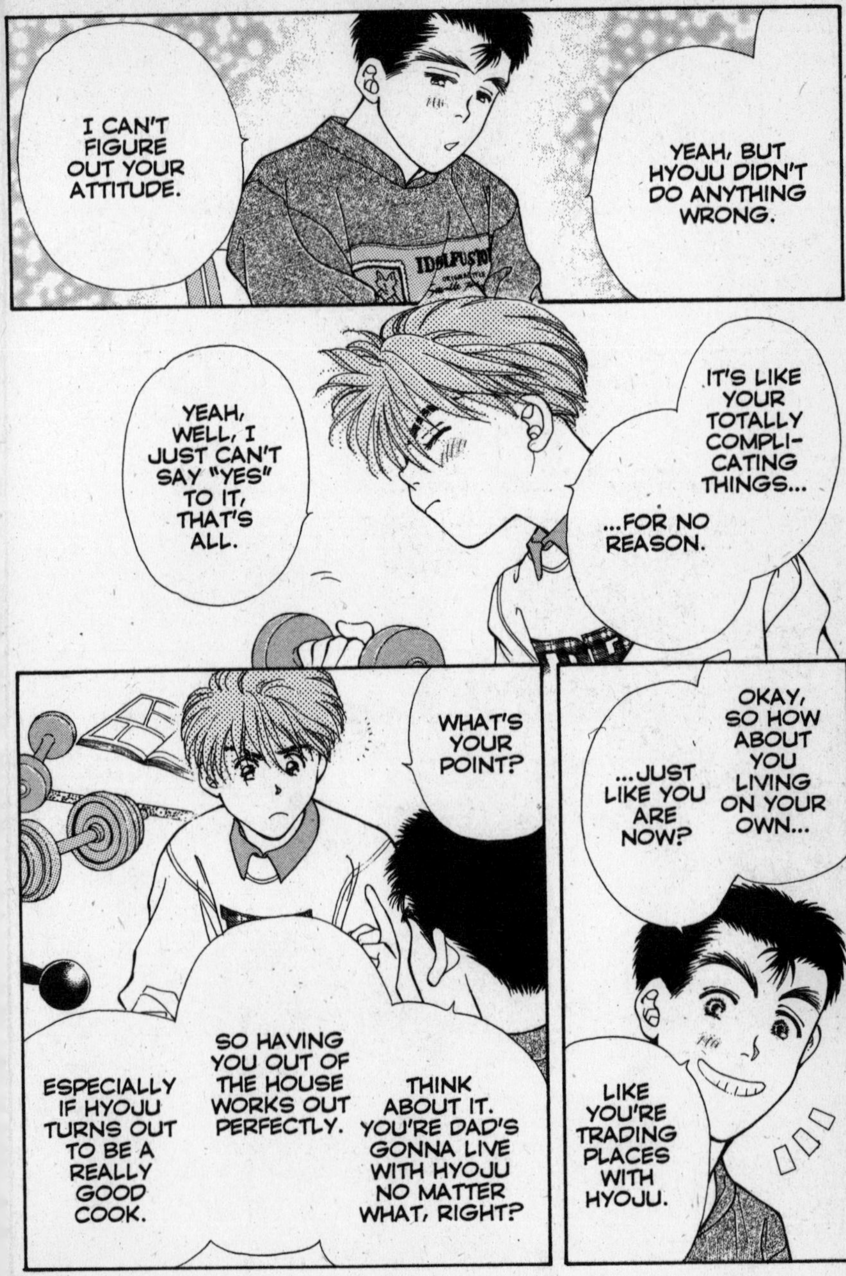
YEAH, BUT HYOJU DIDN'T DO ANYTHING WRONG.
I CAN'T FIGURE OUT YOUR ATTITUDE.
IT'S LIKE YOUR TOTALLY COMPLI-CATING THINGS...
...FOR NO REASON.
YEAH, WELL, I JUST CAN'T SAY "YES" TO IT, THAT'S ALL.
OKAY, SO HOW ABOUT YOU LIVING ON YOUR OWN...
...JUST LIKE YOU ARE NOW?
LIKE YOU'RE TRADING PLACES WITH HYOJU.
WHAT'S YOUR POINT?
THINK ABOUT IT. YOU'RE DAD'S GONNA LIVE WITH HYOJU NO MATTER WHAT, RIGHT?
SO HAVING YOU OUT OF THE HOUSE WORKS OUT PERFECTLY.
ESPECIALLY IF HYOJU TURNS OUT TO BE A REALLY GOOD COOK.

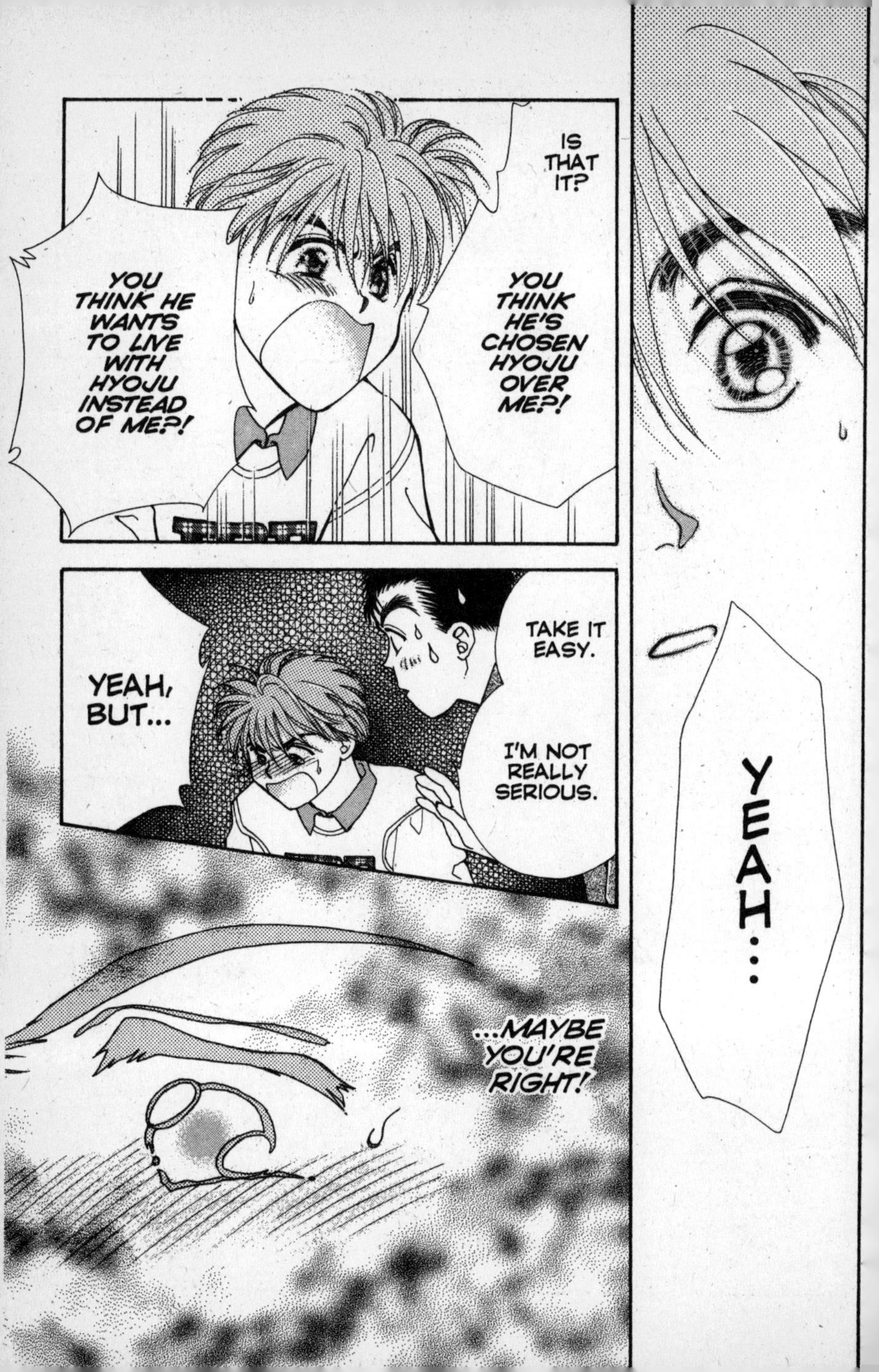
YEAH...
IS THAT IT?
YOU THINK HE'S CHOSEN HYOJU OVER ME?!
YOU THINK HE WANTS TO LIVE WITH HYOJU INSTEAD OF ME?!
TAKE IT EASY.
I'M NOT REALLY SERIOUS.
YEAH, BUT...
...MAYBE YOU'RE RIGHT!

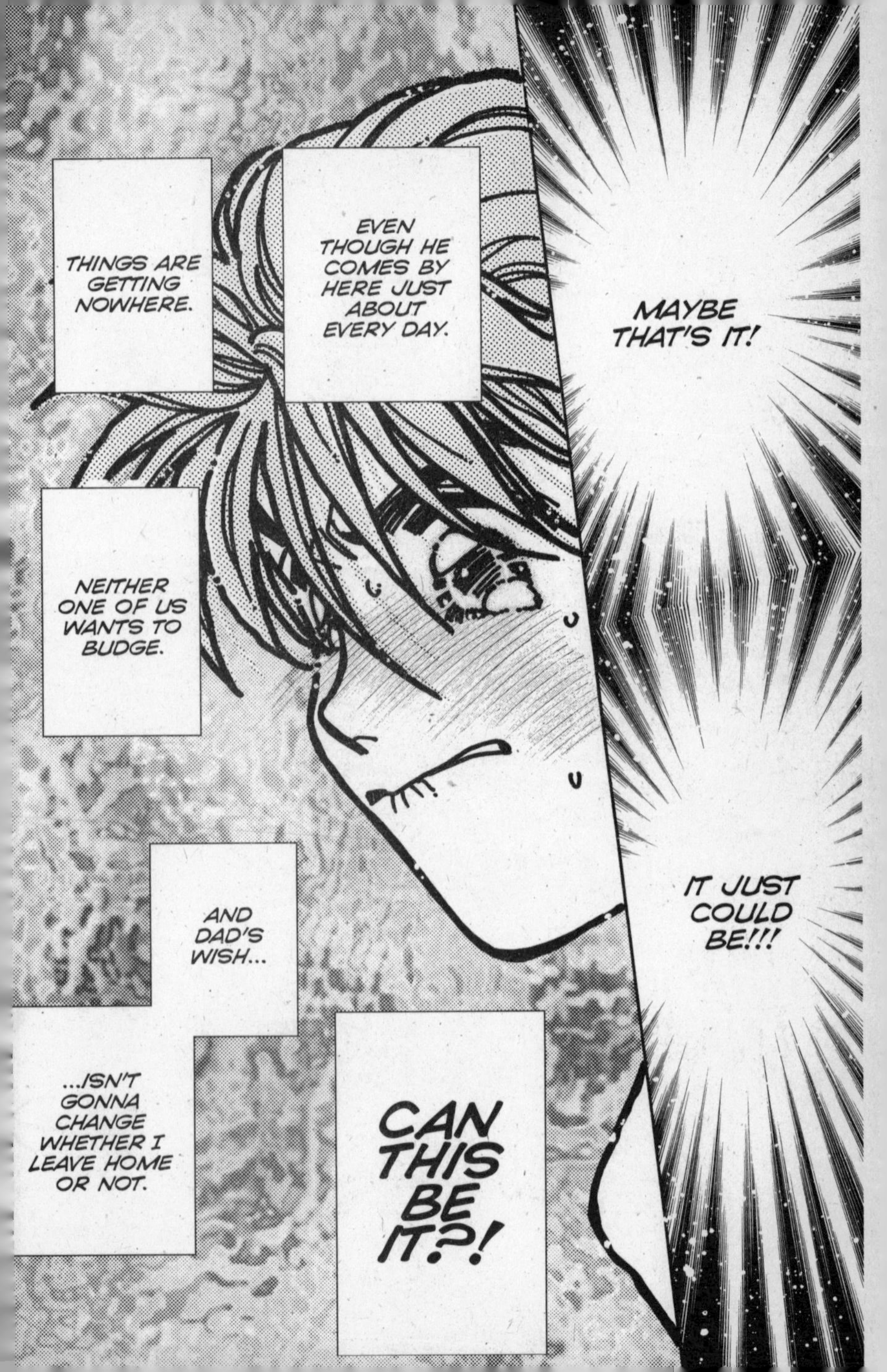
EVEN THOUGH HE COMES BY HERE JUST ABOUT EVERY DAY.
THINGS ARE GETTING NOWHERE.
NEITHER ONE OF US WANTS TO BUDGE.
AND DAD'S WISH...
...ISN'T GONNA CHANGE WHETHER I LEAVE HOME OR NOT.
CAN THIS BE IT?!
MAYBE THAT'S IT!
IT JUST COULD BE!!!

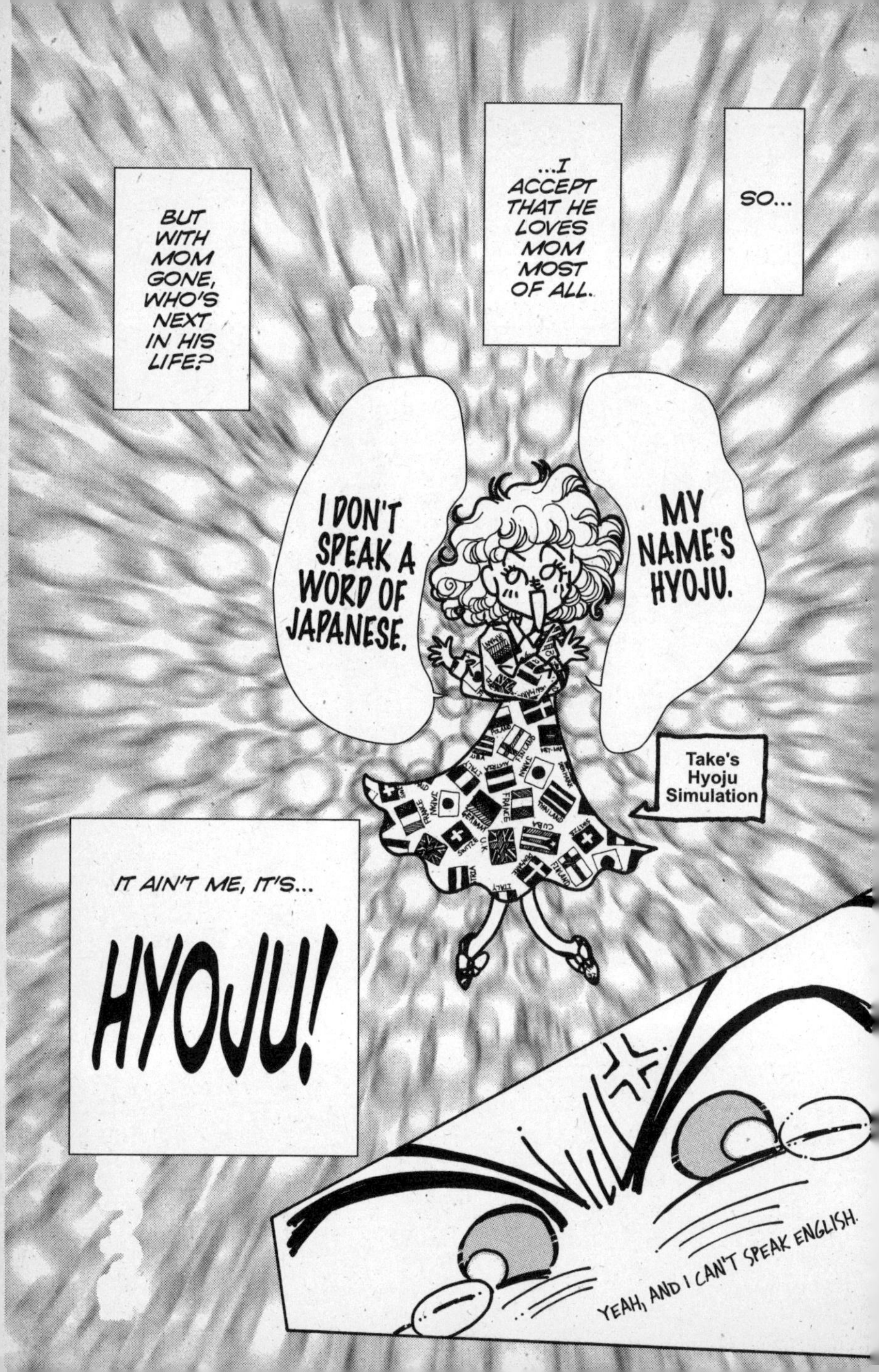
SO...
...I ACCEPT THAT HE LOVES MOM MOST OF ALL.
BUT WITH MOM GONE, WHO'S NEXT IN HIS LIFE?
MY NAME'S HYOJU.
I DON'T SPEAK A WORD OF JAPANESE.
Take's Hyoju Simulation
IT AIN'T ME, IT'S...
HYOJU!
YEAH, AND I CAN'T SPEAK ENGLISH.

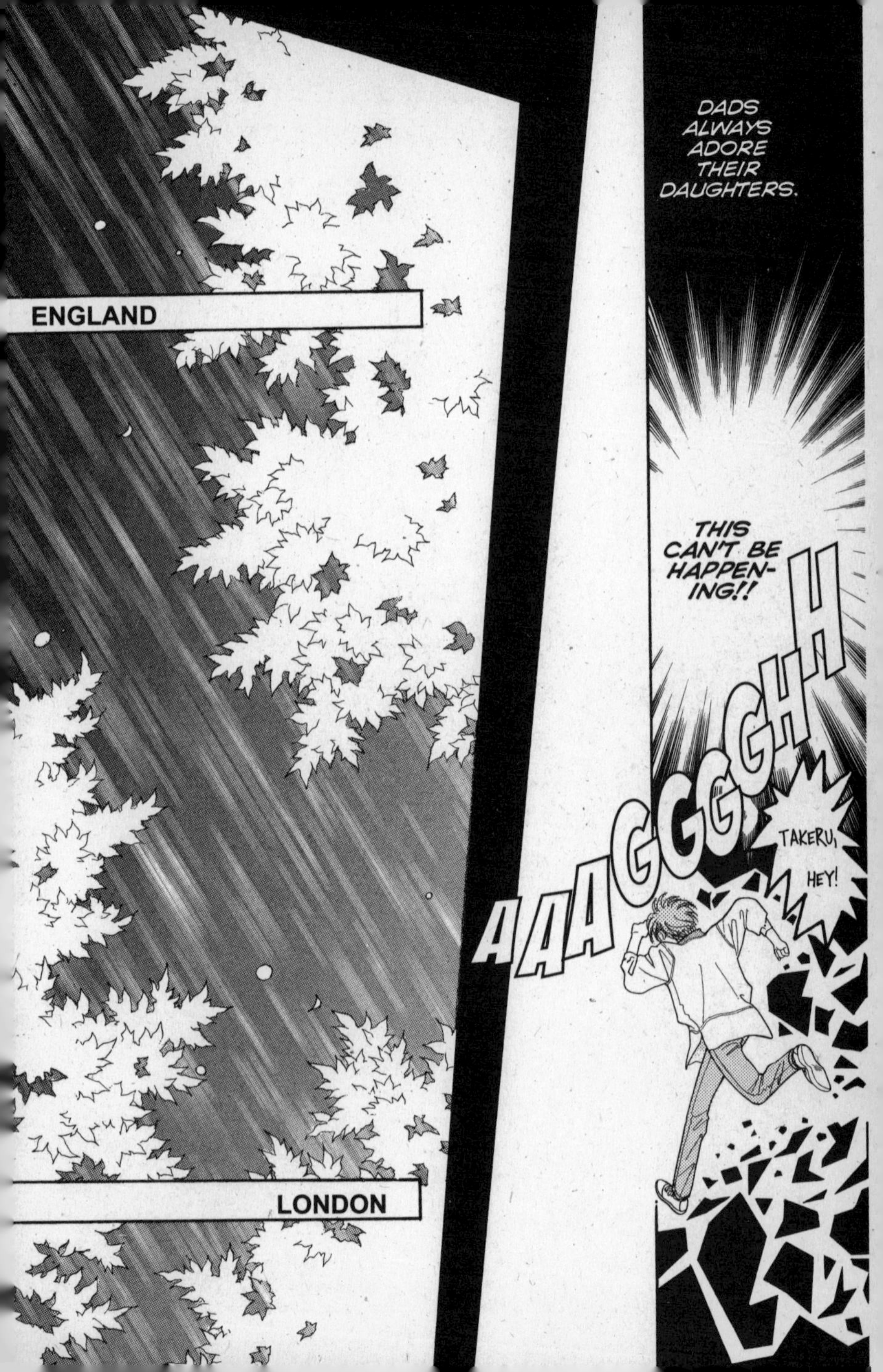
DADS ALWAYS ADORE THEIR DAUGHTERS.
THIS CAN'T BE HAPPEN-ING!!
AAAGGGGHH
TAKERU, HEY!
ENGLAND
LONDON

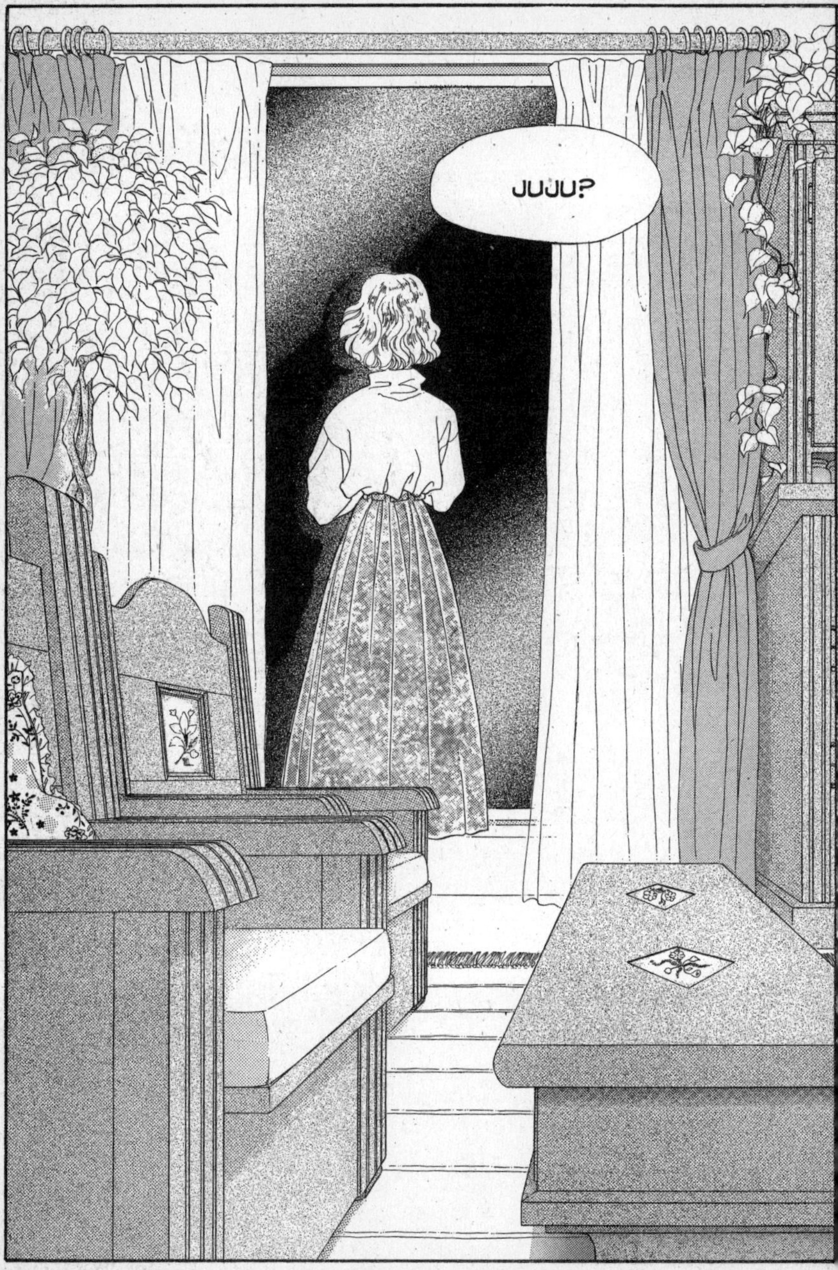
JUJU?

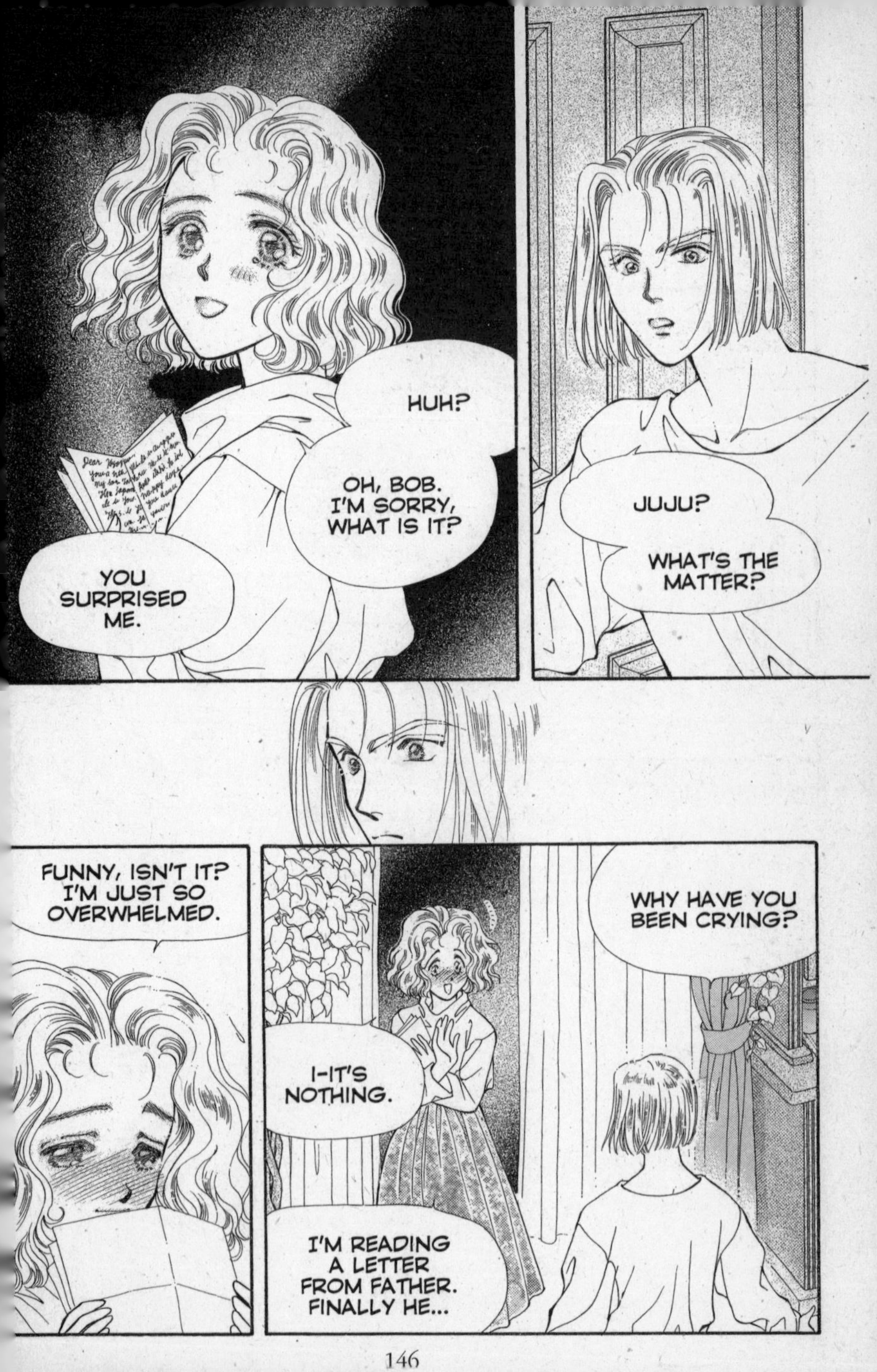
JUJU?
WHAT'S THE MATTER?
HUH?
OH, BOB. I'M SORRY, WHAT IS IT?
YOU SURPRISED ME.
WHY HAVE YOU BEEN CRYING?
I-IT'S NOTHING.
I'M READING A LETTER FROM FATHER. FINALLY HE...
FUNNY, ISN'T IT? I'M JUST SO OVERWHELMED.

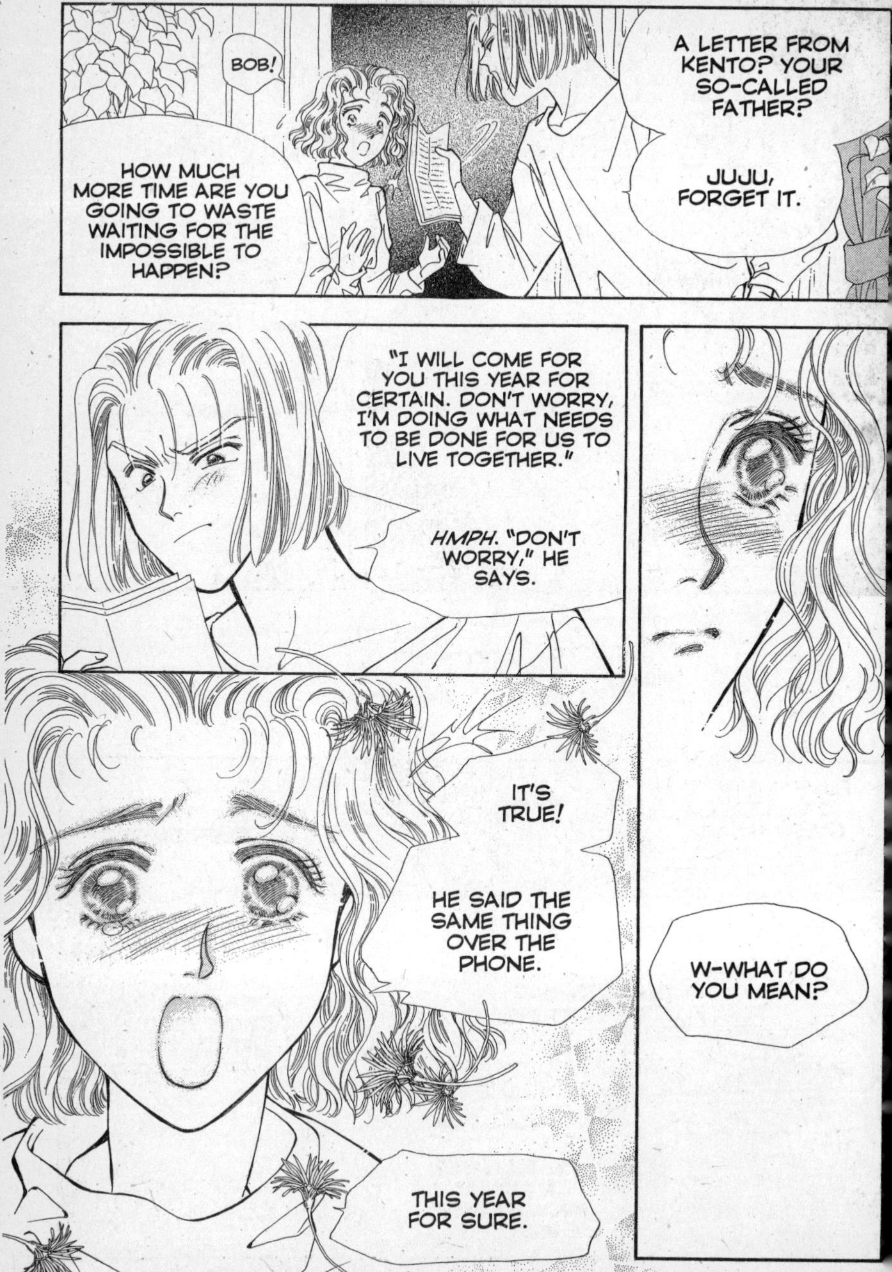
A LETTER FROM KENTO? YOUR SO-CALLED FATHER?
JUJU, FORGET IT.
BOB!
HOW MUCH MORE TIME ARE YOU GOING TO WASTE WAITING FOR THE IMPOSSIBLE TO HAPPEN?
W-WHAT DO YOU MEAN?
"I WILL COME FOR YOU THIS YEAR FOR CERTAIN. DON'T WORRY, I'M DOING WHAT NEEDS TO BE DONE FOR US TO LIVE TOGETHER."
HMPH. "DON'T WORRY," HE SAYS.
IT'S TRUE!
HE SAID THE SAME THING OVER THE PHONE.
THIS YEAR FOR SURE.

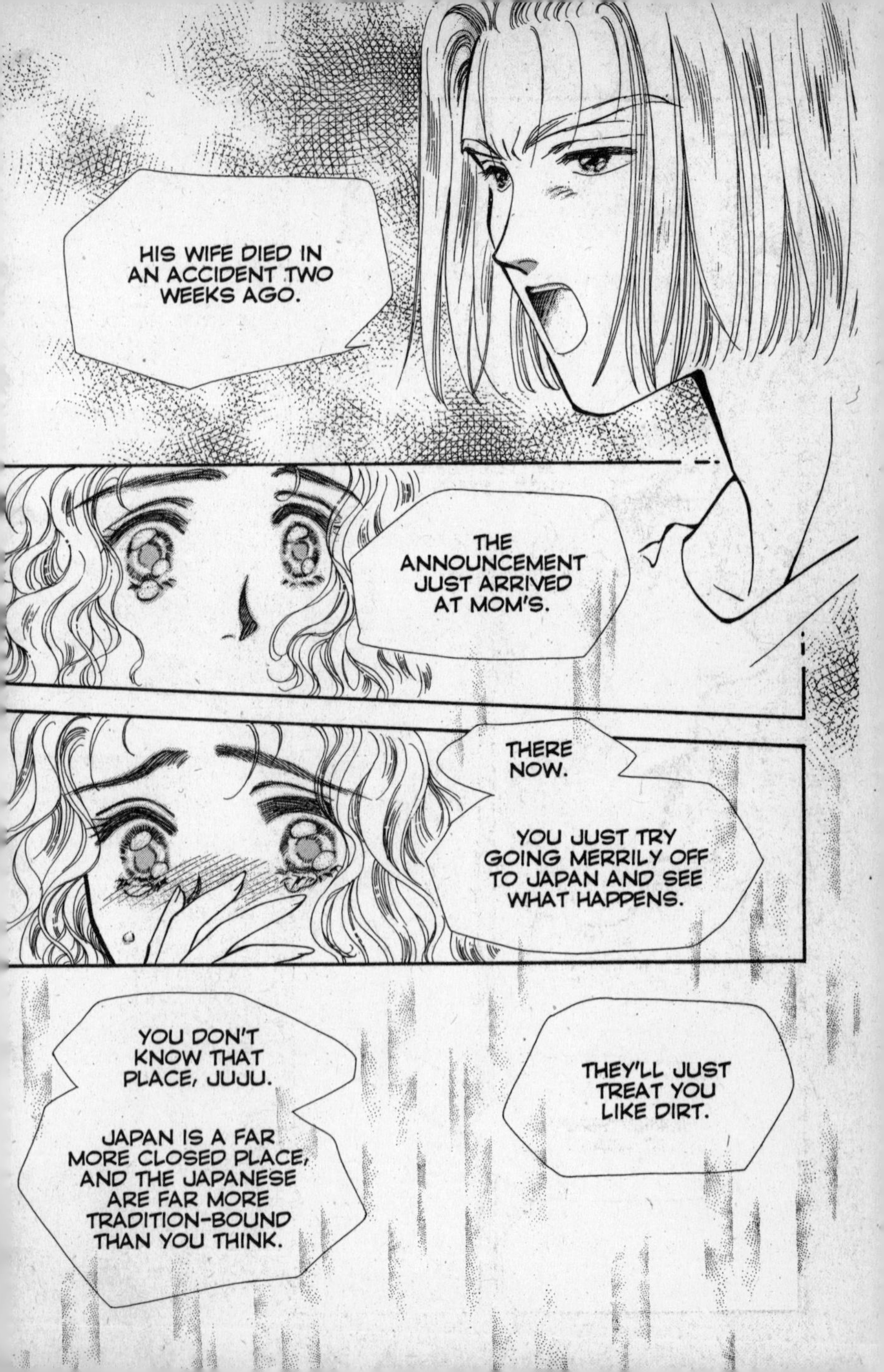
HIS WIFE DIED IN AN ACCIDENT TWO WEEKS AGO.
THE ANNOUNCEMENT JUST ARRIVED AT MOM'S.
THERE NOW.
YOU JUST TRY GOING MERRILY OFF TO JAPAN AND SEE WHAT HAPPENS.
THEY'LL JUST TREAT YOU LIKE DIRT.
YOU DON'T KNOW THAT PLACE, JUJU.
JAPAN IS A FAR MORE CLOSED PLACE, AND THE JAPANESE ARE FAR MORE TRADITION-BOUND THAN YOU THINK.

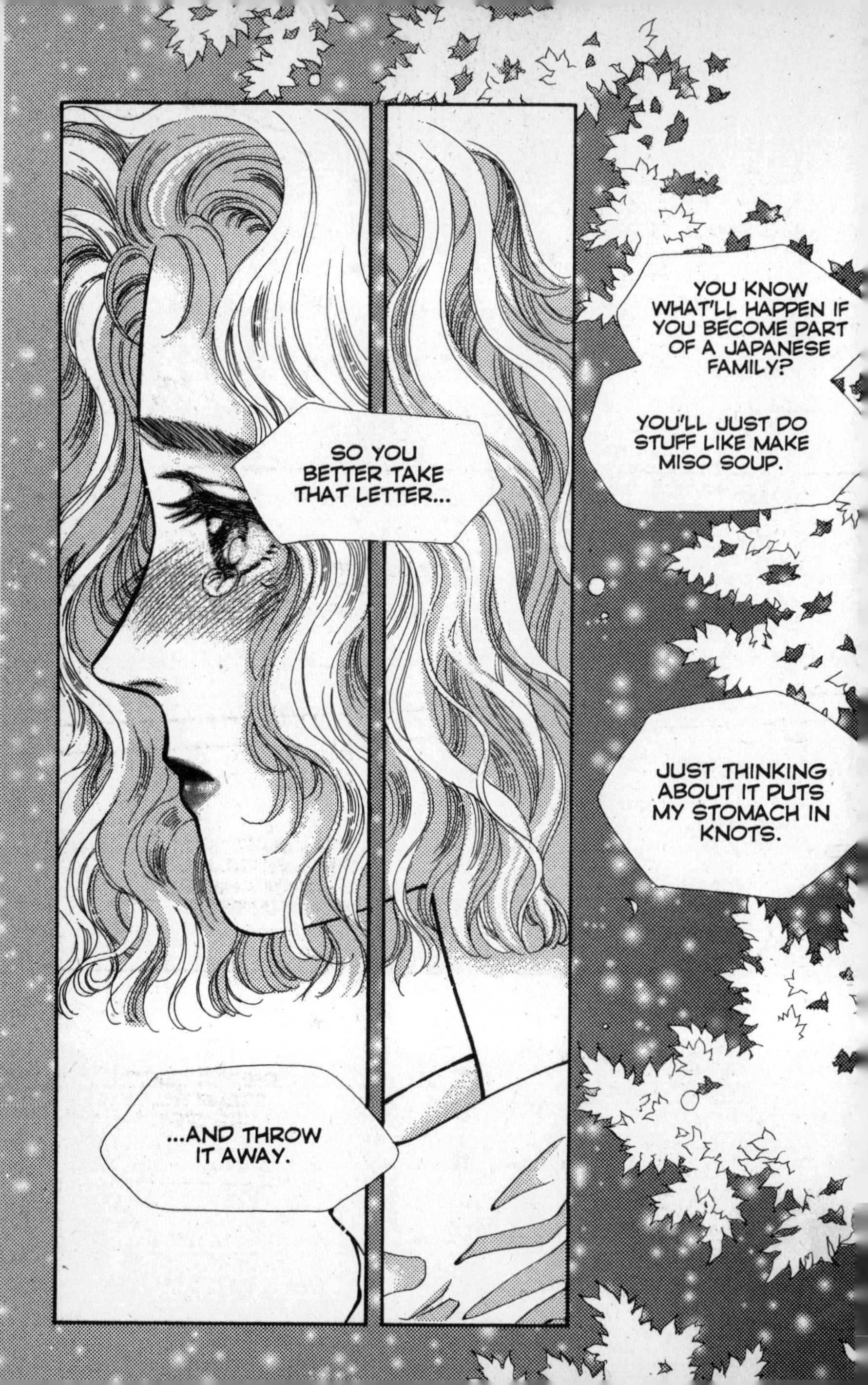
YOU KNOW WHAT'LL HAPPEN IF YOU BECOME PART OF A JAPANESE FAMILY?
YOU'LL JUST DO STUFF LIKE MAKE MISO SOUP.
JUST THINKING ABOUT IT PUTS MY STOMACH IN KNOTS.
SO YOU BETTER TAKE THAT LETTER...
...AND THROW IT AWAY.

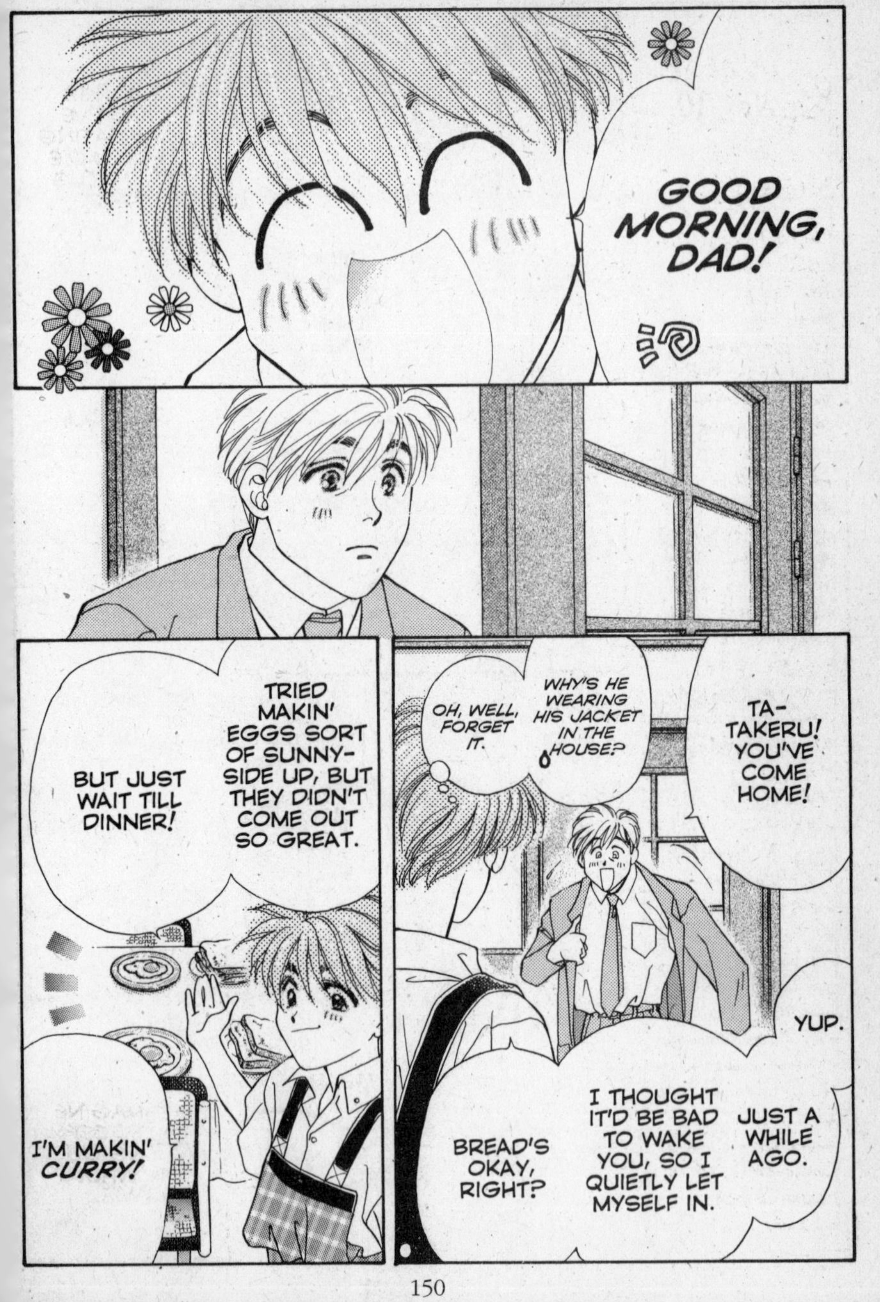
GOOD MORNING, DAD!
TA- TAKERU! YOU'VE COME HOME!
WHY'S HE WEARING HIS JACKET IN THE HOUSE?
OH, WELL, FORGET IT.
YUP.
JUST A WHILE AGO.
I THOUGHT IT'D BE BAD TO WAKE YOU, SO I QUIETLY LET MYSELF IN.
BREAD'S OKAY, RIGHT?
TRIED MAKIN' EGGS SORT OF SUNNY-SIDE UP, BUT THEY DIDN'T COME OUT SO GREAT.
BUT JUST WAIT TILL DINNER!
I'M MAKIN' *CURRY!*

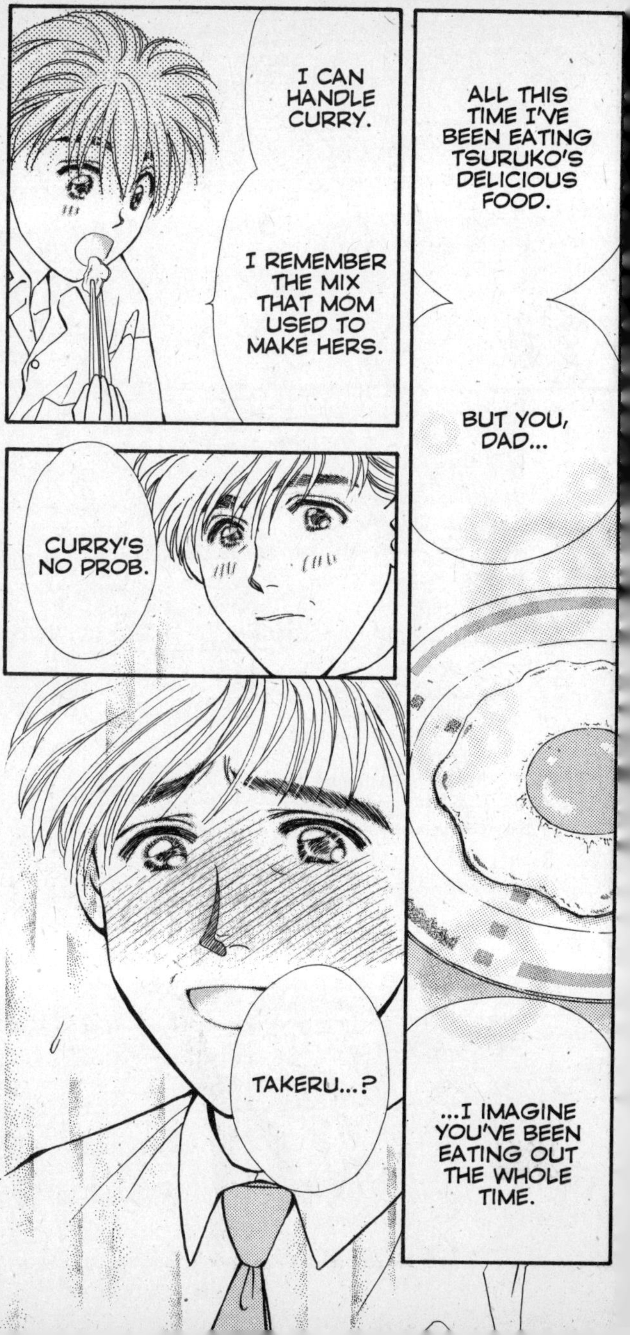
ALL THIS TIME I'VE BEEN EATING TSURUKO'S DELICIOUS FOOD.
BUT YOU, DAD...
...I IMAGINE YOU'VE BEEN EATING OUT THE WHOLE TIME.
I CAN HANDLE CURRY.
I REMEMBER THE MIX THAT MOM USED TO MAKE HERS.
CURRY'S NO PROB.
TAKERU...?

1/4 Sidebar No. 10

≡10≡

When you look up the word "tower" in the dictionary, you'll find something like "a tall, four-sided structure for observation." It just happens that before I started this series I climbed a high tower together with my staff called Tokyo Tower, probably the highest tower around these parts. I've always loved to gaze at the night sky from atop high places. And since I've been doing manga, I've always turned my gaze to the night sky whenever I'm working on a new story. At times like that, I think how I want, more than anything, a tower of my own. A tower can't be a tower as long as it has a roof over it, and I think right now what I really want most of all is to find a tower I can climb up whenever I want. Or maybe I'll even build my own.

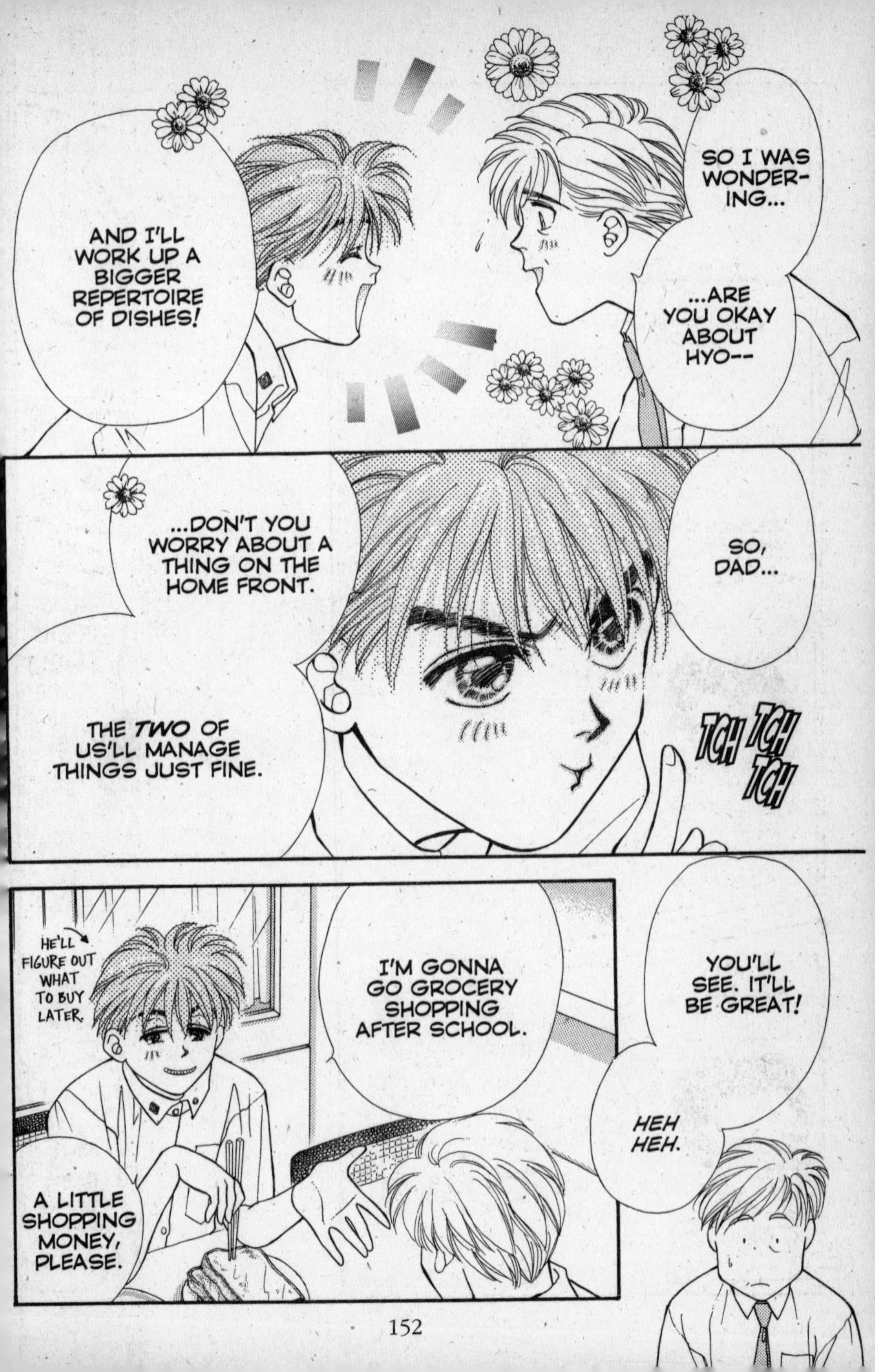
SO I WAS WONDER-ING...
...ARE YOU OKAY ABOUT HYO--
AND I'LL WORK UP A BIGGER REPERTOIRE OF DISHES!
SO, DAD...
TCH TCH TCH
...DON'T YOU WORRY ABOUT A THING ON THE HOME FRONT.
THE *TWO* OF US'LL MANAGE THINGS JUST FINE.
YOU'LL SEE. IT'LL BE GREAT!
HEH HEH.
I'M GONNA GO GROCERY SHOPPING AFTER SCHOOL.
HE'LL FIGURE OUT WHAT TO BUY LATER.
A LITTLE SHOPPING MONEY, PLEASE.

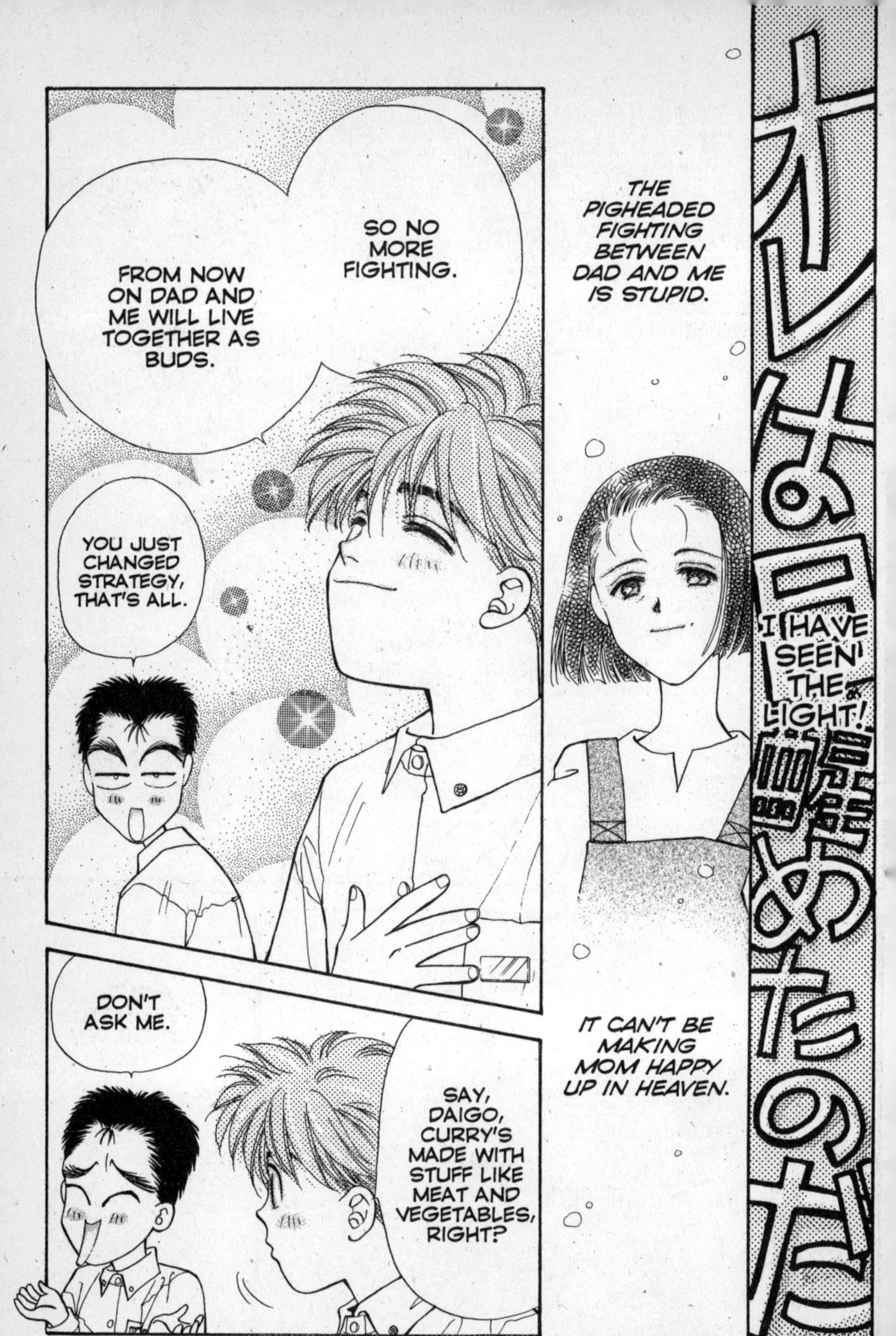
THE PIGHEADED FIGHTING BETWEEN DAD AND ME IS STUPID.
IT CAN'T BE MAKING MOM HAPPY UP IN HEAVEN.
I HAVE SEEN THE LIGHT!
FROM NOW ON DAD AND ME WILL LIVE TOGETHER AS BUDS.
SO NO MORE FIGHTING.
YOU JUST CHANGED STRATEGY, THAT'S ALL.
SAY, DAIGO, CURRY'S MADE WITH STUFF LIKE MEAT AND VEGETABLES, RIGHT?
DON'T ASK ME.

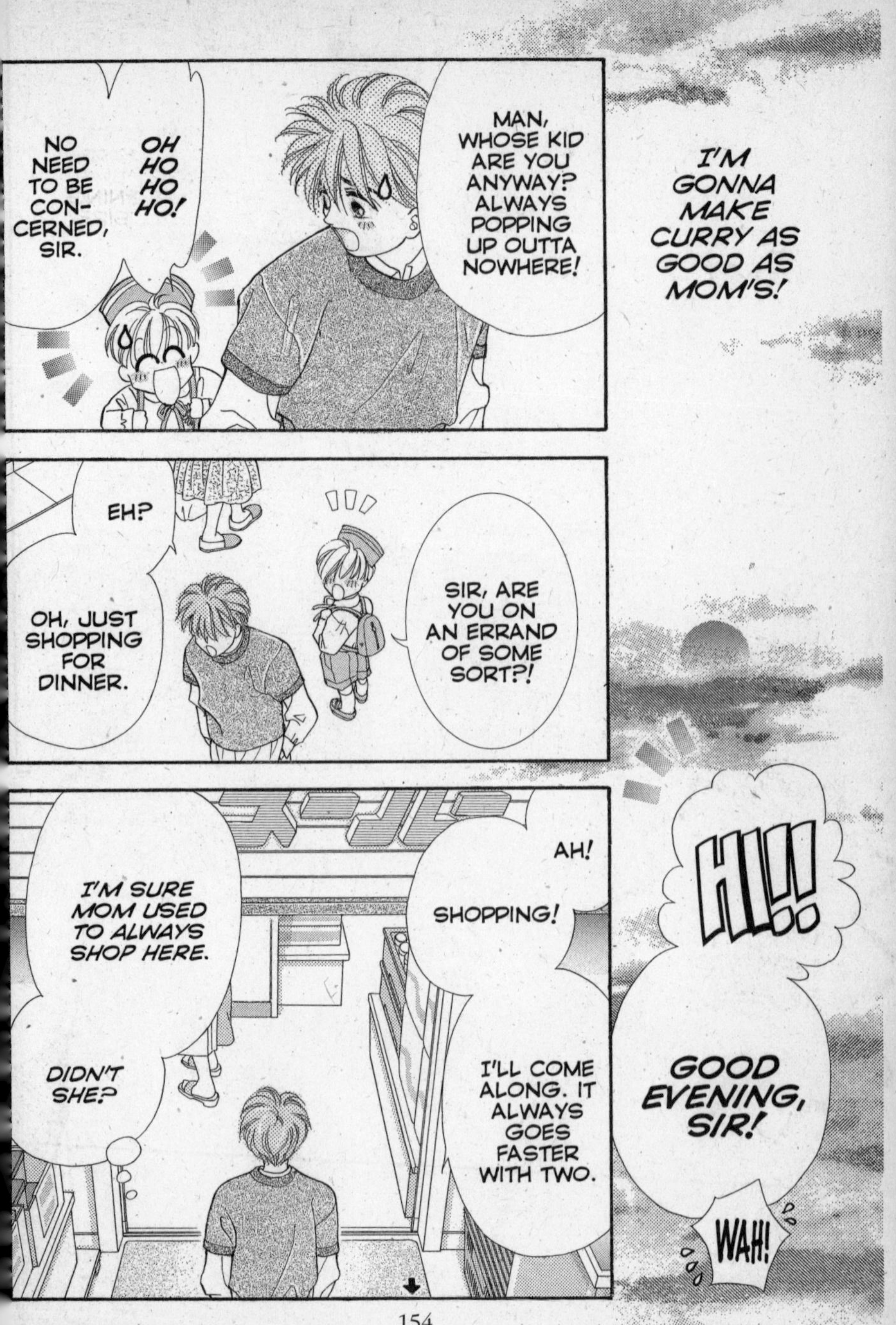
I'M GONNA MAKE CURRY AS GOOD AS MOM'S!
HI!!
GOOD EVENING, SIR!
WAH!
MAN, WHOSE KID ARE YOU ANYWAY? ALWAYS POPPING UP OUTTA NOWHERE!
OH HO HO HO!
NO NEED TO BE CON-CERNED, SIR.
SIR, ARE YOU ON AN ERRAND OF SOME SORT?!
EH?
OH, JUST SHOPPING FOR DINNER.
AH!
SHOPPING!
I'LL COME ALONG. IT ALWAYS GOES FASTER WITH TWO.
I'M SURE MOM USED TO ALWAYS SHOP HERE.
DIDN'T SHE?

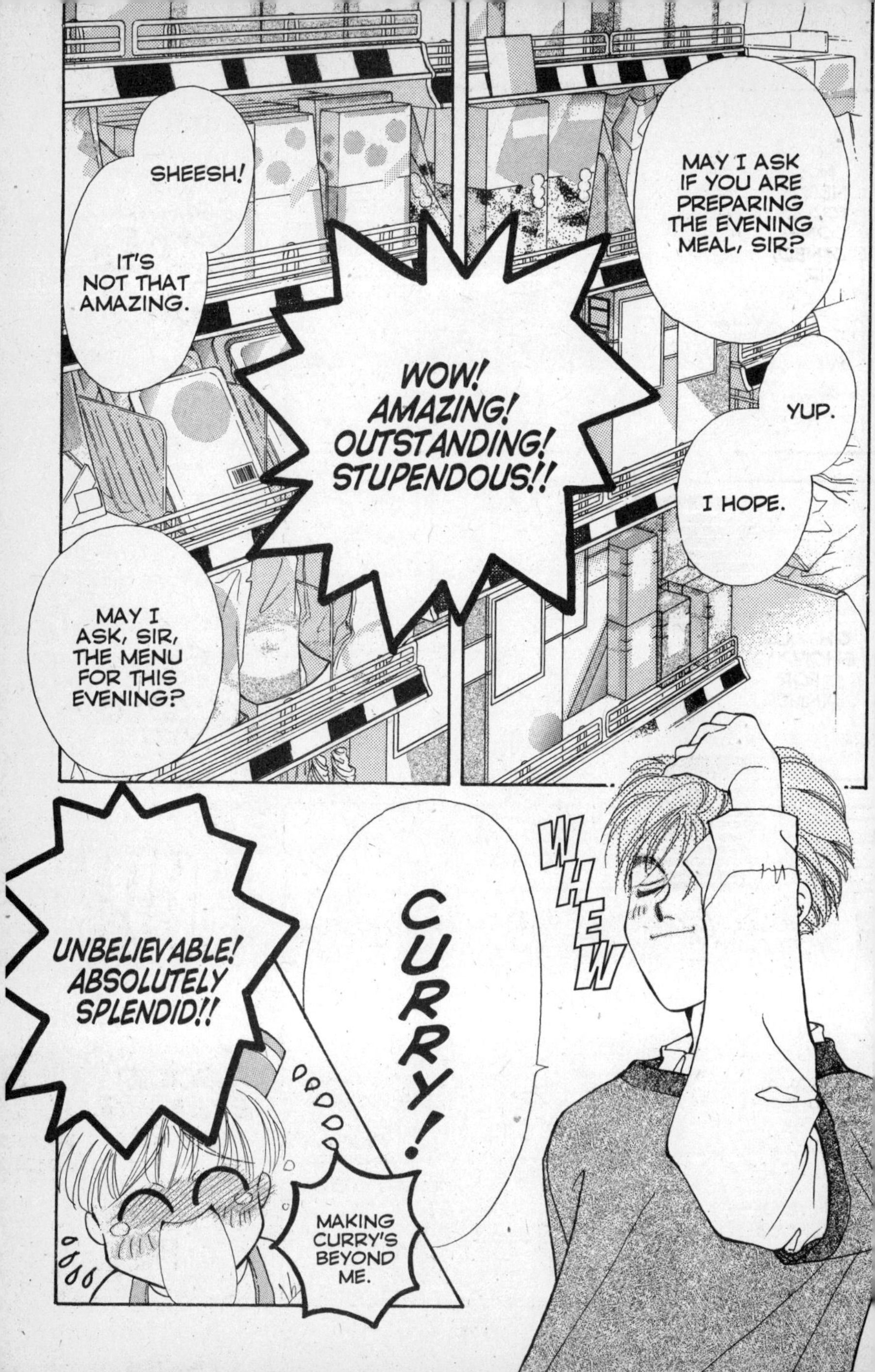
MAY I ASK IF YOU ARE PREPARING THE EVENING MEAL, SIR?
YUP.
I HOPE.
WOW! AMAZING! OUTSTANDING! STUPENDOUS!!
SHEESH!
IT'S NOT THAT AMAZING.
MAY I ASK, SIR, THE MENU FOR THIS EVENING?
WHEW
CURRY!
UNBELIEVABLE! ABSOLUTELY SPLENDID!!
MAKING CURRY'S BEYOND ME.

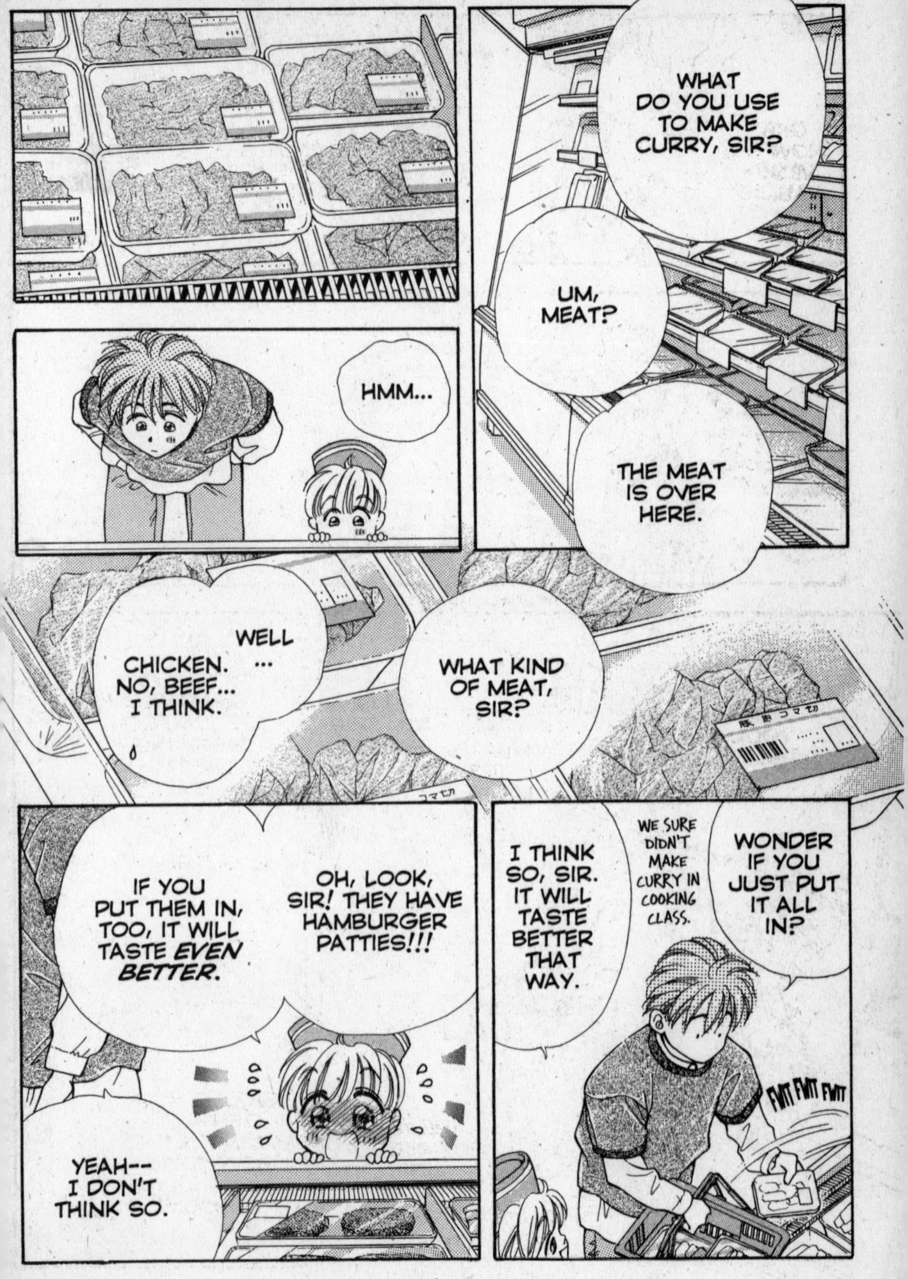
WHAT DO YOU USE TO MAKE CURRY, SIR?
UM, MEAT?
THE MEAT IS OVER HERE.
HMM...
WHAT KIND OF MEAT, SIR?
WELL ...
CHICKEN. NO, BEEF... I THINK.
WONDER IF YOU JUST PUT IT ALL IN?
WE SURE DIDN'T MAKE CURRY IN COOKING CLASS.
I THINK SO, SIR. IT WILL TASTE BETTER THAT WAY.
FWIT FWIT FWIT
OH, LOOK, SIR! THEY HAVE HAMBURGER PATTIES!!!
IF YOU PUT THEM IN, TOO, IT WILL TASTE *EVEN BETTER*.
YEAH-- I DON'T THINK SO.

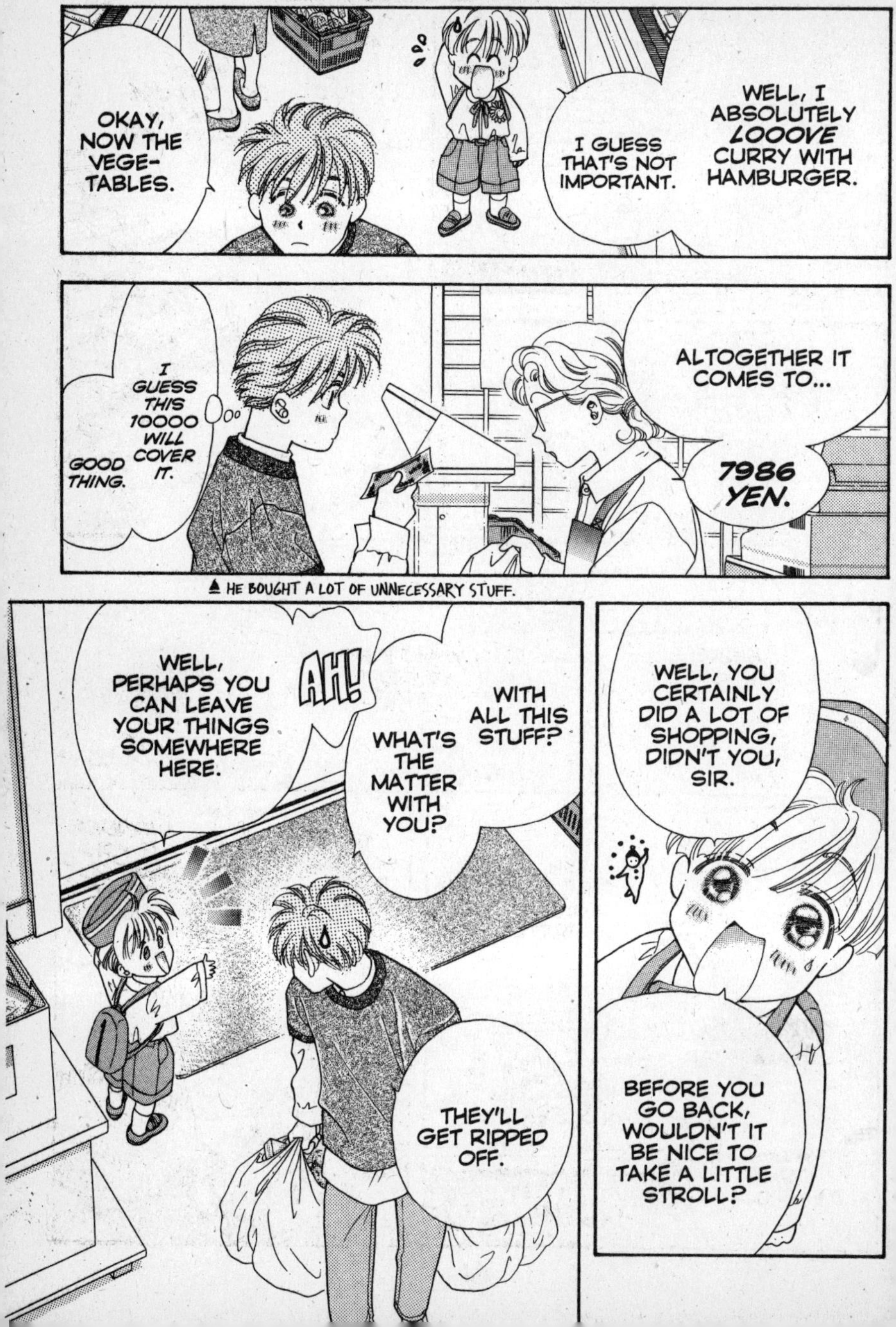
WELL, I ABSOLUTELY *LOOOVE* CURRY WITH HAMBURGER.
I GUESS THAT'S NOT IMPORTANT.
OKAY, NOW THE VEGE-TABLES.
ALTOGETHER IT COMES TO...
7986 YEN.
I GUESS THIS 10000 WILL COVER IT.
GOOD THING.
HE BOUGHT A LOT OF UNNECESSARY STUFF.
WELL, YOU CERTAINLY DID A LOT OF SHOPPING, DIDN'T YOU, SIR.
BEFORE YOU GO BACK, WOULDN'T IT BE NICE TO TAKE A LITTLE STROLL?
WITH ALL THIS STUFF?
WHAT'S THE MATTER WITH YOU?
AH!
WELL, PERHAPS YOU CAN LEAVE YOUR THINGS SOMEWHERE HERE.
THEY'LL GET RIPPED OFF.

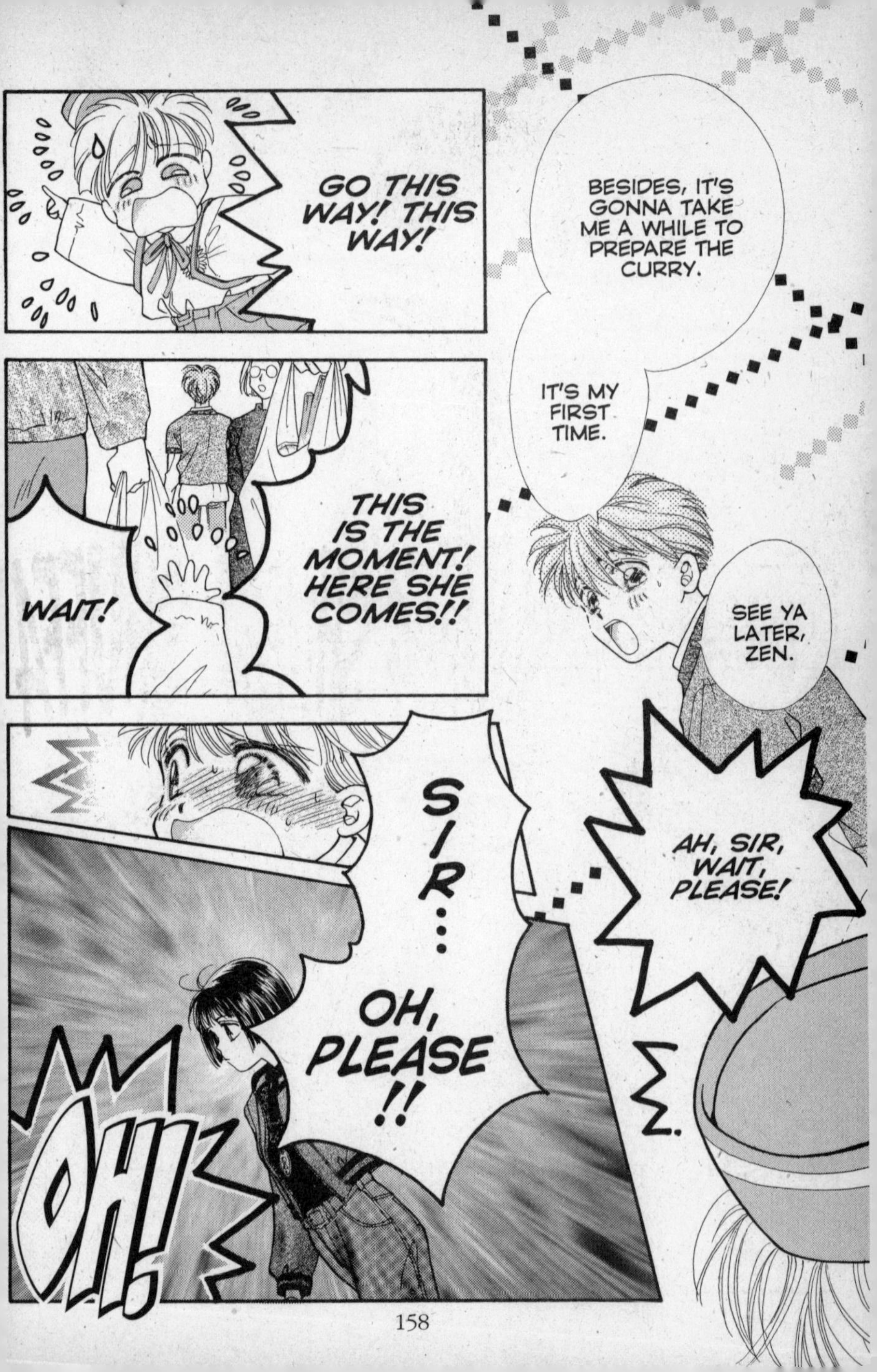
BESIDES, IT'S GONNA TAKE ME A WHILE TO PREPARE THE CURRY.
IT'S MY FIRST TIME.
SEE YA LATER, ZEN.
GO THIS WAY! THIS WAY!
THIS IS THE MOMENT! HERE SHE COMES!!
WAIT!
AH, SIR, WAIT, PLEASE!
SIR...
OH, PLEASE!!
OH!

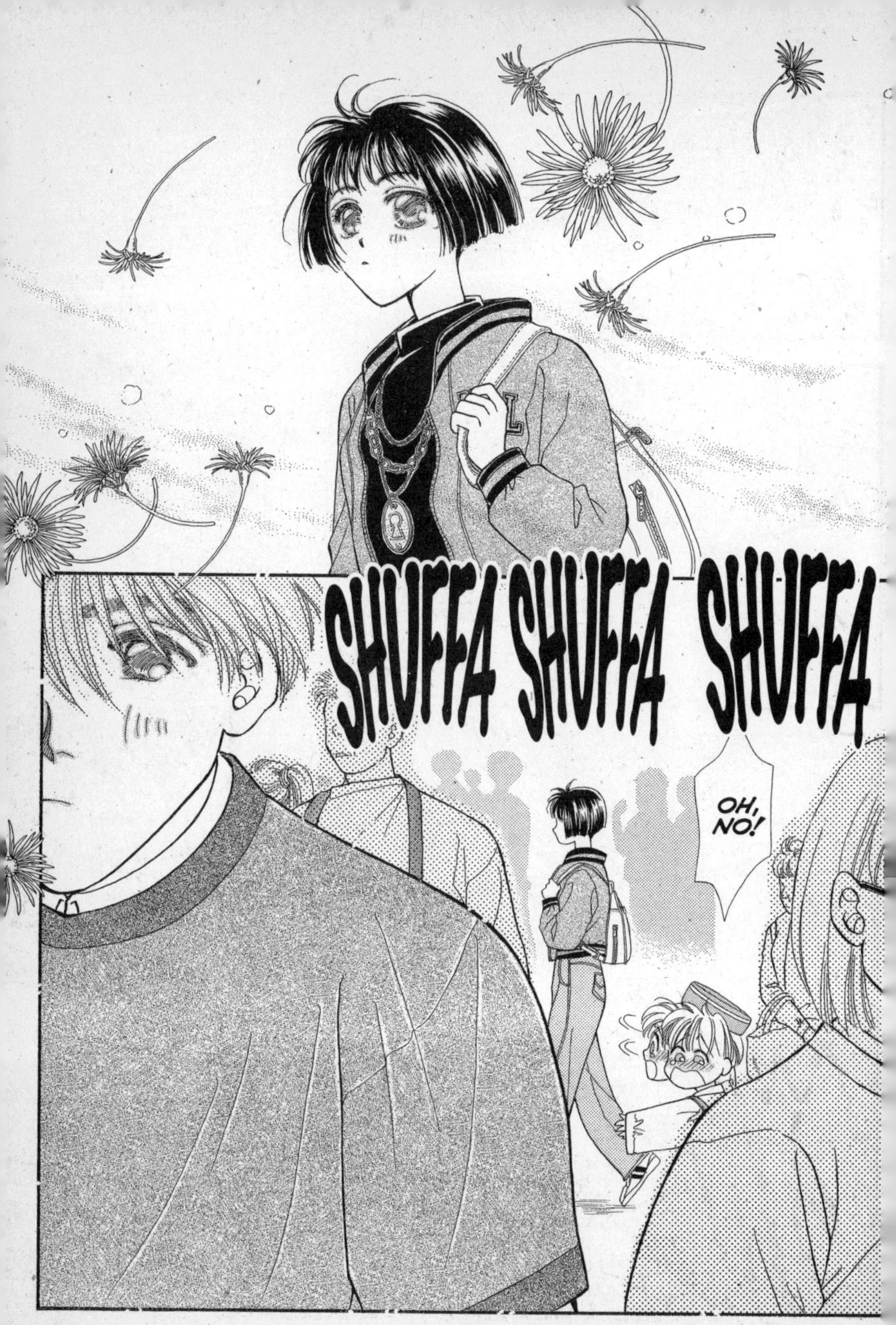
SHUFFA SHUFFA SHUFFA
OH, NO!

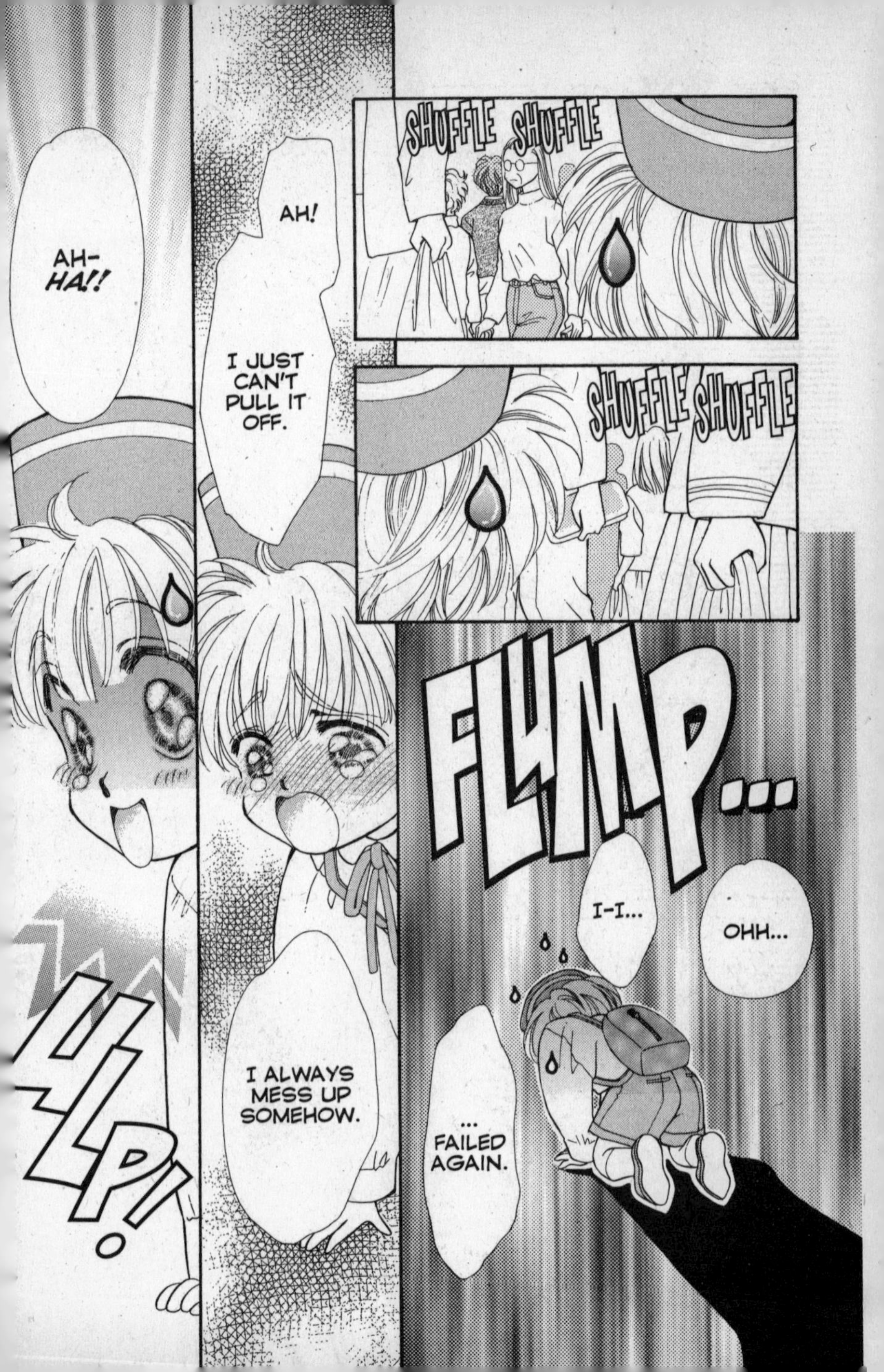
SHUFFLE SHUFFLE
SHUFFLE SHUFFLE
FLUMP...
OHH...
I-I...
...FAILED AGAIN.
AH!
I JUST CAN'T PULL IT OFF.
I ALWAYS MESS UP SOMEHOW.
AH-HA!!
ULP!?

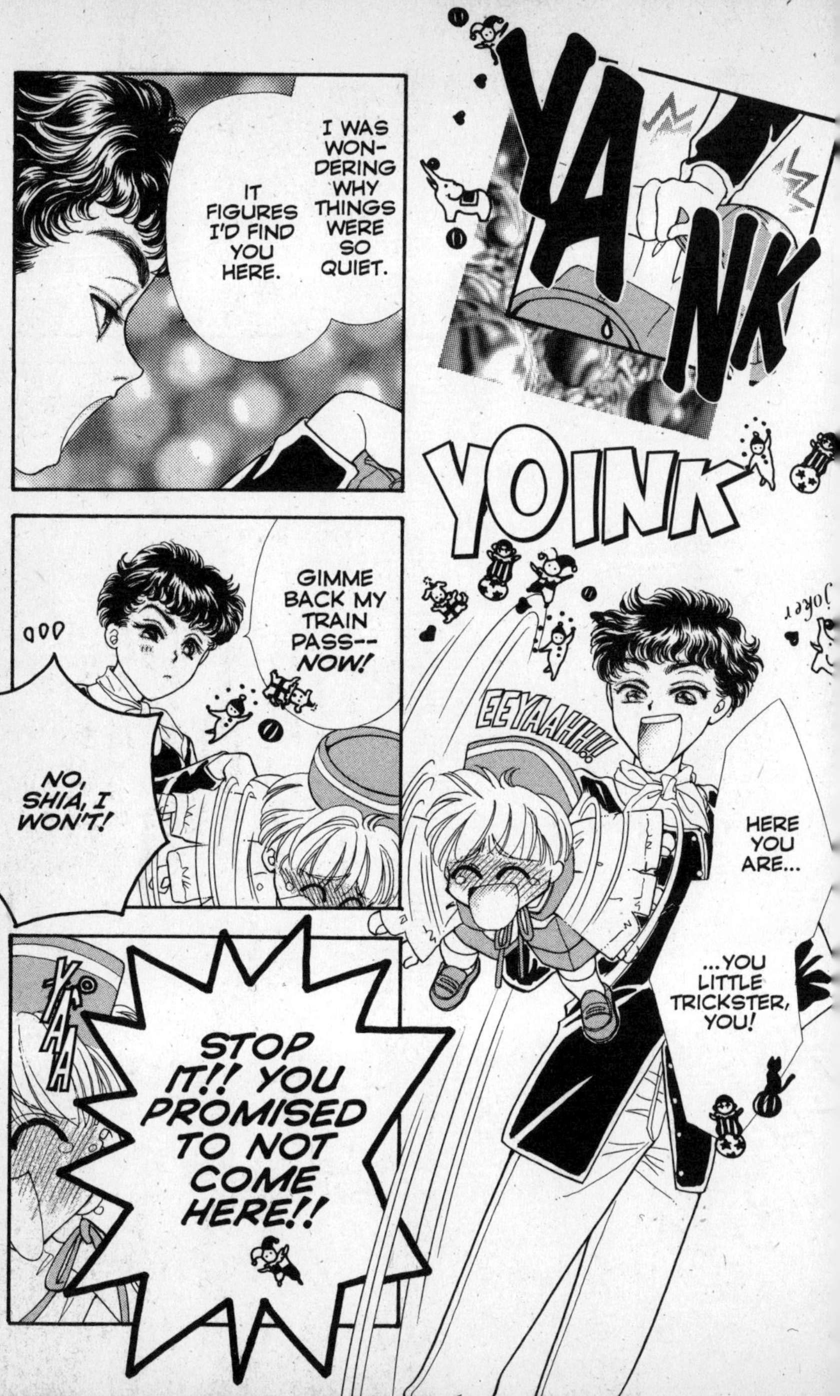
YANK
I WAS WONDERING WHY THINGS WERE SO QUIET.
IT FIGURES I'D FIND YOU HERE.
YOINK
EEYAAHH!!
HERE YOU ARE...
...YOU LITTLE TRICKSTER, YOU!
GIMME BACK MY TRAIN PASS-- NOW!
NO, SHIA, I WON'T!
YAAA
STOP IT!! YOU PROMISED TO NOT COME HERE!!

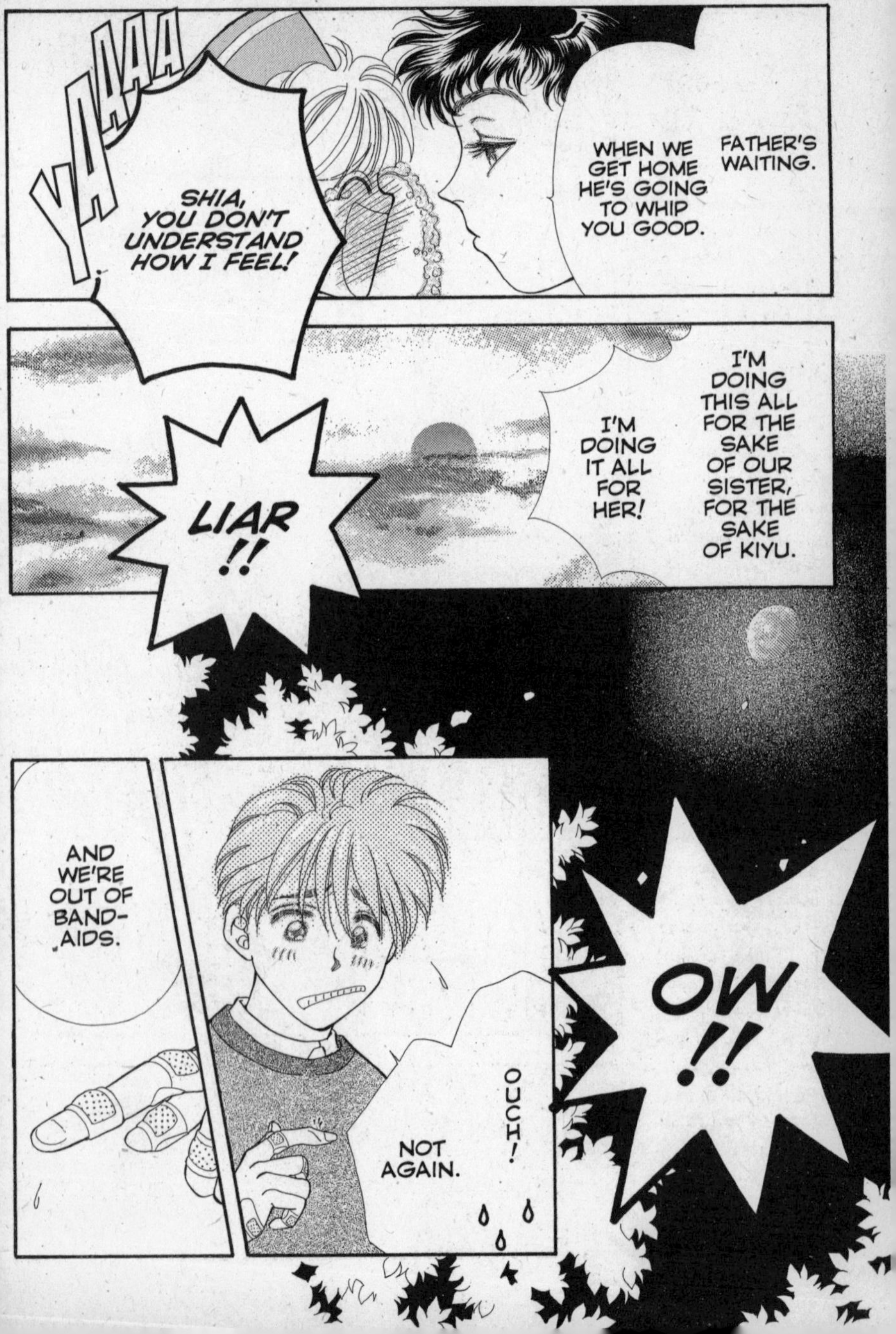
FATHER'S WAITING.
WHEN WE GET HOME HE'S GOING TO WHIP YOU GOOD.
YAAAA
SHIA, YOU DON'T UNDERSTAND HOW I FEEL!
I'M DOING THIS ALL FOR THE SAKE OF OUR SISTER, FOR THE SAKE OF KIYU.
I'M DOING IT ALL FOR HER!
LIAR!!
OW!!
OUCH!
NOT AGAIN.
AND WE'RE OUT OF BAND-AIDS.

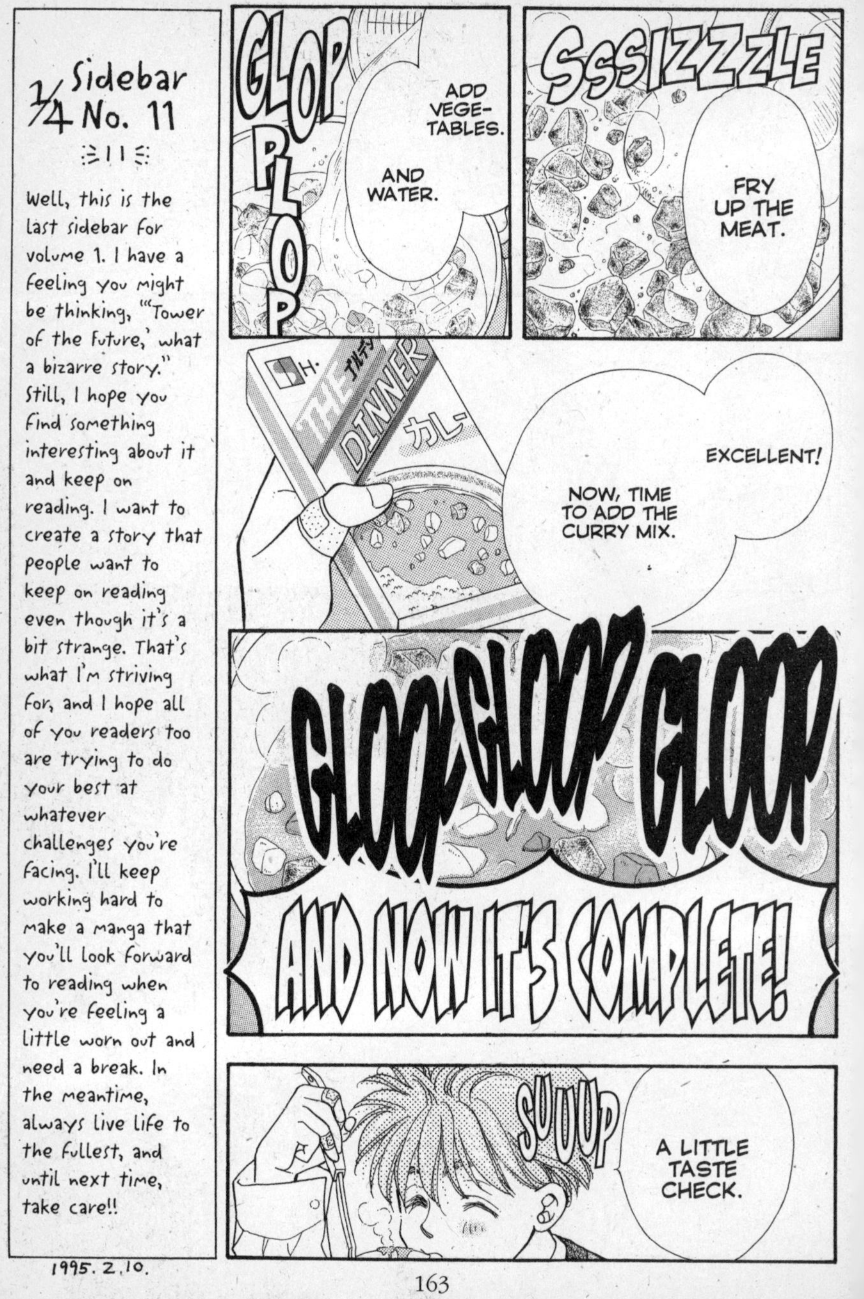
SSSIZZZZLE
FRY UP THE MEAT.
GLOP PLOP
ADD VEGETABLES.
AND WATER.
THE DINNER
カレー
EXCELLENT!
NOW, TIME TO ADD THE CURRY MIX.
GLOOP GLOOP GLOOP
AND NOW IT'S COMPLETE!
SUUUP
A LITTLE TASTE CHECK.

1/4 Sidebar No. 11

Well, this is the last sidebar for volume 1. I have a feeling you might be thinking, "'Tower of the Future,' what a bizarre story." Still, I hope you find something interesting about it and keep on reading. I want to create a story that people want to keep on reading even though it's a bit strange. That's what I'm striving for, and I hope all of you readers too are trying to do your best at whatever challenges you're facing. I'll keep working hard to make a manga that you'll look forward to reading when you're feeling a little worn out and need a break. In the meantime, always live life to the fullest, and until next time, take care!!

1995. 2.10.

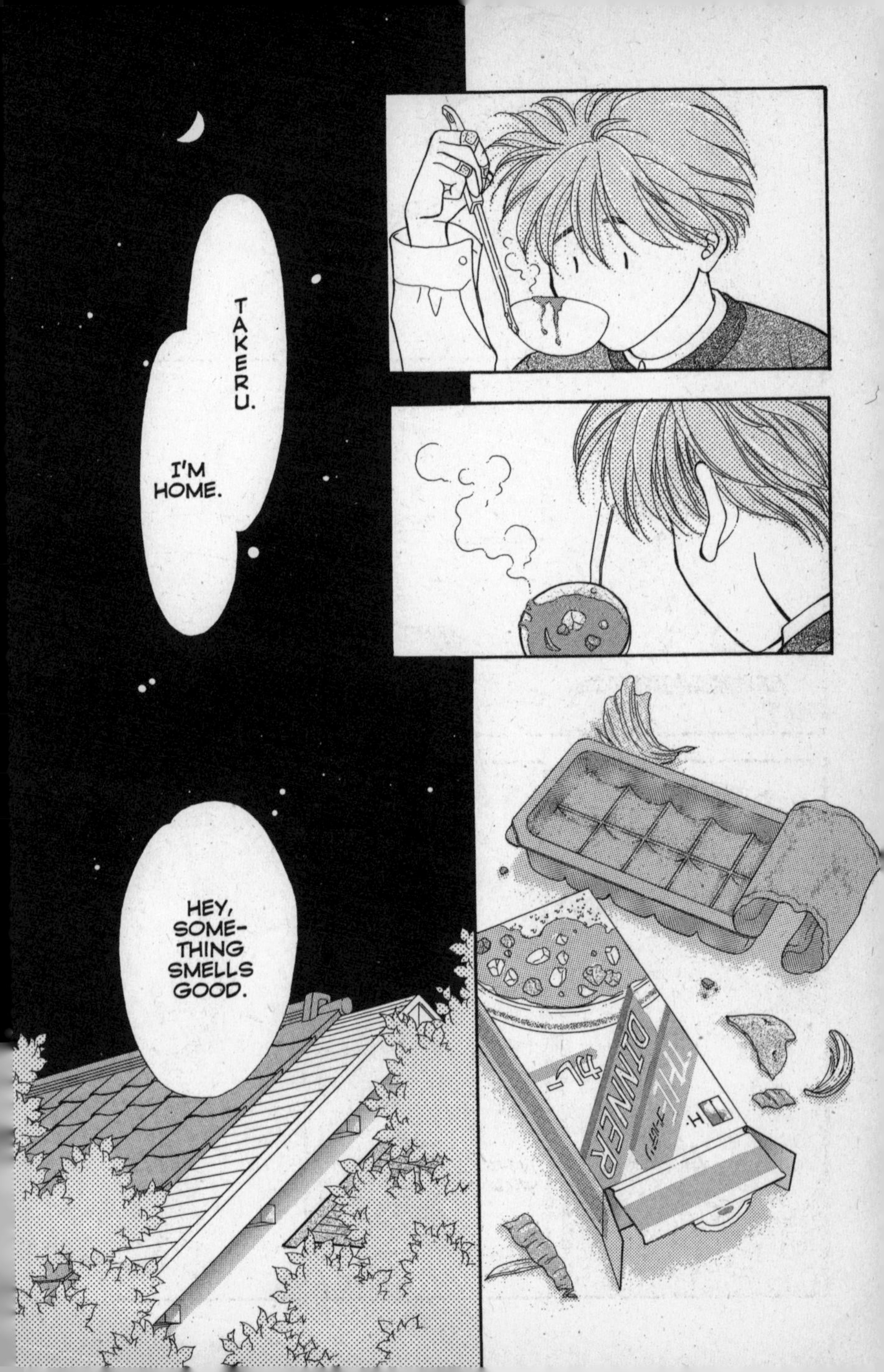
THE DINNER
カレー
TAKERU.
I'M HOME.
HEY, SOMETHING SMELLS GOOD.

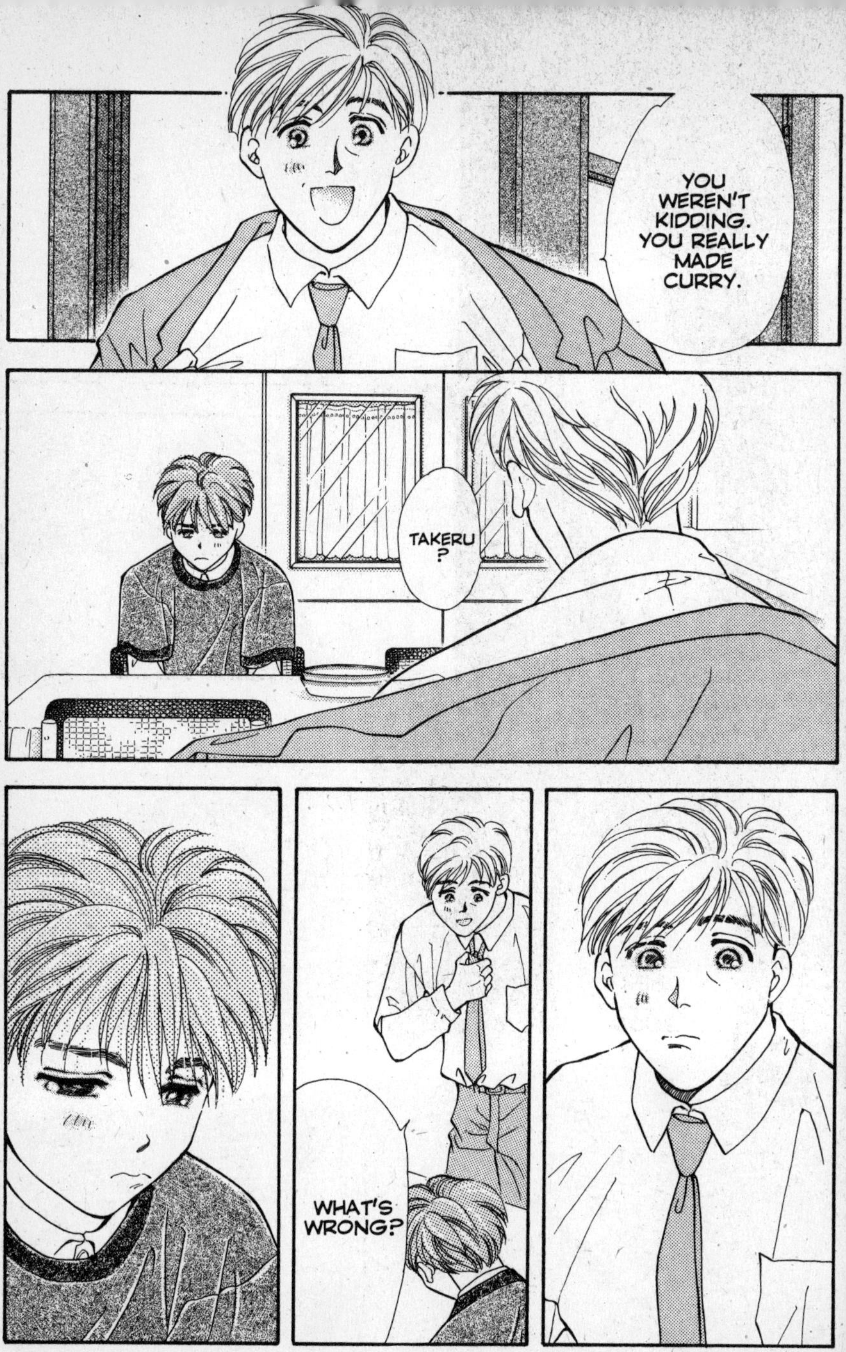
YOU WEREN'T KIDDING. YOU REALLY MADE CURRY.
TAKERU?
WHAT'S WRONG?

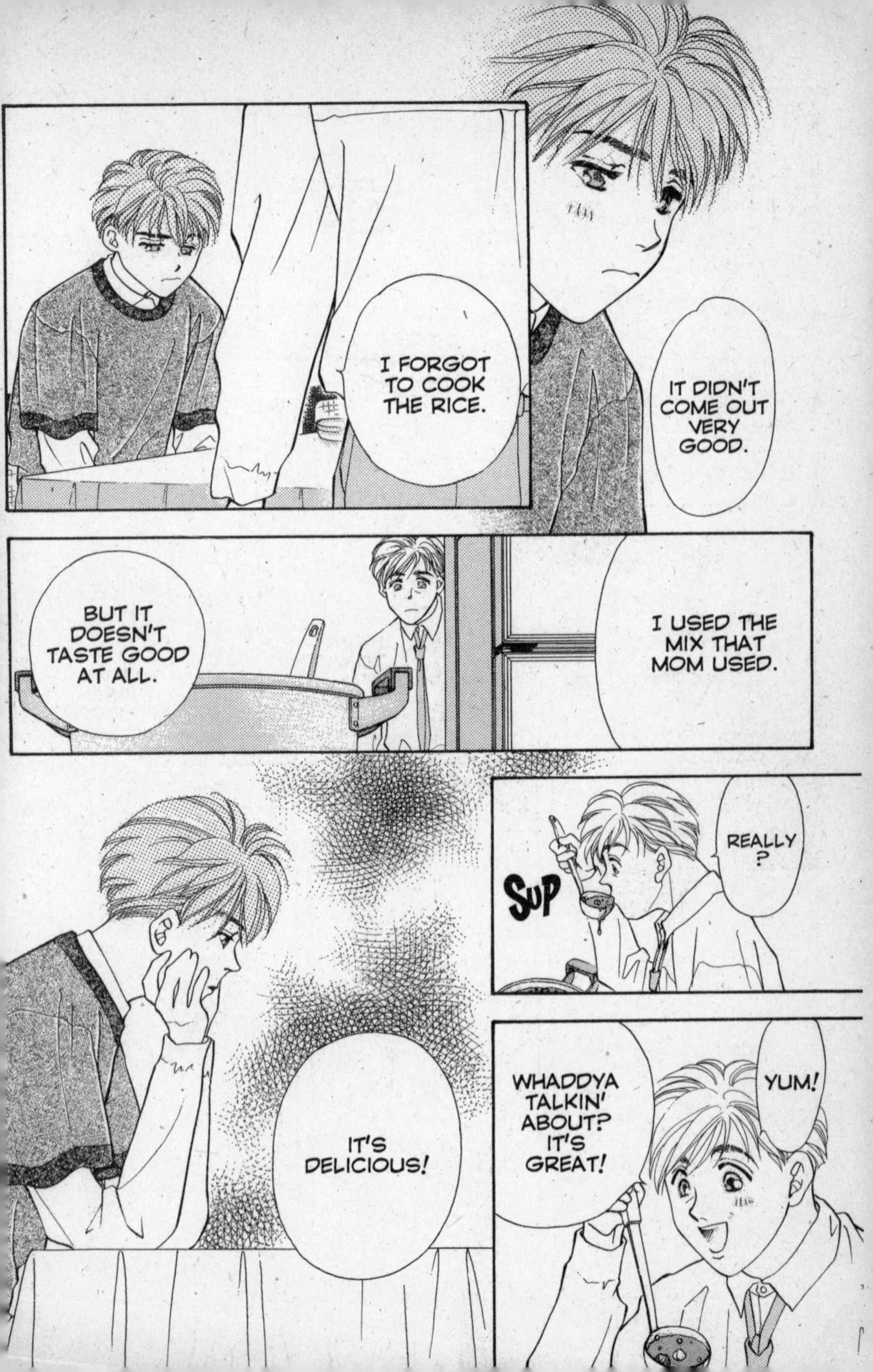
IT DIDN'T COME OUT VERY GOOD.
I FORGOT TO COOK THE RICE.
I USED THE MIX THAT MOM USED.
BUT IT DOESN'T TASTE GOOD AT ALL.
REALLY?
SUP
YUM!
WHADDYA TALKIN' ABOUT? IT'S GREAT!
IT'S DELICIOUS!

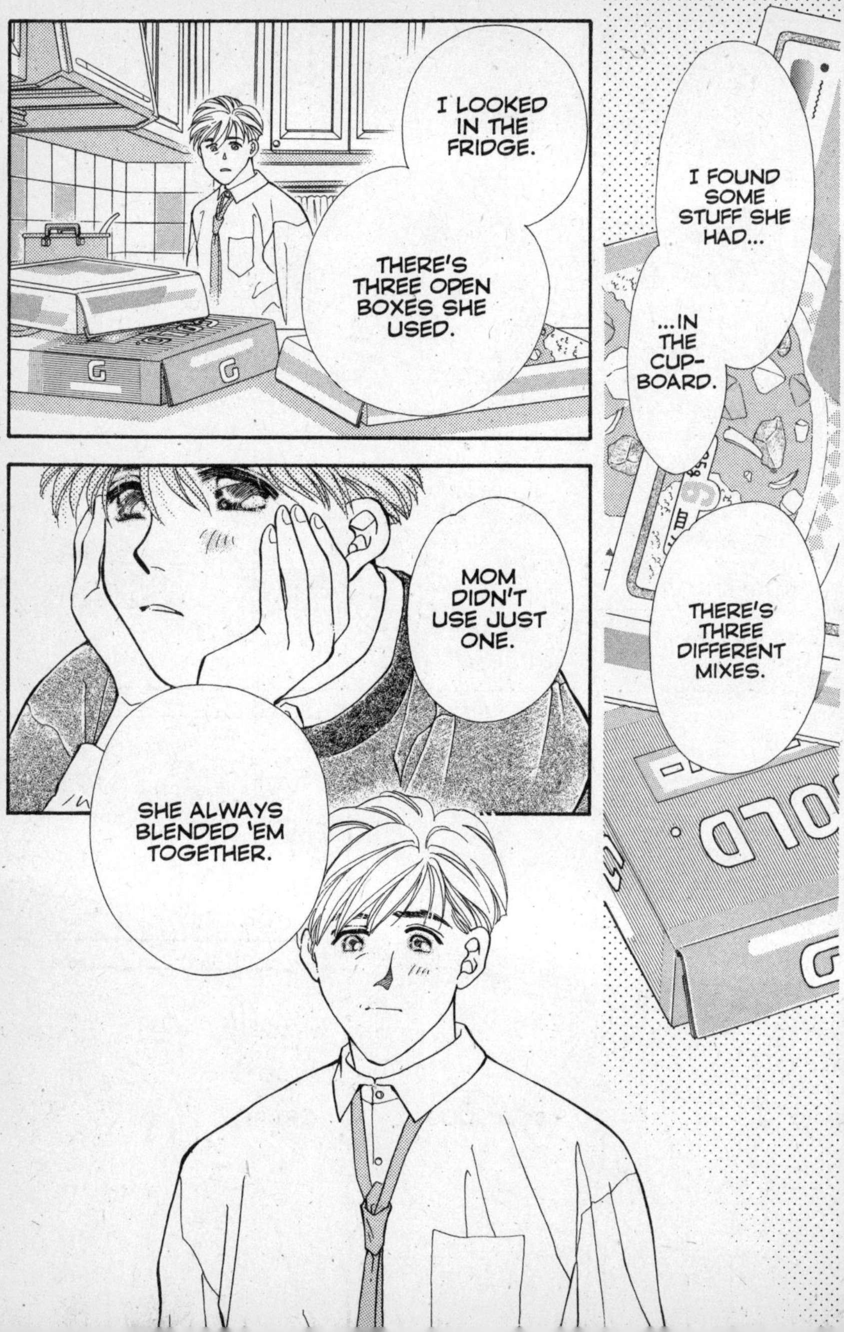
I FOUND SOME STUFF SHE HAD...
...IN THE CUP-BOARD.
THERE'S THREE DIFFERENT MIXES.
I LOOKED IN THE FRIDGE.
THERE'S THREE OPEN BOXES SHE USED.
MOM DIDN'T USE JUST ONE.
SHE ALWAYS BLENDED 'EM TOGETHER.

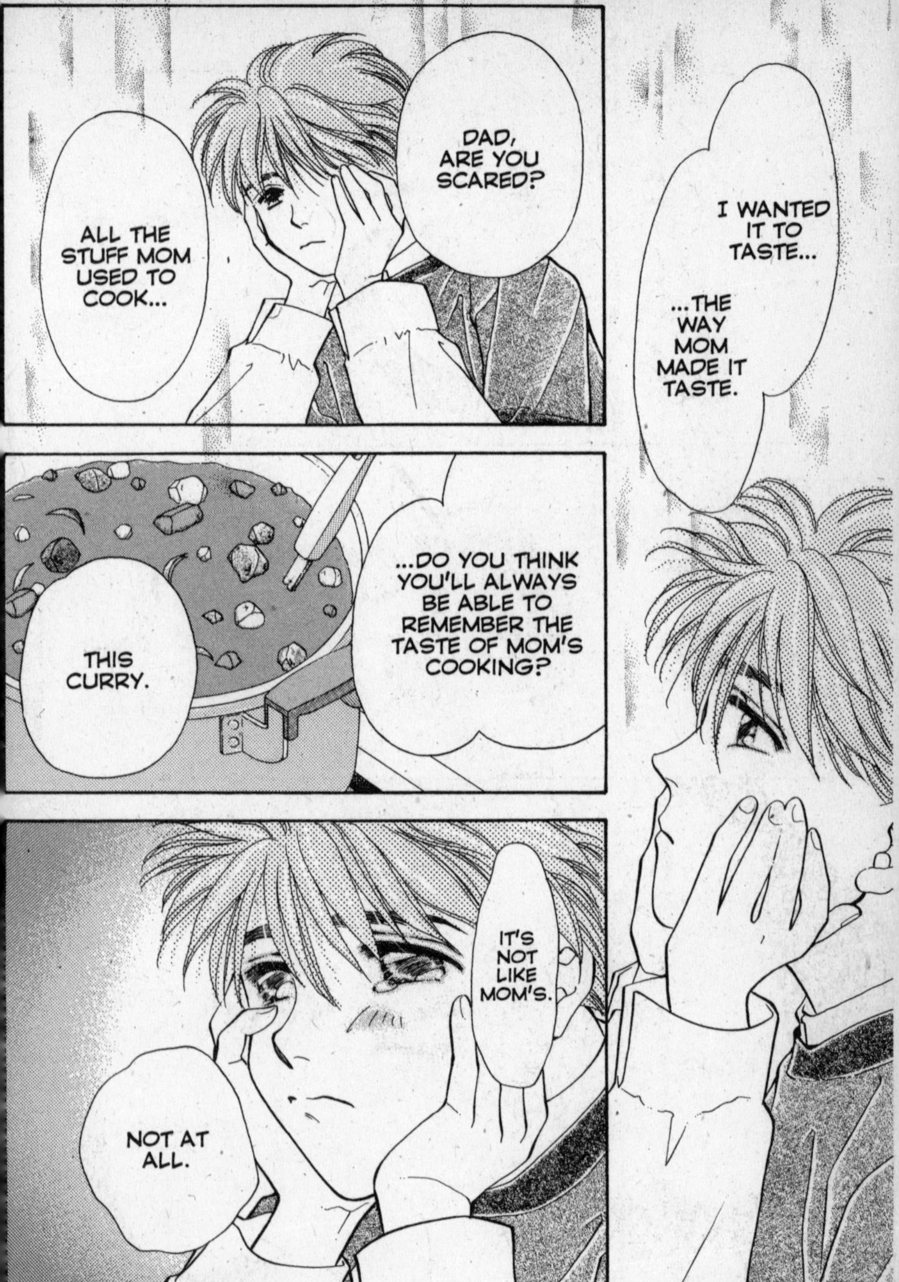
I WANTED IT TO TASTE...
...THE WAY MOM MADE IT TASTE.
DAD, ARE YOU SCARED?
ALL THE STUFF MOM USED TO COOK...
...DO YOU THINK YOU'LL ALWAYS BE ABLE TO REMEMBER THE TASTE OF MOM'S COOKING?
THIS CURRY.
IT'S NOT LIKE MOM'S.
NOT AT ALL.

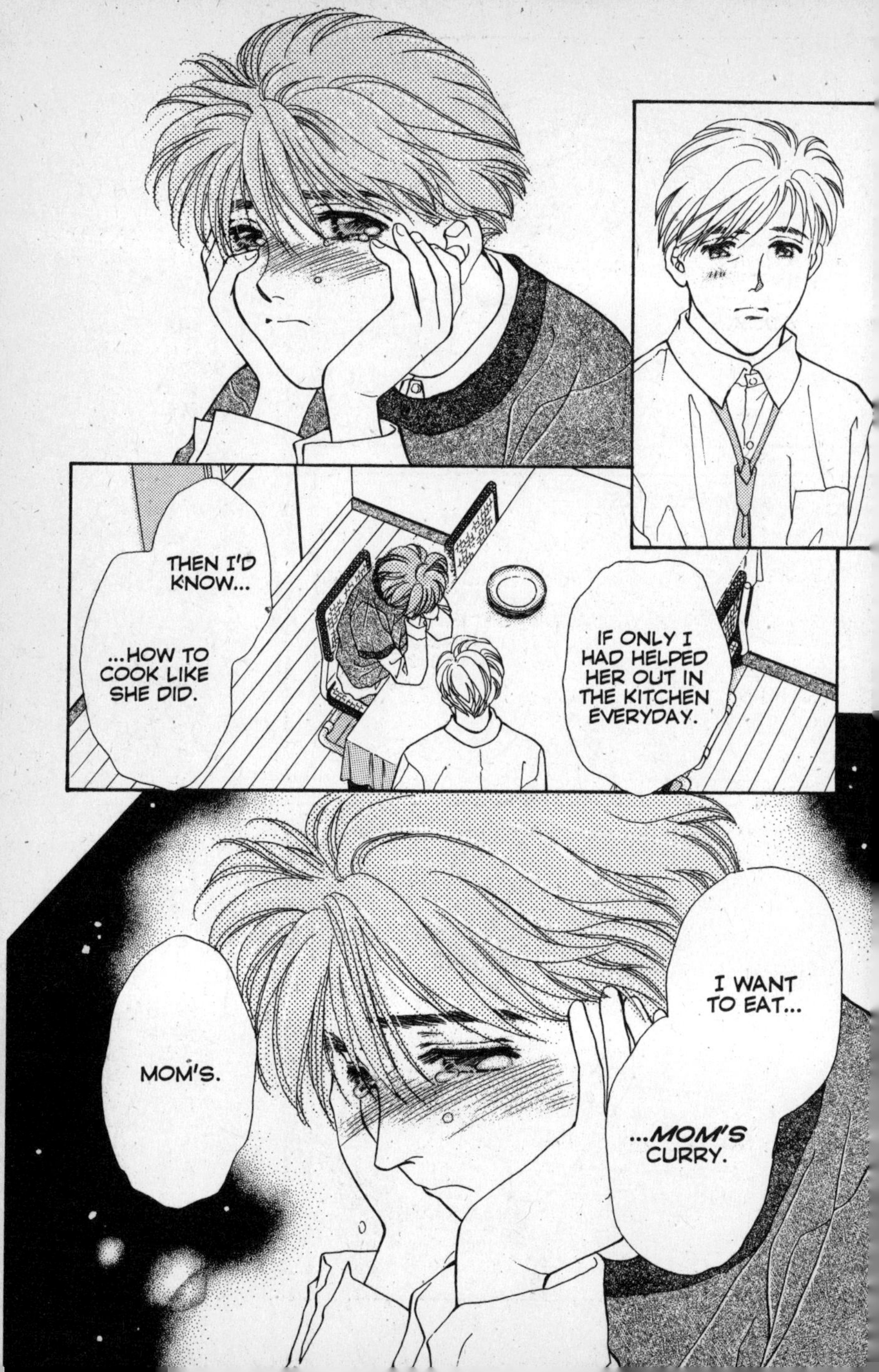
IF ONLY I HAD HELPED HER OUT IN THE KITCHEN EVERYDAY.
THEN I'D KNOW...
...HOW TO COOK LIKE SHE DID.
I WANT TO EAT...
...*MOM'S* CURRY.
MOM'S.

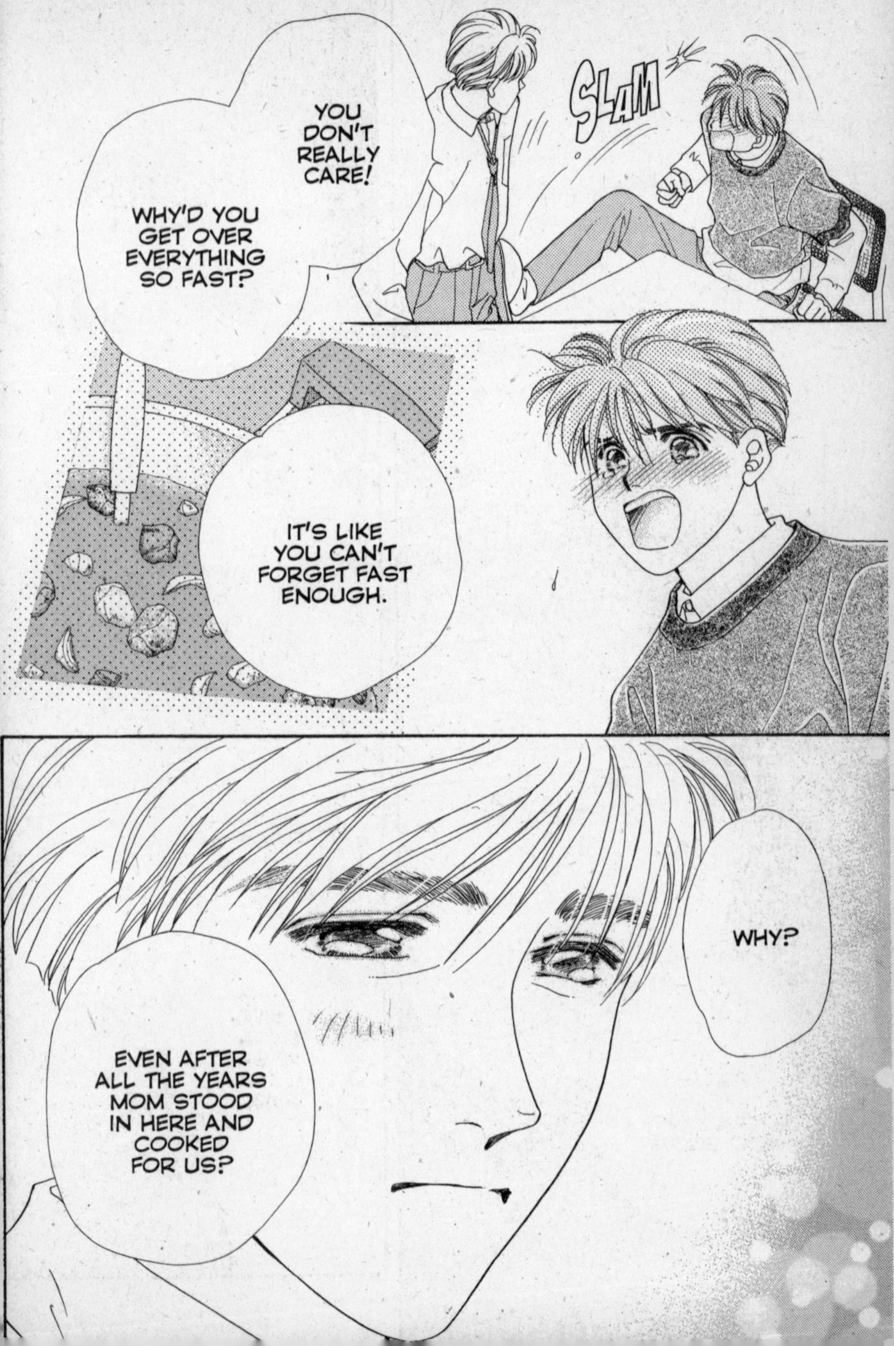
SLAM
YOU DON'T REALLY CARE!
WHY'D YOU GET OVER EVERYTHING SO FAST?
IT'S LIKE YOU CAN'T FORGET FAST ENOUGH.
WHY?
EVEN AFTER ALL THE YEARS MOM STOOD IN HERE AND COOKED FOR US?

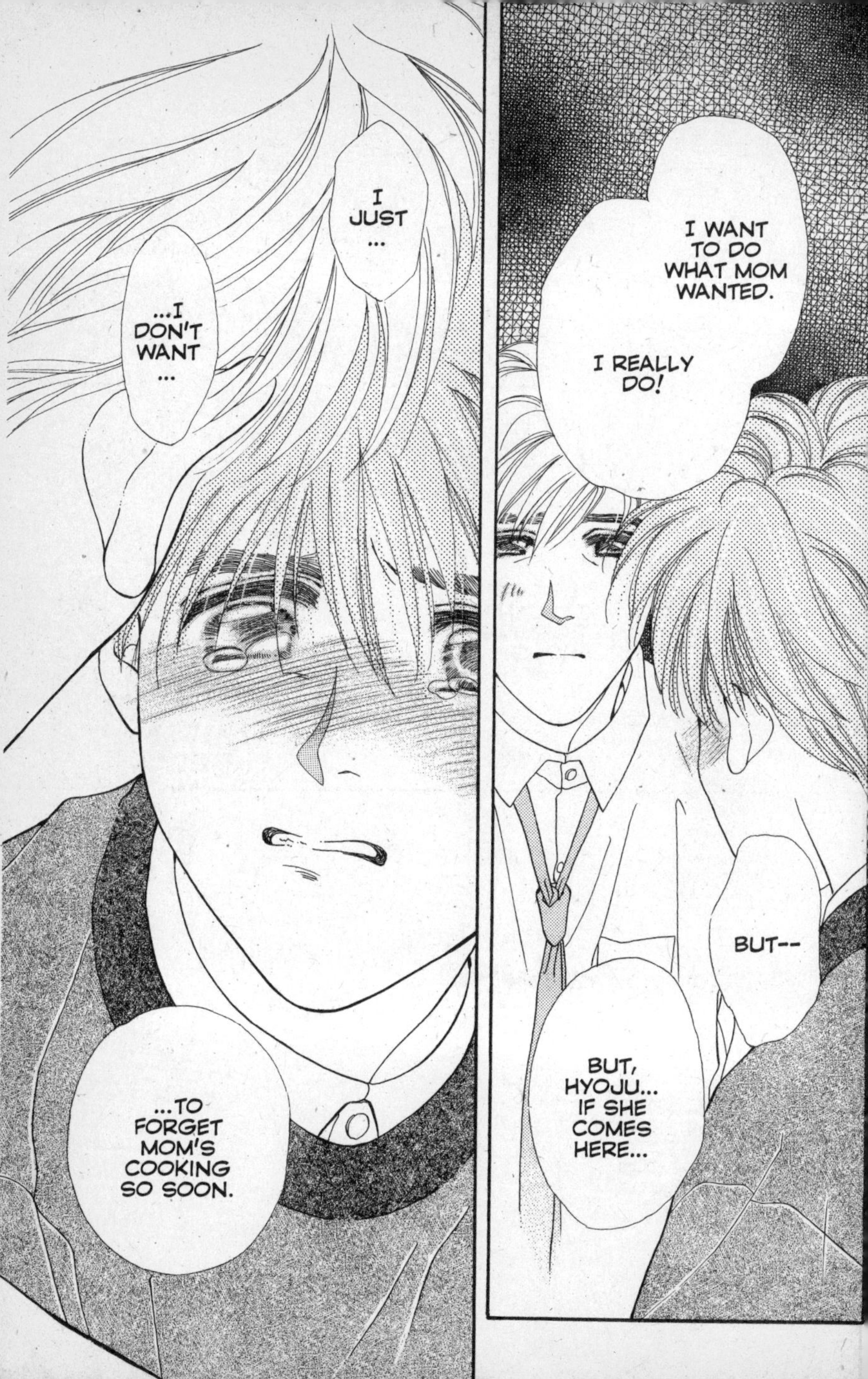
I WANT TO DO WHAT MOM WANTED.
I REALLY DO!
BUT--
BUT, HYOJU... IF SHE COMES HERE...
I JUST ...
...I DON'T WANT ...
...TO FORGET MOM'S COOKING SO SOON.

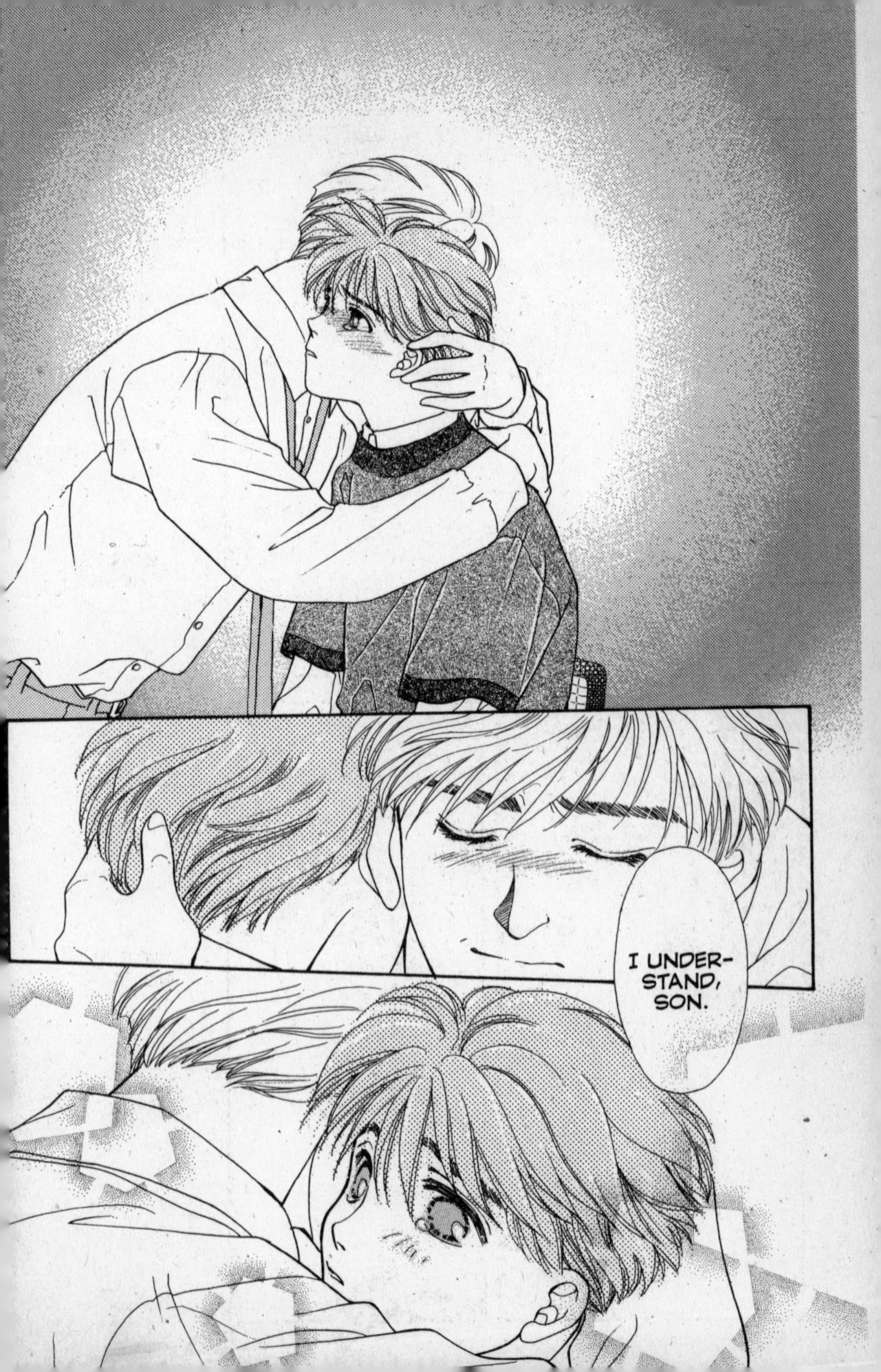
I UNDERSTAND, SON.

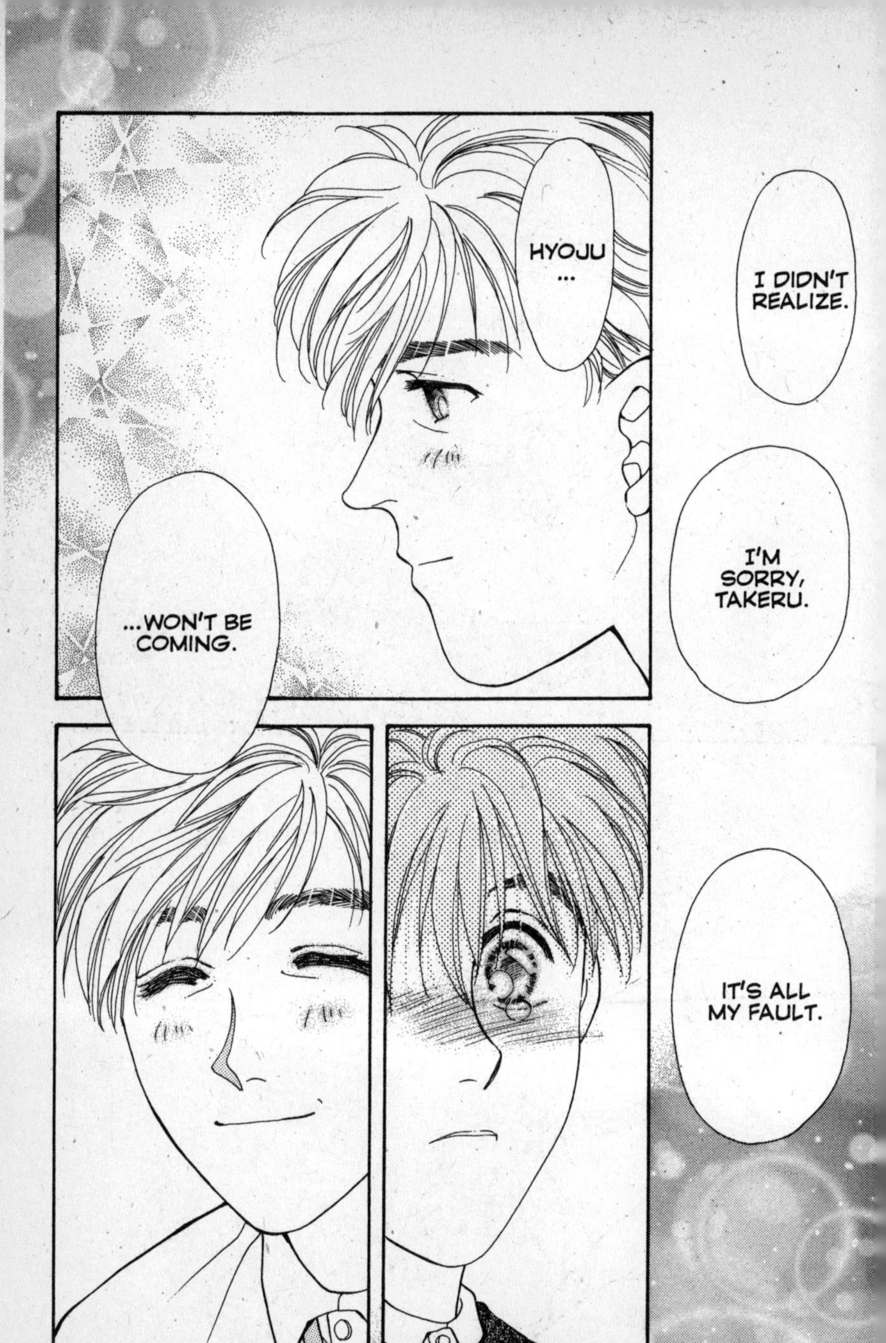
I DIDN'T REALIZE.
HYOJU ...
I'M SORRY, TAKERU.
...WON'T BE COMING.
IT'S ALL MY FAULT.

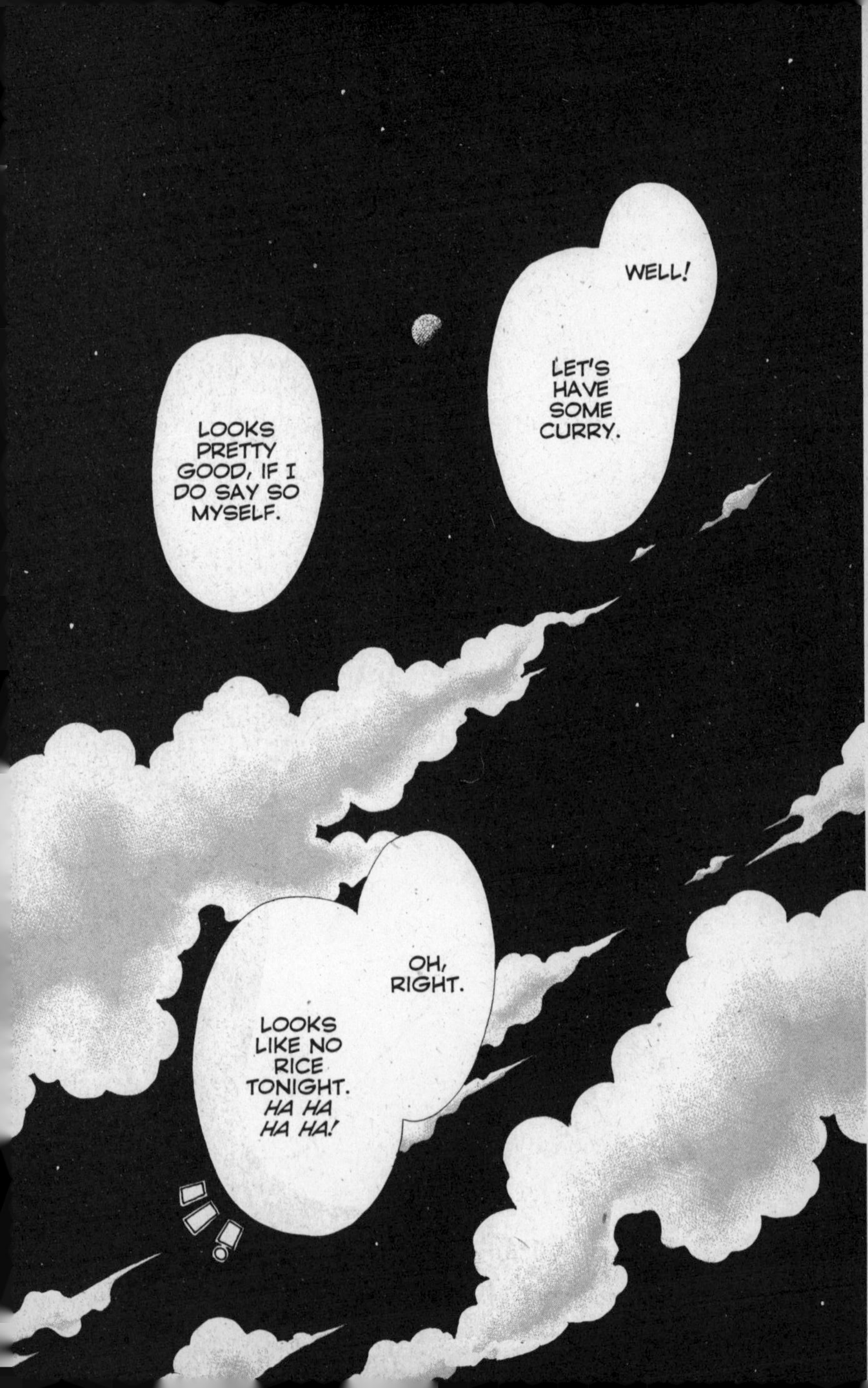
WELL!
LET'S HAVE SOME CURRY.
LOOKS PRETTY GOOD, IF I DO SAY SO MYSELF.
OH, RIGHT.
LOOKS LIKE NO RICE TONIGHT. *HA HA HA HA!*

cmx

TOWER OF THE FUTURE

By
Saki Hiwatari

VOLUME 2

Coming in Feburary

Still shocked by his mother's deathbed revelation, Takeru puts aside his anger and shame to grant her final wish. He agrees to allow Hyoju, the once-secret daughter of his father's first relationship, to come live with them. But only-child Takeru has a lot to learn when it comes to making room for the newest member of his family. Hyoju, too, has lessons to learn: born and raised in a foreign land, she must begin to adjust to her new life in Japan and the brother she has never met.

cmx

Jim Lee
  Editorial Director
John Nee
  VP—Business Development
Hank Kanalz
  VP—General Manager, WildStorm
Paul Levitz
  President & Publisher
Georg Brewer
  VP—Design & DC Direct Creative
Richard Bruning
  Senior VP—Creative Director
Patrick Caldon
  Senior VP—Finance & Operations
Chris Caramalis
  VP—Finance
Terri Cunningham
  VP—Managing Editor
Stephanie Fierman
  Senior VP—Sales & Marketing
Alison Gill
  VP—Manufacturing
Rich Johnson
  VP—Book Trade Sales
Lillian Laserson
  Senior VP & General Counsel
Paula Lowitt
  Senior VP—Business & Legal Affairs
David McKillips
  VP—Advertising & Custom Publishing
Gregory Noveck
  Senior VP—Creative Affairs
Cheryl Rubin
  Senior VP—Brand Management
Jeff Trojan
  VP—Business Development, DC Direct
Bob Wayne
  VP—Sales

MIRAI NO UTENA © 1994 Saki Hiwatari All rights reserved. First published in Japan in 2003 by HAKUSENSHA, INC., Tokyo.

TOWER OF THE FUTURE Volume 1, published by WildStorm Productions, an imprint of DC Comics, 888 Prospect St. #240, La Jolla, CA 92037. English Translation © 2006. All Rights Reserved. English translation rights in U.S.A. arranged with Hakusensha, Inc., through Tuttle-Mori Agency, Inc. The stories, characters, and incidents mentioned in this magazine are entirely fictional. Printed on recyclable paper. WildStorm does not read or accept unsolicited submissions of ideas, stories or artwork. Printed in Canada.

 DC Comics, a Warner Bros.
Entertainment Company.

Glenn Rich – Translation

Jonathan Tarbox – Adaptation

Vanessa Satone – Lettering

Ed Roeder/Larry Berry – Design

Ben Abernathy – Editor

ISBN: 1-4012-0814-2

190318